NAPOLEON'S MASTER

NAPOLEON'S MASTER

A Life of Prince Talleyrand

DAVID LAWDAY

THOMAS DUNNE BOOKS
ST. MARTIN'S PRESS ⚝ NEW YORK

THOMAS DUNNE BOOKS.
An imprint of St. Martin's Press.

Maps by Reginald Piggott

www.thomasdunnebooks.com
www.stmartins.com

Library of Congress Cataloging-in-Publication Data

Lawday, David.
    Napoleon's master : a life of prince Talleyrand / David Lawday.
        p. cm.
    Includes bibliographical references and index.
    ISBN-13: 978-0-312-37297-2
    ISBN-10: 0-312-37297-3
    1. Talleyrand-Périgord, Charles Maurice de, prince de Bénévent, 1754–1838.
2. Statesmen—France—Biography. 3. Diplomats—France—Biography. 4. France—History—1789–1815. 5. France—History—19th century. I. Title.

DC255.T3 L39 2007
944.05092—dc22
    [B]

2007031017

First published in Great Britain by Jonathan Cape, Random House

First U.S. Edition: November 2007

10 9 8 7 6 5 4 3 2 1

To Noëlle

CONTENTS

N

North Sea

ENGLAND

R. Thames
London
Portsmouth

English Channel

Channel
Islands
(Br.)

Le Havre
Rouen
R. Seine
Paris

Calais
Arras

Amsterdam

UNITED NETHERLANDS

Brussels
BELGIUM

LOWER
RHINE
Cologne
R. Rhine

LUX.
SAAR
Mainz
LOWER
PALATINATE

Metz

Rennes

Fontainebleau

Tours
Orleans

Nantes

R. Loire

Valencay
Poitiers
Bourbon-l'Archambault
Autun

Dijon
R. Saône

Strasbourg

F R A N C E

Limoges

Chalais
Bordeaux

R. Garonne

Bay of
Biscay

Lyons

Berne
HELVETIA
(SWITZERLAND)

Pau
Toulouse

R. Rhône

ITALY

Genoa

Aix
Marseilles

R. Ebro

SPAIN

Perpignan

CORSICA
(Fr.)

Mediterranean
Sea

——— Boundary of France 1789
.... Following Treaty of Vienna 1815
– – – 'Natural boundaries' desired by Talleyrand

0   50   100   150   200 miles
0   100   200   300 km

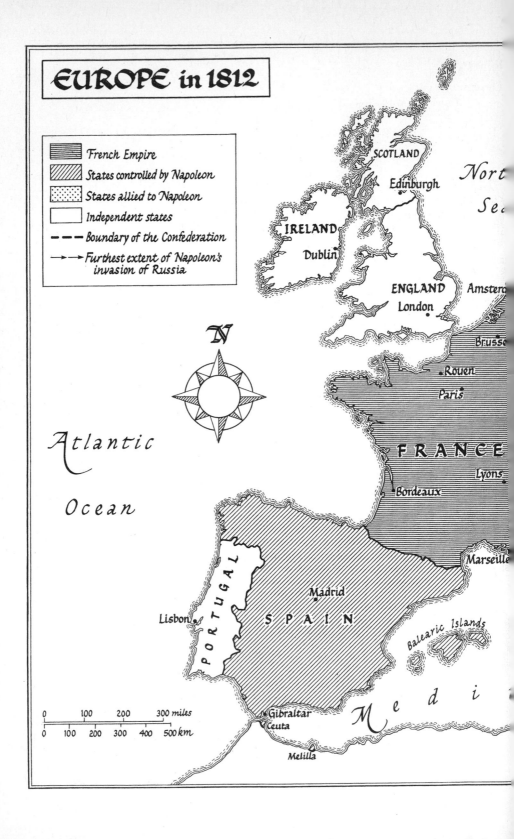

EUROPE in 1812

Legend:
- French Empire
- States controlled by Napoleon
- States allied to Napoleon
- Independent states
- – – – Boundary of the Confederation
- →→ Furthest extent of Napoleon's invasion of Russia

SCOTLAND
Edinburgh

Nort
Sea

IRELAND
Dublin

ENGLAND
London

Amster

Brusse

Rouen
Paris

Atlantic

Ocean

FRANCE
Lyons

Bordeaux

Marseille

PORTUGAL

Madrid

SPAIN

Lisbon

Balearic Islands

Gibraltar
Ceuta

Medi

Melilla

0   100   200   300 miles
0   100   200   300   400   500 km

NORWAY
Christiania
Stockholm
SWEDEN
Baltic Sea
St Petersburg
Moscow
Sept–Oct
1812
Vitebsk
Smolensk
Riga
DENMARK
Copenhagen
Kovno
Vilna
RUSSIA
Hamburg
Danzig
PRUSSIA
CONFEDERATION
Berlin
Warsaw
GRAND DUCHY
OF WARSAW
OF THE
Prague
RHINE
EMPIRE OF
Vienna
HELVETIA
Buda••Pest
AUSTRIA
ITALY
ILLYRIAN PROVINCES
Belgrade
Bucharest
Black
Sea
OTTOMAN
Sofia
CORSICA
Rome
KINGDOM OF
Naples
Constantinople
EMPIRE
SARDINIA
NAPLES
SICILY
Ionian Isles (Br)
Mediterranean Sea

ILLUSTRATIONS

1. Talleyrand in 1808, copper engraving after a painting by François Gérard (*akg-images*).
2. Talleyrand, aged sixteen, portrait by unknown French artist (*Giraudon/ Bridgeman Art Library*).
3. Talleyrand's shoe, with iron strut to support his club foot (*C. Recoura/ Culture Espaces, Château de Valençay Collection*).
4. Talleyrand at the coronation of Napoleon in Notre Dame Cathedral, 2 December 1804, detail of a painting by Jacques-Louis David, 1806–7 (*akg-images/Erich Lessing*).
5. Emperor Napoleon in coronation robes, copy of a painting by François Gérard, 1805 (*akg-images/VISIOARS*).
6. Napoleon at Bologne, contemplating an invasion of England, September 1803, watercolour by Job (*akg-images*).
7. Napoleon in 1812, painting by Jacques-Louis David (*akg-images*).
8. Joseph Fouché, portrait by unknown French artist (*Photo RMN/© Gérard Blot*).
9. Gouverneur Morris in 1808, portrait by Thomas Sully (*© Atwater Kent Museum of Philadelphia, courtesy of Historical Society of Pennsylvania Collection/Bridgeman Art Library*).
10. The Comtesse de Flahaut with baby Charles, her son by Talleyrand, painting by Adélaïde Labille-Guiard, 1785.
11. View of Valençay (*Culture Espaces, Château de Valençay Collection*).
12. Madame de Staël, *c.* 1810, painting by François Gérard (*akg-images/Erich Lessing*).
13. Talleyrand's wife-to-be Catherine Grand, painting by Elisabeth-Louise Vigée-Lebrun, 1783 (*Metropolitan Museum of Art, New York*).
14. Dorothea, Duchess of Kurland and Sagan, contemporary painting by Anton Graff (*akg-images*).
15. Dorothy, Duchess of Dino, portrait by Catherine-Caroline Thévenin (*Photo RMN/© Gérard Blot*).
16. The Congress of Vienna, 1814–5, engraving after Jean-Baptiste Isabey (*Archives du Ministère des Affaires Etrangères, Paris/Archives Charmet/ Bridgeman Art Library*).
17. Napoleon at Fontainebleau on 31 March 1814 after receiving the news of the Allies' entry into Paris, painting by Paul Delaroche, 1848 (*akg-images*).
18. Louis XVIII, portrait by Jean-Baptiste Isabey (*Photo RMN/© Thierry Le Mage*).

Paris 1809

In mid-afternoon on the last Saturday in January, five imperial dignitaries are gathered in the Emperor Napoleon's private salon at the Tuileries Palace, waiting for him to descend from his bedroom. A chill wind off the Seine rips around the front courtyard of the palace. Napoleon has summoned his chief counsellors at short notice after a headlong gallop to Paris from the Pyrenees. The five men are wary. What made Napoleon dash back like this from his warring in Spain? Five hundred miles and more on horseback in barely five days, and over rutted winter roads. It shows a terrible sense of purpose. They can guess at the conqueror's mood: it will not be placid.

The dignitaries rise as the emperor enters, plumper than they have known him despite his exertions. Strangely calm, he starts discussing public perceptions of how his military campaign in Spain is going. Idle tongues in Paris speak of failure, he says. Well, they are wrong. The war is succeeding. As he talks his counsellors take their seats, all except one. The man still standing is the emperor's diplomatic brain, the most artful negotiator in all Europe. He stands at the fireplace in high imperial vestment, bewigged, powdered, the model of a bygone France, an elbow propped on the mantelpiece to take the strain off his club foot.

Still outwardly calm, Napoleon reminds the five that he requires their absolute obedience. He has heard, he says, that people have been scheming for his fall in his absence, people of high rank. The police have warned him of possible assassination plots. He has held power for ten years, conquered the whole of Europe. England alone eludes him. And now this! People he has honoured scheming to get rid of him!

Napoleon's self-control snaps. He bounds across the study to the figure leaning on the fireplace, enraged by his nonchalant stance. He raises a fist, waving it before his quarry's powdered face. 'You are a liar, a coward, a man without faith. You do not believe in God; all your life you have failed in your duties, betrayed everyone, tricked everyone. Nothing is sacred for you. You would sell your father.'

Not a muscle moves in the other's face. His impassiveness only incenses Napoleon the more. 'What are you planning? What do you want? Tell me, I dare you! I should break you like a piece of glass; you deserve it. I have the power, only I despise you too much to take the trouble.' For a moment Napoleon turns away, consumed by anger. Then, abruptly, he turns back, his rosebud mouth curling. 'Why haven't I had you hanged from the Carrousel railings? There's still time. You are a . . . a . . . a shit in a silk stocking.'

The target of the wondrous imperial insult is Talleyrand – Charles-Maurice de Talleyrand-Périgord, prince, bishop (defrocked), statesman, diplomat, imperial elector and much of rank besides – and it is a scene that leads inexorably to the undoing of the greatest conqueror since Julius Caesar. For most of ten years they have been partners, on top of the world together. Talleyrand is more familiar than most with Napoleon's temper fits. But this is the bitter end. His face has remained a mask throughout the attack but as Napoleon stamps out of the room the mask at last speaks, in a measured bass tone: 'What a pity, such a great man and so ill-mannered!'

Talleyrand gathers his cane and departs, leaving his fellow high courtiers reduced to stunned silence. From this moment on Talleyrand makes the fall of Napoleon his mission. It is not personal vengeance that drives him, it is hunger for peace and a return to the civilised world he prizes.

I know why I am drawn to Talleyrand. Though he faces grave and momentous tasks, it is often hard to suppress a smile in his company. He has flaws, extravagant flaws, and when he accepts them as such he contrives to live easily with them, convinced they count for nothing beside his worth. He lives a constant dilemma at the pinnacle of power and does not always come down on the side a man of his rank ought. Aside from the true monsters of history, few world figures have managed to achieve as mottled a reputation as he.

He is himself a monster of sorts. Yet what turns people against him is his humanity; he has too many sides for lesser mortals to cope with. He lives through the most dangerous age Europe has known – directing it, surviving it, moulding it – without batting an eyelid. Give him a dozen hard kicks from behind, says one who knows him well, and nothing in his face will betray the slightest discomfort to those in front of him. The twinkle in his eye is always there, though it often has to be imagined. For Talleyrand is a performer, a supreme performer. The English come to call him 'Old Talley', which speaks of suspicion but also of admiration for the performance. His astonishing self-control is often put down to cynicism, heartlessness or some other unlovely trait. Its origin lies elsewhere. Life's great game for this most aristocratic of statesmen is never to give the game away, and he plays it well – so well that few have matched him then or since in the art of putting the world aright.

One thing I as an Englishman have sensed when delving into his extraordinary life and his still more extraordinary relationship with Napoleon is that to grasp Talleyrand is better to grasp that elusive race, the French. Anyone looking for the hand that created today's highly unusual Europe – unusual because it is more or less united, at peace with itself and, with luck, disposed to stay that way – could do worse than track back to well before the war-weary pragmatists of 1945 and start with Talleyrand. If there is anything more than coincidence in the fact that he dies just as Queen Victoria mounts the throne for the longest reign in Britain's history, it is that he has been intrigued all his life by the British system and has wanted to borrow from it to strengthen the French one. Since his diplomatic accomplishments close to two centuries ago, the British and French, hereditary enemies so long accustomed to being at each others' throats, have never again warred against each other. This is no coincidence.

And on a still broader stage, how many times have I stopped short when exploring Talleyrand's epic struggle against Napoleon's imperial overreach and thought, aha! yes, if only our world's lone superpower at this outset of the twenty-first century were to lend him an ear. He identified for all ages the ultimate foible of empire. The alert he sounded two hundred years ago to a military genius who bestrode a vast empire of his own making rings all the bells:

> I attest that any system which aims at taking freedom by open force to other peoples will only make that freedom hated and prevent its triumph.

If Talleyrand isn't heard loud and clear, it may be that he comes across as a little too ungodly in other matters to be thought entirely trustworthy. Born in 1754 into one of France's noblest houses – the Talleyrand-Périgord line goes back to the ancient Counts of Périgord, sovereign rulers in western France through the Middle Ages – he stands out among world statesmen over the past two centuries and stamps himself upon modern times. Yet in terms of the amount of abuse attracted by a Frenchman, not even Vichy's wretched Philippe Pétain during the Second World War can touch him. In the furious view of many of his contemporaries, as of critics to this day, he is the prince of vice – turncoat, hypocrite, liar, plotter, voluptuary, flatterer, gouger and, to make matters worse, highly successful at them all.

3

He isn't simply masking his emotions, the detractors say, he has none. Even the club foot he drags painfully through life counts against him on this scorecard; if he has a single principle, they charge, it is to serve his own interests. The insult hurled at him above by the Emperor Napoleon, whom he also long serves, though not so faithfully in the end, still sticks to Talleyrand. It says more, though, of Napoleon on his downward spiral to humiliation and defeat at Waterloo than it does of Talleyrand.

Talleyrand's disdain for emotional display hardens jumpier hearts against him during what must count as the most pulse-racing age in Europe's history, surpassing in long-term impact the Russian Revolution and the Hitler blight. At the outset the French monarchy, older than England's and still absolute, is on its last legs, sapped by liberal thinking without and by scandal within. With his wigs and powders, Talleyrand seems so much a product of this *ancien régime* that it comes as a shock at first to find him riding the wave of revolution that turns world history on its head. Political ambition and a liberal outlook fired by the times propel him into the fray. His sixty-year public career spans the rotting *ancien régime*, the Revolution of 1789, the Terror, Napoleon's endless wars across Europe, the unstoppable spread of the Napoleonic empire, the emperor's dramatic fall, monarchy restored (twice) and further revolution besides – most of which occur as Britain and Europe's other main powers, Russia, Austria and Prussia, are at war with France.

By force of circumstance he lives as an exile in the United States of America, itself newborn of revolution, as well as in England. Exile encourages him to make allowances for Anglo-Saxon prejudices, which is generous of him since the English display the worst of theirs when the guillotine hangs over his head. After England, the sanctuary he finds in the early United States is a hard landing for a man reared on the blueblood brilliance of the Paris salon, a man said to write the finest language ever penned in world affairs (his worst detractors may allow this). In his reports on the raw America he comes to inhabit he is as astute in assessing its chances of growing rich as his compatriot Alexis de Tocqueville is a little later in assessing its political possibilities. He recognises the US will one day become a 'great people'. But he never quite understands the American spirit; cussed American honesty and self-righteousness in time confound him.

The age he lives in is one of social decomposition on the grand scale. To have lived through it as an ordinary citizen would have been daunting enough. Talleyrand hobbles in its vanguard: leading participant, architect, guide and at times its helpless plaything. He is too human for most others to accept easily. Surely, they're thinking, a man of his influence and rank can't have so many faults. His eccentricities increase their qualms: he rises close to noon, retires the night half over, overdoses on face powder and scent, daily inhales two beakers of water through the nose and snorts forth the intake before shocked visitors to avoid headcolds, and he sits playing cards at times of peril with an insouciance to match Sir Francis Drake's.

Whenever possible Talleyrand serves power regardless of who holds it, and always at the top of the pile. The king of turncoats, then? I'm not so sure. In his memoirs he notes with his habitual understatement, 'I placed myself at the disposal of events'. The ambiguity of the grand figure that is Talleyrand is a leitmotiv of this book, for ambiguity seems to me a central part of French character, along with a certain trust in reason. Talleyrand does in fact have principles and one of them in particular resonates right through his life. It is this: only fools never change their minds.

In weighing Talleyrand's 'treason', a familiar accusation thrown his way, I've found myself listening not entirely by chance to John Maynard Keynes, whose economist friends have a habit of holding to pet theories even when they are shown to be wrong. 'When events change,' Keynes memorably observed to an obdurate colleague, 'I tend to change my opinions. What do you do?' What does Talleyrand do? Major events overtake each other so fast in his time that it would have been an insult to his own liberal intelligence to ignore the changes they bring. The reference to Keynes is relevant because Talleyrand is an enthusiastic student of economics, a new science in his youth and one that will stand behind every major policy he is to follow. As the young Talleyrand turns over new ideas with fellow intellectual gadabouts in Paris, Adam Smith is publishing *Wealth of Nations*. The book's fame soon spreads to the Continent. Economics seems the right companion for the social ideas of the Enlightenment lately advanced by Voltaire and Rousseau. To Talleyrand, human wealth and happiness derive from industry, enterprise and commerce – all of which he believes depend on flourishing trade between France and mercantile Britain. This in turn requires peace in Europe.

Yet the same Talleyrand comes to lend his diplomatic arts to an alternative method of coalescing Europe: Napoleon's way, by force of arms. He is Napoleon's foreign minister, negotiator and policy guide (in so far as Napoleon ever allows anyone but himself to steer his actions). The Talleyrand–Napoleon relationship is mutually faithless. It can't be otherwise since the relationship is based on a hopeless contradiction: Napoleon lives for conquest, Talleyrand abhors it. France can only ruin herself, he believes, by expanding outside her natural frontiers; the risk applies to all countries that covet territory belonging to others. So he constantly attempts to put a brake on the warrior emperor. His warnings are masked, however, with such outrageous flattery for Napoleon's courage and glory that the emperor may not know which to heed – the brake or the caress – until Talleyrand at last stops him dead to put an end to it all. When he fails to get his way with Napoleon, he goes along with him – but always in the hope of influencing him further down the line. His flattery becomes pitted with irony. On news of one of Napoleon's most resounding later triumphs in battle, his laconic congratulatory dispatch reads: 'I wish to consider this victory the last your Majesty will be obliged to win.' The message between the lines is that victory only makes sense if it leads to all-round peace, not extended dominion.

Talleyrand's tie to Napoleon is extremely complex, and part of the knot is the emperor's generosity. The erstwhile man of the cloth, a high liver, is not made to resist it. Property and titles are showered on him. On the emperor's back he moves up to a grand mansion in Paris where he can feast the highest dignitaries of Europe, he takes a magnificent chateau in the provinces, is raised to the post of Imperial Grand Chamberlain and made a prince (initially of unknown Benevento, an Italian statelet filched from the pope in which Talleyrand will never set foot). He is surely aware of the comic opera side to such elevation, but his impassive temperament helps him to treat it with the necessary gravitas. His home is the epicentre of Paris society, his table the best in the capital, hence in the world, and the new titles carry welcome additional income.

Talleyrand lives dangerously. This is what makes him a performer. In all but the cut of the sabre it is Talleyrand quite as much as the Duke of Wellington who halts Napoleon. Hence the charge of treason.

Those who find the case against him open and shut fail to convince. Talleyrand can plausibly claim he has no blood on his hands. If he is not always the gentleman, he is, despite the thrust of his tongue, a gentle man. His 'treason' exists in defending civilised values through thick and thin, against all odds. This requires a different kind of courage which in the end proves invincible. It is his legacy and it is a large one, not just for France.

This book is not a history of revolution and war, though I hope to have kept the historical picture clear through the heady year of 1789 and through the wars, glory and tragedy that followed. As to dates, I have dropped the stirring *Messidors*, *Thermidors* and *Brumaires* that coloured the months of the French Revolution in blood and putschery in favour of plain Junes, Julys and Octobers. The imaginative revolutionary calendar stayed in use for fourteen years until 1806, close to halfway through Napoleon's rule, and was finally abandoned because Napoleon decided it harked back to times his people ought to forget and because it inconvenienced French trade. I judged it inconvenient for readers too, and I daresay Talleyrand would have agreed.

The book, then, is not a history of the times; it is the story of Talleyrand, as rich in personal ups, downs, foibles, eccentricities and physical trials as those of any world figure I have come across.

Though I first vaguely encountered him in school history classes, I came to meet him at close quarters quite by chance – during a stay in 1990s Berlin, well after the Wall came down, where the pavement stall of a second-hand bookshop off the Kurfürstendamm revealed, wedged between German volumes, a pair of dusty French hardbacks recounting his tormented youth and his exile in America. I was mildly surprised to find those two books on offer there in Berlin. Talleyrand couldn't be a local favourite, for the France of his day was in the habit of wielding the military stick against the Prussians, not, as has often happened since, receiving it. I must anyway have been homesick for Paris, where I actually lived, because having picked out the two volumes I was unable to put either down. They introduced me to this strange figure and set me on his longer trail. While his person is the heart of this book, its backbone is the perverse and addictive relationship with Napoleon, the imprint of which is hard to miss on the world of today.

I won't claim to have unearthed previously unknown things about Talleyrand in tracking him from Berlin to the stupendously rich archives of the Bibliothèque Nationale in Paris, by way of the vaults of the French foreign ministry, the British Library in London, the Library of Congress in Washington, DC, and the many Talleyrand homes, the grandest of which is the chateau of Valençay deep in the pastoral Berri region of France. The challenge has been to peel the cover off the hidden things. For his track also passes through a crop of candid memoirs by his contemporaries who have often spiteful, always perceptive views on him, and through the lives of those contemporaries themselves: Germaine de Staël, Metternich, the Duke of Wellington among others. The earth has been well turned by professional scholars, though the last esteemed biography in English was published in 1932 by Duff Cooper, a lovely writer who became Britain's ambassador to France after the Nazi occupation. In Duff Cooper's time, though, the Talleyrand earth wasn't so well turned, which left him in the dark on certain matters.

Issue must now be taken with that majority of historians, Cooper included, who have taken as gospel Talleyrand's story of his club foot, which he claims was caused by a childhood fall from the top of a cupboard. The story is false. He was born with it, as any modern pediatric bone specialist will attest; infants don't snap bones in a minor fall. To clinch matters, a contemporary painting of a Talleyrand uncle with a club foot has recently come to light. The childhood fall story is a terrifying sop to family pride, a fable spun by family shame. Moreover, there can now be little doubt that his relations

with women were broadly platonic, which conflicts with his standard reputation as a serial womaniser. Talleyrand likes women. He loves women, the
brighter, comelier and more talkative the better. But in his libertarian age,
when it seems next to unavoidable even for a man of moderate sexual drive
to plant his seed, he would quite as soon have his women clustered around
him in a lively literary salon as lying in his bed.

Still, Talleyrand is the most elusive of subjects. His own memoirs are an
enigma. They are a joy to read for their flowing language but ultimately fail
to satisfy. They are wickedly good on the art of diplomacy and on the sovereigns, statesman and rascals who inhabit his world. The trouble is that, typically, they uncover little of what goes on inside him. They are an exercise
in concealment at which he is highly skilled, having spent all his life at it.
They take us through the critical points of his career behind the same
hooded gaze he adopts with adversaries, giving away almost nothing of
himself. And like all memoirs, Talleyrand's are not to be trusted. Omission
is a ready defence. Where he feels uneasy over his course of action or where
he may leave himself open to attack, he omits the issue entirely or dismisses
it in a throwaway sentence – except where he goes to great lengths to defend
himself against taunts of his involvement in a notorious assassination.

His truer self comes out in private correspondence, where he can be
bewilderingly open and one almost wants him for his own sake to shut up,
given the risks he runs. And what a flow of personal letters he keeps up.
The Talleyrand mails hum. He lets loose a daily barrage of confidences,
appraisals and bits of advice to society women, fellow statesmen, financial
partners and of course to Napoleon himself. Fortunately a good many of
the letters have been collected and published since his death. He will also
reveal himself in the set pieces of Parisian society: in conversational spar-
ring at the dinner table, in an outburst at whist, in the busy gossip of the
salon with smart women around him, waiting to be intrigued. Virtually none
of this figures in his memoirs, but fortunately it is recorded in memoirs
penned by others, often by observant high society hostesses, the political
chatterboxes of Paris, some who hate him, some who are lost to his charm.
And what hostess of either persuasion can reject a man who maintains the
highest standards of taste and style even when circumstances may point to
lowering them? A familiar story spun about Talleyrand in frenzied revolutionary times – apocryphal, I fear, and therefore not meriting a direct place
in this life but reaching to his essence all the same – features an exhausted
Jacobin radical bursting into his study, clearly in need of sustenance.
Talleyrand hands him a glass of cognac, which he starts tossing down his
throat. Talleyrand, aghast, interrupts him:

'No, no, no, that is not the way to drink cognac. One does it like this.

One takes the glass in the hollow of the hand, one warms it, one shakes it with a circular motion to liberate the scent, then one raises it to one's nostrils, one breathes it in . . .'

'And then?' sighs his panicked visitor.

'And then, Sir, one puts one's glass down and one discusses it!'

I own to a certain favouritism towards Talleyrand on this count, authentic or not. Hear today's educated French people in dinner table discussion and someone, seeking to impress on one subject or another, will soon break in with: 'As Talleyrand said . . .' Then they're off, each venturing a version of some pearl of wit he is supposed to have uttered. The result is that he has to take credit for more badly mangled aphorisms than ever entered his head. This is the kind of dubious honour that, in English, Shakespeare and Churchill are obliged to bear. There is, moreover, a further count on which it is hard to deny Talleyrand sympathy. It is that the battle he won against Napoleon was in the end unfair. Unfair, that is, to Talleyrand. For in French hearts it matters little what hardship and misery Napoleon caused France. He gave the nation glory, lasting glory. Posterity permits no one to best Napoleon, as the map of today's Paris shows. The capital of the nation which Talleyrand ultimately rescued lives in eternal tribute to the destroyer he rescued it from. Spoking out from the massive Arc de Triomphe, a testament to Napoleon's military genius, run avenues with names that tell of his victories; the busy Place de la Concorde exhibits Napoleon's martial souvenirs in bronze and stone; from atop his column on the central Place Vendôme, the conqueror continues to command the city; his tomb at Les Invalides commands the river Seine. And Talleyrand? He has a single street named after him, a short alley in the Left Bank government quarter behind the present foreign ministry.

Scots, Welsh and Irish will take exception to being lumped together in this book with the majority of the inhabitants of the British Isles as 'the English', and to having the lands they live in called England. I apologise. To people like Talleyrand with roots in the *ancien régime* – and to Napoleon as well for that matter – the act of union between England and Scotland (1707) was still just raw enough in the mind to leave them thinking of the singular old enemy across the Channel in the age-old manner. As for union with Ireland, this was only being hammered out in their time. So Talleyrand and Napoleon, like their compatriots, never called the British nation anything but *les Anglais* or Britain anything but *Angleterre*, and because of the number of direct quotations concerning them in this book it would have been confusing to do otherwise. In subtler ways, to have gone for political correctness with 'British' would have ill conveyed Talleyrand's thinking, though it is a little strange perhaps that the French to this day continue to designate all Britons in everyday speech as *les Anglais*.

A word on the world as it appears in this book is also in order. The majority of its inhabitants, particularly those living east of Suez, won't locate themselves in the 'world' Talleyrand shapes and reshapes. To him the world is Europe; his concern is power, and Europe in his day is where world power begins and ends. The United States, whose future weight Talleyrand nonetheless foresees, is so new as to be left to herself once he manages to end his exile there. The Ottoman Empire exists purely to be played off against tsarist Russia. The rest of the planet is good chiefly for European colonisation, a jealous pursuit in his times.

Finally, money. Given Talleyrand's appetite for it, it has a potent place in this book. The currency Talleyrand was most interested in was the *livre* (pound) under the *ancien régime*, which became the *franc* after the Revolution and kept the same nominal value. It is well nigh pointless to make value comparisons with today's money but those who insist on trying to make some sense of Talleyrand's wealth may wish to evaluate his *franc* at a good £2 sterling – three-to-four euros or US dollars.

ONE

Born to Count

Talleyrand's parents were an unusual couple. His mother Alexandrine, the daughter of a Burgundian marquis, was six years older than his father Charles-Daniel, the stripling Count of Talleyrand-Périgord. Though both hailed from France's high aristocracy and were serving at the court of the Bourbon monarchy in Versailles some thirty years before revolution overturned their world, they were hard up. Family wealth that others of their rank took for granted stubbornly eluded them. In the case of Charles-Daniel, it was bestowed on an older half-brother. Inheritance rights at times went disconcertingly wrong in the tangled Périgord chain. Alexandrine's dowry, though solid, permitted few luxuries. There were chateaux in the provinces to compensate, but in Paris the young couple had barely enough to keep up the minimum living standards of their class: a mansion, servants, a carriage, mountains of linen. Furthermore their residence on the Left Bank, in the shadow of the church of Saint Sulpice, a step from the Seine, was a family home in the widest sense: it was rented in the name of Alexandrine's mother, so that sundry other relatives had lodging rights as required. The predicament seemed to burn itself into the tissue of their son born in the Paris home on 2 February 1754. Charles-Maurice de Talleyrand-Périgord would forever be obsessed by wealth, by both the lack of it and the amassing of it. He too was unusual. He was born with a club foot which neither parent cared to acknowledge as such.

Talleyrand arrived in the world fifteen years before Napoleon Bonaparte, who was born into the clannish small gentry of rugged Corsica, then practically a foreign land. Their worlds were so different as to make a future partnership the wildest of improbabilities. Each man, when he came to know the other, was forever aware of the gulf in class, breeding and upbringing, though only Napoleon much mentioned it.

The Talleyrand-Périgords were the stuff of France's *ancien régime*. It was a wonder any of their line proved able to find their way when the old order ceased to exist. The age Talleyrand was born into was not one of momentous change, but it was agitated all the same. Europe was on the brink of what would come to be known as the Seven Years War, a worldwide struggle in which France and Britain were, as usual, on opposing sides and which soon stripped France of her colonial possessions, including her prized lands in North America and India. Otherwise the long-reigning French king, Louis XV, ruled the country according to the unbudging feudal concepts of his Bourbon forefathers, and only the ruinous outcome of the war, plus the wanton extravagance of his court, showed signs of unsettling the established order. A greater danger did exist, though it was more subtle. It came from a determined and talented school of freethinkers.

Everything Talleyrand's parents undertook was directed by aristocratic tradition. Charles-Daniel was sixteen when he married Alexandrine, a capable young countess of twenty-two with a convent education behind her and a light indoctrination into Paris society and the arts. The marriage was made because it was high time for a girl of noble birth to have a husband on reaching her twenties. Although Charles-Daniel's financial situation was not all his Burgundian bride's family hoped for, his prospects appeared bright. He was in line to become a colonel in the king's grenadiers with a regiment to his name, a tribute to his fine lineage. This he traced back to the early Middle Ages when Counts of Périgord were sovereign rulers over a picturesque chunk of western France lying just above Aquitaine and the Bordeaux vineyards, centred on the Dordogne valley. The lords of Périgord were fully aware of their status. One of them, Adalbert, had a set-to over rank with Hugh Capet, France's first king. Family chronicles recorded a roosterish clash between the two at the close of the tenth century when Hugh Capet sought to bring the Périgord champion under his sway. 'Who made you Count?' inquired the king. 'Who made you King?' retorted Adalbert.

While grand, the Talleyrand-Périgords weren't strictly speaking every inch as grand as they felt. They were an offshoot of Count Adalbert's direct line that died out in the fifteenth century. The titles they bore had changed to Prince of Chalais and Count of Grignols, though Count of Périgord crept back into use with royal assent as the years went by and Talleyrand always figured somewhere in the family name. Often pronounced *ta-i-ran* – a variant that came to be favoured by Napoleon with his strong Corsican brogue – the name Talleyrand was a valorous sobriquet awarded to one of the medieval Périgord rulers for skill in scything through enemy ranks (from the French *taille-rang*).

It is true that our Talleyrand's enemies would delight in questioning his lineage as he rose above them, but this was spite. There could be no serious argument: his best inheritance was a great name. He was proud of it and it lent him a natural superiority he had no need to boast about. In later life he simply recalled that his father and mother were not wealthy, but that they held positions at court which if well used might lead them and their offspring as far as ambition ran.

With Alexandrine busy at Versailles as a lady-in-waiting and Charles-Daniel occupied by soldierly obligations, the couple had little time to take a close interest in the infant son, even if it had occurred to them to do so. Parental coddling was poor form, particularly in aristocratic houses. The duty of parents of high rank was to prepare the ground for their heirs' advance as adults, to secure positions for them, arrange a good marriage and enhance their fortunes. This entailed taking a serious interest in them when they turned fourteen or so. Infants could be ignored. Charles-Maurice was in fact their second child. A sickly first son was to die in early childhood, leaving Charles-Maurice as first heir. Two more sons would arrive. Still, our Talleyrand might well have expected his parents to be more conscious of the mood of the times than they were. For although the *ancien régime* was set to survive for a good three decades yet, the spirit of freethinkers with their liberal ideas on social reform filled the air. The country fizzed with new thinking on most matters. The Enlightenment was in full flow. Rousseau, Voltaire, Diderot and the *philosophes* were persuasive heralds of change, as most of the court at Versailles dimly realised, and they paid for their open-minded sins. Troublesome intellectuals were imprisoned, banished, even stoned. Books they wrote were not merely banned but in some cases burned. Still, if Jean-Jacques Rousseau's reforming notions on how to educate children were about to open the window to tenderness and to draw a large audience, the Talleyrand-Périgords weren't listening. They seemed impervious to the Enlightenment.

Frigid parenting was as much to blame as the club foot for the infant Talleyrand's exclusion. For excluded he was. What was more, none of his brothers was held apart in childhood as he was. He did not remember seeing his parents until he was four years old, and then only briefly. Even allowing for blanks of memory from such an early age and the likelihood that his mother at least kept an eye on him, he was scarred by his treatment. He took it as cruel indifference on his parents' part. Virtually from birth he was farmed out to a wet nurse in a scruffy north Paris suburb near Saint Denis. His exile upheld custom, but lasted uncustomarily long. His story was that during his time with the wet nurse he fell from the top of a cupboard where she'd placed him and broke his right foot, which she left unattended. Though the story was invented he stuck with it throughout his life, except when ribbing the squeamish (to them he said his foot was bitten by a stray pig when his nurse was attending to a passing manfriend). Publicly his family adopted the fall-from-the-cupboard yarn, as did his contemporaries and historians thereafter. Recently, however, a colour portrait of the time resurfaced of a first uncle wearing a tublike shoe plainly made to correct a club foot. Talleyrand's defect was congenital. Surgeons today virtually rule out the possibility that the misshapen right foot – later likened to 'a horse's hoof with a claw tip' by a woman devoted to him – could have resulted from a fall in the home at an age when bones hardly ever break or leave serious deformities if they do. Talleyrand certainly sensed that family shame over his condition consigned him to the wilderness of Saint Denis. His 'accident' changed the course of his life.

Plainly it posed a problem for his youthful father, the count. When the first son died, Charles-Maurice became rightful heir to the family estate, sparsely endowed though it was at the time. Being first in line in a noble house booked him for high service in the king's army. But he did not have a soldier's legs; he was not officer material. The family was in a funk. By Talleyrand's later account, it was left to chance in the person of another uncle, a naval grandee, to reunite him with his parents. The seafaring uncle had grown curious about his nephew's whereabouts. Perhaps in the long hours at sea he had been reading Rousseau. He found the boy in a grimy working-class back yard, dressed in tatters and chasing sparrows on a makeshift crutch. Shocked, he took the ill-clad child and presented him to his parents as they were receiving guests at their Paris residence. How could they abandon the scion of a great family to such squalor? The uncle's accusation was embarrassingly clear as he pushed the boy forward, saying, 'Go on, my lord and nephew. Kiss this lady. She is your mother.' Talleyrand later recalled the occasion as the first time he saw his mother and father. The reunion did not last long. At six he was sent off for a protracted stay with his great-grandmother in her chateau in the heart of the Périgord region close to Bordeaux, still unable to understand the seeming indifference of his parents.

The Bordeaux stagecoach he boarded with a new nurse took seventeen days to reach Chalais, the family's Périgord seat, a journey now made in four or five hours by car. The ride was grindingly rough and wearying. People of rank did not use the regular stagecoach; they took the post chaise, which was more expensive but more comfortable for being better sprung and could cut the journey by half. This second exile opened the child Talleyrand's eyes, and his heart. His time with his great-grandmother, the Princesse de Chalais, engraved on him a sense of ancient lineage and family grandeur of which he'd known nothing until then. It was an authentic, natural grandeur, and the more gracious for that. The mistress of Chalais, a busy septuagenarian, had a special aura: she was the granddaughter of Jean Baptiste Colbert, the chief minister to the Sun King, Louis XIV, and she was so much at ease with herself and her position that she spent more time fending for others than for herself. Her small heir with the bad leg at once took her sympathy. She showed him love and the boy felt it. He was consoled. She gave him the interest and warmth he lacked, and he gratefully responded, hopping around after her in the corridors of the old chateau to see how she lived and what she did. The princess was only too pleased to instruct him. Chalais was a sombre medieval pile but there was plenty of activity around. She was the first lady of the province; the greatest sin she could have committed was not to be generous and courteous towards her inferiors, from the local gentry to the peasantry. Lesser nobles returned the respect she showed them by paying her warm homage, and local country folk from all around sought her help when needed, particularly when they were unwell. 'The manners of the nobility in Périgord resembled their old chateaux,' Talleyrand would remember. 'There was something grand and stable about them; not much light but what light there was came softly. With deliberate slowness they advanced towards a more enlightened civilisation.'

A troop of elderly counts and squires paid court to the princess, widowed not two years before her great-grandson's arrival. Some of the gentlemen were related to her, others took up regular functions, such as accompanying her to mass in the parish church. She had her personal pew before the altar. Beside it she installed a small seat for Talleyrand. After mass, he followed her into a spacious hall in the chateau she called the 'apothecarium'. The hall was lined with shelves and tables containing pots of various ointments and powders which the chateau had concocted over the years, and giant bottles of elixirs and syrups refilled annually by the village doctor and the priest. In closed cupboards were supplies of bandages and rolls of finest linen of different cuts and sizes. Outside the hall sat ailing villagers and peasants who wanted help, and the princess and her limping heir passed between them with a greeting for everyone before entering the larger room, where she took up position in a velvet armchair in front of a black lacquered desk, wearing her Sunday bonnet and a small fur around her neck and shoulders, whatever the season. Her senior chambermaid called in the sick, one by one. A pair of nursing nuns inquired of each patient the nature of their illness or injury, then proposed a remedy. The princess considered their prescription and picked out the pot containing the proposed cure, whereupon the gentleman who had accompanied her to mass went to fetch it. Talleyrand, who had a chair beside the black desk, held out lengths of linen for his great-grandmother to cut into bandages and compresses of suitable size. It was a weekly rigmarole he loved to take part in. He spent two years at Chalais. After a time he knew which pot cured what and how to fend off a head cold: it entailed the noisy sniffing in and snorting out of water he would practise all his adult life – to the astonishment of those around him.

It was music to his child's ears to hear visitors to Chalais saying that the Talleyrand name had always been revered in the region. They would tell him his grandfather had given them their land; such and such a Talleyrand had built the church; such and such a Talleyrand lady had given their own wife a crucifix. Great families never change, they'd say, and he would surely grow up to be as great. At Chalais he learned to read and write, and if the religious side of life at the chateau failed to enthuse him, the book and pen side did. What makes a person the way he is? Talleyrand saw it perhaps more clearly than most, for he was aware that his personality was deeply marked by his early childhood. Against the shame of his club foot and his parents' indifference he could set deep pride in his lineage gained from the stay at Chalais. To the first his reaction was to hide his emotions, to turn his face from injury and insult; on account of the second he was forever aware of a natural superiority over most who crossed his path.

During his absence at Chalais his parents pondered and made a critical decision, though they declined to enlighten him on it for a while. At the age of eight, he returned to Paris by the same jolting public stage – seventeen days once more, to the very hour. He watched the old princess weep as he left and, for all his child's resolve to keep his feelings under lock and key, this time his own tears ran. By his account he was met at the Paris end of the exhausting journey not by his father, whose career was now advancing owing to his appointment as equerry to the Dauphin, the first in line to the throne, nor by his mother, but by a family valet who took him straight to an inner-city boarding school where his place had been reserved. He was used to such things by now, but still he was struck by the suddenness of his transfer to school, the direct move from stagecoach terminus to unfamiliar college without so much as a day spent in the family fold. He recalled: 'I was eight years old and my father's eye had yet to rest on me.'

He hadn't been long at Harcourt College, an august Paris establishment founded in 1280 to cater to the education of the aristocracy, before his parents informed him of their decision: due to his club foot, his career rights as first in line in the family order were to pass instead to a newborn brother who arrived in the family just after his return from Chalais. He might have guessed something disadvantageous was in store when his parents named the brother Archambaud after a sovereign Count of Périgord descended straight from the famous Adalbert. As a name Charles-Maurice was courtly enough, but Archambaud had true dynastic weight. The decision was final. Archambaud would carry the Périgord banner in the king's army; Charles-Maurice would enter the Church in accordance with the nobility's second-in-line traditions.

The dispossession was a huge blow to the boy as he moved through Harcourt. To be robbed of the rights of primogeniture was a humiliation. Worse, he hated the idea of joining the clergy. He already knew he wasn't made for the Church, despite the chances it offered the highborn. The parental decree was the sternest of tests for his newfound strength, his ability to conceal his emotions. He moved things around and upside down in his adolescent head. This, then, was why his parents hadn't taken him into the bosom of the family! All along they'd resolved it was in the family's best interests to place him in a calling for which he was ill-suited – and how could they have found the courage to tell him so if they'd kept him living in the family home? The somersault of logic permitted him to sympathise with his parents' plight, even to re-invent his exclusion from the home as proof of their love for him. For all his misgivings about the Church, here was a good Jesuit in the making. By turning things on their head it was easier for him to swallow his objections and put a blank face on suffering. It shaped a fundamental view of his in adulthood. He told himself: 'The first of all qualities in life is the art of showing only a part of oneself, of one's thoughts, one's feelings, one's impressions.'

Talleyrand's account of his childhood – the sole running record – no doubt erred here and there regarding the degree of his parents' coldness. Letters written by his mother revealed that she took him with her on several occasions to care for chronic leg pains caused by his deformity at the little spa town of Bourbon-l'Archambault, a watering place the Talleyrand family patronised near Vichy, a three-day carriage ride from Paris. Still, schooling him at Harcourt was no act of compassion. The establishment was indeed only a stone's throw from the Talleyrand home in Paris, but its rules were such that he could leave just once a week to visit the family on condition that he was accompanied by the novice priest attached to him as personal tutor. These meetings were brief; they took place over a Sunday meal. They invariably ended with a nugget of parental advice which sounded off-hand to his tender ears: 'Be good, my son, and make your tutor happy.' The rest of the week's schedule also followed an unchanging course: up at 6 a.m. each day, prayers at 6.15, private study until breakfast at 7.45, classes from 8.15 to 10.30, mass in the school chapel, catechism instruction, more private study until noon, lunch and recreation, classes from 1.30 to 4.30 p.m. (5 p.m. in summer), snack, further private study until 8 p.m., prayers, bed at nine.

Talleyrand was lonely at Harcourt. This was not because he made no friends or because his limp brought overmuch taunting from classmates, but because the school's churchly bent inspired solitariness. An older cousin of his was there; others in his family had been there before him. It was in fact the first time he had been in the company of boys of his class. One he grew close to was Auguste de Choiseul, a nephew of the Duc de Choiseul, one of the great statesmen of the age. The duke was now in charge of French external policy: he was the king's minister of war following a good run as foreign minister. What fascinated the boy Talleyrand about his classmate's uncle was that, first, he was a great man who somehow seemed within reach, and second – though this seemed a vaguer wonder at the time – he held great power while also being a friend of the *philosophes* and freethinkers. The duke's skill in marrying the ways of the old order with modern ideas certainly caught the boy Talleyrand's fancy, for he later wrote a personal study of the duke, his sole venture into political biography. For the time being, though, he was content to sit next to the talkative nephew during meals in the refectory. Auguste de Choiseul, an irritating lad at times, would remain a close friend all his life.

Talleyrand never excelled at Harcourt. He plunged into classical studies, philosophy and theology, faring well enough to meet the single demand his parents made on him at the end of his weekly visit home. His tutor did stay 'happy' with him, or at least did not complain to his parents. Only as he ended his seven years at Harcourt did he come face to face with the future his parents had remodelled for him. They sent him to Reims to stay with his youthful uncle Alexandre-Angélique, his father's brother, who had like-wise been dispatched into the priesthood, in his case most willingly. The uncle was already adjutant to the Archbishop of Reims, a cardinal, and was himself preparing to take over both these ranks at the summit of the French Church. Reims was the premier archbishopric in the realm. The object of the trip was to encourage Talleyrand, now fifteen, to think positively about the career imposed on him. To keep up appearances the family sent him to Reims in a post chaise, which picked him up at Harcourt. It wouldn't do to embarrass an archbishop-in-waiting by having his nephew step down at the episcopal palace in Reims from a public stagecoach.

This was 1769, the year Napoleon was born in rustic Corsica, and Talleyrand was finally travelling in style. What was more, by way of coincidence that meant nothing to him then, he felt a certain kinship with the man who had lately brought Napoleon's island birthplace into France. That man was the Duc de Choiseul, the model diplomat in Talleyrand's young eyes. The first building pieces in the improbable future relationship between Talleyrand and Napoleon seemed already to be dropping into place.

The natural sense of superiority that Napoleon would always envy in Talleyrand received a further lift from the stay in Reims. Life in the arch-bishop's palace was luxurious, though he had to wear a black cassock to please his uncle, which gave him less pleasure. The high clergy such as his uncle, who came from France's noblest houses by royal appointment with a nod from the pope, were extremely well rewarded. A large proportion of the country's 130 bishoprics were controlled by just a dozen great families; churchmen of bishop's rank and above thus inherited annual incomes such as those received two centuries later by the more self-indulgent chief exec-utives of major business corporations. It was some compensation for the disadvantage of being kept out of the king's army and out of immediate reach of the royal favour.

The young visitor to Reims was able to appreciate all this. Furthermore, he was fond of his uncle and admired him. Yet something still jarred. Churchly pomp and rite disturbed him. Was the sacrifice he was being asked to make worth it? In Reims he found highborn women beginning to look at him in a new, disarming way. He was a good-looking youth, pale, fair-haired, with regular features and a slightly upturned nose. In the women's eyes, as far as he could tell, his limp didn't detract overmuch from his appeal. He fretted endlessly over his predicament. He still did not want to give in. He simply wasn't suited to the religious life. In the end, though, his defence mechanism took charge: act indifferent, never show suffering. It was the only way. Besides, life in the Church was freer than its rules suggested. In practice there weren't many constraints. Bishops jumped into amours and sired offspring with the intemperate dash of cavalry officers, scarcely bothering to hide their out-of-church activities. They were, after all, of the same class.

After a year spent in Reims seeing what life in the Church held out for him, Talleyrand was not converted. He was, however, resigned. There was no escaping the family plan. On his return to Paris in the spring of 1770 he entered the seminary of Saint Sulpice, a stone's throw from where he was born, to prepare for the priesthood. He was sixteen years old.

TWO

In the Black

If the vows Talleyrand now contemplated seemed a straitjacket, the seminary of Saint Sulpice was freedom compared with life at Harcourt. The adolescent entrant, sporting the seminarian garb of black knee-breeches and black silk frockcoat, had plenty of time to himself. Saint Sulpice was largely reserved for sons of the aristocracy destined for the highest posts in the Church. The institution was walled in on all sides, with courtyards and gardens in the middle, but there was little to stop its young inmates from stepping out into the street and communicating with the fashionable Left Bank district of Saint Germain outside. It was a district full of shops, townhouses and ministries of the king's government, and it was the place to be for those who liked to air their views on the state of France. The seminary head and its teachers, wise to the power of new thinking and the threat it represented to the Church's ancient methods, went some way towards adapting their instruction to the times.

Even so, Talleyrand considered himself miserable. He couldn't get the loss of his family rights out of his mind. The insult preyed on him. Now that he was a young man the seeming unfairness of his demotion due to a deformity that was none of his fault made him not just resentful but angry. He kept himself to himself. 'I spent three years at Saint Sulpice almost without speaking. They thought I was aloof and often reproached me,' he would recall, exaggerating his plight. Little did they know; he was simply brooding. For truer to say, Talleyrand benefited enormously from his years at the seminary and came to enjoy it more than he allowed. He in fact spent not three but four years there, including the time needed to take his baccalaureat in theology from the nearby Sorbonne University. He did not shine at straight religious studies. Perhaps that was fore-ordained. 'They want to make a priest of me. All right! You'll see, they'll be making a terrible one,' he told fellow seminarians with dark glee. As it was, philosophy and the wider field of theology were at the heart of the syllabus and they were a sound basis for a good many careers, even outside the Church. He established his

own learning agenda, based on Saint Sulpice's enormous stock of thirty thousand books, some of which may not have met with the pope's approval. He
tucked himself away with books recounting explorers' voyages, storms,
mutinies, the more perilous and risky the better. 'I devoured the most revolutionary books I could find,' he recalled, 'feeding on history, rebellion, sedition and upheavals galore.' Did he have a sixth sense of what was coming in
France? This, in any event, was useful preparation for it.

There was also the girl he observed regularly at mass in the church of
Saint Sulpice. She came on her own. She was pretty, with a simple, modest
way about her that appealed to him. He wanted to talk to her but couldn't
pluck up the courage. She had barely looked his way. He was now eighteen
and his knowledge of women was limited, as far as arousal was concerned,
to wandering looks he had received from lady guests at his uncle's residence
in Reims. The hags who smiled his way at fireworks displays he'd been to
in his seminary vestments on public feast days in Paris hadn't much tempted
him. Besides, strictly speaking he was heading for a life of celibacy. Priests-
in-training like himself were already addressed as Father, which seemed a
certain drawback. He was Father Périgord. It was hard to get used to.

A nicely timed Paris downpour eventually came to his aid with the girl at
mass. He'd come to the church with an umbrella, the kind then in fashion
that opened inside up. Seeing her standing in the church doorway after the
service waiting to brave the rain, he overcame his shyness and offered to share
it with her. The innocence with which she accepted his offer somehow encouraged him to slip his arm into hers and limp alongside her. Her rooms were
not three minutes from the church and they had hardly begun talking before
they arrived. She invited him to climb the steps to her quarters to shelter
from the rain. There was a fireplace in the cramped apartment and once they
were sitting there drying off she told him who she was. The information was
an extra dart of excitement for Talleyrand: she was an actress at the Comédie
Française, a debutante. Her family had obtained a place for her in the king's
troupe against her wishes; she really hadn't wanted to be an actress at all.

Talleyrand was completely taken. He and the girl were in the same boat.
He was being forced into the Church against his will; she had been forced
into the theatre. The two of them smiled over their common lot, rueful
accomplices. The girl's name was Dorothée Luzy. Young and demure though
she looked – 'pure', as Talleyrand remembered her – she was older than he,
already past twenty, and was playing mostly parlour-maid roles at the start
of her Comédie Française career. By his account it was she who invited him
back the following day to renew acquaintances. He was not to know it, but
she was not so pure as to lack an elderly manfriend who rented her rooms
for her. No matter. She was Talleyrand's first love. Soon he was hobbling

over from the seminary to see her almost every day, not bothering to keep their liaison a secret either from his masters at Saint Sulpice or from local shopkeepers. They were a neighbourhood couple, seen everywhere together.

This was risky for Talleyrand, and he surely realised it. Aside from the fact that this sort of relationship wasn't part of the seminary code, the renown of the Comédie Française couldn't dispel the broadly accepted notion that the stage was for coquettes, and the Father Superior at Saint Sulpice grew increasingly upset with Talleyrand on both counts. He had it in mind to expel the wayward young aristocrat; the fault was not sin alone, it looked more like revolt. There were reasons for lenience, however. Sulpice authorities shrank from the scandal of an expulsion. They also wanted to keep on the good side of Talleyrand's uncle, the prospective archbishop of Reims, who followed the religious side of his nephew's seminary career with close interest.

Thanks largely to his devout uncle, who manipulated the levers of holy privilege without fuss, Talleyrand received his baccalaureat in theology from the Sorbonne a full year ahead of schedule. A surplus of talent was recorded as the reason for this success. The diploma was his exit ticket from the seminary, but also his pass into a life which still filled him with the darkest doubt. At Saint Sulpice, once over the sullen start, he'd probably learned more than most about how to conduct himself in society. However, his uncle wanted him back in Reims to advance his churchly career without further ado.

The dread moment occurred on April Fool's Day 1774. Talleyrand was just twenty. A provincial bishop lined up by his uncle to administer the religious orders did so with due care, without bullying. Talleyrand heard him offer the traditional let-out that would forever after swirl in his mind. Until this moment he remained free! Once he took the vow there was no breaking it. He would be locked in God's service for good. Committed to celibacy. But there was still time to reflect, and he should do so. Should he decide to persist in his holy resolve, then in the name of the Lord he must advance and . . .

Talleyrand advanced. He knelt before the bishop, displaying not the slightest sign of the awe, trepidation and disgust that turned within him. By now he knew what he was doing and he would make the most of it. He had overcome his horror the night before when his friend from schooldays, Auguste de Choiseul, found him in tears, the soul of despair. Clearly Talleyrand was taking the whole thing with the utmost seriousness; he wasn't comforting himself with thoughts of the lax habits of highborn churchmen of the day. Choiseul implored him to turn away if the prospect grieved him so deeply. It was too late, said Talleyrand, collecting himself. His family expected it. There was no going back. The emphasis he put on family expectations no doubt rang a little hollow in his ears as he took his religious orders that day. Neither his father nor his mother attended.

His first steps in the Church, as under-deacon, were rapid. His uncle saw to it that within a week or so he was named a canon at Reims cathedral, then by early autumn he was made abbot of a handsome Reims abbey, a proxy post where he took the income without having to take up residence. This helped assuage his worst qualms about the Church. The Reims diocese was exceedingly wealthy. Together the posts brought him some 26,000 livres a year, a good one hundred times what a Paris worker earned. For a young man still involved in studies, with a master's degree in theology to take before his ordination as a full-fledged priest, his financial security was at once assured.

This was a prime concern of his already met. Still, it hardly stemmed his desire for fortune. A fortuitous bonus at once followed, with the death of Louis XV. In June 1775, just two months after Talleyrand took his vows, Reims cathedral staged the ancient religious rites for the coronation of his first son, Louis XVI, in an explosion of pomp and splendour of a kind France would never again show its kings. Louis XVI was to be the last absolute monarch by divine right. Revolution saw to that. But the ceremony gave Talleyrand a perfect chance to acquaint himself with the all-powerful court. Talleyrand's father was present this time, fulfilling a coronation walk-on role conferred by Périgord family rank. The new under-deacon looked on impassively. For all the brilliance of the occasion he saw its laughable side. Yet at the same time the pageant exalted the France of which he felt himself a special part. Just to be present was to sense his natural right to lead the affairs of a nation whose history was in his bones. He was fated to be in charge; there was really never much doubt about that. Only in retrospect did he see the pageant for what it was. He recollected, 'Never has so brilliant a springtime preceded so stormy an autumn, so grim a winter.'

At the time, though, the coronation was a first chance to mingle with the grandees of the Versailles court and with the priestesses young and old of Paris high society. Among the golden throng were the new king's two younger brothers, whom he met and from whom he received a passing word of acknowledgement. How could he possibly foresee the difficulties he would face in tangling with the pair of them as the old France came crashing down and they in turn, thanks to him, became kings, though of a lesser order and much later on?

A young man of the cloth with Talleyrand's high prospects wasn't chained to his living. The Church was easy-going as regards residence rules. By the time winter set in he left provincial Reims to find lodgings in Paris. With his Church income he was able to rent a comfortable two-storey Left Bank house on the Rue de Bellechasse in the Saint Germain district. The house had six windows overlooking a crossing from where the Rue de Bellechasse led down to the Seine. The move was a return to his seminarian pastures, but the ground rules of life had rather changed in his favour. To begin with, relations with his parents and brothers, who lived nearby, were on an entirely different footing. His new rank brought down fences erected during his childhood. He was able to sue for better terms with his family, first with his mother, whose company he now sought and moreover enjoyed, also with Archambaud and a second younger brother, Boson. He took a hand in supporting his brothers despite Archambaud's leapfrog to the rank of first Périgord heir, which in financial terms at least was a hollow honour. All in all it was a curious family coming-together, not so much a family reunion as a making of acquaintances.

More to the point, he now entered Paris society. The talents he honed in this small, excitable, back-biting, power-conscious world were those that Napoleon, when the time came, most admired and envied. They were talents that made him indispensable to Napoleon, who had no sense of them himself. Their application was infinitely broader than the small world that shaped them. Talleyrand was a serious young man in the main. While affecting well-born insouciance, he was capable of the most diligent concentration. He now began the two-year pursuit of a master's degree in theology, a level of scholarship required of an aspiring prince of the Church. This increased his interest in books, and he began putting together a library which impressed a set of highborn friends he made on his social rounds. They took to gathering at his home most mornings at around eleven o'clock for a late breakfast to discuss the great issues of the day. Gone was the solitary Talleyrand of boyhood. The transformation struck everyone who knew him. The feeling of rejection, the resentment, lay behind him. He had a new, more elastic approach to life: it could buffet him, wound him, but he would ride the bumps. From his encounter with books at Saint Sulpice he developed a passion for precious ones, and he spent a small fortune on them. The books he collected were not simply objects of delight; they were, he liked to think, an investment. He loved the binding, the print, the texture of the paper. His collection ranged from history, literature and the economy to the erotic, which he unblushingly lent out to his new friends.

His interest in the issues of the day was best satisfied, though, by plunging into the frothier delights of Paris society. There was no contradiction here: it was the way of his class. To hell with theology, he told himself. On with life's pleasures. This was part self-indulgence, part fashionable pretence. Everyone was chasing pleasure. Yet he seldom lost sight of his serious pursuits. In precisely the two years allotted to him, he took his theology degree and was ordained a priest. At once he became a vicar-general at Reims, a rank with an impressive ring.

The formal last step into the Church was less of a trial for him than taking his initial religious vows. The heat of his inner crisis had cooled. He could see it now. The Church did not have to be a dead-end career for someone like himself with French history in his veins. More than a century had passed since men in scarlet like Richelieu and Mazarin, cardinals both, stood at France's summit and shaped Europe by the tip of their mitre, but there was still a role for a prince of the Church. Indeed theology had its own virtues. There was, as it happened, no better drilling ground for the profession Talleyrand was to exercise in life. For the benefits of theological training weren't necessarily of a moral order. What it did was to instil orderly, logical thought – in particular the dialectical art of setting up one's questions in such a way as to be able to answer them without fear of being bested, a definite edge in any argument. Talleyrand knew this. If he pretended to close his eyes to it, it was because the pursuit of pleasure on the one hand and progress through the power structure in France on the other had never dovetailed quite so agreeably as they did in the wilting final decades of the *ancien régime*.

Paris society was where the two met. Its mood was increasingly open. Rousseau was in full liberal flow until his untimely death in 1778, the year Talleyrand was ordained. Voltaire's provocative legacy was a feast spread before the elite's eyes. Adam Smith's *Wealth of Nations* transformed thinking on the economy and was at once devoured by young French intellectuals, Talleyrand among them, who wanted a fresh view on the world. A malicious volume entitled *Les Liaisons Dangereuses* was on the writing pad of an unknown army officer named Choderlos de Laclos to plot the moral free-for-all of the age and to skewer its participants. The monarchy, being absolute, wasn't happy about any of this, but in seeking to stop it merely found that it had to put up with it. This was the time when the French monarchy was drawn incongru-ously into the American War of Independence on the side of American rebels intent on setting up a republic. Royalist France was no more enthused by the creation of a republic across the Atlantic than royalist England was. But the wave of liberal thinking, together with the chance to confront England and punish her for having seized huge French territories in North America, sent France into war on the American side. The war in uncharted America was a draw for young French idealists. Boson, Talleyrand's listless youngest brother, took himself there and for once gave a good account of himself.

Such were the issues that embroiled the salons of Paris where the youthful Father Périgord made his debut. It took time to make a mark, but Talleyrand possessed excellent entry credentials. The aristocratic hostesses recognised him as one of them. All he needed was to create a salon persona for himself.

At the coronation rites in Reims he had met three young society women, two duchesses and a viscountess, all married to worthy older husbands and none of them much older than he, who now took him in tow and, in turn, between their sheets. The Duchesse de Luynes, the Duchesse de Fitz-James and the Vicomtesse de Laval each had her own bubbling charm and opinions on events of the day, and, what was more, regularly opened her home as a literary salon. He was to remain friends for life with all three. If he used them shamelessly, even ungratefully at times, they didn't seem to mind. From the start they found something seductive in the highborn priestling with the golden hair, cool blue eyes, the pale face and the limp. They too could be shameless. Social vices weren't tragic: women of their rank enjoyed much liberty in their private lives. Married women in particular changed lovers with the weather if they wished. Not all their freedom was spent on cuckolding ageing husbands and casual amours; there was also a deep thirst for knowledge and a busybody urge to put the ideas of Rousseau and fellow modernisers into practice.

The end of the eighteenth century in France in the run-up to revolution was a time of exceptional ease and pleasure for the privileged classes and Talleyrand lived it to the full. He fully realised how lucky he was. 'Those who did not live before 1789 do not know the joy of life,' he recalled. But he wasn't too young to miss its glaring ambiguities; indeed, he explored them endlessly with the gang of new friends he had in Paris. How to reconcile the life of privilege with the notion of equality contained in the new thinking? How to match high society's generosity of sentiment with its absence of principle? The court at Versailles with the needs of the people? The age was one of unsurpassed elegance with little clue where it was headed.

The salons where Talleyrand enjoyed his evenings, often staying for supper, weren't primarily debating chambers for political issues, though the emphasis swung further and further that way. He lived at the time the Paris restaurant first appeared, often providing quite high-quality cuisine, though restaurants were still too unfamiliar a feature of the street to be relied upon. He never went to one. It wasn't that he steered clear of them, rather that he didn't think of going there. People of his class either ate at home or at a salon where they had a role to play, or were devising one. Most salons sought to keep up their original literary bias. Salon-goers read from books and articles they themselves were writing or from books written by others that were making a stir and tugging at prejudices. Readings from Rousseau's *La Nouvelle Héloïse*, a confirmed favourite by now, still brought sobs from guests and set off emotional debates on love and the purity of sentiment. Science, art, economics, religion all competed for attention with salacious gossip about the royal court, though the young Talleyrand soon learned it was unwise to get overexcited and publicly wander too far out of line in discussing the king and his family. Versailles had ears. Better to snip at the court than slash at it. Or leave the task to court figures themselves. Even the stiff Jacques Necker, a Swiss banker and long-serving French finance minister, could unwind in a salon: France's finances were in a tailspin and it was plain to all, particularly to Talleyrand and his circle, that alternatives existed to policies the king was pursuing but that he was scared to change them for fear of further undermining his position.

The Neckers ran a salon of their own where their precocious daughter Germaine was styling herself to take over as hostess. On marrying the Swedish ambassador to France the doughty Necker girl became Madame de Staël, a prodigious political authoress whom Napoleon came to dislike intensely. Germaine looked forward to Talleyrand's visits to the family salon. In her intriguer's eyes he had precisely what appealed to her: he was both exceedingly clever, she thought, and ambitious. Not only that. She found him 'the most impenetrable and indecipherable of men', quite an admission for a young woman who believed she knew most things. No one helped him more than she when he needed it. In return he went to her bed, which his friends found brave on his part.

Talleyrand delighted in the company of women. He found their wit quicker than that of most men. And they were extremely useful. The kind he met could put in a good word for him in high places. All the same the true salon heavyweights were men. They held high positions, many of them, and were privy to the latest twists in royal policy. They knew who was in favour, who was out. Now he regularly bumped into his schoolfriend's distinguished uncle, the Duc de Choiseul, whom he had looked up to without ever meeting when at Harcourt. By now the duke had retired from government. Talleyrand was disappointed to find him less inspiring than he'd expected. There was a little too much of the court toady about him. But he was struck by insights the duke insisted on offering on how to run the country and he held the advice in mind for all time. 'In my ministry I always got people to work harder than I worked myself,' Choiseul confided. 'You mustn't get buried under paper, you must find people to handle it for you. You govern the affairs of a nation by a gesture, a sign, by putting in the comma that makes sense of everything.' The old duke was all for spending time in salons, though, and he counselled: 'A minister who goes out in the world can pick up signs of danger at any moment, even at a reception. What can he grasp when shut up in his office?'

There were large salons and small ones for Talleyrand to frequent, bold ones and timorous ones, famous ones and deliberately intimate ones. They were mostly reception rooms in grand Paris townhouses with fireplaces and banks of couches and armchairs, often with adjoining rooms in which to exchange confidences or advance a promising liaison, with candles shedding soft light on powdered heads and rouged cheeks, and perhaps a string quartet at work. Salon air was sometimes a little stale, indeed rank. For both sexes believed in freshening themselves up by spraying more scent and more powder on old. Even then the atmosphere was distinctly preferable to the odour of the streets outside, so that salons altogether made inviting venues for those who liked talking, listening, flirting, flaunting their wit, knowledge and high manners, or just sitting around and imbibing the atmosphere. Since newspapers were subject to royal censorship, the most titillating political and social news circulated in the salon. What Talleyrand heard there didn't compare in inflammatory venom with what appeared in pamphlets penned by agitators on the Paris streets, but it nonetheless had a delicious edge to it which his class better understood. The theatrical good manners of the salon much appealed to him: they permitted boldness, enabling one to pass off the most mischievous dig as a compliment. The spirit was very consciously droll. Talleyrand was amused to hear younger men than he addressing young women in the third person. (Would she perchance agree to read this poem? Would she allow me to take her arm?) With his own adjustments, Talleyrand made extreme salon politesse a weapon from the start of his career and used it to advantage all his life. He kept it razor sharp for Napoleon.

Then there was the elegance of dress, a further salon requirement that suited Talleyrand, who took great care with his attire. He contrived to look spruce in black priestly garb and when he chose instead to wear city clothes, which he often did, he cut a fancy figure in blue habit, white waistcoat, chamois leather breeches, silk stockings and snow-white cravat riding fashionably high up the chin. He wasn't the only priest about town. In that, he was well upstaged. He particularly enjoyed dropping by at the residence of Madame de Montesson, who had a certain notoriety through being the mistress of the Duc d'Orléans, the head of France's reserve royal house, rival to the reigning Bourbons. At Mme de Montesson's a cast of Catholic bishops, often accompanied by the Duc d'Orléans himself, took part most evenings in risqué plays composed during the day by their lubricious hostess. As Talleyrand gleefully remembered it, Madame de Montesson's salon hovered 'on the far edge of decency'. The hostess played the harp between her legs.

Salons were luxury clubs at a time when little other relaxation and casual entertainment was available to Paris society. Invariably they were named after the homeowner's wife or mistress. The hostesses set the tone for a free-for-all of intellectual preening at which the most welcome calling card, together with polished manners, was wit. Hostesses competed for wit. The most tigerish of them dispatched their personal carriages the length of Paris to fetch guests they could count on to provide a sharp performance.

Talleyrand won an early reputation as a wit, though he might be forgiven for wondering why. For his first evening social call he personally preferred a small, intimate salon of a dozen or so guests, perhaps because he came to value the tactical silence as the sharpest weapon in discussion. Yet his salon persona was established at a large one. The occasion was his first visit to the residence of Madame de Boufflers, a sumptuously appointed home that left new guests agape. A regular caller there was the Comtesse de Gramont, a vinegary grande dame of the salon circuit who took it in mind that evening to bellow across the salon to Talleyrand that she hadn't seen him before. Why, she wanted to know, had she heard him gasp 'Ah, ah' as he entered the salon? The great room hushed. Eyes turned on the young priest. It was plain the countess aimed to ridicule him. 'I believe you misheard me,' Talleyrand replied gravely. 'I didn't say "Ah, ah", I said "Oh, oh".' The room broke into laughter. Talleyrand was silent for the rest of the evening. Thereafter his salon invitations multiplied. He was a wit. He himself wasn't sure, though, that what he felt to be his 'miserable' off-the-cuff response hadn't been pure nonsense. The reputation he acquired he put down rather to the cool manner and reserve he practised displaying. He wasn't one for Gallic hand gestures and arm circling. Indeed he rejected such accoutrements to conversation as the worst enemy of wit. They were one thing that irritated him even now about his good friend Choiseul, a helpless arm waver. 'As with all people who make a lot of gestures,' Talleyrand noted, 'he is amused by what he says and repeats it. In old age he'll be impossible.' Poor Choiseul.

Talleyrand's own reputation wasn't entirely built on reserve. It also grew from a gift for sharp repartee, from an ability to cut to the heart of outlandish events and characters in a single telling phrase, and from the subtle nuances of his courtly language. Then there was the twinkle barely visible in his impassive gaze, plus a way with courtesy and charm in dealing with women that bewitched most hostesses. As one of them noted, a little warily: 'It was impossible not to grant him your favour, impossible to grant him your trust.' All the same they thirsted for flattery and he was ever ready with the potion.

By 1780, when Talleyrand was twenty-six, he had assumed a demanding Church administrative post. This was again thanks to his thoughtful uncle. The post of Agent-General of the French clergy effectively made him captain of the priesthood's national union. As such he was its representative in dealing with the royal court. The task was to defend the interests of the clergy on all fronts. Though the post was co-held with a priest of similar rank, he was young and inexperienced to hold so highly visible a position. The eyes of the nation's nervous priesthood were trained on him. In view of his busy social programme, which he did not intend to abandon, there were some doubts at first that he would have time to fulfil the function effectively.

The brainstorming breakfasts he hosted at his house were still an important part of his day, as well as his salon rounds. His continuing passion for gambling meant regular late-night sessions of whist, his favourite card game. He took to whist and spent endless hours at it because it had all the elements that appealed to him: chance, uncertainty, guile and the prospect of winning a decent pot to supplement his Church income. By his reckoning he won a good deal more than he lost. Hiding his hand appealed to him. It seemed a good rule to apply to professional life, which he unfailingly did. It wasn't much different from hiding his emotions, and achieved much the same effect on others. Whist for heavy stakes was played mainly in casinos, which weren't strictly legal under the *ancien régime*. The Duc d'Orléans, never one to accommodate rules made by the Bourbon court, hosted a casino which he passed off as a salon where Talleyrand often dallied. Even the regular literary salons set out a table or two for card players, so that when Talleyrand wasn't at a casino or at the Orléans residence he usually ended up at one of these. Late nights – most often continuing until 3 a.m. for hardbitten whist players – ruled out early rising.

His late breakfasts for intellectual friends were joshing and sometimes rowdy sessions with curious minds competing to score points. The morning was a let-down if it failed to come up with some sort of remedy for the regime's latest ailment. Intellectual jousting wasn't all they came for. Even at this hour Talleyrand made sure he provided a fine table. He brushed it off at the time as 'any old fare', his code for a carefully concocted meal. He had acquired a personal valet by now, a fine fellow named Joseph Courtiade who was a year older than himself. Courtiade, who wore black tights and a black redingote to express the dignity of being in service to a rising churchman, saw to his creature comforts. He always had a supply of fresh linen ready to satisfy his master's dress demands, the high white cravats, white shirts and ample undergarments by which Talleyrand swore as his defence against chills. Avoiding colds was a near obsession with him. The breakfasts he and Courtiade organised – early luncheons in effect – were a preview of future achievements in hospitality which Talleyrand's contemporaries couldn't pretend to match and which Napoleon shrewdly came to employ to his own benefit; anyone Napoleon wished to impress, from high statesmen to monarchs, he would send to Talleyrand's table.

Breakfast regulars included his schoolfriend Choiseul, now a traveller and budding ambassador; Comte Louis de Narbonne, a brilliant young man about town and son of Louis XV from the wrong side of the royal sheets; Armand de Biron, an adventurous young duke already returned from fighting the

American War of Independence; and Pierre-Samuel Dupont de Nemours, a business brain Talleyrand listened to closely because he was full of schemes for doubling friends' money with investments. (Dupont's heirs would become pillars of American industrial capitalism.) There were more of them in Talleyrand's morning set, most notably Honoré de Mirabeau, ten years older than he, a passionate and wildly ugly nobleman from the south who let off romantic steam on France's social failings to the point where the rest of the group berated him for monopolising their sessions. Talleyrand was a little disdainful of Mirabeau, though not without affection for him: the older man was a hothead, full of ideas but only half in control of himself, a failing that enabled Talleyrand to toy with him in debate, which he rather enjoyed. How could he foresee that the panting Mirabeau was about to dominate a revolution with his oratory, while his breath held out?

The morning group's guru was Isaac Panchaud, as extravagant a figure as Mirabeau in his way. Panchaud, a Swiss by origin, was a banker and economic theorist who flatly disagreed with practically everything anyone who was running the king's treasury did. With Panchaud in full cry, there was no more provocative a course on political economy to be had in Paris than a Talleyrand breakfast. This wasn't dry theoretical stuff; for Talleyrand it was 'full of charm'. French ministers used Panchaud as a consultant on and off to familiarise themselves with what they might have been doing but weren't. Economics was a new science which Talleyrand vaguely believed, when first immersing himself in it, would increase the general prosperity and improve life's comforts. He described Panchaud as a genius: 'He married the broadest, sharpest, most passionate wit with perfect reason. He was the master of every kind of eloquence.' Beyond his golden tongue, Panchaud's first speciality was in fact financial speculation and what later financial artists came to call venture capitalism. Stock markets, currencies, bills of exchange, government credit, capital movements were all wells of profit for the risk-taker.

With his hunger for wealth, speculation of this kind naturally appealed to Talleyrand; he began investing in earnest. Grasping the complexities of financial markets via Panchaud was an asset Talleyrand used to advantage in other ways too. It helped him in the Church work he now faced, which turned largely on finance. It gave him an itch to involve himself in France's floundering finances, which he did by proffering reports of his own to the king's finance ministry, currently run by the hard-pressed Comte Charles-Alexandre de Calonne, who appeared to welcome the priestly assistance. It was Talleyrand who devised a plan to refloat the faltering establishment that preceded a genuine central bank. The secret, he insisted, was to keep lending rates low and the money supply high. The experienced Calonne was impressed.

While there was something naïve in Talleyrand's worship of Panchaud, something which certainly had its roots in the desire to amass wealth for himself, the schooling set him on a definite political path. There was a steady philosophy behind Panchaud's schemes. In finance he was a convinced Anglophile, and so, if only in outlook, an accomplice of the enemy; he knew English financial institutions inside out and admired them. Free trade was the basis of his theory, a firm English principle upheld by a vigilant Royal Navy. In September 1783, then, as the American War of Independence came to an end and France and England signed their own peace closing it out, the time looked ripe to Talleyrand to move his country in England's free-trading direction. Siding with the American colonies had cost France dear. The French treasury was ruined. Though France was more populous than England and inherently rich, its economy lagged far behind. Talleyrand now picked up free trade as his banner and carried it for the rest of his days. Economics, in his reckoning, was divided between two schools: one, followed by the *ancien régime*, to its detriment, saw agriculture as the source of all wealth and tax revenue for the state; the other saw prosperity in untrammelled free trade. Talleyrand's belief in open trade drove an impossible wedge between himself and Napoleon in due course, since its first purpose was unrestricted trade with the very country whose lines of commerce Napoleon went to extreme lengths to cut. To Talleyrand, the hereditary foe had to be France's first partner; there was no way round it, it was the key to peace in Europe.

Somehow, despite his many activities, Talleyrand managed to satisfy the clergy he was fully engaged on their behalf as Agent-General. And in his incisive manner, he was. His capacity for hard work was tested to the limit. He worked through the night when necessary to get important letters out. He was adept at cutting to the marrow of clerical concerns. It wasn't a question of being religious, it was a question of being practical. It was also an immersion in statecraft. If it was strange that the most reluctant of priests was acting as chief representative and defender of the priesthood, Talleyrand declined to agonise over the contradiction. He was taking his chances as they came now. A bishop's mitre was in his sights. His pedigree plus his forbearing uncle would see to that – unless a helpful salon hostess with influence at court were first to oblige. It was the king who appointed bishops, with only an after-nod from Rome.

Through the Church the clergy owned a good quarter of all land in the kingdom, with revenues higher than the royal treasury's. Yet the clergy, the first of France's three estates – coming before the aristocracy and the bourgeoisie – was on the defensive. Public opinion was increasingly hostile to its power and privilege. The *philosophes* had made it the butt of their ridicule. As the stodgiest pillar of the old order, the Church seemed particularly vulnerable. Now it feared the monarchy could start confiscating its vast properties to avert financial ruin resulting from France's military engagement on the side of the American rebels. The war was ungrateful. The making of the United States was the unmaking of old France.

Talleyrand tackled the threat head on with the silken courtesy he made his trademark. He wrote directly to the king's foreign minister, the lofty Charles de Vergennes: 'Your sincere love for religion is too well known, Sir, and I am too well persuaded of your respect for the laws, of your fairness, of your breadth of understanding, and of the prudence and wisdom of your views to find the slightest cause for alarm in these wild and indiscreet reflections.' Listen to the diplomat. Presumptuous though it was for the youthful Church functionary to go straight to the top of government, the flattering language worked. Talleyrand's young shoulders carried a mature head. The great Vergennes assured him he had no secret intention to harm the clergy.

Talleyrand bubbled with ideas to improve the clergy's standing in public opinion. Some fell on their face. The royal lotteries that raised money for the king's purse struck him as a disgrace. As a gambler himself, he spied the crookedness that had crept into the organisation of the lotteries and, somewhat archly in view of his own predilections, pronounced them immoral. His proposal was simple: the Church would buy the royal lotteries in order to close them down. Each year it would pay the king a sum equivalent to the size of the lottery take. Thus would the Church re-emerge as protector of public morality. The bishops balked, however; they weren't keen on throwing the Church's wealth away. It was a pity. Talleyrand had looked forward to composing the wording of his quirky proposal to the king, assuring himself: 'It would have been superb.'

In five years as Agent-General he had to deal with serious discontent among the clergy over the class chasm within the Church. The vast majority of priests were humble country curates living on a shoestring with only their Church lodging for comfort. The luxury that soured public opinion was enjoyed by the few. Around 90 per cent of the vast Church revenues went to bishops and other high-ranking ecclesiastics whose remuneration in wealthier dioceses was colossal. The pittance the princes of the Church passed down from their incomes to curates in their charge ignited angry debate verging on rebellion among the lower order. Talleyrand negotiated a rise in the traditional hand-me-down to head off a revolt. Personally, he was on the wrong side of the chasm as regards equity, but he rationalised the move by conducting a Church census that illuminated opaque corners of ecclesiastical tradition. A questionnaire he addressed to every diocese in the country established each and every function they had, how many hospitals, almshouses and schools they ran, how much they cost, what property they owned, what they earned and what they spent. His census was rather like the examination of an entire country's finances in minute budgetary detail. The Church probably knew more about itself than ever before. Admiration for the young Agent-General overflowed the day he completed his term before a national assembly of the clergy in 1785. Clerics voted him a personal reward of 100,000 livres. Talleyrand had moved the Church on without destabilising its traditions. His shortcomings in piety never counted against him. He had every reason, it seemed, to expect to be elevated to bishop, or even straight to archbishop, as further reward.

The wonder was that his concentration hadn't stalled midway through his stint as representative of the clergy. By then he was as assiduous as ever in his salon pursuits, but his choice of venue narrowed. Most evenings he was drawn to an attractive apartment in the Louvre Palace. The first floor apartment was originally reserved for artists patronised by the court but was now made over to one Comte Alexandre de Flahaut and his bright young wife Adelaïde, thirty-five years his junior. The count was a benign military duffer whose brother was Director of Royal Buildings, a post holding the key to grace-and-favour lodgings. By agreement with her husband, who was mostly absent, Mme de Flahaut was free to advance her social life as she wished; at the age of twenty-two she was running her own small salon in the Louvre apartment with licence to pick and choose her admirers. Her guests were drawn by her free spirit and beauty. She herself was not of aristocratic stock – her merchant father had bought his way into the king's service – but she had other attributes: a literary flair that helped her launch a spiky genre in autobiographical novel writing, plus, by one close admirer's account, 'the most beautiful eyes in the world'. Furthermore, she claimed never to have slept with her husband, which seemed to increase her allure.

When Talleyrand first looked in at her salon in the autumn of 1783 he was at once taken. From then on he was there most evenings. His devoted presence delighted her in more ways than one. His reputation as a salon performer – the wry mix of churchman-on-the-rise, charmer, man about town and aspiring statesman – was already made, so that his presence increased the appeal of her little salon. Gadabout economists now gravitated her way; Calonne, the finance minister, liked to drop by, no doubt invited by Talleyrand who managed to sandwich between his duties to the clergy a regular function at the ministry, where he served as a creative mind on tax reform. Then there were more intimate reasons for his presence. When Mme de Flahaut gave birth to a son two years later there was no doubt in anyone's mind, certainly not in hers or Talleyrand's, that he was the father.

Talleyrand was thirty-one. In all but giving the child his family name, a step his priestly situation prohibited, he recognised it as his – as did the breezy Adelaïde, though this didn't deter her from turning her temptress eyes on others. For his part, Talleyrand loved his son and took care to see that he had every chance to succeed. He was christened Charles after his natural father, lest there were any remaining doubts over who sired him.

Talleyrand was a particular breed of womaniser. He would no doubt have accepted the general label, but only according to his own sense of it. People who wanted to bring him down when revolution came branded him a lecherous reprobate, a favourite tactic among zealots. But to have a mistress, or mistresses, was a routine part of being a man about town. In Talleyrand's circles no stigma attached, rather the contrary. Well-born women of his time, particularly married ones, were free with their favours. Because his family had forced him into the Church, he wasn't much concerned about its tighter rules. None of his conquests ever appeared shocked or otherwise put out by the idea of sinning with a priest. The fact was that on the eve of revolution the French Church was a lot less fussy about the celibacy of the highborn clergy than it was supposed to be. Talleyrand certainly liked to seduce. Powdered, perfumed and nobly dressed, he was able to draw women around him into a delicious circle of flattery spiced with an amusing dig here, a flicker of mockery there, and always an elegant assessment of the issue under discussion which no one could trump. A young countess who saw a lot of him, who was on her guard, wrote that she was drawn to him 'like a bird fascinated by the eye of the snake'.

His own definition of love revealed most about him. As he felt it love for a woman was: 'The ambition to possess, to reach your goal, the joy of making others jealous, the glory of success, the grief of being deprived. All our faculties are involved in this passion, that is why it absorbs us so entirely.' The joy in making others jealous said a lot. His sentiment was hardly charged with animal passion. This was no goat speaking, not even a romantic. Perhaps his physical deformity restrained him. Adelaïde de Flahaut herself, in a confidence to a relentless suitor, Gouverneur Morris, the American ambassador in Paris, said Talleyrand was tender rather than virile – '*suaviter in modo* as opposed to *fortiter in re*', as Morris smugly noted in his forthright diary. To hold women under the spell of his charm was the pleasure Talleyrand sought. He was a gallant, one who delighted in having gracious women around him and who needed their company but for whom seduction wasn't the means to an end; it was the end itself. He understood better than most the part women played in politics. Women *are* politics, he repeated over and over.

So it was unfortunate, if predictable, that a womanly scheme to promote him beyond his own immediate ambitions should now fall through. His sights were set on a rise to bishop, with luck to archbishop. But a grande dame of the Paris salons, the Comtesse Louise de Brionne, a court priestess twenty years his senior, had purpler ideas. He'd spent enough time flattering and entertaining her lately to earn her political favour. She thought he should rise straight to cardinal. Knowing the power of women, he placed some hope in Mme de Brionne's machinations despite her eccentricities, the first of which was that she wore her face rouge in four horizontal lines arcing from the eyes to mouth level. This lent her an oddly superior air which commended her to the visiting King of Sweden whom she persuaded to intercede with the pope on Talleyrand's behalf. Mme de Brionne couldn't see below cardinal. Her cousin was a cardinal; why not her brilliant protégé?

Alas, it was not so easy. A sniff of the court wind told Talleyrand he was not in high favour at Versailles where the last word on such appointments lay. He might be a prize turn in the salons but he was no angel in court eyes. His more radical ideas on financial reform counted against him, as did reports to the court from devout Church leaders on the dissolute existence they believed he led. His uncle chose to stand back in this instance. To make matters worse, Queen Marie Antoinette had a sudden down on Mme de Brionne.

Talleyrand, champing at the bit, was left to eye more realistic chances. Likely bishoprics were always coming up. But it was a frustrating time for him. Just to calculate the wealth forfeited by the lost cardinalcy upset him. He resided in some faintly laughable station between aspiring cardinal and family man. To be with Mme de Flahaut and his infant son was agreeable enough, however. It was a change of social pace. And it somehow eased the tensions of trying to secure a diocese. The couple dined together most evenings with the baby asleep beside them. He fussed over the child and its mother. There would be no repeat of his own childhood. Rousseau's heritage was at work.

Following the triumphant term as clergy representative, a full frustrating year of semi-conjugal bliss went by before Talleyrand heard the promising news, in 1786, that the Archbishop of Bourges, an important hub of the Church south of the Loire, was in seriously failing health.

He at once began a whispering campaign to the effect that he was first in line to succeed the sickly prelate. The more he touted his prospects the surer he became of getting what he wanted. 'They are talking of the archdiocese of Bourges for me,' he wrote to Mirabeau. 'It's a good position . . . the archbishop is in apoplexy. They don't think he'll last more than two or three weeks.' But the good archbishop defeated such hopeful predictions. Twelve months later Talleyrand was still waiting, his hand pressed to the prelate's pulse. 'My archbishop is in a hopeless state,' he now advised his friend Choiseul. 'They say he has gone. The most active remedies are no help.'

It was unusual for Talleyrand to be so frank. Friends he invited to share his frustrations must have felt the pathos. It was a critical moment in his career, and the court was evidently stalling him. The Archbishop of Bourges died as predicted, but the vacant post went to another. Talleyrand was mortified. He was left ruing the prospect that there would be no further movement at the top of the Church for a long time. He wasn't far from losing hope. It was a time when the privileged reached the top rung well before middle age, and his own years now entered his disappointed reckoning. He was thirty-four. 'Nothing is turning out as I want,' he wrote to Choiseul. 'This is not a happy time for me, my friend. But it will change. I shall wait, although some perhaps will find that a man of thirty-four who has always been active in affairs and attended, single-handed, to the business of the clergy during five years – and what is more received praise for doing so – deserves a little better treatment.'

He was brimming with ideas on finance, governance, education, practically every area of statecraft. These were the affairs he alluded to. Surely there was a place for him! What else was a Périgord to do? He was well aware of the turmoil mounting in France outside the world he inhabited, though his last close shave with the lower orders went back to his wet nurse's back yard and to ailing peasants queuing for a cure outside his great-grandmother's 'apothecarium'. His interest in ordinary people's problems was almost entirely theoretical, informed by a liberal outlook taken from the Enlightenment. But when he wasn't fretting over how to obtain his elusive bishopric, he involved himself in all the manoeuvring and scheming that was going on within the political class in Paris to find practical answers to a gathering sense of crisis.

For now the price of bread had doubled in two years. Poor harvests and food shortages had poisoned the popular mood. The nation seemed on a knife's edge. It wasn't the first time in recent years that France had sunk into glowering depression. Joining the Americans in their war of independence had emptied the royal treasury. France was bankrupt. Anything could happen. Hatred for privileged classes and contempt for the court were rising, and the bourgeoisie – the merchants, lawyers, doctors, entrepreneurs – were in step with the malaise. The pamphleteers were pumping out vitriol against the higher orders. Twice in 1788, in the summer and the autumn, the army opened fire on angry crowds in the streets of Paris. Provincial parliaments, where the middle classes had some say, were repressed.

Talleyrand observed the disaffection and sympathised with some of it. 'A brand new power has formed in France, that of public opinion,' he recognised. But it was not mature, carefully weighed opinion; it was impetuous and raw. That made it dangerous in his view. Moreover, it was particularly ironic that the leading targets of ill feeling weren't united in confronting the public wrath; they were in conflict with each other. Authority was crumbling.

Talleyrand's gambling mentor, the Duc d'Orléans, faced down Louis XVI in a chamber of nobles, warning the king his orders were illegal unless supported by their vote. Talleyrand was stupefied. It was the first time a prince of royal blood had tackled royal authority head on. The duke was exiled to the provinces for his pains. Then the nobility rebelled against royal power over the need to convene a States-General, an exceedingly rare national assembly bringing together the clergy, the aristocracy and the people, to deal with the crisis. Versailles was against a States-General; the last one had been held close to two centuries before. But the aristocracy wanted a session of the ancient emergency assembly in hopes it would dominate the three-sided proceedings and cement its own position.

Did Talleyrand deserve better treatment? Fate seemed to think so, for a few months after the Bourges fiasco the Archbishop of Lyons died and, although Talleyrand did not step straight into his mighty shoes, he stepped into those of the man who replaced him, the Bishop of Autun, a prestigious but sleepy diocese in Burgundy. Even then he owed his ascent to his father, who begged the king to relent, having extracted a promise from his son to cut down on the financial speculation, gambling and boudoir activities that seemed to be obstructing his progress in the Church. In signing Talleyrand's nomination, the king observed: 'This will put him straight.' The new prelate's promises, as the king's forked comment implied, were tactical – subject to modification – though his father wasn't to know. Charles-Daniel de Talleyrand-Périgord died two days after securing his son's nomination, aged fifty-four and plagued by debt. If Talleyrand wasn't numbed with grief, it was because he had barely known him. The head of the family's last act on his eldest son's behalf was the only one that truly benefited him.

At his consecration as bishop on 16 January 1789 Talleyrand displayed deeper emotion. He fainted. A bad cold that confined him to bed only days before may have affected him, but less humdrum matters were surely also involved. He turned ghostly white and crumpled to his knees as he stretched out his palms to receive the holy oils. The ceremony was suspended until he recovered. Minutes beforehand he had vowed to preserve, defend, strengthen and promote the privileges and authority of the Holy Roman Church.

Was all this tactical too? For once his emotions got the better of him. He was not, and never would be, impervious to the mystery of the Church. Perhaps, also, he had received a vision of what that same eventful year had in store.

THREE

A Good Revolution

Napoleon, by remarkable chance, preceded Talleyrand to Autun. For all its rich medieval masonry and its Romanesque cathedral, the Burgundian burg was a tranquil backwater where paths were most unlikely to cross. But these were, as ever, shaky times for Corsican nationhood and Napoleon's father, with the foresight of the island gentry, had thought it best to give his son the trappings of Frenchness. When not yet ten years old, Napoleon was dispatched across the Mediterranean in the New Year of 1779 and enrolled at the school attached to Autun cathedral. Autun was chosen only because Napoleon's father had an influential French military acquaintance whose nephew was then the bishop there. Otherwise there could hardly have been a more implausible destination for a Corsican lad, who counted no more than an archdeacon among his godlier relations. Napoleon's task at the cathedral school was to learn French, of which he knew precious little; his own language was a twanging dialect of Italian. His teachers did their best, but he retained a strong Corsican accent throughout his life and his subsequent mastery of Europe never extended to French spelling, in which he made endless howlers. Napoleon spent four months being schooled in Autun before progressing to military schools in likelier locations.

The day Talleyrand arrived there to take up the bishop's mitre, Napoleon was serving as a nineteen-year-old gunnery lieutenant in the king's army – back in Burgundy once more, by further coincidence, and stationed quite close to Autun. He was engaged in putting down local peasant riots. Such actions were difficult for the young Corsican to undertake. They were an immediate foretaste of the violence it would take to try to beat back a national revolt for which he had some sympathy. He was dismayed by the corruption at Versailles and the monarchy's failure to respond to the national mood, yet at the same time he was far from wanting to eliminate the monarchy altogether. The solution for him was a constitutional monarchy, which was precisely what Talleyrand had in mind.

Talleyrand's promotion to bishop came just in time for him, too, to engage directly in the turmoil threatening France. The winter of his churchly content was astonishingly harsh. No one remembered such cold; in Paris the Seine froze over and the nation itself seemed frozen in resentment. Louis XVI, a stubborn man, was forced to give way on the States-General. Bowing to the nobility, the king summoned the rare assembly to meet on 4 May 1789. For Talleyrand and his statesmanlike aspirations, pontifical rank offered a timely bonus. It ensured him a seat in the emergency parliament and a hand in shaping France's fate. He was, by right, a deputy for the clergy. All he needed was the formal backing of his Autun diocese for the stand he would take. This was a niggling obstacle but it had to be traversed; none of the lesser clerics there knew him or his political ideas, though rumours had certainly spread from Paris about his lifestyle.

The new prelate set out to win them over. It was already mid-March – less than two months before the opening of the States-General – when he arrived in the Burgundian market town and vowed, as required, to take the Church of Autun as his spouse. He cut a grand figure in purple, walking with a cane he now used most of the time. The cane lent him an extra aura of authority. He set about holding dinners for the priests and canons of the province of a luxury and style they'd never before witnessed. He was the ultimate Parisian grandee descending on the lowly, and his priestly subalterns were a little afraid of him. Having feted them, he tested their provincial views with a manifesto he intended to put before the States-General as the policy of the Autun diocese. It was a digest, clear and eloquent, of his own liberal position formed over countless breakfasts with his friends at his Paris home. The main propositions were these: from now on nothing could become law without the solemn consent of the people given by an elected parliament; private property rights were unconditionally guaranteed; no one could be deprived of their liberty, even briefly, except under the public law and never by arbitrary order; freedom of expression was sacrosanct; all punishment under the law was the same for all classes of citizens; all tax privileges were abolished; public finances were to be restored not by raising new taxes, but by increased receipts through the abolition of tax privileges and through treasury loans.

All told, the Talleyrand manifesto called for an end to absolute royal power. If it was adopted, the *ancien régime* was finished. Democracy was to try its wings. It was a demand for an open society. Monarchy could no longer ensure order, so it had to be reformed. Public order, in Talleyrand's view, was the key to civilisation.

The clergy of the Autun diocese, still in awe of their new captain, duly elected him as their deputy to the States-General. Their well-wishing proved a little overwhelming, since he felt obliged to show his gratitude by

responding to their entreaties for him to say mass at the cathedral. He stumbled through it, quite unfamiliar with the task, as all present painfully
witnessed. Talleyrand left Autun one month to the day after his arrival, and,
due to circumstances both stressful and impossible to foresee, never returned
to the diocese. All the same the attachment proved indelible, largely to his
chagrin. For though he gloried in the highest secular titles as time went on,
those who wanted to bring him down a peg and cast him as a traitor to the
Church continued to address him with a nudge and a wink as 'Bishop of
Autun'. Only from his valet Courtiade did he acknowledge the address with
any satisfaction. Courtiade never dreamed of bringing his master down. He
was so proud to see Talleyrand in purple that he addressed him as
Monseigneur in place of Monsieur from the day he took the bishop's oath
and held to it through thick and thin.

Talleyrand's place was in Paris. The great assemblage of France's three orders
was now only three weeks off. He had serious reservations about the way it
was shaping up. It seemed obvious that its 1200 deputies were too numerous
to make it manageable. And the division was wrong. For it was also obvious
to him that there were, for political purposes, two orders in the land, not three.
Nobles and high clergy were in effect a single order since they were the selfsame class. Commoners and rank-and-file clergy were the other. But the
presumption behind the States-General was that clergy, nobles and commoners
would each have a third of the seats. And now the king had stepped in to make
things messier. Because he had come to regard the nobility itself as hostile and
presumptuous, he decided to allot half the seats to commoners and just a
quarter each to aristocrats and the high clergy. So the people's representatives
had the upper hand from the start.
    Talleyrand might not have quarrelled with this had he been less aware
of the category of people the lower order was electing to represent it. 'They
were almost all lawyers,' he noted, 'the kind of men whose frame of mind,
owing to their profession, generally makes them extremely dangerous.' This
was an exaggeration. One in four was a lawyer, and though lawyers were
indeed by far the largest single category it could not have worried him that
the principles they advanced were very close to those carried by his Autun
manifesto. Nonetheless he was prescient. Zealous legal minds were soon to
confront him with dangers that very nearly cost him his life.
    The upshot of the unwieldy States-General was that within weeks the
commoners transformed it into a National Assembly, a parliament made to
override royal power. Lower clerics and a liberal minority of bluebloods rallied
to the new parliament. Outmanoeuvred, the king sought to kill it at birth by
calling in troops to disband it. The royal counter-coup failed disastrously,

leaving the monarchy still in charge of executive government in theory, but in fact entirely at parliament's mercy. The conservative majority of nobles was likewise at the commoners' mercy.

This wasn't quite how Talleyrand had wanted things to go. His inner ties with the *ancien régime* and the sovereign order were visceral and he was obliged to take account of that. However far he went in support of people's rights and liberties, the old order was in his blood. He couldn't resist contacting the court at Versailles to press the king into taking the one step that would salvage the monarchy – to remake himself as a constitutional monarch. Talleyrand took the English system as his model, proposing a house of commons to share law-making duties with a house of lords made up of ranking clergy and nobles. But it was too late for such tinkering. The rumbustious National Assembly was set on writing its own constitution and what place the king might find in it was at best unclear.

Whatever the monarchy's ultimate fate, Talleyrand decided there was no standing aside from the great upheaval. 'I placed myself at the disposal of events,' he wrote. This gave him considerable leeway. He would swim with the tide, save what could be saved of what he prized. What he prized most was a civilised life, and all he knew was that France had to be at peace with herself to achieve it.

On 14 July of that year, 1789, a maddened street crowd stormed the Bastille prison in Paris, raising popular insurrection to full-scale revolution. Jules Michelet, a romantic historian of the revolution born in Paris as it raged, sought with hindsight to grasp its meaning:

> At this decisive moment the whole world was watching, observing with uneasy sympathy the progress of our revolution, conscious that France at her own risk and peril was acting for the entire human race.

Talleyrand took a less romantic view. He had his own interests to pursue, but it was also the time when his concern for France's interests came to the fore. He did not confuse the two. He was steadfast in following his own interests; he was at least as steadfast in following those of France. In the Talleyrand temple the two credos cohabited peaceably. When they conflicted, as they might, the record showed he sought to put France's interests first. They were in his Périgord bones. Still, it was always possible to look for some ingenious way to satisfy both. In the weeks leading up to the fall of the Bastille, he busied himself proposing laws to the new assembly and courting moderates to rally support for his projects. Politically, he had few scruples about leaving the clergy's ranks and joining the people. In terms of power, the nobility and the clergy were finished. Now it was vital to prevent revolution from going to extremes. He placed his chips on compromise. To a whist table hostess who questioned his alacrity in siding with the people, he counselled: 'Please accept the truth; after the way we lived the revolution taking place in France today is indispensable. This revolution will end up being useful.'

He moved on a wide front, bombarding the new parliament with proposals on issues he felt strongest about, from democracy and financial reform to education and weights and measures (the last a pet subject of his because he wanted France to adopt the same system as England in order to drive the trade relations he hoped could turn the bankrupt French economy round). Except on weights and measures, he was remarkably successful. As a performer, he was the opposite of his emotional friend Mirabeau, a fiery orator who sided with the commoners from the outset and harangued the National Assembly into staying put when the king tried to disband it by force. Mirabeau was a wonderful rabble-rouser, a hothead made for revolution. He fired hearts. Talleyrand was calm and thoughtful, almost to the point of tedium in his deep-voiced public delivery. Policy was his strength, presented in clear, reasoned language everyone could understand. It was not his tone that galvanised events, it was his mastery of language and a readiness to take the bull by the horns. Michelet's contemporary, the historian Charles Augustin Sainte-Beuve, who disliked Talleyrand the man, acknowledged his role: 'The Bishop of Autun showed himself from the very first day to be one of the most enlightened and perspicacious minds of the age.'

Making the parliament work seemed to him the priority. Its members had no grounding in democracy aside from fancies floating in their heads. In an early speech Talleyrand gave a course in practical politics, setting out the rights, duties and moral responsibilities of an elected representative. Deputies needed to be sure what they were there for. They were indeed there to represent their constituencies, but they must do so with a free mind. It wasn't their job to follow instructions dictated from their base; instructions on how to vote in general ran counter to the principles of a democratic assembly, where free deliberation on the issues was essential, otherwise laws wouldn't stand up. Nor should deputies walk out of the assembly if deliberations weren't going their way. A 'prodigious number' of deputies seemed, he said, to misunderstand these principles. Talleyrand's motion was adopted.

When it came to France's disastrous financial situation, for two hours he stood before the assembly on his one good leg, arguing the case for floating a massive state loan. Could France raise a loan when it had no credit? Wouldn't that simply plunge the country deeper into debt? The dilemma split the best financial specialists. Talleyrand's minutely reasoned analysis came to this: a government loan was worth trying as long as interest rates were kept low and France's creditors had cast-iron guarantees they weren't about to be bilked. Motion adopted.

All along he showed rare lucidity in confronting a financial crisis that few of those caught up in revolution had the slightest idea how to tackle. His end view was that all the ingenious schemes designed to put things right – paper money, bond issues, coupons and much else – wouldn't get to the root of the crisis. 'Now that all the efforts of wit and ruse are exhausted,' he was soon telling the assembly, with despairing humour, 'it is time for straight honesty to replace genius.' He proposed a simple state book of accounts 'managed by good sense and good faith'. This was homely advice coming a shade incongruously, as all hastened to observe, from a gambling man of shaky faith, but it received plaudits. His reputation as a statesman was on the rise.

Paris society life went on remarkably unchanged at the outset of the Revolution, considering the violence in the streets, the sprouting army checkpoints, the irreparable crack in the throne and the shift in power from Versailles to the people. Though it looked more and more like wishful thinking, the liberal upper class – the salon class – stuck manfully by the notion that the new age was a joyous start to something better. Certain precautions were, of course, useful. Talleyrand dropped his bishop's attire, allowing his pectoral cross to retreat from his shirtfront to his underlinens. Ecclesiastical insignia seemed to conflict with the general mood. The Church was no less a target for the anger in the streets than the aristocracy was. Indeed it was largely regarded as the same bad thing.

Despite it all, salon life continued. Talleyrand was drawn to the Necker home, a hive of political gossip and intrigue where daughter Germaine ruled the roost as Mme de Staël. Perhaps it was the competition she represented, but he felt brilliant in her company and his conversation excelled. She was impressed. 'If his conversation were for sale, I should ruin myself,' she said. It was at the Necker salon that the latest chatter on who would get which of the ministerial posts in the king's last-ditch governments was heard. As a result of his showing in the assembly, political gossip put Talleyrand himself in the finance ministry. Nothing was sure, though he did weigh up the pros and cons of taking the post at that unruly stage. In fact it was not to be. Missing the finance ministry was all to the good. The fiasco of the king contin- uing to name government ministers was bound to tarnish those he named.

The salons tried hard to hold on to their gaiety as the mood hardened outside. Talleyrand attended, with dwindling enthusiasm, masked dinners hosted with all the lavishishness of old except that bluebloods now entertained themselves by imitating the working class and behaving down. A brash woman shopkeeper seated next to him at one such function who called herself plain Mme Denis turned out, on unmasking herself, to be his friend the Duchesse de Luynes, one of the free spirits who had taken him in hand at the coronation of Louis XVI. His relationship with Adelaïde de Flahaut also claimed his time. Even after making an appearance at the Necker salon, he still went to her apartment in the Louvre most evenings. But something was going wrong. That bothersome American, Gouverneur Morris, was trying to cut him out. What was more, he showed not the slightest guile or sensitivity about it. Talleyrand would have ignored him if he weren't a man of influence. So pleased with himself! So bouncy! He seemed to throw himself around. In between trading in tobacco and wheat, Morris was America's official representative in Paris working directly to George Washington, first president of the brand new United States. He was Washington's eyes and ears in the capital and, Talleyrand had to allow, an interesting fellow to discuss things with. Learned, too, for a colonial. His curious first name derived from a past French Huguenot intrusion into the Morris family, but he was wholly American. It was said his pen had put the last dots and commas to the constitution of the United States and he himself put it around that he fathered the American dollar.

Still, it irritated Talleyrand to have to cross the American on the stairs practically every time he went to the Louvre. The two of them had problems in getting up and down to Mme de Flahaut's first-floor abode. Morris had lost a leg after a careless attempt to stop a runaway horse back in New England and, like Talleyrand, used a stick to walk. Adelaïde seemed to have a weakness for the lame. Talleyrand rarely mentioned his infirmity, though it fatigued him. The robust Morris, balding, with a plump underchin, acted completely unperturbed by his. He was always laughing about tripping in the street and 'barking' his wooden stump.

Morris kept an undiplomatic diary in the months before and after the fall of the Bastille in which he tracked Talleyrand's activities. This wasn't difficult in view of their constant encounters. Furthermore, Morris had more than enough of the American snob in him to take to the salon circuit as if born to it. After his initial brushes with Talleyrand he jotted down an opinion of him: 'sharp-minded, cunning, ambitious and malicious'. Rivals never did shower each other with compliments. He drew this opinion mainly from the Necker salon, where Talleyrand continued to shine and earn Mme de Staël's brash devotion. It was now the most crowded salon in Paris, though the wit unleashed there tended to pass Morris by. 'Conversation too brilliant for me,' he noted in his diary. 'I am not in this constellation.'

All the same the American was delighted to be in Paris at this perilous, unpredictable point and he hoped the Revolution would succeed. Yet he often seemed more interested in wheat deals and the ladies than in revolutionary politics, observing with unending glee the easy mores of the time and imagining (more often than not, to his disappointment) a woman's faintest courtesy to be an invitation into her bed. It was his joyous view that most hostesses were sluts. Beside such amusement, politics could grate. 'Go to Mme F (Flahaut),' he noted in late April. 'They are in the midst of politics which I am tired of. After supper the bishop of Autun reads us the protest by the nobles and clergy of Brittany and during the lecture I very uncivilly fall asleep.'

What kept Morris wide awake was an intense though outwardly civil contest with Talleyrand for Adelaïde's generous favours. The malice he saw in the bishop seemed absent from their competition. Not only did they bump into each other on the stairs, they often found themselves dining *à trois* on either side of her. She enjoyed playing them off against each other. She told Morris that Talleyrand was importuning her, and no doubt said the same of Morris to Talleyrand. The American was there to bed her, which he claimed to achieve during perhaps one visit in three, provided she wasn't unwell, which her servants too often told him she was. The bishop, much attracted by her, was more there for her lively company and to see his son. Adelaïde had a nose for politics and he liked to run his latest plans and speech drafts past her. Morris was convinced Talleyrand was incapable of satisfying her sexual needs (it was she who told him the bishop lacked *fortiter in re*). He believed he could wean her away from Talleyrand entirely if he wished, 'but he is the father of her child and it would be unjust'.

The rivals' habit of bursting in on each other in compromising situations seldom ended in anything more hostile than a frustrated stare. Adelaïde's aged husband was never there, so she would merely shoo her servants out of the apartment before moving into action. 'The moment her women leave, the Bishop arrives,' a balked Morris reported on one otherwise promising occasion. 'He lays down his hat and cane and takes a chair in the manner of a man determined to stay – and I think with the intention to perform the part allotted to me.'

Why didn't Talleyrand spend more time putting France aright in the assembly? Morris wondered. Why didn't the American devote more time to settling America's debt with France? wondered Talleyrand. Only once by Morris's account did Talleyrand display real anger. The American ambassador had barged into a family reunion which Talleyrand had evidently been cherishing – a dinner with Adelaïde and their little son who had returned only that day from a long stay in the country. Affronted by the American's untimely entry, Talleyrand rose from the table, took his cane and left without a word. Adelaïde burst into tears. She didn't want to alienate the father of her child. She was 'married in heart' to him, she told Morris.

At other times he and Morris seemed to do better than tolerate each other.

The American promoted Talleyrand's credentials to become finance minister and claimed he talked him up across Paris for the post. He told Talleyrand that although he seemed the right choice he did have one weakness in finance: he lacked people around him who understood hard work and had a passion for it. Talleyrand appreciated the American's interest, tiresome though it sounded. The implication was that he himself was lazy. It was true that he got up late – it was his habit – but his parliamentary output alone should have convinced Morris he was anything but workshy. On the role of finance minister, Morris further permitted himself to offer Talleyrand 'a few hints' on general principles that could bring a nation wealth and happiness. Their source, he sermonised, was to be found in the human heart. Talleyrand listened attentively to the transatlantic moralising, or made a play of doing so, which delighted his lecturer. Adelaïde's face glowed with satisfaction, the American noted, whenever she saw him and Talleyrand seated beside each other on her couch heartily supporting each other's opinions. Talleyrand had by then turned listening into an art; there was no surer way, he saw, to gain the talker's good-will. His rule was: 'To be amiable in society, one must allow oneself to be told what one already knows.' Morris was a terrible know-all.

It was disappointing for the Frenchman that Morris did not live up to his hopes as a man of influence. He was of no help in enabling him to speculate on America's debt to France, which looked like a chance to turn a large personal profit. Nor did he invite him to participate in what he was spinning as a highly lucrative property development back in the United States. Further disappointment was to follow. Just when Talleyrand came to need a favourable American recommendation, his fellow cripple became his character assassin.

The Church would not let go of Talleyrand. The need for reform was blindingly clear. The Church was the object of rising popular loathing, directed mainly at its pampered hierarchy. Since no one, literally no one, knew more about the workings of the Church than he did, he found himself in a squeeze. It was inevitable that his fellow princes of the Church would hate him if he took the initiative, but equally inevitable that parliament would hate him if he did not. Faced with a 'repugnant' choice, he allowed his feelings for France to decide the matter; they told him to follow the march of the nation with all the risks it presented. 'Provided I remained a Frenchman, everything was all right,' he told himself.

The reform he sponsored was so novel as to define the break with the old order. His solution was to nationalise the Church. The state would assume ownership of Church property throughout France and auction it off as it saw fit, paying clerics a salary from the proceeds. Since Church property represented close to half of landed wealth in every province of the country, yielding an annual income of up to 100 million livres nationwide, nationalisation would go a good way towards rescuing the state from bankruptcy. If Talleyrand's antidote for national bankruptcy made him the most astute of political craftsmen in the eyes of the reformers, in the eyes of the Church hierarchy it made him Judas incarnate. For here was one of the Church's own, a captain of the clergy no less, stripping it at a stroke of the colossal material power it had built up over centuries. He was playing to the crowd at the Lord's expense.

If the torrent of abuse he received from fellow high churchmen shook him, he didn't show it. On the contrary, he seemed quite proud of it. He told the assembly: 'I am almost alone among those in my order to support before you principles that appear opposed to his own interests.'

He employed the best of Jesuitical reasoning to push the measure through. Were the clergy the owners of Church property? Not in the regular sense of ownership, that was clear, for priests couldn't sell the property for their own benefit; it was in their keeping only by virtue of their religious function. In keeping for whom? For the nation. So the true owner was the nation. The takeover, then, was the reversion of property to its true owner. Church wealth had always been national wealth. The clergy were merely the administrators. Priests would be no less revered by their parishioners because they were paid by the state instead of being paid by their diocese. Kings, ministers and judges were paid by the state and no less honoured for that. In the circumstances he might have omitted mention of kings, but his argument carried. The takeover couldn't be deemed a breach of property rights, which Talleyrand himself held to be inviolable and which the Revolution did not yet wish to interfere with. This clinched the argument. Furthermore, when he found himself on the defensive once the wholesale confiscation of Church property got under way in November of that revolutionary year, he answered critics with an argument he could not possibly have put to the revolutionary parliament: he had in fact saved the clergy. 'I am convinced I provided the sole means there is to retrieve it from a dreadful fate, that of total annihilation.' In other words, if nationalisation hadn't been imposed, the assembly would simply have eliminated the Church, as Oliver Cromwell had done in England.

The argument impressed salon-goers, but Talleyrand remained in life-long odium with the Catholic Church, the more so when, only a few months later, he took the lead in wresting the Church from its devotion to the pope. First material ruin, now spiritual ruin. That was how it looked to the devout. In place of their vows to Rome, French priests were required to swear allegiance to the new French constitution just voted in by the National Assembly, lately renamed Constituent Assembly to clarify its task of institutionalising the Revolution.

*   *   *

Talleyrand got a little carried away by his own part in drawing up the revolutionary constitution. He had no doubt that political power went before pontifical power. But only with hindsight did he recognise how far he wronged the Church by pressing it to put the constitution before its holy ties with Rome. He had been appointed to an eight-member assembly committee formed to write France's new constitution on the day after the Bastille was reduced to rubble, and was delighted by the honour. It was the most potent sign yet of his place in controlling events. He sought to stamp all his liberal ideas on the country's new rule book and since the committee was largely at one on its aims he succeeded perhaps better than he expected.

The constitution enshrined the rule of law, government by the people through parliament, the right to property, the same justice for all and – most compelling as a break with the old order – social equality. The monarchy continued in place but with only faint vestiges of its past power. King Louis lost command of the army to the state. Aristocratic titles and privileges were abolished. The French were all 'citizens' now.

Many members of the Constituent Assembly, not just the minority from the old upper orders, found it hard to see in Talleyrand a credible enemy of privilege. But he went through more than just the motions in securing profound reforms. The constitution was preceded by a soaring prologue, a Declaration on the Rights of Man, which he took a direct hand in drafting. Article VI on equality before the law came straight from his pen:

> The law is the expression of the general will. All citizens have the right to take part, in person or through their representatives, in making the law. It must be the same for all, whether as protection or punishment. All citizens being equal in the eyes of the law, they have equal access to dignity, rank and public position according to their capacities . . .

With its emphasis on freedom of conscience and freedom of expression, the declaration was a compendium of what impressed him most in the ideas of the Enlightenment *philosophes*. Before long the Rights of Man document was enthralling all Europe, in admiration but also concern, for it contained a palpable whiff of American liberty-taking. Moreover, it had the effect of pressing the assembly into further efforts to bring the Church to heel. That Roman Catholicism should continue as France's state religion now seemed to conflict with man's rights. Talleyrand scolded his Autun diocese on this point when its priests objected to abolishing the Church's formal status as the religion of the land. 'Any manner of constraint as concerns religion is an attack on the first of man's rights,' he wrote to them. From there it was only a small step to forcing the clergy to take their oath to the constitution rather than Rome, which is just what the assembly insisted upon.

Now Talleyrand was more deeply implicated than he wanted to be. Forcing the clergy to abandon allegiance to the pope was as much a violation of their individual rights as was forcing a Frenchman to be a Catholic. But it was too late. He was convinced the Church needed top-to-bottom reform. The takeover of Church property hadn't really calmed popular hostility. On the clergy's side, however, exasperation grew with each speech he made. Out of the exasperation flowed insistent rumours that Talleyrand was speculating on the confiscation and resale of Church land to turn a large profit for himself. It was certainly a juicy proposition for an investor and such propositions did not escape his notice.

When the time came for clerics to take the oath to the constitution, all but three bishops refused. Talleyrand was one of the ranking trio to transfer his oath. Since so few bishops agreed to break with Rome, he personally swore in two pliant priests as bishops to get the pontifical ball rolling for the new non-Roman Church. Clerics who resisted were considered to have resigned, which meant forfeiting the income the state now provided.

Plainly he was uneasy about his role in the breach with Rome. In retrospect, he called it the greatest political blunder committed by the Constituent Assembly. Committed by himself, he might have said. But oaths were two a penny in an age of revolution. They weren't to be taken too seriously, he decided at the time. In a self-exculpatory letter to Adelaïde de Flahaut, he wrote: 'If my brothers in Jesus Christ weren't fools, they would follow my example. They would think a little more of making the people's lot a happy one and burden themselves less with their scruples and their duties towards Rome. After all the oaths we've made and broken, all the fidelity sworn to a constitution, the nation, the law, the king and this, that and the other, how important is one more oath?'

The tone was airy. It was a tone he reserved for occasions when he was unsure of his ground.

Talleyrand's overall efforts to keep the assembly on a moderate track were, broadly speaking, well received. Well enough received at any rate by a majority of deputies so that by February 1790, little more than six months after the fall of the Bastille, they elected him president of the assembly. This put him by rank at least at the head of the revolution.

It was an odd place to be for an out-and-out aristocrat with high rank in a reactionary Church, especially since the parliament was boiling with conflict and animosity between rival revolutionary factions. Jacobins held the radical left with their support for the city poor and the peasantry, Girondins the middle ground with their loftier reforming ideas. Though Talleyrand veered towards the Girondins and courted the Jacobins, he belonged to neither camp. He was, observed the English historian Henry Bulwer-Lytton, a contemporary many years his junior, the personification of the liberal-minded upper class that was about to be the first victim of its own philosophy.

But not yet.

Talleyrand's political networking skills were evident, the object of both admiration and scorn, as was his ability to advance by flattery. Beyond that he was proving himself a liberal all-rounder. He regarded the chance to change *some* things as an invitation to change *everything* on which he had formed a strong opinion. While Gouverneur Morris continued to distract him by unsettling his domestic life, he deployed the sum of his knowledge as though he had accumulated it solely to saddle it up for action. The freedom of religion he espoused wouldn't work unless resident Jews, mainly originating from Spain, Portugal and the Avignon region in the south, were awarded the political rights of which France then deprived them. There should be no different citizenship for Jews, he argued – it had to be the same as everyone else's. Narrowly, the assembly agreed and fully integrated Jews into French civil society by decree. The initiative was a risk for Talleyrand since anti-Semitism in the public domain was neither gentle nor uncandid. The reactionary press berated him. One paper screamed that he preferred to be 'the rabbi of a sect of usurers than the pontiff of the religion of Jesus Christ'.

Human rights were Talleyrand's constant hobby horse. He proposed a grand project – born of his Enlightenment prejudices – to launch free public education throughout the country. This caused an excited controversy, in both parliament and Paris society. The Church's grip may already have been decisively weakened, but many still found it hard to accept the idea of formally removing schooling from her jealous hands. The reason he wanted to make education available at no cost under the state's wing was that he believed it had to be open to every child in the land if France was to prosper. A 216-page report on education – massaged by the busybody Madame de Staël – was the largest plan he put to the assembly and if there was one item above all others that answered lingering accusations that he was lazy, this was it. If such suspicions persisted, it was only because his unhurried manner and hauteur – the signs of his breeding – encouraged them.

His public education programme became law, though not at once (not until a century later in fact). Instead, the obvious reason for his rise to the assembly summit was a stirring apologia for the Revolution he delivered to deputies just a week before they made him president. Previously he'd assured his salon friends, with anxious optimism, that the Revolution would be 'useful'. Now he reached out to ordinary Frenchmen with a burst of parliamentary oratory that sounded incendiary coming from him and caught the revolutionary assembly's fancy for that.

He began by drawing up a triumphal inventory of the parliament's work, starting with the constitution. What of the rights of man, abused and insulted for centuries! 'These rights are re-established for the whole of humanity in a declaration which will forever be a rallying cry against oppressors and a law for lawmakers themselves.' Talleyrand had never sounded more passionate. He turned on the critics and carpers, foes of the Revolution from his own class. We have destroyed everything, they say! But only because everything needed rebuilding. We have gone too fast! Only by tackling all abuses at one go could France be rid of them, for partial reforms ended up reforming nothing. Our parliament has been tumultuous and disorderly! What matter, as long as the resulting decrees were wise. It had its head in the clouds, reaching for unobtainable perfection! Such accusations merely aimed at perpetuating old abuses. No nation as old and corrupt as France could be born anew! Nonsense, the nation was rejuvenated the day it resolved to be reborn in liberty.

Talleyrand's harangue also carried a more conservative sting in the tail, a call to public order. He sharply condemned violence and killing carried out in the name of revolution, and the harassment of the king. Such things were unworthy of the extraordinary exploit the nation had accomplished. 'Under the empire of the law, let the word vengeance disappear. Courage, perseverance, generosity, these are the virtues of liberty. We ask them of you in the name of this sacred liberty, the sole conquest worthy of man.' He raised the tone still higher. 'Do not dishonour the beautiful deed which the annals of the world have recorded in our name. What have you to fear? Nothing, no, nothing but dark impatience. You have granted so many centuries to despotism, now wait a few moments longer, your liberty is worth the wait!'

This was unusually straight talk for Talleyrand. It reflected a certain confidence in his position, but also his deep concern that disorder on the streets and in the provinces was running out of control – in short, that the Revolution was going wrong. King Louis himself, Talleyrand insisted, despised despotism. With his royal powers clipped, he was quite the wrong target for popular vengeance. The king deserved to be left in peace. Talleyrand's end goal remained a constitutional monarchy, though he was clearly less and less sure it would come about. In the privacy of the salons he was calling French royalty 'an ever dwindling shadow'.

The Talleyrand rhetoric that so often enthused parliament was sent to parish curates throughout the land to be read as their Sunday sermon. It was distributed in the name of the assembly so that those devout curates who complied did so without knowing the identity of its author, which no doubt improved the reading it got. As a booster for revolution, Talleyrand was an enigmatic figure. He threw the words freedom and democracy around with some enthusiasm but without blind zeal, for he knew what he meant by them. His two selves came into it: the aspiring one with France and the commonweal uppermost; and the acquisitive, luxury loving, self-interested one he served because it wouldn't go away. Gambling was part of the second self, an addiction he couldn't fight. 'I never loved it, and I particularly blame myself for not sufficiently resisting its seduction,' he wrote in a defensive reply to a Paris newspaper which questioned his fitness to be assembly president. This was untrue. He loved it. He knew his two selves very well, supported them both and furthermore was able to distinguish between them with a clarity others often missed. The method was not to let either self obstruct the other. Both got their chance. In the unlikely event it came to a contest between them, his sense of history allowed the aspiring self through the gate first. The other could always catch up.

Which Talleyrand came first through the gate as the first anniversary of the fall of the Bastille arrived was nonetheless a close call. The Revolution needed a party: some colossal popular celebration to show itself off. Why deny itself a good time! It was yet to turn bloodthirsty in righteous Jacobin hands. The rights of man were still a creation of sheer wonder. Michelet's vision of France acting for the entire human race, at her own risk and peril, filled the common man's heart with pride – even though France's neighbours, England to the fore, in fact saw things quite differently and were itching to reverse the Revolution. The purpose of the celebration which Talleyrand, as assembly president, outlined to deputies was to stir the nation's patriotism by its immense size and to impress upon enemies of the Revolution that any attempts to bring it down were utterly pointless. Here was Talleyrand not only at the head of the Revolution but its grandmaster of ceremonies. What better man to front the anniversary party? Reformed aristocrat, man of God, constitution man and revolutionary assembly man wrapped in one.

He proved inventive at the task. It could not be a miserly affair consistent with the country's financial ruin. What was headlined the Federation Fete had to be heroic. A million people were expected, the biggest public gathering ever witnessed on European soil. The site was the Champ-de-Mars on the banks of the Seine where the Eiffel Tower would one day stand. Talleyrand had the huge esplanade excavated, tunnelled, mounded, amphitheatred, bannered, flagged, tented. Tens of thousands of labourers took spades and earthmoving machines to it. Atop a pyramid mound at the heart of the field rose an altar from which Talleyrand himself would say mass to the nation, Louis XVI included. The king had to be present. Incredibly, he was still head of state.

The 14 July 1790 did its best to thwart Talleyrand. The rain came down in a ceaseless deluge. Dense black rainclouds pelted the festive awnings on the Champ-de-Mars. The vast crowd was a heaving ocean of umbrellas. The endless anniversary cortege with representatives from every province and county town in France was drenched as it snaked in from the Bastille. When at last there came a break in the downpour, Talleyrand was ready to play his part. In full pontifical robes, mitre and cross in hand, alone, mastering his limp, he advanced behind a column of white-surpliced priests to the foot of the altar mound. He was a novice at saying mass, as the painful experience in Autun reminded him, but he'd been rehearsing this performance in private for days and was confident he could carry it off.

Just where the mound rose he spied an old salon acquaintance, the Marquis (now General) de La Fayette, hero of the old order's war against the English in America. La Fayette was a fellow liberal whose reputation had sunk due to his political dithering, but he retained enough weight to be military governor of Paris and was positioned in full military dress regalia below the altar, on watch. As Talleyrand passed La Fayette to the solemn beat of a hundred drums he whispered, 'Ah! It's you. I beg you, don't make me laugh.' Proceeding to the altar with all sang-froid, he turned to face the king's blue and gold velvet dais and said mass in a deep voice, calling to the throng, 'Sing, weep tears of joy, on this day France is united anew.'

Talleyrand plainly did not take the day as seriously as he exhorted his fellow citizens to do. The organisation he took seriously. Organising big occasions larded with pomp and grandeur became a speciality of his, a talent Napoleon would much rely on, regardless of cost. Otherwise his performance at the Federation Fete was the sham to which he made poor La Fayette privy. The best he could claim was that the Revolution needed a celebration and to that extent he had served the interests of France, his first goal. To pose as spiritual leader of the nation was another thing. It wasn't Talleyrand at his best, especially since he was already set on handing in his mitre and resigning as bishop. The personal prestige the immense ceremony offered was no doubt what attracted him most. There he had stood, alone before the world. It certainly marked him out. The mystical patriotic side did not wrap him in contemplation for long. Immediately after the great event he changed into city clothes and went straight to the gaming tables. It was his lucky day. He broke the bank, summoned his carriage and rode forth, pockets bursting with gold, to his friend the Vicomtesse de Laval's salon to exhibit his winnings. Buoyed by the salon's admiration, he returned to the casino and made a second killing. Awash with more gold and banknotes, his hat chockful, he again summoned his busy coachman and returned once more to Mme de Laval's to savour his fortune, sighing, 'Remember, it's 14 July.'

Talleyrand was never happier than when he felt rich. He insisted on living the life of a rich man, particularly when he had no money, which had happened in the past and would happen again. He was good at whist but could run up heavy debts through gaming-table losses.

Through it all, living the life of the rich was his principle. 'Never be a poor devil,' he counselled a high civil servant friend. 'I have always been rich.'

Out of political rectitude, the Constituent Assembly in which Talleyrand established himself barred deputies from keeping their seats when it broke up, its constitution-writing job done, and resumed life in the autumn of 1791 as the Legislative Assembly, a doughtier body with aroused Jacobins in control. The new parliament's task was the grittier one of running the revolutionary ship. Talleyrand suddenly found himself out of national politics and out of the limelight. Instead he sat in the Paris city parliament, which had a front-row seat in revolutionary events and assured him of continuing income from statesmanship. All in all, not counting his fortunes at whist and the gaming tables, he would have been no less well off than before but for a second change in his situation: he resigned his bishopric.

It was time. The nationalisation and sale of Church land plus the furore over the clergy's switch of allegiance to the revolutionary constitution so exasperated the Vatican that at length the pope took a stand against Talleyrand. As villain of the French piece in papal eyes, he received notice of excommunication. His sins were heresy, apostasy and a string of further unpardonables. He feigned indifference to the papal blow. As usual, the pose concealed inner anguish. For some time he had been in a high state of nerves over his bishop's rank. As he saw it, it placed him in imminent danger, physical danger, from two sides. Frenzied royalists issued scarcely disguised death threats against him in the press for 'treachery' towards the Church and his class. At the same time, street fury directed against lordly prelates hadn't abated.

That winter Talleyrand seemed as close to panic as his nature permitted. At noon one day he stumbled white-faced into Mme de Flahaut's apartment and thrust an envelope into her hands. Inside the envelope was a scribbled will. The inevitable Gouverneur Morris was there to witness the scene. Talleyrand, he noted, was seized by a horrible fear of death. The American might be counted upon to pull him down in Adelaïde's eyes, but this wasn't simply another Talleyrand performance.

After his toying with resigning as bishop, the actual step came as a relief. His position in the Church had never been anything but a practical matter. He'd never wanted to be part of it. His fellow aristocrats were not exactly models of steadfastness either. His helpful uncle, the Archbishop of Reims, had fled the country at the first sign of danger to his kind. So had the king's brothers. Now the upper orders, constitutionally stripped of titles and reduced to plain 'citizens', were emigrating in their thousands. At least he was still in France. This was what counted for him. From the outset of the Revolution he'd considered the matter long and hard. 'I reflected for a long time,' he wrote, 'and came to the decision I would serve France as France, whatever situation she was in.' The regime of the moment was one such situation; France an enduring fact.

There were important things to be done, even outside parliament. In April 1791 his flamboyant colleague Mirabeau died prematurely and the flame of one kind of revolution went out. The golden tongue that once enthused and exhausted the Talleyrand breakfast club had ultimately made Mirabeau a popular hero of the Revolution and his sudden death was a huge blow to many of the things Talleyrand stood for, not least his goal of a democracy headed by a constitutional monarch (why not a converted Louis XVI, if he could accept it?). Moreover it was pretty clear that Mirabeau had been working with Louis to this very end, though he'd kept it secret from his co-revolutionaries. However exuberant his language, Mirabeau was the voice of soft revolution; he left a vacuum to be filled.

Gouverneur Morris urged Talleyrand to take up Mirabeau's symbolic role, but it was asking a harpist to bang the drums. Talleyrand couldn't play Mirabeau. Mirabeau brought people to their feet with one drumroll, then had them back on their feet with the next. That wasn't Talleyrand's style. He had reached the top of parliamentary life, but not because he was popular. He had no illusions about that. He had got there because he had ideas and could formulate them. He was no kind of demagogue. With his limp, his cane and his superior air he was hardly the symbol of a brave new France. He'd had his ups and downs with Mirabeau but he shared his ideas, particularly on the monarchy. The Revolution must reform the monarchy, not get rid of it. It at once dawned on Talleyrand that Mirabeau had been the king's last chance of survival and now that chance was dead. 'Now I must think of how not to be buried with it,' he wrote to Mme de Flahaut, mentally preparing himself for the onset of a French republic. He was concerned for her safety, for she was a stauncher royalist than he. She must at least pretend, he told her, to be a convert to republicanism.

Even so France was still in need of a government with responsible ministers and it was the king's last charade, nullified as he was by Jacobins in parliament, to name them. Talleyrand had the job of foreign minister in his sights. Despite past disappointments and the fact that a nod from the king was no longer France's most bankable asset, his desire to be a minister seldom waned.

It was a mad situation. Nobles with experience of running France were fleeing the country, yet there still seemed room at the top for liberal-minded bluebloods who broadly shared Jacobin views. His good friend Narbonne from the days of those scintillating breakfasts at the Rue de Bellechasse was named minister of war under Jacobin auspices. This looked promising. If stories circulating about his financial doings put the finance ministry out of Talleyrand's reach, his foreign ministry aspirations faced less obvious obstacles. He had thrown his diplomatic hat into the ring in the closing stages of the Constituent Assembly, though in retrospect he realised that his aspirations might have sounded rather narrowly focused. It was the old story. His overriding objective was close relations with England. All good sprang from that. It was the inescapable conclusion of his liberal mind.

The trouble was that he was beating his powdered head against the wall. The monarchies of Europe, not least Britain's, were uniformly opposed to the French Revolution and their first aim was to reverse it. Undaunted, Talleyrand had beseeched the assembly to turn to England: 'We must at once establish the grand pillars of eternal fraternity between France and England.' This was more than a political stance; behind it was a life view. Talleyrand was an epicurean. For him a civilised life was one of industry rewarded by riches that ensured a certain ease and comfort blessed by a fine table. Such prizes were to be won only through unhampered economic relations with England, the dominant trading power. For good trade relations it was necessary to have peace; for peace it was necessary to have stability, for stability sensible governance free of extremes. In this he was a determined Anglophile. Rivalry with Britain was fruitless. Alliance was central to any world balance. Thus he asked two things of the Revolution: to ensure peace, first and foremost with England, and to avoid extremes. He imagined his own life view would suit most of his compatriots. It was the mark of a civilised man to wish on others the good he sought for himself.

Such were the credentials he had put forward for the foreign ministry post. Alas, the supposed excesses of his private life continued to get in his ministerial way, despite his compendious intellectual contribution to the Revolution. The foreign ministry too eluded him. When it did, he took on a task with the blessing of Narbonne at the war ministry that appeared to him to be France's first international priority. He left for London to try to put England onside with the Revolution. It was a thankless task.

FOUR

Saved by a Passport

As Talleyrand departed for England, Napoleon, now twenty-two, stood foursquare behind the Revolution, as far as it had gone. He took the soldier's oath to defend the constitution by the sword. For a time he was transferred to a new militia, the National Guard, raised by parliament to keep order in the country as civil war erupted from province to province and royalists bared their teeth. There was bloodshed everywhere, with regular troops and the new guard at times confronting and killing each other out of conflicting loyalties or sheer confusion. Louis XVI was blocked when attempting to flee abroad (he was only a short ride from Germany, disguised as a valet, when police halted his all too distinguishable Bourbon carriage) and placed under palace arrest in the Tuileries. The royal respite was brief: within weeks the Paris mob broke into the Tuileries with Louis inside and made him wear a funny cap symbolising liberty; then, soon afterwards, on 10 August 1792, overstepping the desire to humiliate, they captured the palace amid carnage and looting.

Napoleon didn't like what was happening to the king, but he got on with his job. He was a soldier. What he regretted most was the breakdown of leadership. Strong leaders were a near obsession with him. He'd made up for the lacunae of a military school education with his own assiduous assault on political history, studying the lives of Alexander, Hannibal, Caesar, Cromwell and their like until late in the night and writing out a careful précis for himself of each book he read. To such a young mind the leadership vacuum in France and the disorder it fed was intolerable. Danger loomed from outside the country, too. Austria and Prussia, lance bearers for the European monarchies, declared war on France to overturn the Revolution and soon their troops drove across the Rhine and on to French territory.

Napoleon wasn't part of the revolutionary army that scored a barely hoped for victory over the Austro-Prussian invaders at Valmy in September 1792, a victory which entirely changed the course of events in Europe since it put the Revolution aggressively on the offensive. A struggle to preserve France's frontiers became an itch to expand them.

It fell to Napoleon to face not Austrians and Prussians but other foreign troops, this time the British, and his exploits launched his victor's reputation. The anti-revolutionary citizenry of Toulon, France's Mediterranean naval base, had invited British forces to occupy their city to defend their cause and the English fleet obligingly locked up the port. The battle for Toulon was a desperate affair rooted in the civil strife tearing at the country. Back in the regular army with the rank of captain, young Napoleon devised a last-ditch gunnery officer's plan to blast the English fleet out of the port. Strategies tried by more senior officers to retake Toulon had failed. Napoleon advanced a new tactic: if the British could be dislodged from a hill fortress commanding entry to the port, the English fleet would be at the mercy of his artillery. With two thousand men, his horse shot from under him, Napoleon helped take the fort in hand-to-hand combat. His reward was promotion to major and a bayonet halfway through his thigh. He warned off doctors who wanted to amputate, but was still on his knees when directing the bombardment that expelled the fleet. The lifelong souvenir of his first battle against a foreign foe was a deep scar left by an English bayonet.

The reception Talleyrand received from the English was less violent, but nonetheless cooler than he'd hoped. England and France were not formally at war, but relations could scarcely have been worse; they were so low that France had no ambassador in London. He reached Dover on a blustery day in early January 1792 accompanied by his old associate Biron, another veteran of the Rue de Bellechasse breakfasts and still an adventurous military man. Biron's somewhat indelicate side mission, sanctioned by Narbonne, was to buy four thousand English horses for the revolutionary army and have them shipped to France.

Despite his more than passing interest in taking on the foreign ministership at home, Talleyrand hadn't needed pushing to go to England. At heart he realised that a post at the top of a government appointed, ever more ludicrously now, by a trapped king was unlikely to do his reputation any good. He recalled, 'I wanted to get away for a while. I was tired, disgusted, and though I knew the mission had little chance of success, I accepted.' There was indeed a limit to the powerful urge he felt to stay in France in hopes of moderating things. His 'disgust' grew out of the bloody disorders that seemed to be running ever further out of control. The Revolution, he feared, had gone mad and looked unlikely to regain its reason. He'd taken pains to get to know leading Jacobins in the legislature, among them Maximilien Robespierre and Georges-Jacques Danton, lawyers who thought they'd taken things in hand and aimed to proclaim the republic. As former assembly president, he'd personally discussed the virtues of republicanism with the righteous Robespierre and wasn't in outright disagreement on the principle despite his preference for constitutional monarchy. But the mood of anarchy made a mockery of principle. How would the brave word 'republic' restore order? Robespierre was a cleanser; he wanted to punish.

At the time, Talleyrand felt rather more positive about his mission to London than he later remembered. The aim was to talk Britannia, who ruled the waves, into remaining neutral if France fell into war with the continental monarchies and also to make sure that England and France continued to recognise each other's overseas possessions in India and the Caribbean. He was buoyed by the feeling that in France, even as the Revolution careered out of control, there was careful respect for the English who had gone about achieving their freedoms not only a lot earlier but to clearer purpose. Furthermore, there were plenty of high-up liberals on the English side who sympathised with French revolutionary ideals and wanted Prime Minister William Pitt, their Tory opponent, to take a more sympathetic stance. Pitt, five years Talleyrand's junior and already at England's helm for a decade when the Frenchman arrived, seemed a man who could be talked to on matters of political change. He was a reformer himself at heart and an enthusiastic supporter of free trade with France who only turned obdurate when after-tremors of the upheaval in France prompted him to concentrate on national security.

To be sure, Talleyrand did not arrive in London without serious handicaps. He was not to know quite how badly his name had suffered as a result of criticism put about in London by aristocratic refugees who detested his part in hobbling privilege and promoting the break with the *ancien régime*. His name, alas, was mud. The London press was in its usual scabrous mood with regard to foreigners. On the other hand his muddied name was known, and well known. He was undeniably a grandee. His shock value ought to be enough to win him an audience. Valdec de Lessart, a frightened man who landed the unappetising job of foreign minister in his place, wrote to him, 'It is precisely because it is so extraordinary for you to go that you are right for this mission.' And beyond the shock value, he was an Anglophile eager to express his leanings, an accomplished charmer, plus a match in terms of lineage for any of the governing English bluebloods.

Talleyrand took up residence in Golden Square, Soho, and, once he'd installed Courtiade to look after the supplies of fresh linen, he set about diplomatic networking. His habit was to operate by astute use of patronage under the advanced French method of giving and receiving personal favours, but this seemed an unpromising approach in the circumstances. He was further hampered by lack of official status, a disadvantage that arose both from the absence of formal French diplomatic representation in London and the secretive nature of his mission. He was neither government minister nor ambassador and he soon found that Pitt was minded to use his lack of official status to insidious effect. The prime minister refused to receive him on that very ground. Pitt also made sure that members of his government remained out of bounds, except for Lord Grenville, the foreign minister, who allowed Talleyrand a series of wary interviews in which the French visitor grasped the chance to say he'd always upheld England as the natural ally of France.

Largely, though, Talleyrand's successful political contacts were confined, as a result of Pitt's coolness, to liberal Whig opposition figures. He befriended the Whig party leader Charles James Fox, the ex-foreign minister Lord Lansdowne, the dramatist Sheridan, the social philosopher Jeremy Bentham, without forgetting to satisfy more personal interests by examining the lie of the land with financial and business leaders in the City. His welcome in these quarters no doubt inspired him to fire off enthusiastic dispatches to the foreign ministry in Paris. 'My view remains that your best ground is England. In our circumstances, it is only there that I see terra firma.' And again, 'Two neighbouring nations of which one bases its prosperity chiefly on trade and the other on agriculture are bound by the eternal nature of things to understand and enrich each other.'

But when Pitt briefly relented and gave him an acidly polite interview, the practical prospects scarcely brightened. Pitt let him know he couldn't deal with France as long as it had no viable government. After half an hour Pitt ribbed him by saying it was time to end their talk because a visitor with different ideas was waiting to see him. It was Gouverneur Morris! The American had come from Paris to try to scuttle a rapprochement between France and England which he judged contrary to American interests. Talleyrand had wind of Morris's intentions through Mme de Flahaut, who was furious with the American for his high-level meddling and in this instance flew to the defence of her 'husband in heart'. Pitt enjoyed the situation. He told Talleyrand with a stiff grin that the next time they met he'd know rather more of his intentions than he did so far. 'Delighted,' said Talleyrand. 'For my part I'm going to see Mr Fox to know more of yours.'

A strange lull ensued in his contacts with Paris. The mails went down. His lucidly written dispatches on how to proceed on the England question brought not a peep in reply for three weeks. He was highly vexed. At length he was reduced to penning a short communication. 'So you are not writing to me,' he wrote to de Lessart. 'I don't understand. It's a bad thing, I swear.' Keeping in touch was vital because Talleyrand, while truly sympathetic to the cause of Anglo-French friendship for itself, was out of tune with the underlying Jacobin reasons for agreeing to his London mission. What Jacobin leaders wanted was a clear road, without English obstruction, to take revolutionary war to the Low Countries and thus steal an advantage in impending hostilities with Austria, the sovereign ruler there. This collided head on with Talleyrand's philosophy of peace. In his unanswered dispatches he warned against any French incursion into the Low Countries, knowing that it could only menace traditional English commercial links with Antwerp and Amsterdam and sabotage his chances of holding England to neutrality.

When de Lessart eventually resurfaced, it was with the feeble excuse that he'd needed to show Talleyrand's letters to the helpless king. His silence was in fact understandable. De Lessart faced arrest for failure to pursue the Revolution's aims with sufficient alacrity and knew he was about to be removed from his post, as was Narbonne from the war ministry. His actual excuse was too damp to draw a reply from Talleyrand, who was by then in bed with the first of the bad colds he caught in London and in no mood to communicate further.

Biron's condition was worse. The horse purchase ran into trouble. The English dealer who contracted to sell him four thousand horses complained that the bills Biron sought to pay with were worthless and sued him for debt. Biron was at once imprisoned under England's tyrannical debtor laws, which sent Talleyrand hopping between unresponsive English ministries trying to free him. Pitt stalled. To the delight of the London press half the bills Biron presented were shown to be fakes, as Talleyrand conceded, though no one was able to work out how his companion came by them beyond hints that they were palmed off on him by unscrupulous exchange dealers. Talleyrand saw the hand of London's resentful French émigrés behind it. It was a good week before he secured his friend's release, by which time the sale had fallen through. The episode was deeply embarrassing for Talleyrand, increasing the distrust he already encountered in London government and newspaper circles.

Things might have gone better if Talleyrand had been on his best salon form. This was impossible. London society, aware of his reputation for wit and delicious indiscretion, expected too much of him; he spoke English not badly but it was hard to be brilliant and to unleash the *mot juste* in someone else's language. His fallback was to listen and be devastatingly polite, which could be confused with arrogance. The English wanted raillery from him, not clever silence.

He returned to Paris on 10 March 1792 after a two-month stay in London and then talked his way into going back there six weeks later in the company of a young diplomat, a modern-minded aristocrat who would hold the rank of ambassador so as to make negotiations more formal. The younger man, the Marquis François-Bernard de Chauvelin, was of course to act under Talleyrand's orders, a ruse which was quite transparent to the English. Talleyrand became the puppet master and for a time enjoyed the role. During the brief return to Paris he had cemented his position as a man of peace with some determined lobbying of the increasingly aggressive assembly. He urged it to vote a law upholding the absolute principle of non-intervention by France in other countries' internal affairs. In the atmosphere of the moment this was setting himself up as a bollard in the path of the revolutionary war chariot. The assembly swerved round him, but news of his efforts did him no harm in London. Knowing how the English side revered royalty, he also composed a letter that Louis XVI addressed directly to George III appealing for a new era in relations that would 'command' peace in Europe. It was a long shot, absurd in view of Louis' plight, and Pitt wasn't impressed. Pitt's secret policy was to isolate revolutionary France, to wait and see how the Revolution developed further and be ready to act if necessary, all the while agitating with funds and spies in support of France's active foes.

Nonetheless Talleyrand had his reward. In late May Pitt's wait-and-see strategy led him to sign a declaration of neutrality. In the prime minister's mind it was a holding measure and Talleyrand must have sensed as much. Still, he believed he had forced England's hand and couldn't resist a little preening. His negotiating tactics had been 'not unclever', he hastened to remind those in charge at the foreign ministry in Paris. They should make sure the Paris press gave full cover to his exploit and that he received personal glory. His name should appear prominently in the reports. He wasn't shy to say why. 'I insist on the name part because I need a good reason to be absent from Paris and I know none better than very good work accomplished elsewhere.' Normally when he wrote things that were liable to embarrass or endanger him if made public, he asked the recipient to burn his letter. This time he didn't. An honest plea to be kept away from the Revolution apparently fell into his non-inflammable category.

The fresh gloss on his name failed to prolong Talleyrand's absence. An uncompromising provisional government newly installed in Paris soon demanded his return, and although he stalled a while he couldn't postpone it for long without running the risk of being listed as an émigré, now a crime under revolutionary law. It didn't help that his mission appeared to be accomplished.

The Paris he returned to in July 1792 wasn't the Paris in which he had shone. The best salons were closed, the gaming tables folded, the style and elegance almost invisible. War fever and street killings squeezed out the graceful life he knew. His civilisation was sinking. He saw no place for himself in the prevailing anarchy. The savage assault on the Tuileries Palace by an armed mob on 10 August made up his mind for him. The crowd slaughtered the king's Swiss guard almost to a man and looted the palace; Louis himself narrowly escaped a public lynching and his physical survival was left to the whim of Jacobin politicians, who for the time being held him in prison. What happened on 10 August was a climax to all the disorders that had gone before, and it could not be read by anyone who had been part of the old order as anything but a sign of grave personal danger. Events were already becoming a hideous blur to Talleyrand, but he wasn't blind. If he hadn't so far seen himself in mortal peril, he did now. Looking ahead, he packed up his precious library and sent it to London. He could not pack himself up and do likewise. Straight flight was out of the question. That would make him an outlaw, which in turn would make it impossible for him to recover his place at France's head when things cooled down, as they inevitably would some day. He helped his friend Narbonne and others to make a bolt in secret across the Channel but rejected the chance to go with them. Adelaïde de Flahaut also got out with their son Charles. What Talleyrand needed was a passport to leave the country with the Revolution's formal permission.

But passports were exceptionally difficult to come by in these times, particularly for aristocrats. Talleyrand needed nerve and guile to proceed with his enterprise. He protected his rear with a judiciously argued declaration he thought it useful to put into the mouth of the provisional government – a memorandum to foreign courts explaining the background to the king's brutal downfall on 10 August. The idea was to help Jacobin leaders stay on speaking terms with Europe's aggrieved monarchies, not least England's. Louis XVI, he wrote, had lost all public confidence; he had foolishly undermined the new French constitution 'in which he occupied so fine a place'; he had resorted to heavy bribes in a scandalous effort to subdue the 'ardent patriotism' that threatened him. In sum, Louis was a bad lot.

Again this was not Talleyrand at his best. The language clearly didn't chime with his actual view of things. However, its revolutionary ring might just strengthen the less than solid reason he hit upon for requiring a passport. The ticket he came up with was weights and measures, the pet idea he'd pursued in the Constituent Assembly. Wouldn't France and, indeed, the whole of Europe gain from the adoption of a single system of weights and measures in place of hundreds of curious local traditions? And what more important convert to unity could there be than England, the queen of commerce! It was an eminently useful idea, but the time was hardly ripe for sideshows and Talleyrand knew it. A stronger pretext for demanding a passport might have been the need to tend to the shaky neutrality he had extracted from England. Alas, he had twice been to London on that grand errand and he knew that asking to go back a third time wouldn't work.

Thus he tramped on his cane between government ministries, making his awkward case late into the night. He perused his thick book of political contacts for those who owed him favours, only to discover that all of them had left Paris. The authorities were a wall of non-compliance, either through reluctance or sloth. Talleyrand sensed his personal peril mounting. There seemed no understanding of his earlier role in promoting the Revolution's reforms. Extremists in parliament were braying about his loyalties and time was running out. The guillotine was already hard at work, gearing up for the Terror. A net seemed to be closing around him. Robespierre and his friends were on the point of transforming the assembly once more, this time into a National Convention designed to establish a republic and bring down the guillotine on its political foes, real and imaginary.

It was ironic, then, that a leading Conventioneer – the same Georges-Jacques Danton with whom he'd guardedly discussed prospects for the republic – became Talleyrand's last hope. Danton was one of the broader minded radicals and had just then taken charge of the Revolution, heading the provisional government's executive council as minister of justice. The Talleyrand contact book at last paid dividends. Less forgetful than most, Danton held him in esteem for his part in drawing up the pre-republic constitution and the Rights of Man. Also they had sat together and frater-nised in the local Paris assembly. By the end of August, Talleyrand was reduced to doorstepping Danton, who merely smiled at his weights and measures scam, having heavier matters to deal with. On 1 September, as midnight neared, he sat patiently in a waiting room at Danton's justice ministry, endeavouring to maintain his celebrated sang-froid. Outside in the Place Vendôme workers were installing machinery to demolish the statue of Louis XIV, the Sun King. A Jacobin parliamentarian who saw him sitting there reported: 'I came upon the bishop Talleyrand in leather breeches and boots, a round hat, a short coat and a ponytail . . . He was friendly to me and realised how astounded I was to see him at the justice ministry at this hour. He said it was because he was leaving that very morning for London on a mission for the executive. He had come for papers which Danton was to hand him from the executive council.'

Talleyrand remained in the waiting room until 1.30 a.m. before departing empty-handed, observed the Jacobin, who was touched by the encounter.

But humiliation was by then of small concern to Talleyrand. His innate self-assurance could deal with that. He dressed down into the common man's leather breeches for his passport hunt. The ponytail was a gesture to revolutionary fashion: severe times demanded severe coiffure. A further nervous week went by, however, before Danton, who had a warmer heart than the icy Robespierre, at last produced the passport (mischievous tongues said he received a bribe from Talleyrand, who swore that no such thing occurred). The wording of the executive order that went with the passport was a little slapdash but no less precious for that: 'Freedom of passage to London for Maurice Talleyrand on our orders.' In the coinage of political self-preservation the last three words were made of pure gold.

The passport most probably saved Talleyrand's life. It took him eight days to reach London via army checkpoints, country highways crammed with refugee priests, women and children, and scarce cross-Channel transport. No sooner was he reunited with his library in London than revolutionary crowbars prised open King Louis' private safe in the Tuileries and out spilled the royal correspondence. A pair of letters, penned by a royal counsellor more than a year earlier, pointed to secret links between Talleyrand and the king. Talleyrand was portrayed as pledging loyalty to the king and offering him his services. Since this purportedly occurred at a time when he was campaigning hard for a constitutional monarchy and was convinced not only that it was the best thing for France but that it was workable, his solace for the king seemed neither very surprising nor out of order. But the people's crowbars were insensitive to such logic.

Members of the new Convention clamoured for Talleyrand's arrest. He defended himself vigorously from his haven in London, protesting that he had not once had direct contact with the king. His contacts were with members of the royal household and had nothing to do with motives imputed to him, his main purpose having been to secure grace-and-favour lodgings for a deserving artist he admired. This sounded as convincing as his weights and measures story and would have been rather too much for the Convention to swallow even if its members hadn't been intent on hauling him before revolutionary justice, whatever his defence. Accordingly it decided there was strong evidence to bring charges against him and ordered his arrest.

The extra sting was that his name went straight on to the dread émigré list he had manoeuvred with such energy and guile to avoid. The arrest warrant covered seventeen members of the Talleyrand-Périgord family, his mother included, though almost all of them had already fled the country. The description the police gave of Talleyrand read: 'Five feet three inches [the passport correctly made him two inches taller]. Long face [it was in fact more round than long], blue eyes, regular nose slightly retroussé. Limps in one leg, right or left.'

While such hit-or-miss identification was no immediate threat to his liberty in London, the cruel swerve in the Revolution's attitude towards him closed off the influence he still hoped to preserve in France. Nonetheless his statesman's interests were shifting from the economy to diplomacy as a result of his negotiating experiences with the English, and he sought to keep his hand in as best he could in Paris by recommending an international policy to his saviour Danton. He did so in a comprehensive memoir into which he poured much hard work and thought and which, alas, now risked going unheeded. This was exasperating, since the exhaustive paper laid out in his most lucid language his formula for peace and prosperity. Furthermore, it contained all his thinking on what the increasingly aggressive Revolution must avoid. He wrote:

> We have at last learned that true primacy, the only useful and reason-able kind, the sole primacy that befits free and enlightened men, is to be master in one's own house and never to entertain the absurd notion of being master in another's. We have learned, a little late no doubt, that for states as for individuals real wealth consists not in seizing or invading the lands of another but in increasing the worth of one's own. We have learned that all territorial expansion, all usurpation by force and guile – those things by which our old and illustrious prejudices have measured rank, primacy, strength and superiority among coun-tries – are merely cruel games of political unreason, false calculations of power that end by increasing government costs and problems and diminishing the happiness and security of the governed.

France, he argued, must never seek to expand her frontiers or incorporate even willing neighbours. 'She must remain circumscribed by her own bound-aries: she owes this to her glory, to justice, to reason, to her own interest and to the interest of peoples who wish to be free with her.'

Master in one's own house! That was the thing. It was the essential basis for general wellbeing. Conquest, then, was the ultimate folly. As for alliances, they could work only if they departed from the traditional formula designed to threaten third countries, or to defend against them by military means. The old forms of alliance, Talleyrand argued, were merely arrangements made among kings conspiring against peoples. All that was gone, or very nearly so. Any alliance the new France entered must be designed to advance human liberties among partners so as to create 'new sources of commerce and industry satisfying the needs and activities of the human race'.

The bluntness of Talleyrand's warning against conquest sounded coura-geous, foolhardy even, in view of his present position. Revolutionary armies had invaded and occupied the Low Countries and the French masses were feeling good about it. Yet here was the essence of all his thinking on diplo-macy: his opposition to the lust for empire and territorial expansion. In time it would put his relations with Napoleon to the ultimate test. However, since his forthright memoir reached Danton and the provisional government at just about the time the king's telltale safe sprang open, its immediate destination was the Revolution's back drawer.

Talleyrand wasn't quite without funds in London. Profits made on stock markets and speculative enterprises in Hamburg, Amsterdam and London itself during the adventurous years under Panchaud's tutelage remained a source, albeit a dwindling one. But he was cut off from the handsome income in France that had allowed him to live at the high tempo he desired and this concerned him. He rented a pleasant house on Kensington Square, just off Hyde Park, and settled down to renewing his contacts with highly placed Whig liberals and, whenever possible, with Prime Minister Pitt's diplomats. His objective, he informed a diffident foreign ministry in Paris, was to be 'useful' to France. He still saw his role as working to keep England honest on neutrality, though it also crossed his mind that he might advise the London government on events in France and where they might lead. It was a grind. The problem wasn't English apathy (Pitt's agents shadowed him closely), it was his thankless position. Not only was he without official rank, this time he had no official mission.

His main companions were liberal-minded French refugees holed up in a charming semi-stately residence called Juniper Hall, near Dorking in Surrey, an easy carriage ride from London. The residence belonged to a hospitable English family by the name of Philipps. But it became a haven for that class of French princesses, duchesses and counts who had chosen to see the progressive side of the Revolution and had tried to make the best of it before having to flee for their lives. They were an open-minded minority among legions of less liberal French émigrés – arch-royalists in the main and every bit as suspicious of Talleyrand as Pitt himself was. The reactionary majority loathed Talleyrand for his role in creating the new constitution and he returned the sentiment. The Juniper Hall community, on the other hand, welcomed him with open arms. His friend Narbonne and one or two others from the old Paris breakfast crowd were there, as was Adelaïde de Flahaut.

He began spending more time there than he did at Kensington Square, though his relations with Adelaïde were no longer as cosy as they'd been in Paris. A chill had set in. The blame didn't lie with Gouverneur Morris alone. Adelaïde had escaped to England under the intimate protection of the son of Lord Lansdowne, the liberal peer and one-time foreign secretary whom Talleyrand had befriended at the outset of his first stay in London. She made no secret of her romance with Lansdowne's heir, which miffed Talleyrand besides throwing a small cloud of embarrassment over his relations with an otherwise sympathetic Lansdowne senior, who had graciously extended him an open invitation to stay at his country estate whenever he wished. There seemed something incestuous about Adelaïde's affairs. She'd brought Talleyrand's son Charles with her to England and put him in an English school, which satisfied Talleyrand. But she was also penniless, like most of the Juniper Hall community, and was asking him to provide for her. If he seemed reluctant, it was because his own position was increasingly shaky. She was clearly wounded by his hesitancy. But the chances of making money had dried up. Where could he turn? He had taken the step of informing Pitt's Foreign Office that he was well placed to advise on events in France, but had received no reply. The English were hopelessly suspicious. He toyed with the idea of establishing a bank for trade with India where he imagined English colonials to be swimming in wealth. His own material assets were largely in France, facing confiscation by the state. The one asset at hand was his library. He put it up for sale at auction, receiving far less than he'd hoped but enough to keep him afloat. It was sad to part with the wonderful library. The large collection was a passion, though he consoled himself that he'd always regarded it as an investment as well.

Talleyrand was welcomed by the bored inmates of Juniper Hall because of the immediate impact he made. He was a performer, an entertainer. His sharp way with words, his veiled sport of suggesting more than he said, his laconic commentaries on events in London and Paris, his sense of ridicule and his deliciously overplayed old-time courtesies revived their spirits and made them feel at home, particularly the eager women. Since the women outnumbered the men, he was in his element, surrounded by elegant, rouged creatures hanging on his words. These exiled children of the Enlightenment camped in leafy Surrey were desperately hungry for good conversation, new books and music. He supplied the first and had ideas on the rest. Very soon he was the star of the group.

In the Home Counties life of early Georgian England they made an exotic band – displaced bluebloods down on their elegant uppers and pining for intellectual treats. English relations of the Philipps family came by to examine their plumage and join in their cultural pursuits. Talleyrand's charm didn't strike everyone on a first encounter. The writer Fanny Burney, at that time a blushing young sister of the hostess with literary aspirations rather than achievements, wrote in her notebook after meeting him that she didn't like him at all. It was true that he was losing the graceful, slender line of his youth. Now close to forty, he had thickened out, his fine features puffing up and giving him at times an effeminate look. The extra weight seemed to increase his limp. However, a day or so after forming her first adverse opinion the English rose was writing: 'Incredible! Monsieur de Talleyrand has completely won me over. Now I find him one of the most distinguished and charming members of this exquisite company.'

Despite the chill with Mme de Flahaut, he proofread a romantic novel she was finishing and urged her to have it published, which she did. This proved a boon because it sold well and eventually relaxed the financial demands she made of him. Mme de Staël also turned up for several months at Juniper Hall, making a spectacular detour on her way to her native Switzerland. Her aim was to induce Narbonne, her current amour, to take refuge in Switzerland with her until the storm in France had blown over. But she was still besotted with Talleyrand and his talents, and not a little jealous of her latest literary rival, Mme de Flahaut, who she thought was receiving far more of his attentions than her book could possibly merit. The situation was delicate for Talleyrand: here he was with two mistresses of varying degrees of intensity who were apparently ready for a spat. Half in jest, the burly Swiss authoress asked him in front of the Juniper Hall regulars which of the two of them, herself or Adelaïde, he would save first from a sinking ship. His gaze scarcely flickering, he replied, 'You, Madame, would appear to be the better swimmer.'

In truth it was Germaine who now took the higher place in Talleyrand's esteem. The longer he stayed in England, the further his feelings for the flighty Adelaïde diminished, while the friendship with Germaine, platonic but intimate, intensified. He wrote long, anguished letters to her when she got to Geneva about his sense of helplessness as an exile, and wasn't beyond making elegant appeals for her financial assistance (the Neckers were rich and had their wealth in Switzerland). He blew hot and cold about what he might do to oust the fanatical Robespierre brigade whose grip on France had tightened at Danton's expense. He wrote to her: 'I really want to fight . . . I give you my word it would be a great pleasure to beat those scoundrels.' Then again, 'Our quiet émigré role can't honestly satisfy us much longer.' To Lord Lansdowne, though, he confided that he wanted to stay in England a long time because France was now 'a base heap of lies buried in slime'. Where were the free-thinking men of 1789 who had spearheaded the Revolution and the struggle for reform? They were now, he concluded, all too few.

Talleyrand went fishing in Surrey ponds to compose himself. Fishing became his regular pastime, though it was new to him. He sat for hours with his line dangling in dark pond water, calculating whether his meagre funds would outlast Robespierre. The always-be-rich philosophy by which he lived was put to the cruellest test; it was at the best of times as much a mental as a material state of being. A return to a France that had regained her sanity was his first wish, but each piece of fresh news from Paris brought grief. For him, the Revolution had become a total calamity, aimless, rudderless and driven by crazed passions. It had even lost its historical significance, he decided, since there were no lessons to be drawn from chaos. His beloved France had ceased to function. She had lost the liberty he hoped she had gained.

On 23 January 1793, by a vote of the National Convention, King Louis was sentenced to death and guillotined, causing a furore in the royal capitals of Europe. Talleyrand was 'sickened' by the king's execution, which had the perverse effect of sabotaging his situation as an exile. First it triggered England's return to a formal state of war with France, aborting his freelance hopes of keeping England neutral. It also appalled the English to a point where they turned against all agents of France, official, unofficial or having anything remotely to do with fostering the Revolution. It froze the goodwill English liberals felt for 1789. Even the generous Lord Lansdowne found it hard not to allow his unease to play against Talleyrand. For no other Frenchman then on English soil had ridden the tide of change that led to King Louis' execution as publicly as Talleyrand.

He was a sitting target for English abuse. If the English wanted a devil, he was it. Unjust it was, but, as Talleyrand recognised, unavoidable. He confronted it with his trademark impassiveness, smarting inside. Pitt let it be known that he found him 'deep and dangerous', and although part of the prime minister's mistrust no doubt derived from Talleyrand's hobnobbing with Whig liberals – a preference Pitt forced on him by closing off access to the government side – so sinister a label was bound to undermine his position still further.

Then began the Terror unleashed by Robespierre against both holdfast remnants of the aristocracy and political adversaries. From mid-1793 the guillotine went to work without let-up, poisoning the atmosphere in England still further against Talleyrand and taking the lives, among victims close to him, of his brother Archambaud's wife and Adelaïde de Flahaut's long-suffering husband, the Comte de Flahaut, who had the misfortune to be Keeper of the King's Gardens. This was only a prelude to the Great Terror that soon rooted out aristocrats in hiding and dispatched to the guillotine the broader minded radicals who first made the Revolution, with Danton himself destined for the lead tumbrel. The fear and unease that coursed around Europe did not miss William Pitt, who passed a law permitting him to expel foreigners posing a notional wartime threat to security. The Alien Bill might have been drawn up with Talleyrand directly in its sights. It was obvious from the label Pitt pinned on him that he saw him as a spy. Hadn't he deviously offered his services as 'adviser' to the Foreign Office on the situation in France? Hadn't he consorted with the Jacobins? Of the European capitals, London housed more than its share of continental spies and bribe-masters. French royalists were reckless plotters, floating endless schemes they wanted Pitt to subscribe to. Secret diplomacy was an English forte which indeed also appealed strongly to Talleyrand, except that France in her current circumstances was no mistress to practise it for.

On a damp London evening in late January 1794, an hour after nightfall, two men dressed in black knocked at Talleyrand's door in Kensington Square and entered his home, introducing themselves as government bailiffs. They handed him an order from Pitt to leave the country within five days. The expulsion order came without explanation and the silent bailiffs offered none. On reading the order, Talleyrand, without a flicker of emotion, advised the pair he would obey. He was pleased at least with his reaction to the rude intrusion. 'I don't believe I showed the slightest sign of bother,' he wrote to Mme de Staël in Geneva.

Pitt's narrowly targeted attempt to spare England the contagion of revolution was more than a bother, however: it was a catastrophe for Talleyrand. Of the Juniper Hall community he was the sole victim of the Alien Bill. His reading of the misfortune was that Pitt had bowed to pressure from ultra-royalist émigrés who hated him, though he also wrote to Mme de Staël that he believed the Austrian and Prussian courts had a hand in it, which suggested he wasn't unaware of spying allegations laid against him. To his authoress friend he did his best to remain light-hearted and display his usual sang-froid. 'It seems the Emperor [of Austria] and the King of Prussia are afraid of people who go fishing in summer and correct the proofs of a novel in winter. Those were the tasks of this fevered brain whose stay in Europe is so disquieting.'

Despite his first proud reflex, his unprotesting acceptance of the expulsion order, he at once pondered the dangers and disadvantages it involved and made frantic efforts to have it cancelled. Outside England, where could he go? Other European monarchies and principalities where French aristocrats were taking refuge (all his immediate family plus his uncle, the archbishop, had camped in Germany) were in league with England and clearly closed to him. That much was implicit in Pitt's arbitrary order, which effectively cast him as a plague-carrier of revolution and thus a danger to all European monarchies. Dignity alone, Talleyrand later recalled, drove him to battle such 'unjust persecution'. He peppered the English Establishment – from Pitt's close political friends to Pitt himself, and even George III directly – with requests to have it overturned. He appealed to their English sense of justice which he professed to hold in highest regard. How could they accuse him of being a dangerous revolutionary when the ruling Convention had outlawed him as a partisan of royalty? And with deep indignation: 'You would lay on me the dark ingratitude of not cherishing the one hospitable country where I can rest my head!'

Pitt remained unmoved even by this emotional compliment to England, though it rang sincere. The prime minister had an agenda and Talleyrand wasn't part of it, or rather he refused to recognise him as part of it. The task Pitt gave himself was to weather the storm of the French Revolution and steer Britain away from republicanism into the safe haven of limited monarchy. Talleyrand, alas, had displayed too much republican spirit to fit into the Pitt picture. Yet piqued and horribly inconvenienced though he was by England's rejection, Talleyrand never strayed far from his Anglophile beliefs. In his view they continued to shape the fortunes of France and of peace. From the outbreak of the Revolution he'd tried to influence things in such a way that English institutions served as a model for those of the new France. In so doing he'd made the mistake of putting England on a pedestal, which made his reward from Pitt so much harder to accept.

The one relief his protest campaign obtained was an extension of the five-day departure deadline to a month. This gave him a small breathing space to think about his destination. Barring unlikely outposts such as Egypt or India, he had little choice but to make for America to be sure of avoiding arrest. He put a brave face on things. However raw, the United States, as it had just begun to call itself, carried the glow of its own revolution. Also it had the advantage of being at peace with France and by all accounts remained grateful to the French for having helped free Americans from British rule not ten years earlier. Within months of turning forty, he was young enough to try a new life. Americans, he'd heard, were mainly interested in making money, which happened to be a priority he fully shared at this moment. He convinced himself that a fortune awaited him in America. Gouverneur Morris would surely put in a good word for him with George Washington and other Americans of high influence. After all, his peg-legged rival had once backed him to be finance minister of France.

To tide himself over for his start in America he talked London bankers into providing him with a bill of exchange worth $8337, on which they could expect a profit once he settled in and restored his fortunes. The last step was to book a passage to Philadelphia aboard the Yankee merchantman *William Penn* for himself, his valet Courtiade and a fortune-seeking companion from his days in the Constituent Assembly, Comte Briois de Baumetz, who insisted on joining him.

On 1 March, with the *William Penn* about to weigh anchor, he wrote to Mme de Staël: 'This is my last letter from London; tomorrow I shall be aboard. In leaving, my dear friend, I ask you to remember that the one pleasure I can have is to receive your letters.' Despite the riches that beckoned, to be cut off from everything he knew was hard to face. It was a break with the civilisation he cherished most in life and in defence of which he had ridden the Revolution.

FIVE

America

While Talleyrand sailed under duress to America the outlook for Napoleon abruptly turned bleak, as if fate were dealing each man a similar unkindness in order somehow to narrow the gulf between them. Napoleon, now twenty-five, found that the fame and rapid promotion he had won by driving the English out of Toulon left him open to grave republican suspicion. A leap in rank to brigadier general in command of Mediterranean coastal defences failed to protect him from spiteful republican commissars watching over what they held to be the interests of the Convention. Twice they placed him under arrest, a misfortune often amounting to a death sentence in those unpredictable times. The reason for the first arrest was his preoccupation with civil order, which led him to submit military plans to curb the turbulent Marseilles populace. His proposal so injured the feelings of Marseilles representatives to the Convention that they wanted its author curbed instead. The second arrest, some months later, resulted from tenuous contacts he had with bit-part revolutionary figures who suddenly fell from political grace. Since political heads were by then falling like slates from Paris roofs, it came as a huge relief to Napoleon to escape the commissars' clutches and secure his eventual release on both counts.

Nonetheless the passing stigma, coupled with total political confusion as Robespierre himself went to the guillotine in the high summer of 1794, blocked his immediate ambitions. What he wanted more than anything was the command of artillery in the Army of the Alps, a republican force mustering on the Italian border to confront imperial Austria, the power in northern Italy. This was Napoleon's part of the world: the south, the Mediterranean. He longed to get into action there, to fight France's enemies rather than bloody his hands in putting down civil war. Though he was by now a willing republican, he was sickened by the prospect of dealing out death at home. With some gall for a very junior general, he therefore rejected an assignment as gunnery chief in the republican army engaged in destroying royalist forces in

Brittany and the neighbouring Vendée; the command was right, the venue and mission wrong. That impertinence further held him back. Hard as he lobbied his military seniors and the Jacobin realists who eliminated Robespierre, a command in the Army of the Alps eluded him. He was obliged to cool his heels with mounting impatience in a Paris desk job.

It was the autumn of 1795 before Napoleon's chance came to break out, and he seized it. He took a snap personal decision to line up heavy guns in the wet and windy streets of Paris to help a new set of Convention leaders hold back columns of royalist insurgents. This was a climax to the revolution at home and he managed to put his aversion to civil slaughter aside for the occasion. At the personal behest of Paul Barras, a liberal southern gentleman now risen to the top of the republic, he fired on the Paris insurgents. Their rebellion was crushed. His reward from a grateful Barras was a call to take full command of the Army of the Alps, which Napoleon did before the ink was dry on his certificate of marriage to a sensuous young widow six years older than himself named Josephine de Beauharnais. Josephine, a woman about Paris, came from a family of Caribbean sugar planters and was introduced to him by Barras himself, a peacock of a man of ambivalent amorous leanings who was one of her lovers.

Napoleon's lightning thrust across the Italian frontier at the head of the army in his charge stunned Austrian forces. Victory after victory soon made him master of Italy, owing only token fealty to the government in Paris. It was the onset of an age of conquest unmatched since the empire of ancient Rome.

Talleyrand's passage to America in a pitching Yankee merchantman took thirty-eight days. The voyage had an ominous start, not only because the boat had to run for port at Falmouth, Cornwall, in a raging Channel storm two days out of London. He was relieved that the captain chose not to seek shelter and repairs on the French side of the Channel which he had nervously spotted at one point from the heaving deck, certain that he would be arrested if the ship put ashore there. The choice of Falmouth, as it turned out, had a peculiar sequel that also bothered him.

In the Cornish inn where he put up was a doleful guest the innkeeper introduced as an American general. Talleyrand was delighted at the chance to quiz the American on the unfamiliar land he was bound for, but having exchanged courtesies with him he found it impossible to engage him in conversation. Every lead he tried fell flat. Talleyrand attempted to retrieve things by asking him if he would mind writing a letter or so of introduction to people of influence in his homeland. Army generals, after all, were men of stature: George Washington was one himself.

The American shook his head. 'I am perhaps the only American who cannot give you letters for his country,' he said. 'All my ties there are broken.' It was the innkeeper that same evening who supplied the name of the reluctant American. It was Benedict Arnold. Arnold! Even the French knew of Benedict Arnold, the general condemned to death at home for betraying his own side during America's war of independence. Arnold the traitor! The chance meeting shook Talleyrand. He himself was accused of being a traitor by royalists who bore him a grudge for participating in the Revolution, and by priests who reviled him for undermining church power. No charge infuriated and wounded him more. They were wrong; their charges were shallow. He was filled with pity for his fellow inn guest.

It was early spring before Talleyrand sighted the mouth of the Delaware and disembarked in Philadelphia, capital of the infant United States, his hopes of restoring his material fortunes still buoyant after the long crossing. Indeed, he carried much the same innocent hopes of all immigrants to America then and since. First he confirmed for himself, with some glee, that Americans were mad about money. 'Lucre is the subject of all conversation and the motivation of all action,' he was soon writing to Mme de Staël. Just the same he was all too sharply aware of the paradox he presented: the Old-World elitist with the ageless history of France in his bones set down in a raw new land just six years old, dating it from the ratification of the United States constitution. In this view even his limp was a decadent mark of what he was.

Still, a small tribe of French refugees not wholly unlike himself was already established in Philadelphia and with his bankers' draft he rented a small red-brick house in the heart of the city at the corner of Spruce and Second streets. The house was near a French bookshop, lately established by an émigré colleague of Talleyrand from the old Constituent Assembly which served as a meeting place for French bluebloods stranded in the city. The bookshop was a mini-Juniper Hall transplanted across the Atlantic and its founder, the amiable Médéric Moreau de Saint-Méry, was always ready with a good story, topped by his involuntary part in the storming of the Bastille: as chief advocate of the parliament that was then contesting the king's authority, he'd been handed the keys to the Bastille by the maddened street mob whose leaders, so he said, couldn't think who else to give them to, nor he where to put them. All the Philadelphia den lacked was an eager, talkative flock of elegant women. It was a male world with an ambiance not unlike that of the Rue de Bellechasse breakfast set, except for the disorienting, out-of-the-way setting. Still, Moreau served Madeira wine, which Talleyrand favoured over French claret. He drank a good two glasses of Madeira each day for fortification, the first at breakfast.

The population of the United States was then some four million, and one in a hundred of its citizens lived in Philadelphia, an industrious river port of shipwrights, ropemakers, printers, gunsmiths and other busy trades. The Pennsylvania city had twice the population of New York, which itself was booming, but that hardly made it an appealing destination for Talleyrand. He shuddered at its lack of charm and grace. The civic spirit hadn't recovered from a catastrophic outbreak of yellow fever which had killed off Philadelphians at a rate of one hundred per day not six months earlier, descending on the population with the rage of the guillotine in Paris. For some months the plague had reduced the federal capital to a ghost town and, though November frosts at last halted it, the mood in the city was still depressed.

Philadelphia's gruffness extended to George Washington, the new republic's first president, who refused to see Talleyrand. The president knew full well who this new refugee was, but he wanted to keep France and its problems at arm's length. Furthermore, the letters of recommendation Talleyrand carried from illustrious Englishmen, such as his friend Lord Lansdowne and sundry bankers, did not carry anything like the weight of a damning letter which Gouverneur Morris took the trouble to address to President Washington. Whether out of spite or a sense of national duty, Morris warned the president off Talleyrand, his rival in love. 'The Bishop of Autun has a reputation for immorality,' he wrote, 'not so much for adultery, for that has been common enough among clergy of high rank, but for the variety and publicity of his amours, for gambling and above all for stock-jobbing during the ministry of M de Calonne, with whom he was on the best of terms and therefore had opportunities which his enemies say he made no small use of.'

Was it insider trading or adultery that most upset Morris? Either way the pot was calling the kettle black, most mischievously so in his harping on the outdated Bishop of Autun title, which he evidently thought would make Washington think still worse of Talleyrand. American leaders liked to be reminded that they did not share the frivolity of the French. In addition, a Jacobin ambassador fresh from Paris did all he could to blacken Talleyrand's name and warned the Americans against dealing with an aristocratic exile facing arrest.

Denied direct access to the great Washington, Talleyrand compensated for the disappointment by befriending Alexander Hamilton who was in charge of the US Treasury. The two had much in common: each helped frame his country's constitution. Hamilton was a lion in his land for doing so, and Talleyrand greatly admired him. He rated him the equal of Europe's leading contemporary statesmen, Pitt included. Though Hamilton was very close to Washington, having been his dashing military alter ego in the war of independence, he was far from being a Washington yes-man. As leader of the Federalist party which favoured a centralised US government and liberal trade policies, presupposing decent terms with England, he was near in spirit to Talleyrand. The pair's shared passion for the intricacies of finance pitched them into intense discussions on the workings of the world economy, and they listened to each other with deep interest. Hamilton wanted to run his country as a sound business venture. It impressed Talleyrand that he had established a national bank, something he himself had been on the verge of setting up in France. More to the point, anything Hamilton had to say on how to accumulate wealth in America was music to Talleyrand's straining ears.

Land speculation, already an American standby, seemed the surest road to success. The country was a vast virgin forest – but for a narrow band on the eastern seaboard stretching from Maine to the border with Spanish Florida – and even in the most developed states of Pennsylvania, New York and Massachusetts less than a third of the land was cleared for farming. Americans were indeed beginning to spill westwards through the untamed wilderness into Ohio, but half of the territory then comprising the United States was still occupied by Indians. For Talleyrand the task was how to enter the property fray. The thirteen states were subject to vast speculation deals involving American businessmen and European banks. Big banks in Europe, fretting over rising warfare on their side of the Atlantic, aimed to place capital in American land as a shelter from risk. The business was straightforward: home capitalists bought swathes of virgin land on credit from the various states, then sold it for double or triple the price in chunks of tens of thousands of acres to European investors, who sold them on for further profit in smaller chunks to American farmers, property dealers and smaller investors.

The prospect of engaging in this profit chain fascinated Talleyrand, sober though he felt about the quality of life in America. He dreamed up a scheme catering to maharajahs and colonists with fortunes in India, a community to which his fancies often turned. Wouldn't they do better to leapfrog England when placing their wealth and invest it in wide-open America instead? 'There's a lot of money to be made here,' he wrote to Mme de Staël, slipping into the language of the real estate operator, 'but it is for people who have it. If you know people who want to speculate in land here I shall be pleased to look after them. If I had a large number of people giving me their business on commission, we should both make a lot. They would do well because Americans aren't too sure in business, and I would do well because I wouldn't need personal funds to get started. Look into this please.'

His head swam with ideas on how to restore his fortune. There was speculating to be done on trade across the Atlantic. Buying and selling cargoes on commission had promise. Then there was the enduring problem of moving payments from here to there and back again, which he resolved to his own satisfaction (though not conclusively to that of international bankers) by proposing an early version of the traveller's cheque. Still, what was proper coming from him did not sound so pleasant, in his ears, coming from Americans. He found America's admiration for money and the way of expressing it downright crude. 'Luxury has come too soon. When man's first needs are scarcely satisfied, luxury is shocking,' he wrote, pained at seeing the wife of an American banker he knew tossing her tawdry felt hat on to a precious stool made of Sèvres china from the Trianon in Versailles. How the banker came by the delicate work of art he couldn't tell, but the incongruity amazed him. The hat was so ugly, he thought, that a French peasant wouldn't have been seen wearing it. There was something horribly maladroit about luxury in America. Luxury in Europe, to be sure, was at times taken to frivolous excess, but American luxury displayed a total absence of style and refinement. Americans seemed too basic to cope with it. Theirs was a strange nation in most respects, he decided: 'It has thirty-two religions and only one dish – and that is bad.' He didn't say what it was, but it must have been the staple Philadelphia meat and potatoes fare.

His criticisms, even tongue in cheek, no doubt reflected how underused he felt his own talents were in America. At least he knew how to use money. The more ideas he had for procuring it, the more his sights settled on land as the starting point. By now high summer had come to Philadelphia, the air as heavy as hot lead. Talleyrand found it hard to breathe. Each time he inhaled he wondered where the next breath was coming from. It was unbearable. He had to escape. The one condition, in his circumstances, was that wherever he fetched up there needed to be financial opportunity – at least enough to keep him going.

A Dutch banking and property company established in Philadelphia, Holland Land, provided a solution that couldn't have suited him better. The Dutch wanted a reconnaissance party to strike out north for Maine and scout for land-purchasing possibilities. Since Talleyrand had already initiated business contacts with the company he signed up for the mission with the equally unemployed Beaumetz and the faithful Courtiade. The trio joined a Dutch banker-prospector on the journey north, starting with a rough two-day stagecoach ride to New York, thence by mailcoach to Boston and by coaster to the coolness of a fishing village in Maine. The party trekked inland for a week, then doubled back to New York to seek an alternative inland route north through New York state to Niagara Falls. They were prospecting for land, but they were tourists too.

On reaching Albany, then on the verge of becoming the state capital, they received good news. It was early October, a beautiful month in the region, and a town father to whom Talleyrand had a letter of introduction greeted him waving a newspaper. 'Come, come, great tidings from France,' he cried. Robespierre had been deposed, guillotined on the spot. The Terror was over. The news had taken six weeks to reach Albany. For Talleyrand, the first seeds of the possibility of returning home were planted.

Past Albany the journey was on horseback. This was trying for Talleyrand and his club foot, though preferable to walking, the only other means of progress. All the same the intrepid exile's encounter with the untracked wilderness, coupled with the news from home, turned him lyrical. 'I discovered nature coarse and wild, forests as old as the world, the debris of plants and trees that died of age littering the uncultivated soil, others growing in their place and destined to die likewise.' His prospector's imagination also ran wild. As his gaze ranged over the impenetrable terrain, he envisaged in its place cities, villages, canals and slopes covered with cattle and corn. All it needed was perspicacious land selection.

For this part of the journey he had shed town coat, silks and breeches, replacing them with out-of-bounds trapper's gear of thick shirt over long trousers and loose moccasin boots, with a hatchet slung from his saddlebag. A wondrous sight he would have made for his Paris salon harem. In truth, those elegant ladies weren't far from his mind, especially with the turn of events in Paris. As his small expeditionary party hacked at vines and creepers barring their path towards Niagara Falls, with every mile he was conscious of straying too far from the ocean linking America to the real world in Europe. He was also conscious of being too close to Iroquois scalping knives. The local Indians had sided with the English against American colonists and Talleyrand wasn't expecting a warm welcome from the Iroquois in the event of an impromptu forest encounter. He spied some of them at riverside trading shacks and wasn't enamoured. They smelled bad, he wrote in a report to Holland Land, and were not fit for service. They were generally touchy and hostile, though they were nothing that American laws couldn't cope with.

The Talleyrand party spent most nights in the open by a campfire, keeping the flames prudently low so as not to excite the Iroquois. He was touched by the concern for his welfare shown by Courtiade, who made sure he was in sight at all times and cried out 'Monseigneur, Monseigneur' the moment he wasn't. This amused his master no end. Coming from anyone but the loyal Courtiade, he would have found the high church address offensive, almost certainly a smirking insult. Compared with the campfire, they enjoyed themselves better during an overnight stay in a trapper's cabin they came across after a long day's hack through the forest. They settled down to supper with the hospitable trapper, his wife, two strapping sons and daughter, feasting on smoked fish, ham, potatoes, a strong beer and brandy. The coarse alcohol quickly went to their heads and they listened spellbound as the two sons instructed them on beaver hunting: how the fur of beavers was only good at the end of the season, how to lie in wait to kill them, how to split wood to lay traps for them, to attack them when the water iced over so as to snare them when they came up for breath through holes in the ice. Heads afire with brandy, Talleyrand and his friends soon fancied themselves as beaver hunters. They persuaded the two sons to take them on a week-long hunt starting the next day, and only wriggled out of the commitment at dawn, their senses half recovered, by leaving a pile of dollars and shamed apologies with the boys' father.

Talleyrand's brain was afire with more serious matters too. His taste for political analysis and getting to the heart of world problems not once deserted him in America. Underused though he was by his lights, there were not just Dutch land speculators to cater to; there were bankers in London and Amsterdam to report to, and Lord Lansdowne and Whig party associates in London he had promised to inform of political trends in America. The English governing class was now all ears with regard to America because the Pitt cabinet was presently negotiating a trade and friendship treaty which, when ratified by the US Senate in June 1795, fairly defused the hostility and ill feeling resulting from America's fight for independence.

The Anglo-American pact was received with red rage by France, for despite Talleyrand's briefly successful neutrality mission the French were now formally at war with England and in this conflict the revolutionary government in Paris had been counting on America's continued sympathies. Now it was in league with the enemy. Beyond those small matters, Germaine de Staël demanded constant news, and it was vital to keep up with her, not merely because of business commissions he hoped she would send his way through her father. Dimly, at this early stage, he also saw her as an instrument in his eventual return to France, for when she put her mind to something Germaine was unstoppable.

Although Talleyrand hadn't seen the Anglo-American pact coming, what he'd seen of America convinced him that the former colony was inextricably linked with the mother country and certain to remain so. The split caused by independence was bound to heal. In an analysis addressed to Lord

Lansdowne, no doubt based on discussions with his Anglophile friend
Hamilton, he wrote: 'America is all English. That is, England still has every
advantage over France in extracting from the United States every benefit
that one nation can draw from the existence of another.' He recognised a
score of reasons why that was so, starting with the English language, which
was so natural to Americans that they had no way to liberate themselves
from it. Then there was the legal system: American laws and liberties were
taken straight from England's. There wasn't one volume in an American
lawyer's library that wasn't written and printed in England. American
merchants were tied to English credit, as were their transactions. England
was virtually America's sole supplier of all the goods its people ever needed,
or wanted. England's factories and mills spewed across the Atlantic a vast
array of merchandise that undersold anything other European countries
could provide, giving the English an enduring trade monopoly. He concluded:
'Thus it is to England that America aims to be useful. It is also to England
that she can be useful.'

Alas, France, by comparison, did not have much to teach the US. French
ties with the country he judged to be sentimental. They stemmed from
common preoccupations with liberty, and so were superficial. This didn't
stop him giving the English some advice which he thought Lord Lansdowne
might do well to pass on to those in power in London. For the English had
a failing they should mend at once: they should stop acting so superior
towards the Americans. Coming from Talleyrand that was rich, but he gave
the advice, he explained, in England's best interests. In Boston, the city he
liked best in America, he'd listened, for example, to its sons and daughters
of liberty sighing about how grateful they'd felt when the Prince of Wales,
George III's travelling heir, accepted an invitation to a grand ball put on
by Boston society to mark his visit. Everyone had expected the prince to
scorn their festivity. A woman who actually danced with him had fainted
from nerves. All it took to profit from the goodwill towards England which
Americans were doomed to carry in their hearts, Talleyrand reckoned, was
a little less haughtiness from the mother country.

He also had some advice for the Americans. They were hard working and
knew how to make their labours pay. But they concentrated far too much
on business and not enough on agriculture, where he was convinced America's
future lay. He put a proposition to Hamilton. If the Americans, with their
endless land, went all out on farming, they could make an excellent economic
fit with the Europeans. In the Talleyrand scheme of things, Europe was best
placed to provide the luxuries and comforts of life, America the cheaper
basics. This was a 'natural combination' for immense growth in world trade.
Hamilton was not altogether taken. Before such a combination could work

to mutual advantage, Hamilton argued, the US would need to develop its own great marketplaces of the size of London and Amsterdam, or Marseilles.

On returning to Philadelphia from the long jaunt in the wilds, Talleyrand felt increasingly beset by the sense of being underemployed for a man of his rank and ambitions. It wasn't boredom, more frustration. For the good Beaumetz was proving to be a tiresome companion. In a viperish letter to Mme de Staël, Talleyrand complained of his friend's vanity and constant prattle. 'At the age of forty, his oldest friends are people he has known for eighteen months,' he wrote. And it was pretty clear why. Beaumetz talked too much. He had an appetite for business but not an original thought in his head. 'All in all he's better than many, but not up to our friends,' Talleyrand told the authoress.

His compensation for boredom, or more likely for his feeling of being shut off from the world, was an American mistress. The one he chose certainly stood out from the virtuous Philadelphia society matrons with bad teeth he mostly met, who apparently hadn't responded to his charms as readily as the Parisian salon divas, though there was no evidence he'd felt much tempted to exert them. His mistress was a voluptuous woman with rainbow clothes and swinging hips from the Caribbean. A liaison with a negress seemed calculated to shock not only the dominant Quaker folk of the American capital but most of his professional and political contacts: Quaker prudery wasn't to trifle with and segregation of races was taken for granted. If Talleyrand aimed to confirm the adverse prejudices lately fed to George Washington by Gouverneur Morris, he could not have proceeded better. His conduct appeared all the more provocative in light of his prospective election to the American Philosophical Society, whose members included many of the most distinguished figures in the new world, Thomas Jefferson, the future US president, among them.

Philadelphians stood back on the pavement, scandalised, as the grand European exile limped arm in arm with his brightly dressed paramour up and down Spruce Street, the tip of his walking stick drumming out his amused defiance. The match lasted some months, during which he installed the Caribbean belle in his house. He left no personal record of the affair, but his design was no doubt to cause a stir. Perhaps he just wanted public notice. He was, after all, a performer. The Philosophical Society lived up to its name and looked the other way, making him a member all the same.

In the pleasure it gave him, the liaison made some amends for difficulties that kept cropping up in his quest for fortune. He succeeded in staying financially afloat while in America without meeting his initial expectations. A nice commission here and there couldn't hide the fact that his brightest money-making schemes never quite worked out. This was the penalty for having to act as a middleman, not a capitalist. As he told Mme de Staël, there was much money to be made in America for those who had it. To another blueblood woman friend in exile, he concluded that it was a country where honest people could prosper – 'but not as well as scoundrels who, as you may imagine, have many advantages'.

His intuition and acute sense of observation nonetheless won him plaudits from the banking fraternity. Alexander Baring of the London-based banking dynasty wrote to his father from America that he'd seen a lot of Talleyrand during his stay and discovered that he had travelled extensively, had an eagle eye for business opportunities and was more perceptive than any of his fellow exiles. The conclusions Talleyrand drew, Baring said, were remarkably astute and pertinent. 'I have never met anyone so able to make sense of what he has seen and heard. He is an intriguer of the first order who will surely soon play a great role [in France].' Baring Junior couldn't resist an English backhander: 'I absolutely agree with him and have a high opinion of his abilities, though I doubt his honesty.' The irony was that, if Baring saw him as a potential scoundrel, Talleyrand wasn't enough of one by his own lights to grow rich in America.

That a satisfactory level of wealth eluded him was apparent from an exotic pan-oceanic trading scheme he dreamed up with Beaumetz. The scheme was a new angle on the old idea of siphoning off wealth from England's charge in India, only this time it would mean leaving America and installing himself in Calcutta. He was serious about it; passages to India were booked. Beaumetz actually went. Only the latest news from France – and perhaps a better sixth sense than poor Baumetz had about life in Calcutta – stopped Talleyrand himself from going.

News from the homeland kept his analytical powers busy during his nearly two and a half years in America. He pored over the French press despite the weeks and months it took to reach him. At all times he knew just what had been going on in France. He knew that his confiscated property and belongings, all his fine furniture and his wardrobe, were sold at auction, sinking his hopes of recovering them. He knew all about the exploits of revolutionary armies victoriously pressing north and east beyond France's frontiers, and he knew something about a dauntless young general named Napoleon Bonaparte who had crushed a royalist rebellion in Paris. While he considered military conquest a ruinous policy in itself, and held fast to that position, he could still identify with the spirit of independence it was possible to construe as a motive for French military exploits. For the earliest battles were fought and won to clear Austrian, Prussian, Spanish and English invaders from French soil, which could only be a good thing. Carefully, in a letter to the 'Citizen Minister' now running foreign affairs in Paris, he let the new men in power know how he felt: 'It is in reading the story of these victories, in associating myself with the glory of independence, that I have found patience in exile, courage in adversity. Deprived of the right to serve liberty, I at least have suffered for its beautiful cause.'

By this time he was aware he could probably return home without putting his neck on the block. After Robespierre's fall the National Convention lingered on for close to a year through the summer of 1795, increasingly muddled, more flexible in some things, but still by no means lenient towards refugee aristocrats. Emigrés remained outlaws and they faced trial if they ventured home. All the same, to Talleyrand the time seemed propitious to send out serious feelers. His place was in France. If he had to spend another year in America he would die, he wrote in a plaintive note to his Swiss confidante. It was more than just the experience of his second unbearably humid American summer that distressed him; he was impatient to pull his weight in France. Would the passport he'd obtained from Danton clear him? Did it not set him apart from royalist émigrés? He was not an émigré in the outlaw sense. He was not one of them. They took arms against their own country. He did not share their consuming desire to restore the monarchy by force. He wanted order restored to France so that people could live and work in peace.

But it wasn't in his nature to be seen pleading for permission to return. He wasn't going down on his knees to those in power in Paris. He found a transparent way round the problem by having a petition published in the semi-official Paris newspaper *Moniteur Universel*, a publication which wouldn't dare print anything offensive to the Convention. He composed the petition himself in Philadelphia but had a loyal retainer in Paris, a fellow priest, press it on the newspaper for publication, unsigned. The unstoppable Mme de Staël was also part of the scheme.

The petition read by curious Parisians on 3 September 1795 argued that being absent from France and being an émigré weren't necessarily the same thing at all, and certainly weren't in Talleyrand's case. He had left Paris with a government passport 'ordering' him to go to London to forestall a break between England and France. As for the arrest warrant against him, its pretext was entirely frivolous. What sane man would have surrendered himself at the very time Robespierre's tyranny got under way? That would have been tantamount to presenting his head for the guillotine. Now, though, he was ready to put his case to a tribunal. Talleyrand's constant devotion to the cause of liberty, the petition thundered, tied him irrevocably to the fate of the republic.

The pro-Talleyrand machinery was well primed, with Mme de Staël oiling it from the Paris end where she now had leave to live once more. The next day on the floor of the Convention a deputy she lined up to help out, a fellow writer, formally requested Talleyrand's removal from the criminal émigré list. 'I request his return in the name of the Republic which his talents and industry can still serve,' the compliant deputy told the house. A large majority voted to clear him. He was free to return without trial. Pride still prevented him, however, from admitting a role in bringing this highly satisfactory finale about. In November he told Lord Lansdowne he only learned of it when the London *Times* reached America. 'Apparently my friends judged a petition necessary. So be it.'

In fact it was so only because he had engineered it. For at the same time that he wrote to Lansdowne he was writing to Mme de Staël: 'Thanks to you, dear friend, this whole affair is now over. You have done absolutely what I required. I wanted the selfsame Convention that accused me to rescind its decree.' Still, it was not his plan to rush into returning. He told her that he preferred to wait until the following spring, most likely May – for 'a thousand reasons' he did not go into. He signed off with a flourish: 'Adieu, dear friend, I love you with all my heart', gamely pledging to spend the rest of his life near her, wherever she lived. This was not an unusual ending to a Talleyrand letter; it was the kind he at times used to male friends who were riding particularly high in his esteem or deserving of special thanks. Besides being a flowery remnant of *ancien régime* style, the affection it expressed welled both from gratitude and from the intimate camaraderie that came from working closely with another. It was the kind of 'love' he would soon express to Napoleon himself.

From the day he penned the petition to the day he left America for home an entire year passed. His thousand reasons for the long delay took time to deal with: he felt obliged to keep rounding up information on America for London contacts; he had his existing middleman business transactions to tidy up, and new ones to close; not least, he was involved with Beaumetz in refining their great scheme to mastermind trade between America and India (where Beaumetz, having arrived there on his own, ultimately caught a Calcutta virus that killed him). The India project was a forerunner of economic globalisation which Talleyrand spent a long time explaining in a series of carefully reasoned memoranda to American and European bankers.

Mostly, though, he felt extremely insecure about the return to France. His view of a new five-member Directory that took over power from the Convention just weeks after it voted to clear him was not positive. Its dominant member was Paul Barras whom he did not know personally, though he'd heard much about him from the press. He saw the Directory as weak, 'perhaps ridiculous' and unlikely to endure, though with changes here and there he thought it might just make a passable job of things in the short term. But how would the sleek Barras and his motley team receive him? They scarcely looked like harbingers of stability. What was more, reactionary royalists were showing their teeth once more. Supposing they were to regain the ascendancy! That could be fatal for him.

Talleyrand found time to lay out his hopes and fears for France in essays he wrote for a French periodical launched by his Philadelphia bookshop friend, Moreau. To put an oar in with the new men in power, he wrote:

> Lasting tranquillity in France is inconceivable unless peace returns to bring abundance by restoring numerous hands to agriculture, industrious men to manufacturing and useful speculation to commerce. Peace alone can produce the goods to make France one of the most delicious places on earth to live, where arts and pleasures and her soft climate may entice the inhabitants of all other countries, as they have in the past.

It sounded like an all too idyllic goal, a dream, but it was the image of civilisation Talleyrand carried in his head and he never lost sight of it. For the present, though, his unease was compounded by a sensible dread of spring storms in the Atlantic, which he'd once braved when sailing in the opposite direction, and also by the need to find a neutral ship bound for a neutral European port. If he booked a French vessel or any vessel remotely engaged in trade with France he'd be exposed to the piratical wrath of the King's Navy.

By March 1796 he had decided upon Hamburg as his safest disembarkation point in Europe, and located a Danish merchantman to get him there. Hamburg, a free city, was full of refugee French aristocrats and some of them, he reasoned, would be friendly faces. His own family were mostly located well to the south, in the Rhineland, but Mme de Flahaut for one had settled in Hamburg. Even then his plans almost came unstuck. The Danish vessel was so long overdue in reaching New York for the passage home that its agents feared it had gone to the bottom and Talleyrand was obliged to renew his quest for a vessel that suited his conditions. When the Danish ship at last arrived and took him aboard, June was already half over.

Talleyrand's landing in Hamburg on 30 July 1796 brought a further unwelcome reminder that he hadn't succeeded in lining his pockets with gold in America, at least not in satisfactory quantities. Mme de Flahaut, who was looking for financial security, not only recognised his situation but had good reason to avoid him. Indeed, she was very far from being the friendly face he'd envisaged. An emissary of hers came aboard on the final stretch up the river Elbe with an urgent request for him not to disembark but to sail back to America at once. He must not attempt to see her, she said in a panicky Dear John note, because she was about to marry the Portuguese ambassador to Denmark and it would not do for her to be seen associating with a former lover. Talleyrand thought her demand hysterical and stayed for a month in Hamburg, his ties with his son's mother severely frayed. She eventually married the wealthy Portuguese and went on to write further feminist-genre novels under her new name, Mme de Souza. Talleyrand didn't allow the breach to spoil his feelings for his natural son, whose high-flying career he promoted all his life.

In Hamburg, the returning exile toured the commercial banks he'd dealt with off and on in America, withdrawing for immediate living expenses the sum of fifteen pounds from the 'extremely meagre' remains of his Hamburg deposits. This treasure disappeared faster than he would have wished. In the Hamburg inn where he stayed a fellow guest who was leaving for London the following day implored him to read through the manuscript of a book he'd written. Talleyrand wearily agreed and when nodding off for the night halfway through the manuscript he slipped his packet of fifteen pounds between the pages to mark his place. The author rapped on his door at 6 a.m. and asked for his book, saying he needed to leave earlier than expected. Talleyrand awoke in a daze, pointed to his night table and asked him to take it. He wished him a good trip and fell asleep again. Only when he re-awoke did he realise he'd lost his money. He took the loss stoically, amusing himself with the thought that the author received more for his work than any publisher would have paid him.

Though he spent half his stay in Hamburg recovering from a severe chill, it was an ideal place to get a feel for what might await him in Paris, as well as to mull over fresher news than he'd had access to in America. Now the press was full of the irrepressible young Bonaparte's rampage through Italy. This Bonaparte seemed an original, he was a resourceful entrepreneur, and Talleyrand placed high hopes in him from afar. He was a force for order, a good notch above the rest of those hungry for power in Paris. All the same, just to avoid unforeseen problems with such newcomers for the last lap of the return home through Amsterdam, then Brussels, Talleyrand obtained a nicely engraved passport in Latin from Hamburg magistrates casting him as a Swiss merchant, 'Honestus Talayran Negociator Helveticus'. The subterfuge wasn't strictly necessary. Within a year he was France's foreign minister, a gift of the pragmatic Barras who unleashed Napoleon upon the Austrian Empire and most of Europe besides.

SIX

Encounter with a Warrior

At 11 a.m. on 7 December 1797, the foreign ministry on the Paris Left Bank was on its toes. It was a little early in the day for Talleyrand, the minister, to be at his best but he nonetheless caught the eye in the apparel of state which the Directory had designed for him: black topcoat with wide crimson lapels and embroidered sleeves, crimson stockings and waistcoat, an enormous white silk sash, sheathed sword and a hat sporting three large feathers. What the uniform lacked in taste it made up for in gaiety. On the stroke of the hour a carriage bearing a slim, dark-haired young man in the more sober uniform of a republican army general pulled up outside the pillared ministry on the Rue du Bac, and Talleyrand, departing from custom, hobbled out to the steps to receive him. It was the first time that Talleyrand, now forty-four, and Napoleon, aged twenty-eight, set eyes on each other.

Prior to this first meeting they knew each other only through exploratory letters they'd been exchanging since Talleyrand's appointment as foreign minister not five months before. During that time Napoleon was away warring with spectacular success on the plains of northern Italy, a lion in public esteem and to all intents his own master.

Retiring with his visitor to his cosy office, Talleyrand, already well disposed towards him, now seemed captivated. 'At first sight I found his countenance charming. Twenty victories in battle go so well with youth! He was pale, good looking, with a sort of exhaustion about him.' The romance of the soldier registered full tilt with Talleyrand despite his ideas on peace. All those battles won by one so pallid and young! Napoleon in turn congratulated his host on his appointment as foreign minister and told him how great a pleasure it was for him to be able to correspond with someone in France of 'another stripe' from the ruling Directors. Evidently Napoleon too was impressed. The distinction he drew showed that he viewed Talleyrand as a superior being compared with most of the Directors and their gruff acolytes whose reputation for grace and style was not undeservedly low.

Furthermore, Napoleon seemed conscious of the class difference separating himself, the Corsican squire's son, from Talleyrand. He had dispatched his aide-de-camp to Talleyrand's ministry residence just as soon as he arrived from Italy to ask when it might be convenient for the minister to receive him. For the young lion of France this was a genuflection. In preliminary small talk – all that was recorded of the meeting – he noted almost obsequiously that Talleyrand's uncle was the Archbishop of Reims, adding, 'I too have an uncle in the church, an archdeacon in Corsica. He raised me. And you know, an archdeacon in Corsica is like a bishop in France.'

Talleyrand smiled to himself. Napoleon had the makings of a snob. The comparison between his uncle and a Corsican cleric was too ludicrous to be anything but appealing. All the same, Talleyrand believed they had each other's confidence. At this stage it was bound to be built on mutual admiration more than trust.

In the interlude between his return from exile and the meeting with Napoleon, Talleyrand had wrestled to regain his place in France. He was an alien in more than one respect. Things had changed more than he suspected since he'd left. Before, he'd somehow been able to carry off a double life: in the frontline of revolution yet spiritually encamped, like it or not, in the *ancien régime* of which he was part. The Paris he returned to was neither the Paris of the old order nor, he was relieved to confirm, the Paris of gratuitous violence and revolutionary ayatollahs whose clutches he had narrowly escaped. There seemed to be a general public feeling of release from the reign of terror and zealotry, and although everyone was Citizen This and Citizen That – from lamplighter to government minister – it was not a lack of high spirits or pleasure-seeking that disturbed the returning Talleyrand. What concerned him was the ravaged, down-at-heel look of the city, horrific inflation striking at the poor, an explosion of corruption and the dithering of the Directory.

Together it all fell short of the public order he espoused. Paris society had also changed and he took a dim view of it, though he was not unamused. He wrote to his bookshop owner friend in Philadelphia: 'Balls, shows and fireworks have replaced prisons and revolutionary committees. The women of the court are gone but the women of the nouveaux riches have taken their place and the tarts come right behind, vying with them for luxury and extravagance. Around these dangerous sirens buzz swarms of feather-brains we used to call know-alls. Today they are "marvels" who talk politics while dancing and sigh after royalty while eating ice cream and yawning at fireworks.'

Citizen Talleyrand was soon able to mix with people with whom he felt more at home through membership of a new national body called the *Institut*, a hub of intellectual, scientific and policymaking life which was practically the only place where thoughtful work on France's future was at present conducted. On the strength of policies he'd drawn up for the Constituent Assembly on weighty matters of education, finance, democracy and so forth, he'd been elected to the distinguished Institute in his absence, while he dallied over which ship to take home from America. He delivered two reports in quick succession to its crowded meetings, restoring his intellectual renown with each presentation. The first was based on the long study he sent Lord Lansdowne on Anglo-American trade relations, an issue of extreme relevance to a France inhibited in its commerce by a hostile English navy. He crafted his personal experience of America into a thesis concluding that England's business with the United States, far from suffering, had in fact mushroomed since French arms helped the Americans seize independence. America's breakaway was indeed a real advantage for England. Americans consumed twice as much English merchandise as a free nation as they did when a colony; they were bound to England more tightly than before.

It was no good the new French republic thinking it had a fit with the new republic across the Atlantic. 'Everywhere I went in America, I came across not a single Englishman who didn't feel American and not a single Frenchman who didn't feel an alien,' he reported. Any thinking man could see that in England's representative system there was much of the republic, just as there was much of the monarchy in republican America's presidency. Hence Talleyrand bade France not to waste her time trying to break unbreakable bonds.

His second report to the Institute was on overseas colonies and the advantages they offered, another burning issue in view of the fact that foreign possessions had the unfortunate result of provoking rivalries and war between European powers, in particular between England and France. Here he took the view that colonies were a proper outlet for adventurous, frustrated souls (he was thinking of those unable to come to terms with the Revolution) and for speculators, for they would spur French industry. The question was how to replace possessions lost to the English or in danger of slipping from French control in North America and India, and Talleyrand counselled France to go for warm places, already forgetting perhaps that two Philadelphia summers had defeated him.

At the close of the eighteenth century there was still a certain innocence and pure adventurousness regarding the making of colonies which corresponded with Talleyrand's passion for world trade. To him, coastal regions of Africa and its islands looked like ideal venues. They'd be 'easy and appropriate' to colonise because the twofold requirement of any good colony was that it had things that were lacking at home and needed things the mother country made. Most important, colonisation had to be a peaceful, generous pursuit driven by the will to protect, not conquer. Conquest would not produce prosperity. Egypt looked a similarly appealing prospect, so much so that Talleyrand sketched out possibilities for negotiating its cession to France from the Ottomans. Goods it produced were similar to those that came from lands wrenched from French control in America. Talleyrand's was probably the first public call for French colonisation of the huge Nile territory. It had startling repercussions. Whether or not Napoleon took his direct cue from it, once he had conquered Italy and brought the Austrian Empire to heel he decided to set off with an expeditionary army to take the Land of the Pharaohs – not, as Talleyrand proposed, by negotiation.

Talleyrand's performances before the Institute regilded his reputation but were otherwise without remuneration. He needed a government post. As regards income, things were grim for a man of his heavy requirements. The trouble was that he had a very poor view of the only body able to satisfy him, the ruling Directory. Only Barras, who had taken a lead in getting rid of Robespierre and retained the courteous touch of the *ancien régime*, looked at all viable to him. He was aware, moreover, that other Directors disliked him. They were ruffians who couldn't stand his superior air, his tone, his manners, let alone his history of fleeing 'their' revolution. He was in no position to approach them personally.

The ever-ready Mme de Staël again barged forward to help him, this time not solely out of sentimental attachment. At her re-established Paris home one day, feeling particularly rattled about his financial situation, he threw his purse down on her table saying, 'My dear child, that's all I have, twenty-five gold pieces. Not enough to last a month. I don't walk and I need a carriage. If you have no way to find me a suitable position, I shall blow my brains out.' Talleyrand knew her taste for high melodrama. He'd always held that women were more useful than men in resolving this kind of problem. Moved to action, the Swiss dynamo arranged for him to see Barras at the Luxembourg Palace where the Directory met, pushing Talleyrand forward as a natural candidate to hold a top ministry, either foreign affairs or finance. Talleyrand raised a brief protest that a meeting with Barras alone would be irregular, and that he ought to see all five Directors together, but just as soon let the objection slip.

Barras at first resisted, a little fazed by the facial resemblance he noted between Talleyrand and the pallid Robespierre. This was unpromising. After the interview Barras owned to being impressed by Talleyrand's talents and experience but let Mme de Staël know that his fellow Directors were negative. She wasn't put off. 'He has all the vices of the old order and all those of the new,' she insisted, embellishing Talleyrand's references. She knew Barras' improvident tastes. Soon Barras was indicating that he could use Talleyrand to give France a less bellicose look in the eyes of European neighbours while General Bonaparte pursued his rampage. At length the principal Director invited the candidate to dine with him at his home by the Seine in Suresnes, on the west side of Paris. The omens began to look more promising.

Talleyrand arrived at Barras' riverside residence late on a warm July afternoon, finding five places set for dinner but no host. The Director would be late, a servant informed him, suggesting he might want to pass the time reading in the library. After a while two youths came by to check the library clock and Talleyrand heard them deciding that they still had time for a swim before dinner. Not twenty minutes later one of them returned white-faced and dripping, shouting for help. His companion had gone under in a whirlpool and hadn't come up.

Behind panic-stricken servants Talleyrand limped down to the river where boatmen were converging from all sides on the whirlpool, too late. The youth had drowned. It turned out he was Barras' private secretary, a young favourite he'd raised from boyhood as a lover. When Talleyrand returned to the house, Barras arrived and was informed by a butler on the spot of the youth's death. He ran upstairs, sobbing wildly, too pained to greet Talleyrand, who was left to dine on his own. Later, still weeping, he called for his guest to join him. Talleyrand sought to console him, finding 'sweet things' to say that helped calm him down, whereupon Barras implored him to accompany him back to Paris that same night in his carriage. Judging by the attention Barras heaped on him, Talleyrand later recalled, he seemed suddenly to have become the apple of the grieving Director's eye. A few days later, on 16 July 1797, he was named foreign minister. Barras had contrived to swing a three-to-two vote of the Directory in his favour.

With hindsight, mindful of how it looked to be a minister of the fumbling, ill-fated Directory, Talleyrand said with some disdain that he accepted the job not because it amounted to much but because 'it was not impossible to do a little good'. In fact he was thrilled. With greater room to manoeuvre he would gladly have become a Director, for he had eyes on that highest post too. As for his appointment as foreign minister, beyond being a favour from Barras and a reward for his grasp of international affairs, it showed a belated desire within civil ranks to bring France back into the European family of nations before things got out of hand with the military. For that, France needed the services of someone who was at once a true European and a French patriot.

Part of the thrill of getting the post was the remuneration he could expect, which his detractors at once claimed was all that mattered to him. The story spread that he was drunk with joy on receiving news of the nomination, repeating to himself over and over again, 'We shall make an immense fortune . . . an immense fortune . . . an immense fortune . . .' This, supposedly, was in his carriage when he was on his way to thank Barras. It did not sound like Talleyrand, given his horror of appearing crass. But since the story was relayed by his then close associate Benjamin Constant, Mme de Staël's brilliant young writer friend, who was with him in the carriage, it had some credence. It was not, anyhow, an 'immense' ministerial salary he had in mind. It was customary at the time, and had long been so, for those engaged in international negotiations and in seeing to other states' diplomatic desires to take a commission. This was the *douceur* (sweetener) and no continental European power, down to the merest principality, was entirely averse to it. The *douceur* was a currency of negotiation. And, sure enough, no sooner had Talleyrand become foreign minister than the ambassadors of Prussia, Spain and Portugal began shovelling money at him to buy the Directory's favours: large sums running to 100,000 francs and more a time.

He was an expensive appointment for the courts of Europe. Foreign envoys informed their governments that Talleyrand liked money and he did not discourage them in this belief, though he seldom demanded money straight out, preferring to have subordinates bargain on his behalf. To allay possible recrimination at home, the commissions were paid frequently into foreign accounts Talleyrand held in London, Hamburg and Amsterdam. To a financial expert like himself these were safe-deposit boxes. When Napoleon became master of Europe a torrent of wealth would come Talleyrand's way in the form of diplomatic commissions, particularly when he was left to cut and paste German statelets to a pattern conforming to the conqueror's wishes. Was he proud of himself? Money was certainly an ever present concern for him, though naturally he never once alluded in his memoirs to enriching himself in office through *douceurs*. He genuinely considered them an element of diplomacy. He was ribbed – at times vilified – for being venal, but not formally taken to task. By his lights the practice wasn't illegal; it was part of the financial merry-go-round of state, and he chose not to tangle overmuch with its moral aspects. He never wanted to have to rely on a pension from the republic.

Once Talleyrand was able to live the life of great ease and social expansiveness he thought proper for himself and those around him, he had extremely heavy expenses to keep up. To stint on spending when one had money was to his mind a mark of mediocrity, though this did not extend to settling bills. Among his initial outlays as foreign minister was a splendid white carriage that identified him in the streets of Paris. Everyone knew when Talleyrand was riding by. But when the coachbuilder hadn't been paid for his work for a month or so, he posted himself at the ministry gate to present his bill. Talleyrand halted the white carriage on his way out, assuring him, 'Of course, of course, Citizen, you must be paid.' The man humbly thanked him, muttering that times were hard and he would be extremely grateful for the settlement. No need for gratitude, Talleyrand told him, it was his right to be paid.

'But when, Citizen Minister?' the man persevered.

'When!' said Talleyrand. 'You are very curious!'

A greater priority pressed. As foreign minister, Talleyrand needed to treat with Napoleon. He had to take the warrior's measure. On the face of things, since his own credo was that a nation's wellbeing depended on a sound economy, and that this first demanded stability, which in turn required peace, the two men seemed fatefully at odds. To confront the problem Talleyrand used the weapon of old-world courtesy and the rich coating of flattery that went with it. Precisely a week after taking office, he wrote privately to Napoleon on the Italian battlefield, informing him that the Directory had made him foreign minister. It was his first contact of any kind with the young hero and he spent a long time composing the brief letter, sensing how important it would be in shaping their personal relationship. He wrote:

> Awed as I feel in assuming responsibilities of perilous importance, how reassuring it is to know what strength and facility your glory brings to our negotiations. The name Bonaparte alone is enough to smooth away all before it.

From the outset he was silkily engaged in a policy of flattery, the style of which managed to keep it just on the right side of obsequious. Furthermore, he undertook to rush through to Napoleon all foreign policy decisions reached by Barras and his fellow Directors, ending with the flourish, 'The fame you continue to win will often rob me of the pleasure of being first to inform them how you have carried these decisions out.'

The initiative was ingenuous since negotiations were, in practice, all but out of the Directory's hands and thus out of Talleyrand's. For Napoleon had already taken it upon himself to determine the foreign policy of the republic where it touched on his exploits. As Talleyrand came to office in mid-summer, Napoleon was already celebrating a highly advantageous truce he'd personally called with Austria and was now in the act of negotiating a formal peace treaty for signature at Campo Formio, in northern Italy, in the autumn. The signature would be Napoleon's. All Talleyrand could do as minister was dot i's and spur him to keep the Austrian Empire out of Italy altogether from now on, suggesting the Habsburgs might be allowed to make up lost ground in Germany if need be.

Napoleon replied to Talleyrand's private note with a generous though mildly prissy tribute of his own:

Citizen Minister
Your appointment as foreign minister does honour to the government's discernment. It is proof of your great talents, your pure civic sense and your distance from the aberrations that have dishonoured the Revolution.
I am flattered at the prospect of corresponding with you often and thus of being able to assure you of my esteem and consideration.
Greetings and fraternity
Bonaparte

Napoleon seemed to be extending Talleyrand a pardon on any suspicion of entanglement with the monarchy or of plotting with the English against the republic. The minister didn't really need such blessing. Wasn't his expulsion by Pitt evidence enough of his fidelity to the republic? But he still faced constant Jacobin denunciations on both counts, and it was good to know that Napoleon recognised his *pure* civic sense. Napoleon wanted to work with him! Indeed his letter seemed to hint that they might together bypass the Directory, which was scarred by the disastrous aberrations he referred to.

Soon the two of them were corresponding on two levels, one official, one secret. There was no doubt that Talleyrand was enchanted by Napoleon. It would have taken less of a Frenchman than he not to be so enchanted. The glory dazed him. The incredible boldness and effrontery astounded him. Napoleon was a risk taker after his own heart. As someone who loved France and was committed to work for her recovery, Talleyrand readily owned to the 'great hopes' the young general aroused in him; they dwarfed misgivings he must have had about the younger man's political vision. For although Napoleon classed himself a staunch republican, he had his own ideas on how democracy should work. From his camp in Italy he set them out in a long letter to Talleyrand which he made sure was delivered privately.

While finding the contents of the letter 'rather curious', the minister was struck by Napoleon's interest in political affairs and was touched by his attempt to show that there was more to him than barking cannons and campaign maps: he seemed to have statesmanlike potential. The general was no intellectual dunce. He had plainly immersed himself in political philosophy and was able to cite in the letter distinguished thinkers such as Montesquieu, the velvet-gloved scourge of the *ancien régime*, to prove it. On the romantic side he'd consumed Ossian, the source of selfless valour and its misty legends. What Napoleon wanted, in essence, was strong executive power that relegated parliament to the sidelines. The republic was mistaken in thinking of modelling the government structure on England's. In England parliament was the only real representative of the nation, a dyke built against the despotism of the sovereign. In France things were different: the people was now sovereign. The executive, working to a constitution, was best placed to represent the popular will for reasons that would strike any student of France between the eyes: ever since the Revolution, parliament had been chopping and changing the law with such absurd rapidity and incoherence that, in effect, France was now 'a nation without laws, only three hundred drafts'. Napoleon was distressed by the popular uprisings he and fellow generals were regularly called upon to crush. It was humiliating for the largest country in old Europe, a country of thirty million people (upping the actual population by a million or so was a military commander's conceit), to have to resort to bayonets to save herself. A strong executive would put an end to that.

Napoleon's letter had an authoritarian ring which wasn't lost on Talleyrand. On the other hand it was presented as a recipe for restoring public order, which he also regarded as vital. Napoleon asked him to keep the letter to himself. Should he decide to make use of it, he should say it applied to Italy where Napoleon was presently installing a republic in place of Austrian rule. It was obvious, in fact, that it applied to France. Talleyrand could only infer that the young general was feeling his way towards taking charge of the strong executive for which he carefully laid out his case. Nor was the minister entirely put out by the prospect. When Napoleon signed the peace treaty that completed the Austrian Empire's humiliation at Campo Formio on 18 October, Talleyrand brimmed with praise and admiration, writing to tell him that words failed to express France's joy. In his euphoria he coined a new name for the warrior. General Peacemaker! The term wasn't much heard thereafter.

The place in government brought emotional strains for Talleyrand. The first concerned a *douceur* that went wrong; another – infinitely more important as to the impact it had on his life – a woman from the Indian tropics.

The George Washington who snubbed him in Philadelphia was succeeded

as president of the United States in March of that year, 1797, by John
Adams, likewise a father of the American Revolution. President Adams, a
Federalist with pro-English leanings, sought a reconciliation with France in
hopes of putting an end to French attacks on Yankee merchantmen that
were crippling US trade. Ever since the US had restored friendly relations
with England two years before in order to halt post-independence bitter-
ness, French privateers had considered American cargo vessels fair game.
With the backing of the revolutionary regime in Paris, the heavily armed
privateers plundered American shipping mercilessly, capturing hundreds of
vessels and maiming American crews. The US grew frantic over the menace
to its trade and Adams ordered a naval build-up to dissuade the French,
telling the US Congress that France had 'inflicted a wound to the American
breast'. The Adams order was the first sign of America's emergence as a
military power to contend with, and the French, like Adams' Republican
party opponents, heard it as a war whoop. War fever gripped the American
public. It was an ironic situation: two republics, absorbed by their own bold
creation, were on the brink of war. To stop things deteriorating further,
Adams dispatched a three-man negotiating team to Paris, hopeful they could
reach an agreement with Talleyrand, whom he considered to be an expert
on American matters and had met, though scarcely knew, in Philadelphia.

It was a pity that Talleyrand's attachment to America didn't quite match
Adams' hopes. The American negotiating trio, led by a no-nonsense general
from the War of Independence, Charles Cotesworth Pinckney, was kept
kicking its heels in Paris for weeks, with neither the Directors nor Talleyrand
permitting a direct audience. The sole contact came from private representatives of Talleyrand who had certain proposals to make bearing on the
possibility of actual negotiations. Talleyrand personally favoured a reconciliation, the intermediaries told him, but he needed to know what specific
ideas the American side had in mind. Also, Adams had to row back on the
pugnacious stand he had taken against France before the US Congress, for
the Directory viewed his military build-up pledge as a direct threat and an
injury to French pride. To put things in motion, the intermediaries insisted,
Talleyrand required a sweetener of 50,000 English pounds placed at his
personal disposal. This should be attached to a hefty US trade loan to
France, signalling American support for the financially strapped republic.

Pinckney was deeply shocked. He found the proposals at best disre-
spectful. Three separate Talleyrand intermediaries the Americans dealt with –
Pinckney christened them X, Y and Z in reports home – sought to validate
the *douceur* as a 'customary distribution in diplomatic affairs'. If the request
were met and Adams dropped his threatening talk, Talleyrand had 'no doubt
all their differences might be accommodated'. The more Pinckney

balked – arguing that the issue of Adams' bellicose tone would best be resolved in the words of a reconciliation treaty, and that America couldn't lend large sums to a belligerent power without relinquishing her independence – the more X, Y and Z pressed him on Talleyrand's private fee. 'You must pay money, you must pay a lot of money,' he quoted them as saying. The dispute grew heated, according to Pinckney:

Talleyrand's agent: Gentlemen, you do not speak to the point. It is expected you will offer money.
Pinckney: We have spoken to that point very specifically. We have given an answer.
Agent: No, you have not. What is your answer?
Pinckney: It is no. Not a sixpence!

The deadlock worsened when the Pinckney trio was given to understand by the Talleyrand side that they would have to leave Paris unless they stumped up the fee. Talleyrand eventually relented and received the most Francophile of the three, Elbridge Gerry, a politician he'd met in Philadelphia and whom he remembered as a signatory of the Declaration of Independence. Precious little came of it. The Directory soured things even further with a fresh decree that subjected to seizure all neutral vessels carrying English merchandise and banned from French ports any foreign vessel that had even called in at an English one. Americans saw themselves as the act's prime target.

Evidently the scuffle with America wasn't as large an issue for France as it was for Adams. Talleyrand himself was by now busily engaged in trying to keep some overview on Napoleon's negotiations with Austria for the peace of Campo Formio, and had little time for what appeared to him a sideshow. He felt somehow liberated from the Directory by the liaison he was building up with Napoleon through their correspondence, which left him at some freedom to operate as he saw fit.

As Pinckney told it, Talleyrand basely subjected reconciliation between the world's republics to a £50,000 fee. What ingratitude for the welcome America had so recently given him! It did seem a clumsy operation. That it didn't work was the clumsiest part of it. It was clear that Talleyrand hadn't yet found his formidable touch with the *douceur*, which from then on became a smoothly functioning part of his diplomacy. He should have known the Americans hadn't long graduated from their upright Pilgrim Father traditions, at least at government level. They weren't like the bankers, property people and merchants he'd met in America for whom money spoke louder than virtue. It was true that the US paid American Indians to behave themselves. But the governing culture there was different from that of European states, large and small, which made a habit of paying money to difficult neighbours to head off problems.

In the end the US peace mission was aborted, miring Talleyrand in scandal once the Americans self-righteously published their side of the story. This was rich food for royalists who were once more rallying to seize power in Paris and enjoyed spewing venom at Talleyrand whenever they had an opportunity. In fact they criticised him less for the money he sought than for the large sums he now began laying out to live in the lavish style he favoured. He faced down the XYZ uproar with an ingenuous article in the official Paris press noting that ministers weren't responsible for indiscretions committed by irresponsible agents. Quite so. Peace with America was postponed to another day.

The feminine strains were exerted by a woman who was running from the Paris police when she entered his life. He had most likely first seen Catherine Grand in London, since she was living there as an exile during his time in Kensington and at Juniper Hall. The French exile community was a small world and a beauty like Mme Grand could not have passed his notice. Some brief prior acquaintanceship, sufficient to intrigue him, would explain his reaction on the evening this stunning 'Indian' woman with cascading fair hair broke into his foreign ministry residence in tears, imploring him to save her from arrest. The police were chasing her, she said. They had found letters she had written to England; they suspected her of plotting against the republic. Talleyrand was smitten. It was soon after the XYZ affair broke. She came from India. He'd always had a weakness for India, as his wilder business fancies demonstrated, and although the ravishing creature seeking his help was of French stock she had grown up in India and, to his eyes, carried its exotic spell.

Talleyrand was vulnerable. He missed the company of the bright young countesses he was used to having around him with their well-informed chatter. They were few in number these days in Paris, though thankfully they were beginning to come back. For the moment the social round was run by the bourgeois women of the Directory set who struck him as strident and gawky, with more money than refinement. Adelaïde de Flahaut was lost to him. At forty-three, he himself had lost the youthful appeal that kept the countesses flocking around him before the Revolution. Though he was still a good-looking man whose superior air gave him true distinction, the thickening of his face and waist that had started in America wasn't stemmed by the blessed return to French cuisine. At the same time his right leg gave him increasing pain from a corrective boot he wore on his club foot. He walked straighter with it, but an orthopaedic iron strut running from the boot to his calf to keep him steady grew more uncomfortable as the day wore on.

In sum, his Indian goddess could not have chosen a better moment to entrance him. To keep the police at bay he prepared a room for her that same night in his handsome ministry residence. Soon he installed her there, having asked Barras to take the police off her case. 'In all Europe she is the person most far removed and incapable of conspiracy,' he wrote to the principal Director. 'She is Indian, very beautiful, very lazy and the least active of any woman I have ever met.' He would be angry if the police bothered her any further. 'I love her,' he wrote with uncharacteristic zeal, 'and I assure you, man to man, that never in her life has she been involved or been in any position to involve herself in a conspiracy.'

His protestations were not wholly convincing. Catherine Grand's hybrid past divided between Paris and London, which were after all at war, was enough to justify the interest of a nervous police. But his profession of love did the trick. An astonished Barras couldn't refuse him, though Talleyrand no doubt came in time to wish he had. Beautiful she was, with gleaming white teeth, blue eyes, a slender figure and hair so long and full that a blue-blood memoirist of the day, the Comtesse Adèle de Boigne, recalled her using it to spectacular effect at a well-wined dinner party before the Revolution. Mme Grand, it seemed, had come naked to the dinner table with only her tresses for cover. Her performance wouldn't have alarmed Talleyrand. Risqué behaviour in others pleased him. It could not have escaped him that she was a woman about town, a tug to his non-conformist streak. Talleyrand was never shy of rocking the boat, as Philadelphians knew from his cavorting with the gaudy negress.

At this point Catherine Grand's main sin lay in the future: she was to come between Talleyrand and Napoleon; she would be a poison in their relationship. The conqueror disapproved of her and said so openly. His Corsican prudery was deeply offended by her. He thought she not only let Talleyrand down but himself too. All the same, she did have skills, one of them being an ability to attract the sympathies of important men. She used it well, even if Napoleon himself failed to respond. Before establishing herself with Talleyrand she was the mistress for a time of a predecessor as foreign minister, Valdec de Lessart, the same who had annoyed Talleyrand by failing to answer his pressing diplomatic correspondence from London. Clearly, she was able to look after her own interests. It was because of links she'd maintained with men of substance in London, particularly letters she wrote describing events in Paris, that she found the Directory's police on her trail. After meeting Talleyrand she began referring in her tittle-tattle letters to an anonymous '*Piedcourt*' (Stumpy), a code not lost on the police who were habitual letter-openers, obsessed with running down spies. It briefly reignited their interest in her case in view of Stumpy's responsibility for foreign affairs.

But, as Talleyrand assured Barras, Catherine wasn't a spy. Not intentionally. She wasn't up to it. She was born Catherine Worlée in India, near Pondicherry. Her parents were French expatriates stationed at various colonial outposts, her father a port superintendent in the French king's service. At sixteen, barely schooled, she married George Grand, a naturalised Englishman of Swiss birth with a post in the British colonial administration. Grand was a dullard and young Catherine, with her breathtaking looks, soon fell into the arms of one of his English superiors. The resulting scandal went to court where the philanderer, Sir Philip Francis of the Bengal administration, was forced to pay the wronged husband heavy damages. At eighteen, separated, Mme Grand was off to London, thence to pre-revolutionary Paris where she first arrived in 1782 and was never to be short of wealthy admirers offering their protection. By the time she ran into the foreign ministry mansion to seek Talleyrand's she was thirty-six, past youth's first bloom but still a great beauty.

He was bowled over. It was a *coup de foudre* – quite unlike Talleyrand. He was unable to explain it satisfactorily even to himself. And once he'd taken her in he didn't know what to do with her. The truth was that, although she came to live in his house for a dozen years, she didn't matter in his life. She was absent from his memoirs. He spoke less of her than of women he chanced upon during social soirées. Yet she served as hostess at his residence through most of those dozen years and she certainly made a name for herself in that department: she was famous for saying the wrong thing at the wrong time, which often had guests sniggering, particularly the women. The hole in Talleyrand's later memory concerning Catherine Grand suggested more than the discomfort he felt at choosing to live with a ninny. It suggested he himself was bewildered by the choice, by the surge of blood that brought him to take her in, then, not content with a misjudgement, five years later to marry her.

To friends, he owned at first to finding in her 'three exquisite forms of sweetness – her skin, her breath and her character'. But even if these virtues beguiled him – dental care being what it was, it was rare to come across an object of one's desire with meadowmint breath – she simply wasn't one of his kind. She wasn't one of those he loved to have around him: the bright, well-informed women of high birth reared on the Enlightenment who seemed able to pick up clever meanings in his words that he himself hadn't necessarily intended. With her beauty and her silliness, plus the marriage above her station, she was an invitation to bitchiness which Talleyrand's salon companions gleefully accepted. Claire de Rémusat, another blueblood diarist of the time who was far from the unkindest of her detractors, noted: 'She continually wounded Talleyrand with her platitudes and disturbed his peace of mind with her uneven temper.' Temper tantrums were no doubt the 'character' part of those virtues he first found so exquisite, though his glowing initial bill of worth suggested she was most generous with her attentions to him, a home comfort to a busy statesman.

With the Directory, Talleyrand had no *coup de foudre*. He was serving this awkwardly conceived follow-on from the Terror because it was his way back to the top of public life. He felt he had more right to be in government than any of its five members, Barras included. This was a natural assumption on his part, deriving from his class and his sense of oneness with his country's fate. The Directors were mostly vulgar men with narrow perspectives, interested more in serving themselves than France. Their government was an object of popular derision, worse, a target of revolt. In September 1797 it had to arrest two of its own members and scores of dissenting parliamentarians, packing them off to Cayenne in the South American jungle to forestall a coup. But for help from Napoleon, who dispatched one of his best generals from Italy to command the troops in Paris, the government was most likely lost.

The land of the Enlightenment seemed lost in the political murk. Civil war sputtered on, with countryside ranged against towns in the west. Corruption in the administration was rampant. Talleyrand thought it all brought shame on France. But who was he to talk! Wasn't he part of the corruption? Not by his lights. His self-enrichment went by the diplomatic rules, albeit unwritten. He gambled, but that wasn't corrupt either; it enriched or impoverished himself alone. The Directory, on the other hand, was degrading France, not just itself. It couldn't last. The question was, what to replace it with?

The day he met Napoleon for the first time and conversed with him in person, something besides mutual admiration was born. The seeds of conspiracy to change things at the top were already planted in Talleyrand's mind. General Bonaparte's forceful private musings on strong executive power and the diminishing of parliament implied they were also planted in his. He was back from his conquests in Italy to examine the topsoil.

It was ironical that they both owed their position to the man they knew would have to be removed, Paul Barras. As it was, higher things than loyalty to a faltering benefactor were at stake. Public order had to be re-established and Barras couldn't secure it. It occurred to Talleyrand that a proven champion of the republic might do so. Napoleon had similar ideas. In the thought transmission of their first private meeting, their ideas met. The powdered grandee of the *ancien régime* was sure he could keep a rein on the young god with the despotic urges and the lick of dark hair across his brow. Of course Napoleon was no champion of individual freedom; he seemed to regard civil liberty as a niggling matter thrown up by the Revolution. In a recent frank exchange with Talleyrand by mail he'd written: 'I see from your letters you always start out from a false premise. You imagine that liberty will make soft, superstitious, idle, cowardly people do great things. I do not make miracles . . .' Talleyrand had felt vaguely dismayed. Again Napoleon was talking of Italy. But again these were clearly his thoughts on liberty in France.

Against this, Talleyrand weighed up his own advantages. Maturity, experience, breeding, subtlety, knowledge of Europe and the world – all these would permit him to steer the soldier towards his concept of a peaceful France reborn, conducting her affairs not against other nations but in harmony with them. If Napoleon were to win just enough battles to stop those other nations trying to undo France's Revolution, he could then step in as a broker for peace.

It was wishful thinking.

SEVEN

Minister of Civilisation

Napoleon's return from Italy allowed Talleyrand to measure his glory and cause some of it to rub off on himself. The general had been away from France for twenty months, much of his absence overlapping with Talleyrand's stay in America. No sooner had they met and taken admiring stock of each other than Talleyrand stage-managed, at the behest of Barras, a state homecoming for the hero. He did so with a care calculated to increase Napoleon's confidence in him.

The victor seemed intent at this point on projecting a modest republican persona, but Talleyrand's intuition told him that he had, like most military men, a taste for pomp and clashing cymbals, and against the instincts of the Directors he set about satisfying it. Barras wished to place the emphasis elsewhere: on Napoleon the citizen, the valorous functionary who came to the defence of the republic. This would keep the conqueror in his place. 'I recommend you organise things thus,' Barras told him. 'You have the tact.' The Directors were fearful of Napoleon; they realised they couldn't control him. Riven with discord themselves, they were at least united in one thing: jealousy of the general and his patently oversized political ambitions. Without wanting to extinguish the military glory he was heaping on France, they wanted to direct it.

Having received advance notice of Napoleon's arrival, Talleyrand had good time to prepare the homecoming reception by his own lights. On a grey December morning in 1797, three days after his first face-to-face encounter with the general, he staged the ceremony in the grand courtyard of the Luxembourg Palace, the seat of the Directory. Barras and his four partners, resplendent in blue, white and gold uniforms of state, were seated on thrones before a patriotic altar backed by three imposing statues: to Liberty, Equality and – a personal Talleyrand touch – to Peace. To right and left flew enemy battle standards won by General Bonaparte. The sides of the courtyard were hung with scarlet cloth. Outside in the street the cry built into a crescendo,

'Bonaparte! Bonaparte! Long live the Republic!' and to the boom of cannon the hero entered the courtyard on foot, dressed in a simple grey uniform, without spurs, at the head of his own honour guard. Talleyrand, struggling against his limp, brought up the rear, no doubt with the trace of a smile.

He was conscious of the overplay. It wasn't quite the balance the Directors wanted. Moreover, for one horrible moment, balance of any sort deserted the proceedings due to an incident at the back of the courtyard: a government clerk who had climbed to the top of some scaffolding for a better view of events plunged on to the paving stones below, landing with a sickening thud. As fainting women recovered their composure, it fell to Talleyrand to present formally to the government the slim figure who made war and peace practically on his own terms. Calling him plain 'Citizen Bonaparte', he hailed him as the guarantor of peace, the man bearing in his hands the armistice signed by the Austrian Empire. His brilliant place in history was already achieved, Talleyrand said, the admiration of posterity assured. But yet the glory he brought to France belonged to the Revolution! All Frenchmen were victors in Bonaparte!

The Directors sat up on their thrones. This was what they wanted to hear. Talleyrand aimed to calm their fears about Napoleon's ambition. 'No one can fail to see his profound disdain for splendour, for luxury, for display, those wretched ambitions of ordinary souls . . . far from fearing his ambition, I believe that one day we shall perhaps have to beg him to return from the comforts of a studious retirement. All France will be free; perhaps he can never be. Such is his destiny.' To portray Napoleon as a selfless warrior in bondage to the state was a little much coming from Talleyrand, who was more privy than most to the general's views on the shape of government. In the back of his mind, though, was the belief that Napoleon was the right man to restore order. After that, who could tell! Moreover, presenting Napoleon had to be a performance in tact as well as hyperbole, as Barras had recommended. Thus he rounded off his introduction with a strangely violent harangue against England, which the Directory for desperate reasons of its own wanted to invade (it was counting on Napoleon to decamp from Milan to Calais to take charge of the task). Talleyrand concluded:

At this moment a new enemy summons Bonaparte, an enemy famous for its deep hatred of the French and its insolent tyranny towards all the peoples of the earth. Let his genius promptly deal with one and the other, so that at last a peace worthy of the glory of the Republic is imposed on these tyrants of the seas. May he avenge France and reassure the world!

The vindictive language didn't sound at all like Talleyrand's, and only its publication under his name in the official press the next day indicated that it was. The rage, if indeed it was his, seemed contrived to gratify the enthroned Directors, who aimed to prove themselves and enhance their crumbling status by taking the offensive against England. Talleyrand could indeed turn wrathful at times over continuous bullying by the English navy, and could grow quite venomous about it, but in his head he never veered far from the proposition that friendship with England was the key to general prosperity and support for the civilised life he desired. So this was a blip in an otherwise unwavering Talleyrand line towards England.

Napoleon had a rejoinder – the finale to the Luxembourg Palace reception – but it made no mention of England. It was a puzzling, low-key little speech carrying a mild challenge to the five Directors. 'When the happiness of the French people is based on better basic laws,' he said, 'the whole of Europe will be free.' He did not elaborate. Coolly, then, he marked his independence. It was all the Directors could do to force themselves from their thrones with an air of enthusiasm to embrace him. Napoleon was disgusted with their government. Twice he had supplied military force to save it, and he found such actions degrading.

In the winter days that followed, and into the New Year of 1798, Talleyrand shepherded Napoleon around government departments and foreign embassies, counselling him on who was worth seeing and what to expect. Talleyrand was in fact able to blow hot against England without much concern, for it at once became clear to him that Napoleon wasn't intending to lead any invasion across the Channel. As foreign minister, it was better for Talleyrand to huff against the old enemy than to appear pusillanimous. In fact the only way Talleyrand ever envisaged dealing with England was through diplomacy. Alas, an initially hopeful round of peace negotiations had just broken down, giving rise to much clamour on the French side for an invasion, a patently reckless project. The last time it had worked was seven centuries previously, in 1066, when the enemy had no navy.

All the same the Directory went to the lengths of placing Napoleon in formal command of an invasion force – the Army of England as it was called, mustered around Calais and Boulogne – and he rode there in January 1798 to spend a week or so inspecting its prospects. He was not impressed. A mass landing in England was far too risky, he decided. It wouldn't work. Even an invasion via landings in Ireland, where the people appeared hostile to England, wasn't viable. Stirring a worthwhile rebellion in Ireland had already been tried, and had failed.

The truth was that Napoleon had his sights set on a different adventure, one that Talleyrand did favour, in his own manner. In fact the general went through the motions of inspecting the Army of England merely to recognise the military command pressed on him. The direct target he personally had in view at this juncture was not England, but Egypt. For he believed that taking Egypt would not only give France immense leverage in the Orient, it would be a passage to India and a threat to English dominance there. What better way to bring England down in the long run?

Though the idea of taking Egypt had been in the air for some years, Napoleon and Talleyrand came separately to it. Talleyrand made a pitch for its colonisation in his lecture to the Institute as soon as he returned from America, arguing for the trading advantages to be had from mastery of a vast land on the route to India. Soon after, learning in the course of their private correspondence that Napoleon had his eyes on Egypt, he wrote to him: 'In trade what counts is time, and this would give us five voyages [to India] against three by the normal route [via the Cape].' Egypt seemed ripe for the taking because the Ottoman Empire, of which it was part, had lost control to its powerful beys. Talleyrand believed he could square its cession to France with the Ottomans, who had other priorities, not least resisting pressure from tsarist Russia. He would argue that France's intention was to quell the beys. In other words, Egypt would be taken to protect it, not to vanquish it.

To Napoleon, though, the pull of Egypt and the Orient wasn't confined to the prosaic matter of trade, or even to settling scores with England. It fired his conqueror's imagination. This was the world in which Alexander the Great marched. The time wasn't quite ripe for him to make his thrust for power in France, so an alternative mission the size of his soldierly ambitions was required. Of the declared enemies among the European powers, Austria was beaten, Prussia offered no challenge, Russia wasn't in the mood to engage, and England was unattackable. Where else could he reach? Egypt was ancient legend, the right lure for his warrior spirit.

As Napoleon sparred with a hesitant Directory to switch his next command from the dreary Channel to the far end of the Mediterranean, Talleyrand wheeled out his social field pieces to sustain the general's admiration. Bit by bit Paris was returning to happier times, at least for those with rank or wealth, and he was determined to accelerate the process. Life was made for enjoyment, pleasure a first requirement of civilised man. In this, Talleyrand was a true believer.

It was a pity that Napoleon did not much enjoy the social life. This Talleyrand learned from shepherding him around Paris. Napoleon wasn't reared in the capital's salons and was conscious of his limited conversational gifts, as well as his modest origins. As for officerly dash, neither his toes nor his tongue twinkled. Accordingly, the invitations to a sumptuous New Year party Talleyrand threw for him took careful account of his social shyness. The cards announced the party in honour of his bride Josephine de Beauharnais, who was altogether at home in high society and loved to flirt and dance. Talleyrand's party for the Bonapartes relaunched the Paris social scene at a stroke; it was a considered slap at post-revolutionary grey-ness and prudishness. Even Napoleon managed to have a good time, mainly because he saw how delighted his wife was and recognised the high tribute the evening paid him.

The party was held at Talleyrand's ministerial mansion on the Rue du Bac, revamped for the night with countless candles floodlighting its oval staircase and its Italian pillars, rich amber perfuming its salons and exotic plants in every nook. At its balconies musicians strummed; in its gardens rose an Etruscan temple with the bust of Brutus at its portal, an authentic trophy Napoleon had sent back from the Capitol in Rome. Despite the winter season this was the chance for highborn women to re-emerge in silken evening finery unglimpsed since the Revolution. Paris still had beau-tiful heads on beautiful shoulders. A new dance was danced in the French capital for the first time, the waltz – straight from Vienna so recently humbled by General Bonaparte. Everyone who tried it enjoyed the waltz. Talleyrand pared the guest list to five hundred, making sure to invite the most striking young women in Paris. His policy of surrounding himself with alluring women worked to order; they garnished a mix of ambassadors, republican worthies, military officers, the cultural elite and – this was unavoidable – the Directory set.

The Directors themselves had been inclined to give the event their cold shoulder, believing it wise to dissociate themselves from displays of luxury, but in the end three of them attended, dressing down like lawyer's clerks. The fusty wife of one of the trio quizzed Talleyrand on the expense of it all, frowning: 'This must have cost a fortune, Citizen Minister.' Her host gave her one of his brief, expressionless looks. 'Not Peru,' he replied. His curt retort made the rounds that night. Distant Peru was the Eldorado of the age, an imagined treasure house which Talleyrand's detractors believed he had entered since taking over foreign affairs.

To be sure, ministry funds coupled with diplomatic commissions did permit a lavish lifestyle; his outlays, particularly on his oversubscribed dinner table, were growing by the day. That night, though, luxury was not the problem for either Talleyrand or Napoleon. The problem was Mme de Staël, who, in her impatient, intrusive way, entered Napoleon's bad books for life. Talleyrand's authoress friend and occasional saviour threw herself at the guest of honour's husband, having pressed his reluctant aide-de-camp into securing a head-to-head conversation. She wanted to conquer him, to gain influence over him, as was her way, and perhaps also to rib him and show off her superior intelligence. Standing a head taller than the warrior on being presented, she gushed that he was the first among men. And where did he stand with women? So began a perilous exchange in which Napoleon was visibly irritated from the start and was progressively put out.

'Who is the kind of woman you most love, General?' she pressed.

'My wife,' Napoleon replied stiffly.

'And the woman you most esteem?'

'One who best cares for her home.'

'But who would be the best of all?'

'One who has the most children!' he snapped, turning on his heel.

The encounter amused guests, but Talleyrand was deeply embarrassed. It placed him in a dilemma. Napoleon clearly couldn't stand Mme de Staël. To her credit, she had only been acting her ebullient self. Napoleon wasn't good with women; it seemed he couldn't find anything nice to say to them. But it was clear there wasn't room for both the conqueror and the literary lioness in Talleyrand's fold, and thereafter, perhaps half unconsciously but to noticeable effect all the same, he squeezed his ever dependable saviour out. He spoke less well of her, was caustic about her. Personally, he enjoyed provocation, but she was too much.

Talleyrand's tolerance of the Directory diminished by the day. On taking the foreign ministry post he had set himself the task of 'bringing France back into European society', an operation he couldn't define quite that way to Barras and his four colleagues. But it wasn't working out, not as long as they were giving orders. Under the cover of patriotism, they acted bellicose to mask their weakness. He wouldn't have minded becoming a Director himself to show the way and he tentatively lobbied for it, much as he had done when probing in vain for ministerial rank prior to his flight.

By the spring of 1798, Napoleon, with a tip from Talleyrand's diplomatic hand, had convinced the government to back the expedition to Egypt. The Directors still wanted an assault on England but finally saw Egypt as good riddance. It would get the conqueror out of the way, far out of the way, where he posed no threat to their hold on power. By May, Napoleon was off, shipping thirty thousand men across the Mediterranean and somehow avoiding the attentions of the Royal Navy. It was the most eccentric of missions, particularly since the end objective wasn't any too clear. Somewhere in the back of Napoleon's mind floated the grander idea of toppling the Ottoman Empire and taking charge in Constantinople. Talleyrand had a strong premonition that it was bound for failure. He thought the general allowed his imagination to run away with him, forgetting all prudence.

On the eve of his departure Napoleon made a farewell call on Talleyrand who was ill in bed at the ministry with one of the heavy colds that often laid him low. He made clear he wanted Talleyrand to go to Constantinople to square matters personally with the Sultan so that the French expedition wouldn't run into unnecessary obstacles. As Napoleon saw it, this was a vital mission. The urgent request sent the patient's temperature still higher: to expose himself to torture in the Sultan's dungeons did not appeal. He procrastinated. Perhaps a stand-in would suffice? He had no intention of offering himself up as a hostage to the Turks.

On the point of leaving Talleyrand's bedside, Napoleon suddenly stopped and turned round. He was out of money, he said, and didn't know how to procure funds with so little time left before his departure. Talleyrand was astonished. Here was the man who kept the government afloat asking for money! 'Here, open my desk over there,' the patient wheezed, 'you'll find 100,000 francs of mine. It's yours for now. You can repay me when you return.' Napoleon was overjoyed, throwing his arms around the sick minister. Their complicity was cemented at a stroke, though it occurred to Talleyrand that the general was perhaps too well informed regarding his recent access to wealth. If his generosity were to deflect Napoleon from pushing him to go to Constantinople, so much the better.

In fact, Talleyrand was already debating his future as foreign minister. He had the hang of the job; it wasn't that which bothered him. Though his working routine seemed to reinforce the public myth that he was lazy, he didn't mind that either. He took it as a mark of his style, his class. His temperament set him against haste. 'Dress slowly when you're in a hurry' – it was advice he'd picked up from an *ancien régime* courtier in his youth, and it supported his own inclinations; his club foot made him a slow dresser at the best of times. His professional advice to novice diplomats in his charge was, 'Better put off to tomorrow what you can't easily do today. It stops you doing things badly when you are overworked.' His method in preparing important letters, drafts of treaties and official memoranda was to fish out a sheaf of small personal jottings and choice phrases relating to the matter in hand, give them to his clerks with a few words of advice on the tenor he required and the goal he sought, then look the result over and give it his personal touch so there could be no doubt who it came from. If he chose to dictate he did so lying down to rest his bad leg, with his clerk standing over him at a pulpit desk. What distinguished his work, whether private notes to Napoleon or letters to government officials and ambassadors, was the personal tone. A Talleyrand letter was totally unbureaucratic. Simple without being trite, it gave life on the page to personalities and issues he dealt with. He was a good read, and worked hard at it. This was the substance of one of his strongest bonds with Napoleon: the warrior took pleasure in reading him.

But if he liked high ministry rank well enough, the prospect of pursuing his functions with Napoleon running amok in the Orient while the government floundered looked unrewarding. He decided his best course was to resign, though not at once. For a man of peace there wasn't much consolation to be taken from the situation as he saw it. He ranged over the world scene in a typically colourful summary for the Directors. Holland, Switzerland and Italy right down to Rome might be in French hands, but no one liked France; she had no allies who counted for anything. Russia was the most implacable foe, the first to ignite European monarchies against the Revolution under the late Catherine the Great. Now Russia was ruled by the 'imbecilic delirium' of a new tsar, her son. Austria, so recently cowed, was re-entering the lists to renew hostilities – this, despite the fact that the Habsburg emperor was 'weak and melancholic', fearful that the first volley of cannon would bring down his throne. Prussia did not wish to be an outright enemy, but nor did it wish to be a friend. It lived in fear of France, which brought respect but was no basis for an alliance. The best thing was to keep Prussia as far away as possible from France's natural borders: 'Better to give Prussia a few thousand leagues square on its Polish side or the Baltic than on the Elbe or the Weser.'

As for the United States, he considered its neutrality to be a fake, for its disputes with France were endless. The recent renewal of American ties with England was targeted against France. The answer was for France to take an ambivalent stance towards America, 'half friendly, half hostile'. Talleyrand added: 'Any idea of accommodation must be adjourned.' This was pretty much the message that President Adams' three envoys had taken home with them from Paris almost a year earlier, its meaning perhaps garbled by Talleyrand's demands for his *douceur*. The deeper meaning of Talleyrand's ambivalence was that the United States, a fledgling power without history, had little importance for him on the world stage. The Americans would have been aggrieved to hear it, but the French republic's relations with them depended almost entirely on its state of war or peace with England.

So the essential problem was England, 'the soul of the great plot hatched against France'. England, he wrote, 'has fomented, directed and paid successive factions that burst forth to sully the Revolution'. William Pitt's government was insincere in efforts to come to terms with France; all peace missions it mounted were 'ridiculous and pointless'. Why should England desire peace! Her basic tenet was that everything that fuelled war on the

Continent maintained her security. In this appraisal of the world scene for the Directors, Talleyrand fairly frothed against England. Once again it was mostly playing up to their phobias and to public opinion. Some of the ferocity of tone, to be sure, might also be put down to his need to counter constant allegations carried by scurrilous political tracts and newspapers that he had somehow sold out to the English, or, worse, to the royal personage the English harboured, the executed King Louis' brother, who styled himself Louis XVIII. And then there was England's failure to see the obvious. This did disturb him. The English navy had been holding and blocking French ports for centuries. Why didn't the English understand they would be better off trading with France, not against her? Freedom of trade meant freedom of the high seas, which logically meant an end to the domination of the English navy.

The report was as truculent as he ever grew with England, though it derived more from regret and disappointment than from loathing proper. His pen blistered the ministry parchment. He clutched at Gaelic straws. 'Let us pay England back for the damage she has done us,' he wrote, alluding to Napoleon's raid on Egypt and its eventual threat to English domination in India. 'We shall strike at her navy. Who knows whether the navy won't mutiny! A third of its sailors are Irish who must see the English as oppressors and enemies.' (The tirade carried an incongruously gleeful footnote to the effect that he had learned, via the Spanish government, that in the fleet of England's most redoubtable admiral, Horatio Nelson, the crews were almost entirely composed of Irishmen.) 'To resume,' he wrote, 'our position vis-à-vis England is hostile, purely hostile. Before doing business with her we must inflict much damage on her.'

The moment of fury passed. Never again did he publicly use such resentful language against England. Patching things up was always better than ripping them up.

The news from Egypt wasn't all good. The landing in Alexandria at the end of June was successful, the beys were outfought and in retreat, Napoleon in control, but Admiral Nelson spoiled the celebrations. The English navy had caught up with the French armada that transported Napoleon across the Mediterranean. On 1 August 1798, Nelson's battleships set upon the French fleet and destroyed it at anchor close to Alexandria in the bay of Aboukir, stranding Napoleon and his armies in the Orient. Talleyrand at once recognised the dimensions of the disaster. Any hope the republic had of countering English dominance at sea was now dead. Napoleon's 'imprisonment' in the desert gave heart to the many enemies of the republic.

Talleyrand saw Aboukir as the event that emboldened other European powers to stand up against Napoleon in unison. And he was right. England, Russia, Austria and the Ottomans very soon joined forces in a hitherto unlikely chain of military cross-alliances. An active coalition formed. Talleyrand had no regrets at having dawdled over Napoleon's call for him to go to Constantinople; it was much too late for that now.

Aboukir was indeed a thunderbolt. Napoleon realised he had lost all chance of preserving the conquest of Egypt over any length of time. The campaign wasn't without successes of its own – a side brigade of botanists, zoologists, anthropologists and archaeologists he took with him made exciting discoveries, including the Rosetta stone that unlocked the mystery of ancient Egyptian hieroglyphics. His inquisitive scientists profoundly advanced European knowledge of antiquity, giving exploration the kind of push that Captain Cook's scientists had provided on locating Australia not three decades earlier. But cultural glory was secondary to Napoleon, and as he ranged about aimlessly in the Middle East, driving his army up to Syria and back, the martial glory he had brought France in Europe faded fast. There, under other generals, French revolutionary armies were in retreat everywhere. Within months Italy itself, Napoleon's first great prize, slithered from republican control as Austrian forces returned with new heart. The tsar's forces arrived to join the fray. Holland and Switzerland were evacuated. Nothing, it seemed, could preserve French gains.

In Paris, public opinion blazed against the Directors and their ministers, with Talleyrand first in the firing line. Through that winter and the spring of 1799 he was under constant public fire for supposedly dreaming up the Egyptian fiasco and for being a closet agent for the English. His recent public attacks on the English and their suffocation of open commerce failed to blunt such accusations. Unjust they were, but there was more than a grain of truth to them: he suffered from instinctive Anglophilia. Even Catherine Grand, by now a resident of close to a year's standing in his ministerial mansion, might be seen as a symptom.

Talleyrand's urge to resign quickened. In secret, he set about finding ways to replace the Directory, a task that came rather more easily to him now that there was precious little chance of his becoming one of its five members. New room for manoeuvre on the home front opened in May when Emmanuel Sièyes, a thin, high-minded fellow cleric, filled a suddenly vacant place on the Directory which he himself had been eyeing. He empathised with Father Sièyes, though with reservations. The incoming Director was an odd fellow: he lived alone with a wax figure of Voltaire for company. His urgent philosophical pamphlets had driven the progressive phase of the Revolution. There was no denying that Sièyes was the brains behind the constitution which Talleyrand had helped compose to end the *ancien régime*. Lately, though, Sièyes seemed to have grown unnecessarily self-righteous. Talleyrand had received a dressing down from him over news-paper reports that the Prussian ambassador in Paris had extracted a large sum from the Prussian court to pay him to think well of Prussia. In a disobliging letter, Sièyes, then ambassador in Berlin, wrote that he hadn't believed the reports, but that he should do everything to disprove them formally, otherwise their friendship would cease. Talleyrand had been able to finesse his colleague's concern. But the man was too proud and fretful for Talleyrand's liking. Someone had described Sièyes to him as profound. 'Profound?' he'd replied. 'You mean hollow. Very hollow.'

Fortunately that dig, which made the salon rounds, didn't prevent the pair of them from scheming together at this point to find an alternative to the Directory. They were already conspirators of a kind. Apart from the diplo-matic channel they'd shared when Sièyes was in Berlin, they had previously kept in private contact while Talleyrand was in exile, so they knew each other's leanings. In addition, Sièyes was well aware of Talleyrand's complicity with Napoleon. He too appreciated the general. 'We need a sword,' the new Director told Talleyrand. They agreed that the five-man band he was entering had led the republic to grief. Disorder still went unchecked on the streets. The economy was in ruins. Three in four Paris workers were jobless. Civil servants went unpaid. Another royalist coup attempt could be expected at any moment and the Jacobins were re-arming for combat. The rot seemed complete. Barras had gone downhill, 'selling himself to pay for his pleasures', as his cousin, a certain Marquis de Sade, observed of him. To the conspirators a return at this stage to one-man leadership, monarch or otherwise, would be too sugges-tive of a past the French had buried. A triumvirate, they believed, was the solution. It was bound to produce stronger government.

To free his hands, Talleyrand resigned from his ministry in July 1799, telling the Directors that he was the target of constant 'outrages' that made him an obstacle to their government. He signed off, 'I shall always bear the memory, Citizen Directors, of your kindnesses.'

To pay them this courtesy was no doubt a strain, for he did not go without simultaneously delivering a stinging rebuke to the men in charge and their attitude towards countries which the revolutionary armies had so recently conquered. This he unleashed in a written reply to a vexed question on policy from a member of the Council of Five Hundred, the latest version of a lower house of parliament, where anguish over the subsequent loss of territories vanquished by Napoleon and other republican generals ran high. Talleyrand's retort was a clarion call against the concept of 'liberating' other peoples by conquest:

I attest that any system intended to bring liberty by open force to neighbouring nations can only make liberty hated and prevent its triumph.

Napoleon wasn't listening; he was two thousand miles away on the Nile. But this was the Talleyrand creed in a nutshell. What other nations needed from France was an assurance of their independence and a solid constitution and stable government in place there with which they could do business. The revolutionary republic provided none of these. Of course it should fight to the last drop of blood to defend itself, Talleyrand asserted, adding: 'But let it not claim to interfere in the affairs of any other nation, let it respect the independence of all and, as long as it isn't attacked, let it abide religiously by the general rights of nations and its treaties.' This was best for France and best for Europe.

Talleyrand was near unique among contemporary statesman in talking of the interests of Europe. Or even in thinking of Europe as an entity with interests that, if upheld, could work to everyone's advantage. Most statesmen of the age, on the Continent and in England, were fairly straightforward nationalists, preferring not to look past the interests of their own country. He wasn't an idealist in these matters. He knew the ancient rivalries better than most. France was his first concern. But if a genuine balance of power could be achieved in Europe, it was the first step to all-round prosperity.

Napoleon's astonishing reappearance in Paris on 16 October 1799, as the domestic crisis reached its nadir, was a goad to action for Talleyrand, Sièyes and a handful of liberal political co-agitators engaged in the scheme to turn things round. Napoleon escaped from Egypt in the one sound vessel left to him from the Aboukir catastrophe, taking a huge risk in once more running Admiral Nelson's Mediterranean blockade. He left his army behind in the desert, convinced that France needed him more. The impotence of the government enraged him; everything he'd won in Italy was lost. He was also steamed up over reports from an aide – explicit as they were reliable, his wounded heart told him – that Josephine had taken a lover during his fourteen-month absence.

In calmer times Napoleon might have faced a court martial for deserting his army, but now he was untouchable. He was still a national hero, his reputation enhanced, if anything, by contrast with that of a government which had allowed French power to disintegrate while he was away. 'What have you done with the prosperous France I left behind!' he cried. 'I left you peace, I find war. What have you done with my comrades in glory!' It

sounded disingenuous, in view of his own failed adventure, but it strengthened his place in public esteem.

Talleyrand understood that Napoleon was aiming at this stage not for
supreme power but for a situation that allowed him to aspire to it. A triumvirate would fit the bill. Yet another new constitution could then be put in
place in consultation with the Five Hundred and the Council of Elders, a
mild upper chamber sworn to uphold the Revolution. In secret they discussed
the plan, with Talleyrand acting at first as a bridge between Napoleon and
Sièyes, who did not at once take to each other.

It was a perilous undertaking, for the Directory still had fangs: it shipped
political enemies off to steaming colonial prison camps in the Caribbean
from which few returned. Furthermore, as minister of police it had recently
installed one Joseph Fouché, a former mathematics teacher and ruthless
Jacobin who dealt in oppression. As an agent of the Convention when the
Revolution ran into serious obstacles he had executed its adversaries without
qualms, presiding over the massacre of 1700 people in provincial Lyons
alone. Talleyrand noted that Fouché's bloodlust had cooled since then and
he had helped bring down Robespierre, but he remained the nosiest of
bloodhounds with spies on call everywhere. Talleyrand had an uneasy
feeling that Fouché, with his fish eyes and extraordinarily pallid face, was
his match as an intriguer. He was the best there was at police intelligence
work. Having gone to work for Barras, he was now said to be wavering
and considering transferring his loyalties to Napoleon. Such was the drift
of salon talk, but no one knew with Fouché. With a figure like Napoleon
prowling the corridors of power in Paris, clearly seeking a promising outlet
for his energies, it wouldn't be long before rumours of the plot surfaced
and Fouché was certain to be apprised of them. Despite the sympathies
Barras had once shown each of them, Talleyrand and Napoleon knew they
were under suspicion.

One night in early November, a month after Napoleon's return, the two
of them were discussing final plans into the early hours at Talleyrand's new
residence on the Rue de Taitbout on the Right Bank (the move across the
Seine made him a neighbour of the Bourse, an institution that also kept him
busy). The plotters were careful not to commit their plans to paper. At 1 p.m.
they heard a squad of cavalry clatter to a halt outside and carriage doors swing
open. They stared at each other, aghast. Napoleon blanched, as did Talleyrand,
who snuffed out all the candles within range. They were caught! They felt
sure the guard had come to arrest them on Fouché's orders. Talleyrand side-
hopped to the darkened window and looked down. In the broken silence of
the night a team of horsemen and a carriage were indeed drawn up in front
of his house. He waited for a rap at the door. None came. After fifteen minutes

the cavalcade moved on. Barely relieved, Napoleon slipped away to the house he had taken in a neighbouring street. Only the next day did Talleyrand learn the cause of their panic. Afterwards he and Napoleon often laughed about it. Since the streets of Paris were unsafe during the night, the owner of the casino at the Palais Royal paid gendarmes to provide a mounted escort for a carriage in which he took home the gaming receipts each night. The night before, the carriage had suddenly broken down, requiring minor repairs. Talleyrand's house was on the direct route between the Palais Royal and the gaming operator's Right Bank home.

With a small scare behind them, the conspirators moved into action. Talleyrand acted as fixer in the ensuing drama, an event that was in fairly short order to bring the end of the republic and launch a dictatorship, though this wasn't the outcome he presently foresaw. His role was to ensure that Barras stood down without a fuss. The principal Director was primed for it: with all the rumours of a takeover involving Napoleon floating around he feared his time was up. But Barras also knew how to defend himself and when Talleyrand went to his Luxembourg Palace residence to secure his resignation on the morning of 9 November – the very day Napoleon intended to reach for power – he took the dramatic precaution of carrying a pair of pistols in his pockets, together with a million or so francs in bank drafts, to induce the Director's cooperation. He handed Barras a pre-written letter of resignation to sign, which would permit him to leave with honour. To press him, he directed him to the window to look over the street, pointing out soldiers fraternising with crowds demanding the government's departure. Napoleon, he advised, had just taken command of the Paris troops.

Barras signed. Talleyrand kissed his hand and called him a true patriot, the saviour of France. According to Barras, who in retrospect believed he'd been had, his resignation went so smoothly that Talleyrand kept for himself the large sweetener Napoleon thought he might need to ease the head Director out without a struggle.

Pleased with his morning's work, Talleyrand boarded his carriage to cross Paris en route for the chateau of Saint Cloud, a leafy suburb across the Seine where both the Council of Five Hundred and the Council of Elders had decamped for security reasons, supposedly because of uproar in the capital. He was now a witness to Napoleon's boldness. The swift transition to government by triumvirate with Napoleon on the top rung was a flagrant *coup d'état*, in the event bloodless or almost so. The idea of dressing it up as legal and democratic foundered: the Elders gave it their grudging blessing the next day but the Five Hundred, full of Jacobins and royalists with their own agendas, balked to the end.

When Napoleon entered their session to talk them into submission, deputies jostled him, the angriest of them grabbing him by the collar and yelling 'Outlaw! Dictator!' To protect the general, who had blood on his face from scratch marks, his brother Lucien Bonaparte, conveniently deployed as president of the chamber, called in a contingent of grenadier guards who charged the deputies with bayonets drawn. Some leapt from the windows shouting 'Liberty or death'. The cowed remnants passed edicts installing a provisional triumvirate to write a new constitution – the fourth since the Revolution – with Napoleon and Sièyes among its designated members. No one doubted who would assume command.

It was a hard day, among the most tense Talleyrand had endured. In late evening as the dust settled he looked around at the handful of friends and accomplices who lived through it with him. 'Time for dinner, I think,' he said, a faint smile appearing on his powdered cheeks.

Talleyrand wasn't a member of the three-man Consulate which now came into being, with the soldier as First Consul. Since the title derived straight from the power structure in ancient Rome, the winking shades of Caesar were apparent. The role of parliament was reduced, as Napoleon wanted: a passive Senate composed of notables picked by the new master was installed to cushion him from common parliamentary deputies, who had still less power. Talleyrand had fielded far too much public abuse of late for him to aim at being one of the consuls. Napoleon had other ideas for him. And he had ideas for Napoleon. He wasn't especially enamoured of the way the Consulate was created, but the end seemed more important than the means. The need to restore order was paramount, he saw, and Napoleon looked like the only man who could achieve it. Like Sièyes, who finally ducked a consulship, aware that his skill was in writing constitutions rather than wielding power, Talleyrand did not for a moment believe he would be subordinate to Napoleon in anything more than formal rank. In wisdom, experience, subtlety and much besides he outranked the callow general, and that, he told himself, would count most.

EIGHT

Napoleon Breaks His Leash

As First Consul, Napoleon lost no time in asking Talleyrand to take charge once more of foreign affairs, aware how important the post was to his own destiny. He owed him the honour. He seemed to have put aside Talleyrand's contrariness over the mission to Constantinople as water under the bridge. Informing Consulate partners of his choice, he said: 'Talleyrand has much of what is required for negotiations – he has a worldly spirit, he knows the royal courts of Europe, he has finesse in excess, an impassive face which nothing can move and, finally, a great name.' How the list of Talleyrand's talents hung on that last asset. A great name. Napoleon was entranced by Talleyrand's pedigree; his admiration for the ancient bloodline never waned.

Talleyrand was forty-five when he began serving France's new master, who had just turned thirty. He moved fast to cement his influence, contriving to relegate Napoleon's two fellow consuls – Jean-Jacques de Cambacérès, a jurist and ex-Conventioneer, and Charles Lebrun, a financial brain with royalist leanings – to routine administrative affairs to which he believed them suited. Under his breath he called the trio *hic*, *haec*, *hoc* (he, she and it). There was no doubt who *hic* was; Cambacérès, a large, baggy fellow with a homosexual streak, was *haec*, and the rather dull Lebrun *hoc*. Cambacérès and Lebrun were manoeuvred aside at Talleyrand's very first private audience with the First Consul. His words, as recorded by Napoleon's secretary, were a study in corporate self-advancement:

Citizen Consul, you have entrusted me with the ministry of external relations and I shall justify your confidence. But I think I should at once declare that I wish to work only with you. This is not empty pride on my part, I am speaking only of the interests of France. For the country to be well governed, for there to be unity of action . . . the First Consul must take in hand all ministries linked to policy, which is to say Interior and Police for domestic affairs and my ministry for external affairs, plus the two great means of executing policy, War and the Navy. It would be highly suitable for the ministers of these five departments to work to you alone.

The administrations of justice and good financial order no doubt have many links with policy, but they are not as tight. I should add, General, that it would therefore be a good thing to give the Second Consul, who is a most able lawyer, charge of Justice, and the Third Consul, who is equally well versed in financial law, charge of Finance. That will occupy them and keep them amused while you, General, having all the vital components of government at your disposal, may meet the noble goal you have set yourself: the regeneration of France.

This cocktail of hard sense, flattery, patronising humour, effrontery and sheer nerve appealed to Napoleon who swallowed it without further ado. For all his self-imposed reading of history, he remained thirsty for knowledge. Who better to supply it than Talleyrand?

'Talleyrand isn't wrong,' the First Consul confided to Louis de Bourrienne, his *chef de cabinet*. 'You know, Bourrienne, he has got inside me. What he advises is just what I want to do.' Talleyrand would work to him alone, consulting with him every day. Foreign affairs and diplomacy were by nature secret doings, which added weight to the argument. The upshot of the agreement was that Talleyrand rather soon emerged as the second most powerful figure in France, followed at some distance by the dark Fouché who had indeed moved to Napoleon's side on the eve of the coup and thus kept the post of police minister. Talleyrand still didn't like Fouché. He was a sinister, manipulative fellow and through his contempt he couldn't help seeing him as a rival. People said they resembled each other: they had the same heavy eyelids.

Between Talleyrand and Napoleon a permanent duel of quite another kind began, good-hearted, intimate, curiously fond in its early stages. The relationship gave each of them genuine pleasure, developing a fine balance which each worked to maintain. Talleyrand took care to be exceedingly deferential in the old-school manner; Napoleon, still intimidated by his minister's ancient family line and his *savoir-faire*, showed himself eager to hear his view. Talleyrand presented the weightiest of matters with a lightness of touch proper to his class; Napoleon delighted in the finesse of it all, even when he ignored the advice, which was often. And if people had the temerity to speak ill of Talleyrand in the First Consul's hearing, he waved them aside, saying: 'He comes of a grand line, that makes up for everything.'

The relationship lifted the minister into the position of what was known in his *ancien régime* youth as court favourite – the privileged figure who ran the state because of the confidence he inspired in the sovereign and who benefited from all the advantages of power, in particular material ones. If Talleyrand had dreamed of growing rich from Barras' initial invitation to take charge of foreign affairs, he was doubly favoured by Napoleon's generosity. Napoleon showered wealth and titles on him. Years later he recalled that time with unusual candour: 'I loved Napoleon. I was even attached to his person, despite his flaws. At the start I felt drawn to him by the irresistible attraction that belongs to great genius. His generosity found me sincerely grateful. Why deny it? I bathed in his glory and in the glow it conferred on those who helped him in his noble task.'

That noble task, as Talleyrand saw it at the dawn of a new century, was to make fresh overtures for peace with England and with Austria, the two powers that carried the greatest threat to republican France. In January 1800 he went to work by composing a letter which Napoleon addressed under his name to George III in London: it was a personal request for an end to hostilities. A similar letter went to Emperor Franz II in Vienna. The argument Talleyrand put in Napoleon's mouth was that England was spending prodigious sums on bringing republican France to ruin for entirely spurious reasons. Who could doubt that King George recognised the right of other nations to choose their form of government! He owed his own crown to respect for that right. Why should the two most enlightened nations in Europe sacrifice their trade, prosperity and happiness to false notions of grandeur? Behind this logic the First Consul proposed an immediate truce and the exchange of peace negotiators.

Neither England nor Austria stooped to answer the letter, nor even to formally acknowledge its receipt. The rigid Pitt, still in power in London, was unimpressed: it was an effrontery for the leader of a coup, a usurper of power, to be addressing himself to established monarchs. Talleyrand hadn't expected a favourable reaction. But the publicity given in France to Napoleon's gesture scored a success with public opinion at home which in Talleyrand's reckoning had a benign influence on domestic peace, the first condition in his book for peace abroad. Napoleon's reaction to the dual slight was, however, that of the impetuous warrior. He was determined to deal with one foe or the other, and the one he believed he could force into submission was Austria. He had already done so once. That achieved, the Continent could be pacified with a string of treaties, under a pax Bonaparte.

So Napoleon scarcely had time to assume the leadership of France before he was off to war. It seemed unlikely that taking more time for reflection would have changed his natural bent. He did manage, however, to squeeze in a Talleyrand crash course on how to conduct himself in high society. He looked to Talleyrand as his social guide, urging him to give lavish dinner parties and expecting the style and polish to rub off on himself. Some of the more cautious émigrés were now returning home, enticed by the change of regime, the restitution of their confiscated properties and his own signals that they were not only welcome but in line for the Consulate's administrative posts. He needed to learn how to be at ease in such company. Talleyrand's contribution was to move from his Right Bank quarters to a splendid mansion in Neuilly where guests at his lavish parties and receptions were made to feel in the Consulate swim.

Napoleon paid close attention to these soirées, though less than he might have done to the hostess, Mme Grand, whose presence only strengthened his opinion that she wasn't up to Talleyrand's mark. He had heard too much about her past as a woman about town. She had her beauty, but she was putting on weight now, using too much rouge and her conversation was trite. Talleyrand was silently aware of his distaste. Otherwise Napoleon was curious to know exactly who was present at the Neuilly parties, and Talleyrand, no doubt smiling to himself, obliged. He listed women guests for the First Consul with particular care, separating those who danced, the young things, from 'non-dancing' guests, who tended to be the salon divas of Talleyrand's generation, women of letters, fading beauties with much to say for themselves. The 'non-dancing' names invariably recalled the old aristocracy. Talleyrand wanted Napoleon to know that they were the backbone of a successful soirée.

As soon as he felt a little less stiff in society, Napoleon took the initiative in asserting his rank. He moved into the Tuileries Palace, the principal residence of the Bourbons and scene of Louis XVI's humiliations at the hands of the Paris mob. In making the Tuileries his home and working headquarters, the First Consul domiciled the two lesser consuls there as the core of his court as well. The uniform of rank he chose for them was a double-breasted outfit in blue velvet with gold trim. His own was in red velvet.

Talleyrand's influence bore more closely on the First Consul in the ballroom than in his soldiering. By May 1800, Napoleon was back on a black charger at the head of troops crossing the Great Saint Bernard Pass, then a new and risky route into Italy. The army led by the new Hannibal, ill-equipped for the exploit and subjected to atrocious suffering in that glacial spring, descended somewhat fortuitously on Austrian forces which had regained control during his absence in Egypt, and after a string of violent encounters won a decisive victory at Marengo on 14 June.

Marengo made Napoleon master of Italy once more; an ensuing armistice cleared the Austrians out of the lands they held south of the Alps and encouraged Napoleon to set up a republic of Italy – the Transalpine

Republic – adjacent to the French one. Outwardly, Talleyrand's reaction to Napoleon's fresh military glories was nothing short of sycophantic. He wrote to him on the battlefield like a mother peppering her absent son with anguished affection. Recovering from another heavy cold, he wrote to him on the eve of Marengo: 'Now that I'm feeling better with each day, I feel ready to come and join you if you agree. I daresay that if you stay away any longer I shall not only want to be with you, I shall need to be with you.' Again, 'I am not whole when I am apart from you.' And still more arch – this with Napoleon back in Paris reading up on history and political economy to plan his future – he wrote: 'I don't like your library, it's damp, I think, and you spend too much time there: the ground floor doesn't suit you, you are made for the top.' He fretted over the general's safety as well as his health: 'I cannot bear the idea of you coming to harm, first because I love you, then because you are made to create happiness not pity.'

A little later, still not feeling up to scratch, he felt it necessary to prolong the separation from Napoleon by taking the waters at Bourbon-l'Archambault, the distant spa near Vichy which his family had long patronised and where he found reliable repose. The spa waters were flush with minerals that seemed to help his club foot, as well as his chest. In cloying terms that perhaps surprised Napoleon, who wasn't as accustomed as he to *ancien régime* flourish, he signed off a letter explaining his departure: 'Allow me to repeat that I love you, that I am distressed to be leaving you, that I burn with impatience to return to you and that my devotion will only end with my life.'

No doubt he felt awkward about removing himself from the Consulate loop at this early stage and wished to compensate, but even so the intimate language he used to Napoleon seemed to test what was fitting in correspondence at this level of the republic. For one thing it was a patent throwback to pre-revolutionary mores. To close male friends from the old days such as Choiseul, his schoolmate, Talleyrand routinely ended letters with some such flowery line as: 'Goodbye, I love you and embrace you with all my heart.' Mme de Staël, before she fell foul of Napoleon, could count on receiving his assurance of eternal love as his signoff. Love was batted around without great store by *ancien régime* veterans. But times were different now and there was a chance that Napoleon would feel embarrassed. All the same Talleyrand was able to risk it with some confidence. From their earliest exchanges of private letters he had established for himself that the First Consul was sensitive to fond words and flattery, even heavily larded. Also, male bonding came naturally to warriors, and this was a trait which Talleyrand detected in the general despite his own forced diversion from the military career that might have been his. On Napoleon's side, tenderness was part of what he recognised as Talleyrand's ability to 'get inside' him. For Napoleon to hear this superior and normally reserved figure waxing intimate and unguarded in his personal devotion was a caress for his enormous pride as well as a tickle for his minor-gentry snobbery. Furthermore, the fondness was to a great degree heartfelt. Harder French hearts than Talleyrand's melted at the sight of a youthful hero transforming himself into the national saviour. Talleyrand did recognise Napoleon's genius and wanted him to know it. The question was, how could he direct such headstrong genius?

For Talleyrand identified Marengo as a fateful crossroads. It was, to be sure, a boost for French glory at a time when his country's weary soul and ruined economy at last seemed to be on the mend, thanks to Napoleon's accession. But France was the largest nation in Europe (the Russians he regarded essentially as outsiders) and it wasn't out of rejoicing alone that he told Napoleon through his blocked sinuses: 'It is Marengo that will decide the fate of Europe.' For his view, confided to a banker friend, was that there were now two paths open to the conqueror and he sincerely hoped Napoleon would take the right one. He could opt for a federal Europe within which each prince, in the event of a military setback, remained master of his realm, conceding peace conditions favourable to his victor but otherwise remaining independent. And what of the other path? What if he opted for annexation, for incorporating his conquests? The thought appalled Talleyrand. 'In that case,' he said, 'he is launched on a course that can have no end.'

Perhaps so sombre a reading had something to do with his still feeling poorly, for France now embarked for two years on the most hopeful and productive period it had known since the outbreak of the Revolution. The country seemed borne aloft by the confidence it placed in its new leader. The Revolution was over and Napoleon had ended it. At last the steam went out of the fierce uprising in support of the broken monarchy and the Church in Brittany and the Vendée marshes out by the Atlantic; only the dying embers of civil war still burned, though they remained volatile enough.

Altogether, the new century was the chance for a glorious new start. And what matter if this great revival had a reactionary streak! Among his initial acts as First Consul, Napoleon silenced the raucous political press, having Fouché ban most of the capital's sixty or so newspapers, all but a dozen of which stopped printing. Freedom of information and civil liberties weren't part of his agenda for progress. He developed a simple policy on news: 'Each time there is an item of news disagreeable to the government, it should not be published until we are so sure it is true that there is no point in printing it because everyone already knows it.' This didn't quite square with the liberal view held by Talleyrand, who abhorred censorship. But Napoleon's first minister also represented that broad category of the nation that was ready, for the moment, to make almost any concession in order to obtain respite, repose and strong leadership after the violent upheavals of recent years.

As to France's foreign foes, the active coalition of enemies that clicked into place after Aboukir soon loosened in the face of Napoleon's rise and his renewed triumph in Italy. Though their deep mistrust continued, he responded to their apparently diminished bellicosity by signing peace treaties all round, calculating them to be to his advantage. In the end England herself signed a peace. To the more jaundiced English eye, the reconciliation of Napoleon's republic with the rest of the world looked too good to be true, but there it was, on parchment, inscribed in a host of accords bearing the most august signatures of the age. A jittery period of peace opened, with no bets on how long it might last. France's glorious new start under Napoleon seemed nonetheless confirmed.

It all suited Talleyrand. No doubt the situation fell short of the professional definition of peace he made ministry lore for the benefit of his underlings: 'A peace treaty is that which settles all the issues in dispute and thence creates not only a state of peace in place of a state of war but also friendship in place of hatred.' In the present circumstances the spirit of friendship was plainly missing. Still, the broad outbreak of peace gave him an immense amount of work, plus the usual openings for *douceurs*, even if Napoleon, who wanted a direct hand in most things, often kept the endgame in negotiations to himself and had his elder brother Joseph sign key treaties.

Peace with the United States was first to land. Though the US Congress was still livid over the high-handed treatment it had received from the Directory and from Talleyrand's personal financial representatives, Napoleon now adopted a conciliatory position: that attacks on American shipping on the one side and the arming of America against France on the other had simply been a family quarrel. Talleyrand tactfully kept out of the bargaining here, though he sought to redeem himself in American opinion by having a statue of George Washington, who died as Napoleon took power, erected in a main Paris square. Past caring about Washington's uncharitable snub in Philadelphia, Talleyrand wanted the memorial to America's first president to honour 'a people which will one day be a great one and which is today the wisest and happiest on earth'. The peace signed on 30 September 1800 freed the United States to trade at will and left it well on the way to becoming a military power in its own right, albeit a docile one for some time to come, at least on the world stage. Napoleon neglected to pursue the Washington statue proposal. Like Talleyrand, he actually had little interest in America. From now on the pair of them largely ignored it, which soon brought a colossal advantage to its wise and happy citizens, for not two more years went by before the United States more than doubled the extent of its territory due in large part to the inattention of the French pair, who sold off the vast American west for a song.

The armistice with the Habsburg Empire was at the heart of the general reconciliation. Signed at Lunéville in eastern France on 9 February 1801, it consecrated French dominion over Italy and confirmed France's post-revolutionary land border as the left bank of the Rhine all the way to the North Sea, including half the German Rhineland and Belgium. Since Talleyrand saw this as the 'natural' border for his country, his principles weren't unduly trespassed upon. Beyond that, Holland and Switzerland – French-made republics by virtue of the revolutionary wars – settled under Napoleon's wing as protectorates where he could do as he wished. As for the hotchpotch of principalities, duchies, archbishoprics and city statelets clustered in the heart of Germany – the 'German princes' as Talleyrand called them for short – they existed only to be chopped and reordered so as to form an obstruction against the two principal Germanic powers, Austria and Prussia. Talleyrand saw the presence of the German princes as saving France from having to live cheek-by-jowl with a serious rival power.

All the same the armistice with Austria did colour Talleyrand's view of Napoleon. The careful measures the First Consul took to assert himself both surprised and amused him. To tuck away last-minute details, Talleyrand accompanied the Austrian peace negotiator, a Habsburg aristocrat, to the Tuileries Palace for a meeting with Napoleon. The first thing he noticed was that the little Corsican had completely rearranged his reception salon for the meeting. The furniture was removed except for a small table in a far corner at which the First Consul sat studying papers under a single desk lamp. He and the Austrian could scarcely see him when they entered. As they reached his table, he briefly rose then sat down again. With nowhere to sit, the Austrian was obliged to confer standing up. He raised not a single objection to Napoleon's proposals.

Peace treaties of one kind or another then pattered down in placid drops until the summer of 1802: the Two Sicilys, England's ally Portugal, the Catholic Church, Russia, the Ottomans. Talleyrand's diplomatic efforts with Tsar Paul of Russia, Catherine the Great's son, were mercurially supported by Napoleon. In his generous-hearted military manner, the First Consul assembled the many Russian prisoners taken while the tsar's troops were fighting alongside the Austrians during his disastrous absence in Egypt, gave them new uniforms and sent them home without demanding a rouble in ransom.

The most singular peace, the cap on all the rest, was that signed with

England at Amiens on 25 March 1802. It was a stiff-necked affair, for there was still no love lost between the two sides. Pitt, Talleyrand's old nemesis, stood down immediately prior to the negotiations and, although he himself grudgingly came out for peace, the hawks on his Tory side did all they could to subvert it, assailing Napoleon at every turn as a terrorist and tyrant. Talleyrand judged that England condescended to sign simply because she felt isolated by her coalition partners' slippage.

All the same it was an exciting time. Amiens put an end – while it lasted – to the conflict between revolution and royal order in Europe. Curious English travellers flooded across the Channel in thousands to take a look at Paris for the first time in close to a decade and to see for themselves what revolution had wrought. They hoped for a glimpse of the great Napoleon. Was he the hideous gnome portrayed by London cartoonists? As the English public wondered about these things, the English navy relaxed its grip sufficiently to give republican France freedom of the high seas, which Talleyrand saw as the beginning of any true European harmony. The English had agreed to give up Malta; they refrained from trying to reassert their traditional sway over Antwerp, the trading gateway to Europe, which in any case now lay within France's 'natural frontiers'. The French got back most of the colonies they had lost during hostilities.

Talleyrand was so pleased with the result that he permitted himself to be skittish with Napoleon, playing on the intimacy that marked their daily meetings. He was the first to receive a copy of the signed treaty confirming the peace and on that bright March day he placed the precious parchment in the back of his briefcase behind a thick sheaf of routine diplomatic matters he had to discuss with Napoleon. At the end of the meeting, which lasted an hour or so, he delved in his case like a stage magician and pulled out the treaty, saying without a change of face, 'Now, I am going to give you great pleasure. The treaty is signed. Here it is.'

Napoleon leapt to his feet. For weeks he had been waiting on tenterhooks for the signing. 'Why didn't you tell me at once!' he cried.

'Ah, because you would not have listened to all the rest. When you are happy I am unable to reach you.'

Napoleon, even as First Consul, was as volatile and quick-tempered as Talleyrand was imperturbable. The warrior now set himself so much to accomplish on unfamiliar home ground that stress was ever present. The first minister was astonished at his 'incredible activity'. Sometimes Napoleon's work rate alone seemed enough to reform the country. He had set views on the kind of society he wanted. There was his Civil Code to be drawn up to organise that society, a legal rota simplifying rules for marriage, divorce, inheritance and the everyday corners of common law. The court system itself demanded thoroughgoing reform. Public education was put in place within a brand new structure, open to the masses. The administration of the nation was further centralised, with government prefects – a new semi-military class of uniformed bureaucrats – ruling in every reach of the provinces. Napoleon also saw that stability at home would be at risk unless peace were made with the Catholic Church and its head in Rome.

Aside from Napoleon's indifference to free speech and civil liberties, which chafed, Talleyrand was fairly comfortable with most of these issues; indeed, he had personally worked on realising a good many of them since the fall of the Bastille. He had never been happy over the break with Rome: he remained convinced that he had acted to save the French Church, not destroy it. Only he had a horror of rushing into things. Now his first diplomatic task, as he saw it, was to 'negotiate Napoleon' into not letting his headstrong temperament and quick temper make policy.

Their daily consultation arrangement held firm, though it was hard to imagine two more different personalities at work. First their natural timing was out of kilter. Talleyrand still got up in very late morning, usually at around 11 a.m., unless an emergency called. The torrent of private and official letters he worked on far into the night, after his evening whist, dictated a late rise. Napoleon rose at six or seven, obeying his own reveille.

Talleyrand's routine was to go to Napoleon's private office after an elaborate morning toilette, armed with the latest foreign ministry dispatches and official papers. Napoleon read those that took his fancy, discussing details here and there. The minister appeared to listen attentively, rarely advancing his own ideas. His habit was to answer in monosyllables, with a nod or a shake of his powdered head. Méneval, Napoleon's secretary, wondered at the performance. Was it Talleyrand simply being careful? Or did he want to know Napoleon's reactions before stating his own position? If there was an interruption and Napoleon was called away on some other matter, he waved to Talleyrand as he left, 'Try to put all that on paper if you would, I shall be back.'

An hour might go by, perhaps two. Talleyrand would wait there, without beginning to put pen to paper. On his return, Napoleon, showing not the slightest surprise or displeasure at Talleyrand's inaction, gathered the dispatches and reports together and dictated to Méneval his various judgements. Then he asked Talleyrand to have a clean version of his replies ready for his signature the next morning, a chore the minister hobbled off to his ministry to have his clerks complete.

That was a calm day. Méneval wasn't present for their confidential conversations, which could go on for hours at any time of the day or evening. Talleyrand watched out for the sudden angry gleam in Napoleon's eye or an open fit of temper. He could see it coming. A small tic would agitate his right shoulder, an involuntary movement that caused his mouth to pinch from left to right. The general's pale, meditative face could erupt from one moment to the next in a volcano of wrath before subsiding just as fast into smiling good humour. If he was angry during a meeting, he was liable to make bad decisions.

In such cases, at their regular consultation the following day the First Consul would ask him, sheepishly, 'Well, have you sent our letters?'

'No, I was careful not to,' Talleyrand said. 'I would not have wanted to send them without showing you first.'

'Well, on second thoughts, I think it better not to send them,' Napoleon concluded.

The only way to handle Napoleon was to sit on his orders, Talleyrand told Bourrienne, who studied these matters closely. Extreme calm, extreme deference and hard common sense were a match for his Latin tantrums.

Napoleon could be tetchy about all sorts of things. He couldn't resist prodding Talleyrand on his newfound wealth, though he himself was his direct benefactor. Napoleon knew the size of his salary and the allowances he received to entertain foreign dignitaries and Paris society in the high style he himself prescribed. He knew he had a growing household staff to maintain: chefs, servants, gardeners, grooms. So when he inquired into his wealth, Talleyrand knew he was alluding to poisonous gossip about the side commissions that went with his post. This was discomfiting for Talleyrand, but he found a suitable sidestep. Very simple, he explained. He'd bought government bonds the day before the fall of the Directory and sold them the next.

Napoleon could only smile. The quip was a tribute to his own extraordinary feat of changing France's fortunes overnight. He continued to allude disparagingly to the secret commissions from foreign courts from time to time, but stopped putting direct questions about them.

By and large the Consulate was a honeymoon period for Talleyrand and Napoleon. Making peace with the Catholic Church naturally put the spotlight on the defrocked bishop at the summit of the French state. Talleyrand, unfazed by his sensitive position, played the principal part in negotiations with Pope Pius VII, who was fresh in office. Napoleon wanted to revive the Church in France to avoid religious dissension, especially since diehard royalists who now presented his only real threat at home were defenders of the faith. He thought that restoring church worship would further strengthen his public support, though much of the nation had turned away from religion, as he himself had. As leader of the nation, his token nod to worship was to have a portable altar wheeled out at the Tuileries on Sundays for mass, which he limited to twelve minutes during which time he also corrected his correspondence. His understanding of the Concordat signed with Rome in July 1801 was that a grateful pope would henceforth do as he, Napoleon, wanted.

It was far more complicated for Talleyrand. He felt he owed it to the Church to restore the umbilical link with Rome, though he made sure that the Roman Catholic faith wasn't designated under the Concordat as France's 'state religion' or 'dominant religion', as the pope wished. That would have been too much for his belief in freedom of worship. It was restored simply as the religion of the majority of the nation. Churches and non-nationalised Church lands reverted to bishops, beholden to Rome but nominated by Napoleon. More stickily, Talleyrand's personal life entered the equation. However much, or little, weight was given to sin in these post-revolutionary times, he was living in it with a woman who had come to him literally off the street.

This was one of the things Napoleon, with his Corsican prudery, was tetchy about. Talleyrand's informal relationship with Mme Grand struck the First Consul as degrading for his government. The wives of foreign ambassadors – angels of decorum in these matters – were taking a stand against her: some refused to attend official receptions at Talleyrand's residence with a mere mistress acting as hostess. The English were particularly stuffy. Lord Cornwallis, in Paris for discussions leading up to the Peace of Amiens, refused to be presented to her. None of this bothered Talleyrand much, but Napoleon insisted he regularise his domestic situation. What he really wanted him to do was to relinquish a mistress he regarded as a 'tart' and said as much, not always under his breath. He should get rid of her. Failing that, he should marry her.

As an annexe to the Concordat, Talleyrand strove to have the pope absolve him from his priestly vows altogether and grant him secular status. To avoid giving the impression that he was demanding special favours from Rome, he tried to push Pius VII into accepting a broad measure granting lay status to numerous French clerics who had decided to marry following the break with Rome. To treat these men as eternally damned was wrong, Talleyrand asserted. Pius balked at the demand for this general amnesty, but under pressure from Napoleon, who aimed to keep Rome as submissive as possible, he was lenient towards Talleyrand. He not only lifted his excommunication, he granted his return to secular life.

Clearly the ex-bishop had done a good job in convincing papal negotiators that he merited indulgence. Pius sent him what read like a pardon, noting, 'You willingly confess you have fallen into grievous error and you decry the crimes you have committed. You have accepted wise counsel and blushingly ask for the pardon of your beloved Father.' As it turned out, Talleyrand read too much into the pope's words, for a papal bull eventually published after the signing of the Concordat only half met his requirements.

Napoleon chose to broadcast what he also saw as Talleyrand's full liberation from his priestly vows in a government decree declaring: 'A bull issued by Pope Pius VII at the Vatican in Rome on 29 June 1802, by which Citizen Charles-Maurice de Talleyrand, Minister of External Relations, is restored to secular lay status, shall have full and immediate effect.' It would have taken a suspicious notary familiar with divine small print to regard the bull as anything but a licence for Talleyrand to marry, especially as the pope's negotiators knew all about his relationship with Catherine Grand. That was how the French public took it, and that was how Talleyrand decided to take it, though within a very short time he learned that it wasn't how Pius saw it. The Vatican small print was in fact rather concise: Talleyrand's return to secular status was one thing, but no power on earth could undo religious vows taken by a bishop, and that being so the pope was unable to authorise his marriage.

Talleyrand played deaf to the negative background noises from the Vatican. He was no longer quite sure, though, where Napoleon stood. On the other hand, to Mme Grand, who was turning forty, the situation was crystal clear. Now within close sight of a marriage she had long angled for, she was convinced the First Consul would stand in the way. With no illusions about Napoleon's feelings towards her, she prevailed on his wife Josephine to arrange a private meeting with him. Slipped by Josephine into his office through a side door, she fell to her knees sobbing and begged for his blessing. And since Josephine had done what she could to soften him in advance, the tears found a crack in his armour. So be it, he decided. Either she would take Talleyrand's name or leave his house. No doubt the First Consul believed Talleyrand wouldn't go through with marriage, for he continued to smart about it years later after his fall from power, protesting: 'Against my wishes, scandalising all Europe, he married a shameful mistress who couldn't even bear him children.'

Catherine Grand became Mme de Talleyrand-Périgord in a civil ceremony in Paris on 10 September 1802, two months or so after the ambiguous papal bull was issued. The marriage took place in virtual secret with a handful of Talleyrand's oldest friends in attendance, as well as his émigré brothers Archambaud and Boson, back in France under a pardon from Napoleon who condoned the marriage to the extent that he put his own pen to the contract. It was generous to Catherine. Talleyrand had lately been buying properties with his newfound wealth, among them a large Right Bank town-house on the Rue d'Anjou. Provisionally he made this Paris house over to his wife; co-ownership of a lordly estate with a chateau, north-east of Paris in the Ardennes, was a second gift. They were handsome offerings, the tribute of a man most likely still enamoured of a woman he had chosen in the face of near unanimous criticism from his social circle, though he clearly also had it in mind that she would eventually move into her townhouse, which she did. The gift laid the ground for getting her out of his hair as his feelings for her cooled.

The strangest detail of the contract was that it declared Talleyrand's mother 'deceased'. She was in fact in good health, living in exile in Germany and not yet decided whether to return home. The marriage witnesses assumed he was reluctant to involve his mother in the proceedings. Out of respect for her feelings? Out of shame over his wife's inadequate pedigree? For some financial reason or other bearing on inheritance? No one knew for certain. It was hard enough to understand why he entered the Church-damned marriage to Catherine Grand at all.

Paris society was tireless in teasing out the marriage puzzle. Napoleon certainly pushed him to regularise his situation, but Bourrienne, who knew both men well and watched them together, dismissed as absurd the view that Napoleon forced him into it for prudish moral reasons. The purpose, rather, was to remove a ticklish protocol barrier to the salon diplomacy at which Talleyrand excelled. That the proud minister had consented to be pushed was a further gleeful topic. This was galling for Talleyrand who became the butt of salon humour. Speculation grew increasingly tortuous and far-fetched. Catherine knew too much about his financial intrigues for him to throw her out! They were bound by a love child born during their parallel stays in London! (A little girl, Charlotte, declared to be an orphan, did now make an appearance in the Talleyrand household and remained there, always close to the statesman as she grew up. He became fond of her and provided for her, though she was not his flesh and blood; she was the result of an earlier amorous fling by Catherine, who for the sake of appear-ances said she was the child of a penniless French acting couple, stranded in London, who'd begged her to adopt her.)

As speculation went, there was better still. Napoleon wilfully compro-mised Talleyrand in forcing him to marry so as to keep him in line! To humiliate and debase him would ensure his obedience! So the rumours ran. That he had once been bowled over by one of the great beauties of her day, had grown used to her for all her failings and owed her a loyalty he habitually showed his family and most of his personal friends hardly came into it.

It is true that the marriage won him no admiration. Nor contentment. As hostess-in-residence at the receptions and social soirées Talleyrand put on in his expansive prime as a statesman – right through the first decade of the new century – she was the first person guests laid eyes upon, heavily rouged and occupying a seat of honour in the middle of proceedings, though not readily engaging with visitors. As the years went by, Talleyrand's diarist friend Mme de Rémusat tartly observed: 'Talleyrand seemed not to notice her. He didn't speak to her, scarcely listened to her and I think suffered inwardly but resignedly over the burden of this strange marriage.' He was bored by her, uncomfortable. While giving her little of his time, he did, however, find an ironic formula to explain the attachment to friends: 'You would need to be a lover of Mme de Staël to know what pleasure there is in loving a featherbrain.' For once, though, his sharp humour wasn't enough to stay the criticism. The marriage went down in salon lore as the one lapse no one ever expected of him – a lapse of taste. The faithful Courtiade, who never had a bad word to say of his master, remained disconsolate. 'Who would have thought we could have been so foolish? We who have had the finest women at court!'

Talleyrand's method of dealing with the problem was never to discuss his wife. Only when Napoleon had hinted a hundred times that her silliness could harm his diplomatic career did he put his thoughts on record. Napoleon was right to raise the matter, he at length wearily observed: 'A woman of wit often compromises her husband, a witless one compromises only herself.' If neat epigrams did not entirely get him off the hook, fate did. But fate took its time. It was ten years before a younger woman, improbably younger, came along to replace Catherine as Talleyrand's hostess – and this time her aristocratic lineage was every bit as grand as his own.

Despite their intimacy and mutual admiration, Talleyrand ate a good deal of humble pie in the early years with Napoleon. He took pains to be deferential. But there was method in his subservience. With so wilful a character as Napoleon there was no point in confronting him head on; it was a matter of composing with him.

At the very same time Talleyrand was stumbling into marriage, Napoleon was elevating himself to Consul for life. The self-promotion distinctly altered the political picture for France and the world. It was an overt leap into dictatorship. He had just made himself president of the neighbouring Cisalpine Republic, embracing conquered northern Italy, having leaned on Talleyrand to ensure that the Italians made no fuss. In his view the switch to Consul for life in France then became a natural political progression. His European counterparts were all monarchs. How could he deal with them if he weren't on their level? Their permanence was their strength. He needed such permanence. It seemed vital to him, with his life under threat from increasingly bold assassination plots hatched by royalists working with a last-ditch frenzy for the return of the Bourbons.

Napoleon had largely kept his promise to restore order in France. Yet the national revival that took place from the start of his Consulate merely fired some royalists to more daring action. On Christmas Eve 1800, he'd come close to being killed in a terrorist bomb attack on his carriage near the Paris Opera. The terrible explosion killed nine people and mutilated another twenty, but miraculously left Napoleon unscathed. Police minister Fouché, having failed to forestall the attack, caught its perpetrators and had a pair of them guillotined. Fouché branded them royalist extremists. In such men's eyes Napoleon's success as First Consul now looked like the biggest obstacle to a Bourbon restoration.

To discourage the plotting he got the Senate, the tame legislative body established under the Consulate, to proclaim him Consul for life on 2 August 1802. The act followed an overwhelming plebiscite in his favour. Apart from putting him at France's head for good, it gave him the right to choose his successor, which was tantamount to hereditary rule. His calculation was that this would force the royalists to accept once and for all that their dreams were unrealisable. Thereafter, why try to assassinate him? At this point what little remained of parliamentary authority withered away.

Talleyrand could not have failed to see where all this was leading. Nonetheless he supported the momentous change, indeed urged it, for reasons he believed were good for France. To hand so much power to one man, even to one he still believed he could hold to a moderate path, was of course risky. But he had a mission at home to accomplish in parallel with his peace mission abroad. For all his early part in the Revolution, Talleyrand was at heart a monarchist, an unwavering one at that. His republican passions ran no deeper than his belief in the incompetent Directory leaders he'd briefly served. The difference was that the monarchy he wanted for France was a constitutional one, akin to England's. This was a position he'd reached long before the Bastille fell. Naturally it put him at loggerheads for the time being with the exiled Bourbons and their residual absolutist fantasies, but in a country with France's long history, only a monarch, he believed, could embody legitimacy. Any acceptable alternative to the Bourbons thus needed heredity at its core. The more he analysed the problem, the more Napoleon emerged as the answer.

Talleyrand judged that there were three ways to become a sovereign: to be elected as sovereign ruler for a given period, to be elected for life or to be installed by heredity. In France's post-revolutionary shambles it had always looked impossible to reach the stage he desired – the third – without passing through the first two. Provided the Bourbons accepted the proper constitutional constraints, their dynasty might be able to return to the throne one day. They embodied that vital stuff: legitimacy. But that day was far off. For the moment France needed a temporary sovereign to restore legitimacy of rule. Talleyrand concluded: 'The question was not whether Bonaparte had the most desirable qualities in a monarch. He incontestably had those which were indispensable to re-establish monarchic discipline in a France still infatuated by all sorts of revolutionary doctrines. No other possessed these qualities to the same degree as he.'

It was, of course, a colossal gamble. Give Napoleon sovereignty and, from what Talleyrand already knew of his nature, it would be hard to hold him to any restraint. But Talleyrand wasn't going to let the mere threat of despotism halt his dual mission, not when he believed he had the tools to pursue that mission to the end. His strongest tool was the mystical assurance that he carried France's best interests in his bones. Napoleon, he judged, was essentially pursuing his own interests. Each of them had a quite different perception of France. To Talleyrand, France was that sacred, civilised corner of the earth where his ancestors slept; to Napoleon it stretched to wherever his warhorse would carry him and his Roman eagle standards flew.

So Talleyrand gave himself the task of acting as a brake on Napoleon. His fondness for the younger man, which he felt was reciprocated, would help his cause. He would yield to circumstances where necessary, but behind his deference and flattery he would keep pushing and prodding Napoleon to pursue moderation. When he failed, so be it. He would go along with him in the expectation that somewhere down the line he would get his way. It was a warrior's nature to fight and he probably wouldn't be able to stop Napoleon fighting. Even so, it escaped his calculations that the rise to Consul for life would infuse Napoleon with sufficient new pride and bravado to sweep him decisively off the ledge of peace and into an age of imperial warfare such as Europe hadn't known since Charlemagne.

NINE

England's Baggage

Talleyrand arrived late at a reception for the foreign diplomatic corps hosted by Napoleon's wife Josephine at the Tuileries on 13 March 1803. Not an hour earlier he'd been consulting in private with Napoleon and they'd had a difference on policy which caused the Consul to lose his temper. Punctuality wasn't therefore uppermost in Talleyrand's mind. In fact he could have done without meeting Napoleon again that day. But as he thumped into the reception on his cane, the event struck him as exceptionally quiet. The guests appeared dazed. Napoleon, he learned, had been and gone only moments before. There had been a terrible scene with the British ambassador, Lord Whitworth, a newly arrived envoy sent to shore up, if that were possible, the now compromised peace treaty signed at Amiens just one year before.

Napoleon had fairly set upon Whitworth. 'So you want war!' he shouted. 'We've had war for fifteen years, and you want it for another fifteen. All right, you force my hand.' Still ranting, he swung around on the Russian ambassador: 'The English want war! If they are the first to draw swords I shall be the last to sheathe mine.'

On hearing what had occurred, Talleyrand did his best to placate the ashen-faced Whitworth, without much success. The Englishman asked for his passports and said he would be leaving for London. This was more than a setback for Talleyrand; it was a disaster. The moderate approach he favoured in dealings with England was collapsing before his eyes. He'd been pressing Napoleon's ambassador in London not to say or do anything in haste. 'There are very few political transactions that don't benefit from delay,' he advised the envoy. A snap remark, a moment's forgetfulness, could undo years of good work. He knew how to handle the English. 'Never give a direct reply to proposals you receive, or to complaints or unexpected offers. Make yourself as popular as possible. Never refuse an invitation from the head of the City or rich businessmen. Conform to the ways of their society and their conversation, for there are always sure to be members of the government at receptions and meetings to which they invite you.' Now Napoleon had acted in just the hasty, ill-considered manner he abhorred. The incident with Whitworth upset not only the tenuous pact with England but threatened to disable the broader structure of international peace set in place over the past two years.

The immediate cause of Napoleon's rant was England's delay in leaving the island of Malta, which the London government had agreed to relinquish in the Amiens accord. The Consul had been growing steadily more exasperated at the dragging of English feet and now by all accounts he had boiled over, convincing himself that nothing could be done about English domination of the Mediterranean as long as the Royal Navy held Malta. For their part the English resented Napoleon's recent annexation of Piedmont, the territory on the flank of the Alps between France and Italy. Napoleon had simply detached it from Italy, where he also ruled, and incorporated it into France. It wasn't Piedmont itself that mattered to the English so much as Napoleon's will to expand his domains; such high-handedness destroyed the spirit of the Amiens treaty. To English eyes the Consul looked hell-bent on creating an ever widening empire that would surely threaten England's lifeblood, her commerce. The more territory he acquired the more territory was potentially closed to English trade.

Talleyrand couldn't help but see some logic in English fears. London reasoned that it would be dangerously short-sighted to abandon Malta as long as Napoleon continued to seize territory. Besides, he too was peeved with Napoleon over Piedmont. He'd pointed it out time and again: annexation of foreign territory was an error that could only end up damaging France's true interests. In the case of Piedmont, he saw the annexation as a 'monstrous violation' of its people's rights and kept trying to change Napoleon's mind, though in milder language than he used in his personal notes. He judged the general to be driven solely by pride, a pride heedless of his calls for prudence. Here were the seeds of larger discord between the two of them.

Indeed, it was more than likely that 'little Piedmont', which had become the English refrain, was the source of the tiff between Napoleon and Talleyrand prior to the diplomatic reception. For as soon as the Consul had cooled down, he told Josephine he was sorry to have spoiled her event. 'I was wrong. I hadn't wanted to come today. Talleyrand said things which put me in a bad mood and that big fop of an ambassador was the first one I came upon.'

Alas for their partnership, Talleyrand and Napoleon had very different views on the wounded Lord Whitworth's homeland. Talleyrand was at times irritated by England's conduct, as he showed in his fulminations when he first took office under the Directory, but he had great respect for English institutions and saw England as the crucial weight in the European balance he aimed to achieve. Napoleon, on the other hand, was inconsolably bitter. He was obsessed by feelings of enmity. England mocked his soldierly ambitions. The English, he decided, regarded the Amiens peace merely as a pause to regain breath (which wasn't far from the truth). A resumption of war in fact suited Napoleon. He needed to maintain his image of national saviour, which meant that he needed a grave threat to face and overcome. He wasn't a king who inherited his charge by grace of God, he argued in all candour; as First Consul he was obliged to live by 'brilliant action, thus war'.

Once Whitworth repaired home, once Amiens was duly torn up and war redeclared for the umpteenth time in best cross-Channel tradition, Napoleon passed from musing to further raging. 'The English want to force us to jump the ditch, and we shall jump it. They can take a frigate from us here and a colony there, but I shall take terror to London and I can tell you they will weep tears of blood over this war and its end.' In steadier moments, he contented himself with pouring scorn on England's military institutions. He had convinced himself that they compared shamefully with his own: English recruitment was done by emptying the prisons; discipline was cruel; the ordinary soldier's lot was so poor that armies were top-heavy with officers; the officer class was venal with all commissions up for sale; the armies dragged women and children behind them with so much baggage they were unable to manoeuvre. And why did the English hate him so much? Why did they pay all the courts in Europe to be against him? Why, after all, did Piedmont bother England?

Talleyrand respectfully told him why. According to the watchful Bourrienne, most of those who served Napoleon were blindly obedient and so did him great harm. Only Talleyrand was not. It meant that he served him best, in Bourrienne's judgement, and also that he had to field Napoleon's bad temper more than most.

Despite Napoleon's short fuse, the resumed state of war was slow to materialise on the field of battle. It did, however, have rapid side effects, the most significant of which was the doubling in size of Talleyrand's old home in exile, the United States. Under the Louisiana Purchase signed on 2 May 1803, the US extended itself beyond its old Mississippi river limits, across the western plains and the Rockies to the Pacific. The land sale was the largest one-stroke event in American history, and always would be, yet the scale of it was a fluke pinned on a seemingly throwaway remark by Talleyrand.

Louisiana was the courtly name the French gave to that wild slab of continent west of the Mississippi they claimed as theirs after settling at New

Orleans, at the river's mouth, around the year 1700. The French had little idea what it contained or what it was fit for and happily ceded it to Spain half a century later to prevent it falling, like Canada, into the grasping hands of the English, whose American colonies were already encroaching upon it. Little changed until Napoleon's interest was sparked by Louisiana when establishing himself as First Consul. With Spain and its Bourbon monarchy at his mercy and ready to please him, he got Talleyrand to negotiate a secret agreement ceding Louisiana back to France in late 1800. One goal was to build up French trade in the Americas, an ambition Talleyrand naturally smiled upon.

But New Orleans not only looked ideally placed as a commercial hub, it was within close range of the French Caribbean possession of Santo Domingo, where a slave uprising urgently required Napoleon's attentions. He responded by sending an expeditionary army to the colony to put down the insurrection. Unfortunately for the broader Louisiana enterprise, the slave conflict wore on without immediate advantage to either side. The Santo Domingo standoff, ultimately ending in defeat for the French, augured badly for Napoleon's ambitions throughout the region since the Amiens peace accord was already wearing thin and he could expect the English to test him there in the event that it snapped. The English navy would surely make the New Orleans base a prime target once war resumed, and he would be unable to protect it. His solution was to relinquish Louisiana to Thomas Jefferson, Adams' successor as US president, again more than anything to keep it out of England's reach. It was going to be difficult in any event to hold on to Louisiana now that intrepid American settlers were pushing west past the Mississippi and assuming free navigation rights on the river.

The population drift to the west had already moved Jefferson to investigate how the US might acquire New Orleans. All he wanted was the port and a neighbouring slice of Florida, not the boundless wilderness to the west which he considered too burdensome to handle. While the Amiens peace still held, he instructed American negotiators in Paris to make an offer to buy New Orleans – a transaction which Talleyrand of all people at first rejected, informing the Americans that a cash sale was beneath French dignity. At that point Jefferson was quite content to leave all Louisiana, bar New Orleans and the strip of Florida, in Napoleon's hands.

But it was now Napoleon's turn to press. From the moment the Amiens peace fell apart, the last thing he wanted was to have his attentions deflected by the Louisiana issue. Changing his tune, Talleyrand then casually let slip to the American negotiators, 'How much would you give for the whole?' The Americans were astonished. Off the cuff they proposed 20 million francs, an adjusted offer they had in fact prepared for New Orleans alone.

Again the French minister balked, telling them to go away and think about it further. He was back in bargaining mode, claiming that the proposal to sell the whole of Lousiana was 'only personal' on his part and that the enormous territory wasn't yet France's to sell, which the Americans knew was untrue. They guessed he was laying the ground for a *douceur*. Napoleon, in a hurry, apparently thought so too, since he abruptly took the matter out of Talleyrand's hands and handed it to the Consulate's official treasurer, setting his price at 100 million. The final price was 80 million, a quarter of it held back as compensation for US shipping wrecked by French privateers a few years earlier. Had it not been for the on-again conflict between England and France, there was little chance that the US would have spread west to the Pacific within the lifetime of many a president who followed Jefferson. Napoleon fretted more over tiny Malta than he did over what was destined to become one of the richest regions on the planet.

As Napoleon grew in self-importance and adopted imperial airs in keeping with his new hold on hereditary power, Talleyrand enjoyed some of the side effects. Evidence of the First Consul's taste for grandeur was everywhere. He put all streets and bridges where he intended to pass during the day under guard from early morning on, and rode around Paris in an eight-horse carriage with a dashing military escort, followed by six smaller carriages containing his two under-Consuls and government ministers. The familiar you (*tu*) form of address used at the summit of the state under the Revolution was banished in favour of the formal *vous*; court etiquette, graced by court costume, made its return; the noble particle *de* preceding grand family names trotted back from exile.

The most direct benefit that fell to Talleyrand from Napoleon's airs was a magnificent country chateau which the First Consul financed on condition that his chief minister used it to entertain foreign dignitaries as lavishly as possible. Napoleon, still aware of his shortcomings as social host, was frank about it. He said he wanted Talleyrand to have a place of such splendour that kings, statesmen and ambassadors would fight to be invited there. The showplace Talleyrand found for himself in the spring of 1803 was a moated Renaissance chateau built by an aspiring sixteenth-century courtier who wanted his residence to rival the royal chateaux being erected in his day along the river Loire. The chateau of Valençay had dual domes and a Renaissance keep overlooking a lush valley skirted by twin deer forests. The location was perhaps a little further from Paris than Talleyrand might have wished: it was in the pastoral Berri region below the Loire, a good two-day carriage ride due south from the capital. But it had attractions beyond its grandeur that appealed to Talleyrand. As one of the three largest estates in all France, it was a sure wealth spinner. The revenue derived from twenty-three dependent parishes and a hundred farms crossed by vineyards and the two deer forests. A swift horseman took a day to ride round it.

The first thing Talleyrand attended to was Valençay's kitchens. If the food and drink weren't right, the point of Valençay was lost. 'Eating,' he told its cooks and servants, 'is a form of government.' At this stage his Paris duties and the diplomatic work thrown up by the rupture of the Amiens peace prevented him from spending much time at the chateau, but from the arrival of his first guests he made a leisurely round of the kitchens his morning priority. The kitchens and wine cellars were the engine room of proper hospitality, but also a mine of piquant information. He got to know everyone on the numerous kitchen staff, asked after their families, joked with servant girls and quizzed footmen closely on what they'd overheard at the huge dining table the night before.

Such information could be precious since the acquisition of Valençay coincided with the close of a hectic period of diplomacy for Talleyrand. He was engaged in re-ordering the German heartland: the task was to make political sense of the 'German princes' and their innumerable separate lands. The end objective was a confederation of German states. It was a matter of scrapping statelets here, enlarging them there, merging still others or even appending bits to Austria, Prussia or independent Bavaria where this looked sensible. Then there was the problem of settling the level of indemnities to be paid to Rhineland princelings who lost their domains as the French republic pushed its 'natural frontiers' up to their river all the way to the sea. Many of the German princes, historically tied to Austria's Habsburg Empire, came under Napoleon's sway as a side effect of the battle of Marengo, and, since Talleyrand was pulling the diplomatic strings, they and their envoys bore down on Paris and Valençay in hopes of achieving a favourable deal for their domains.

If ever Talleyrand had an occasion to apply the rules of *douceur* diplomacy it was now – and he did not miss it. A contemporary police estimate put his aggregate take from German princes at 10 million francs. The puppet master himself never talked of it, certainly never boasted about it. His interest in making money was to spend it. In time Valençay became a poisoned chalice in relations between Napoleon and Talleyrand. But both were happy with the acquisition in their different ways – Napoleon because it tied his first minister to him about as closely as anyone could be tied, Talleyrand because it reflected his aristocratic rank and made him a very considerable landowner.

Naturally, Napoleon's thoughts were not now concentrated on rural real estate. His problem was how to defeat England. To cross that cursed ditch and march on London was his dream. The rest of Europe, from Spain to Russia, presented no pressing problem: it was either his, beholden to him or rendered placid by his round of peace accords. To realise his dream of defeating England he resurrected the Directory's old plan for an invasion launched from the Channel port of Boulogne, though the outlook wasn't objectively brighter than it had been five years earlier when he'd personally rejected it as unworkable. Moreover, England had knuckled down to war business as soon as the Amiens peace fell through by arresting all French vessels in English ports and reblocking French ports with Royal Navy men-of-war, so Boulogne was by no means a secure embarkation point for invasion. Nonetheless he calculated that if he could assemble three thousand fast vessels there and put 200,000 soldiers aboard, overwhelming force would win out. Within six hours London would be his.

The preparations began in earnest during 1803. His Grand Army moved into the Boulogne zone. His engineers tried exploratory tunnelling beneath the Channel to see if the seabed was easily bored. Scientists put forward all sorts of imaginative schemes for a submarine passage. It was a long shot but if there was a chance to get at the enemy from beneath the Channel and avoid the King's Navy altogether it was worth examining. Napoleon established quarters in Boulogne, from where he commuted to Paris as needed.

Talleyrand was at a loss. Napoleon hated him even to mention Malta and Piedmont. 'He is the most intractable and most stubborn man God ever made,' Talleyrand wrote to a discreet colleague, admiration still peeping through his dismay. But he wasn't going to leave Napoleon to his own devices. In a dictatorship the only chance to make an impact was from inside. For all his experience, finesse and guile, he was not overburdened by introspection. He proceeded by instinct, expecting the way he acted to be right for himself and for France. This meant staying in the saddle.

Talleyrand was invested in Napoleon as fully as Napoleon was invested in him. On the minister's side it was still principally an investment in civil order. Most Frenchmen who had ridden the mad steed of revolution shared his craving, but their number did not include an ever-determined band of royalist agitators who continued to believe, despite Napoleon's Consul-for-life gambit and its hereditary implications, that the only way to restore the Bourbon monarchy was to kill Napoleon. Liberally financed by English agents, the royalists had tried everything to eliminate the First Consul, from the street bomb near the Paris Opera to a botched military landing in Brittany. Rumours, invariably unfounded, that princes of the royal line were hiding in Paris garrets ready to leap forth and regain their heritage, were the talk of the town. Napoleon was more angry than nervous over these continuing threats. They exasperated Talleyrand for two reasons: first because of the civil tensions they inspired, then because it was obvious to him that, although France needed a monarchy, the Bourbons had so disgraced theirs that it was no time for their recall. The Bourbons themselves had become purveyors of disorder.

Of such conflicting elements was made a drama that dogged Talleyrand for the rest of his days.

Though the uprising against the Revolution in Brittany and the Vendée region was by now long quelled in military terms, in rebel hearts it lived on. The arrest in Paris in October 1803 of a trio of Vendée veterans led, through further arrests, then still more arrests, to unusually disturbing and detailed information concerning die-hard royalist intentions. The watchful Fouché wasn't on hand to get to the bottom of things, since Napoleon, with more than a nudge from Talleyrand, had temporarily decommissioned the police ministry a year earlier and put its occupant out of business; his face no longer fitted. It was said that Fouché despised the human race, to which Talleyrand added with a half-smile, 'You can see why. He has studied himself very closely.' Napoleon, realising he had done himself no good by relinquishing Fouché, was now on the point of reinstalling him, but it was a little late. Had he been ensconced all along in his intelligence warren the conspiracy would no doubt have been nipped in the bud long before it reached its fraught conclusion.

As it was, allegations emerged from months of police interrogations that a renowned republican army commander, General Jean Moreau, was preparing to depose Napoleon under the banner of a Bourbon prince who was waiting on France's border to show his colours in the capital. If it was true, it was the gravest menace to Napoleon. For General Moreau was a public hero in the Bonaparte mould: just three years earlier he'd won the battle of Hohenlinden in middle Germany which first routed Austrian forces in the north while Napoleon overwhelmed them in the south. The army loved Moreau. Furthermore, the prince in question was the young Duc d'Enghien, first cousin of the guillotined king, the last of the distinguished Condé family branch of the Bourbons. Enghien, who had intelligence and dash, cut a more romantic figure in popular opinion than the mediocre run of royals. It seemed unwise to try to make Moreau pay with his head, cocooned as he was in army support and no doubt content to play a wait-and-see role. But the prince, barely turned thirty, was a symbolic target which, once struck, might well dissuade royalist extremists from further folly.

At a crisis meeting called by Napoleon to decide what to do about the prince, Talleyrand argued for his arrest. For Napoleon, what clinched the case against the prince was that the police said he was in the company of General Charles Dumouriez, a turncoat army commander who had abandoned the republic to serve the Bourbon cause. But this wasn't properly a police matter, since the Duc d'Enghien was ascertained to be in hiding in Ettenheim, in the theoretically independent German state of Baden just across the Rhine from France. It was a matter of diplomacy, Talleyrand's province. Or at least a show of diplomacy. Thus on 10 March 1804 he served Baden's ambassador in Paris with police notice of a plot against Napoleon's life being hatched in his state and demanded in an accompanying diplomatic brief the immediate arrest of those involved and their delivery into French hands in Strasbourg.

This was a diplomatic blind and Talleyrand knew it. Before Baden had time to respond, he handed its envoy a second note. This one was purely informative, making no excuse for territorial violation: a detachment of dragoons, it said, was to cross into Baden under Napoleon's orders to abduct Enghien and Dumouriez and take them via Strasbourg to Paris. France would not sit back while its enemies sought to assassinate its leader.

The dragoons entered Baden on the night of 14 March, snaring the prince alone. Dumouriez wasn't on hand to be abducted; the rumour of his presence turned out to be farcical, the result of a local police agent's untuned German ear mistaking the name of a Baden-based French marquis called de Thumery for that of the turncoat general. Taken straight to Paris, Enghien passed at night before a military court which knew its verdict in advance. Without further ado he was executed by firing squad in the early hours of 21 March in the Vincennes army fort. Napoleon's written orders wanted it so.

Talleyrand was seized by remorse and unease over the royal execution. He had been able to sit out Louis XVI's end on the guillotine by virtue of his exile in England but there was no escaping involvement, however indirect, in this second royal execution. Now it struck him as despicable: an intolerably vulgar act. At first he hid his anguish behind his habitual mask of coolness. He could scarcely claim he hadn't known just what fate awaited Enghien. And at the hour scheduled for the execution he was playing a late-night whist game at the table of his old salon friend the Duchesse de Luynes. As the duchess's clock chimed half past two, he laid down his hand and muttered darkly to the table, 'The last of the Condés is no more.'

His whist partners were mystified; they hadn't even heard that the prince had been abducted. A white-faced foreign ministry subaltern whom Talleyrand ran into the next day had heard the news, though, and the shock showed in his face. 'What are you doing with your eyes popping out?'

Talleyrand asked. 'What is there to make a fuss about! A conspirator is caught near our frontier, brought to Paris and shot. What's so extraordinary about that?'

Talleyrand had no taste for blood. If not always the gentleman in the sense William Pitt or George Washington meant it, he was a gentle man. Napoleon was a tyrant, but not a cruel one. With him blood was meant to flow on the field of battle. In this case, however, state security forced their hands. Talleyrand was increasingly conscious of the fact that the civil order and government legitimacy he sought for France hung by a thread. If Napoleon were to be assassinated all would go begging. Anarchy would return. He had discussed this concern in private with the First Consul even as police reports on the plot implicating the Duc d'Enghien and part of the army were still being assessed. After their discussion he reflected further and wrote to him: 'People do not properly understand in France or even in Europe that the precious order of things hangs on your person alone, and that it can only subsist and gain strength through your person.' It would be a travesty, he told Napoleon, if people came to think he was a transitional stand-in for the Bourbons. And here, with the Enghien affair, was a perfect opportunity to dispel such worries. Would he let it slip? 'You have the right of self-defence. If justice must punish rigorously, it must also punish without exception. Think well upon it.'

Was this incitement to murder? Not in Talleyrand's mind. His emphasis on justice hardly supposed a kangaroo court and summary execution. Napoleon's unease seemed as deep as his minister's over the outcome. He gave the fatal orders. But as time went by he alternated between blaming Talleyrand for goading him into giving them and taking full responsibility on his own shoulders. On the one hand he would claim that Talleyrand pressed him into arresting a prince whom he didn't know and hadn't even considered a danger; on the other, in his last will and testament, he declared it was his own doing, a necessary step to protect the security, honour and interests of the French nation. 'In a similar circumstance, I would do the same,' he confirmed. The claim that he never remotely regarded young Enghien as a threat was fiction. Much of the reason he gave himself for blaming Talleyrand was the annoyance he felt over his chief minister's vehement subsequent denials of culpability. Two decades later, when Napoleon was dead and buried, Talleyrand was still defending himself against insinuations and innuendoes arising from the Enghien killing. It was a rare issue on which he displayed true passion. His role was purely diplomatic, he insisted, and the sole wrong he personally committed was his second note to the ruler of Baden that made light of international law. In his ultimate judgement on the execution, he claimed absolution with a copyright Talleyrand twist: 'It was more than a crime, it was a mistake.'

At the time, the drama had insidious repercussions, perhaps the most harmful of which was the birth of distrust between Talleyrand and Napoleon. This altered their relationship without disrupting it, for as ever in the course of the past five years their unbroken bond lay in their need for each other. They needed and depended on each other.

Talleyrand at once sought to head off the indignation of foreign courts, with limited success. He instructed his ambassador in Vienna to 'make mockery' of likely Habsburg court protests. Did Austria believe that assassination threats against a country's head of state should be left unanswered? His follow-up circular to all ambassadors gave an emphatic account of the conspiracy. Russia in particular was loath to accept the explanations. Its youthful new tsar, Alexander, placed further questions and demanded satisfaction. In reply, an irate Napoleon had Talleyrand demand to know more about the recent death of Alexander's demented father, Tsar Paul, who hadn't long succeeded Catherine the Great. This cruel rejoinder, alluding as it did to rumours of Paul being strangled to death in his own palace, fed Alexander's enduring distaste for Napoleon. Added to the Enghien killing, it swung Russia away from a certain tolerance towards Napoleonic rule and into a new military coalition that England was even now mounting against France.

At home the repercussions were equally significant. Popular satisfaction over the crushing of the assassination plot outweighed foreign indignation, allowing Napoleon to draw the conclusion he desired. The government propaganda machine was cranked into action. The depth of the conspiracy made a clear case for hereditary rule – a guarantee of stable power protected from insurgents and terrorists.

And so it was. Exit Consul Bonaparte. Enter Emperor Napoleon I.

Napoleon was proclaimed Emperor of the French by the trusty Senate on 18 May 1804. Talleyrand was all for the move to monarchy, but the title of emperor pleased him less. There was something vague and frightening about it. He felt it evoked conquest and expanding frontiers and would probably inspire Napoleon on both paths. 'The combination of ancient Rome and Charlemagne turned his head,' he told salon intimates in weighing the first effects of the switch from republic to empire.

Talleyrand favoured king as a title. King spoke authentically of French history and was reassuring. But Napoleon refused to let his first minister change his mind. In his view 'king' was overworn; it would make him the heir to something, and he did not wish to be the Bourbons' heir. 'The title I carry is grander, a little vague, yes, but it fires the imagination.' The fact was, there had been so much public prattle of late linking Napoleon with Charlemagne and conjuring up a renewal of the Frankish emperor's Western Empire – it was all the talk in the press and the foreign embassies – that the warrior became immersed in it and was determined to swim in the romance.

Defeated, Talleyrand decided to flatter his fancies. In August when Napoleon tried himself for size with a visit to Aix-la-Chapelle, Charlemagne's seat of empire (Aachen in the German exclusively spoken there), he joined him at his destination with a posse of foreign ambassadors who needed to present their credentials to the new imperial court. It was an arch piece of stage management. The symbolism of Aix-la-Chapelle was bound to impress the ambassadors, and their presence would please Napoleon. Informing him of their coming, Talleyrand wrote:

> It will seem grand and just for a city long among the first of imperial cities, always the seat and throne of emperors, the residence of Charlemagne, to know the brilliance of Your Majesty's presence. All of Europe already recognises how close are the destinies of the restorer of the Roman Empire and the founder of the French Empire.

It was hard to know what to make of such hyperbole. He was pluming an aroused eagle. Moreover, there seemed little trace of self-amusement in the flattery. The softly scolding irony that habitually poked through his more outrageous praise – a trusty instrument he employed to hold his own and insert his own ideas – seemed altogether absent. One reason was that the situation had swung. The onset of empire altered the scene; Talleyrand had to fix his place in the imperial court. Stroking Napoleon's vanity ought to help. From the day of the proclamation of the empire he had changed his manner of addressing Napoleon. Now he headed his letters with the lofty 'Sire' in place of 'General' (itself a gracious advance on 'Citizen General'). In his presence, he addressed him as 'Your Majesty'. Napoleon's brood of brothers and sisters were 'Imperial Highnesses', his fellow generals mostly raised to imperial marshals.

The task of explaining the progression from people's republic to French Empire to a wary outside world fell to Talleyrand. He primed his ambassadors to foreign courts with the message that the empire forever joined the destinies of the French nation and its leader, 'shielding both from the caprices of fate and the vicissitudes of time'. It did not change France's relations with other countries so much as it invested her government with a dignity proportionate to her power. It was in fact an advantage for the world, since France had greater political stability to which other countries could better relate.

This was excellent diplomatic spin. It was a pity that the emperor did not respond quite as Talleyrand might have expected to his skilful conjuring, or indeed to his arch flattery. Talleyrand had his sights on the imperial office of Arch-Chancellor which was as high as anyone who wasn't a Bonaparte could aspire in the court firmament Napoleon devised. (The equally grand office of Arch-Elector went by family right to his elder brother Joseph.) It came as a sharp disappointment when the Arch-Chancellor post went to the enduring Cambacérès, whose influence as co-Consul Talleyrand had largely usurped four years before. The disappointment was sharper still when Talleyrand learned why. It filtered quickly through the salons that his wife Catherine did not meet the emperor's standards as spouse for a figure who was to serve as his highest imperial dignitary. Napoleon still despised the former Mme Grand. He wanted his Arch-Chancellor to be addressed as *Most Serene Highness*, which would apply to his wife too. How could Catherine answer to that!

Talleyrand wasn't conspicuously successful at landing the posts he most prized and believed he was right for. Over time he had pressed with varying degrees of urgency to become finance minister, then Director, then Consul, all of which eluded him. His present standing as second most powerful figure in the land was notional rather than official. Now Napoleon made him Imperial Grand Chamberlain, while keeping him at the head of the foreign ministry where he most needed him. To placate hard feelings involving his wife, Napoleon stipulated that an imperial dignitary at the Arch-level could not in any case serve as a government minister. For his part, Talleyrand concluded that to address people like Cambacérès as *Most Serene Highness* was 'quite ridiculous'.

Grand Chamberlain wasn't to be laughed at. It was the top rung inside the Tuileries Palace and added 100,000 francs to Talleyrand's ministerial income. Access to the emperor was immediate and constant, though he already enjoyed that through his ministry post. It made him titular head of the emperor's palace services, his head of protocol and organiser of imperial festivities, ceremonies, receptions and entertainments. There was a slight comedown involved. He had turned fifty. However lavishly he was able to live, there was something ungracious, at that age, about finding himself in the position, ceremonial though it was, of head manservant to a Corsican squire's son. For the descendant of the sovereign Counts of Périgord it was an odd situation which did not go unobserved by the salon crowd.

Talleyrand knew what it was to attempt to make a polished social animal of Napoleon, and he couldn't help feeling there was something a little silly in the endeavours of the man who was now emperor to make his court an attraction. Napoleon let it be known that he wished his courtiers and foreign grandees to find pleasure in being at his court. As Grand Chamberlain, Talleyrand was closely involved in the effort, which was an uphill struggle. He smiled at how the emperor in his peremptory manner seemed to be ordering people to enjoy themselves. To Mme de Rémusat he relayed dryly, 'The emperor isn't joking, he desires that we have fun.'

For formal occasions at the palace Talleyrand wore a Grand Chamberlain uniform designed by Napoleon with an eye on the courtly past. The emperor took the closest personal interest in imperial dress. He favoured velvet, a fabric banished by the Revolution. Everything bespeaking rank had to be made of velvet. This didn't displease Talleyrand, with his *ancien régime* aura. Furthermore, it was a godsend for Lyons, France's second city and silk capital. Napoleon's sartorial whims quickly pulled the city out of an economic crisis caused by the austerity of republican attire. The Grand Chamberlain's red velvet habit and coat of office were lined with white silk, the collar, lapels and edges embroidered in gold, the ensemble set off by a white lace cravat, white silk scarf and sword. This, by the look of it, was a uniform that was trying to make an announcement: from its velvet folds leaked the news of a further stage in empire – a coronation. The Senate act that made Napoleon emperor clearly lacked the ceremony and dignity that a sacred coronation would provide.

To give his empire divine lift, Napoleon became set on coronation rites in the cathedral of Notre Dame. With the Concordat with the Church of Rome in place, the one person of sufficient spiritual prestige to provide such a lift was Pope Pius VII. But this raised awkward questions. Napoleon's troops were occupying the papal states around Rome and the Vatican was naturally little better disposed towards the Emperor of the French than it was towards the Revolution. Napoleon's insistence that Talleyrand himself should draw on his churchly past and twist the pope's arm to ensure that he came to Paris to give his blessing only seemed to aggravate the problem, for although the ex-bishop's return to lay status ended his religious war with the Church, his marriage was forever damned. The confrontation through envoys was embarrassing for both diplomat and pontiff. Pius prevaricated as far as he dared. But running through Talleyrand's pressing reminders that the Vatican was remiss in failing to give a prompt response to Napoleon's invitation was a plain hint that things might go worse for papal sovereignty if Pius did not accept. The invitation was in fact a summons. At length the pope gave way, retrieving a crumb of pride by refusing to be introduced to Talleyrand's wife when he reached Paris for the coronation at the onset of winter.

Having got the pope to Notre Dame on time, the Imperial Grand

Chamberlain's role was to get the emperor there. When he called at Napoleon's Tuileries Palace apartments to accompany him to the cathedral on the great day, 2 December 1804, his fabled composure very nearly deserted him. His face for once twitched at the sight of the emperor. 'But for the solemnity of the moment I would surely have lost my sang-froid,' he recalled. Before him stood Napoleon, barefoot, dressed in white satin trousers embroidered with golden bees, his torso adorned in a robe of purple velvet swarming with more gold bees and lined with white ermine. The Grand Chamberlain had been forewarned of the bees, though not of their profusion: they were a dynastic symbol of France's medieval Merovingian kings which Napoleon had unearthed, with the added attraction that they looked like the famous Bourbon fleur-de-lis inverted. Part of the shock for Talleyrand was that he had never before seen Napoleon wearing a full robe. To hold back his hilarity required an effort of will recalling the absurdly inflated climax to the Federation Fete a dozen years earlier when the glum Lafayette caught his eye.

The coronation itself proved a further strain on the facial muscles. Talleyrand felt a proprietary interest in the empire, indeed regarded it to an extent as his own work. It went in the direction of the legitimacy he desired. The coronation, though, was another matter. This was one grand state event he hadn't been asked to stage-manage; it was Napoleon's personal production. The cathedral nave was draped in royal red and lined with cardboard Greco-Egyptian pillars from which hung Roman imperial standards wreathed in laurel and inscribed with a large N. Having given his blessing, the pope was spared the task of officiating at the sacred climax. Napoleon crowned himself. There was no protocol to go by and he thought self-coronation appropriate, after which he also crowned Josephine, pledging to make his sole objective 'the interest, happiness and glory of the French people'.

Talleyrand's observation post was the altar to Napoleon's left. His mood was captured in a vast fresco of the event painted by Jacques-Louis David, the Revolution's leading artist. David, a master of detail, portrayed him larger than other liveried grandees of the new regime. He was standing, his eyes half looking down beneath a plumed hat, pre-eminent, superior, wearing the trace of a disdainful smile. The look said he was involving himself in Napoleon's splendid event, but not identifying with it. He was his own man; he was keeping his judgement free.

He was also surely in two minds. Here he was at the pinnacle of the nation's affairs at the most testing time imaginable for his diplomatic arts, with shaky peace accords giving way to the prospect of the most gigantic battles Europe had yet witnessed. It would have been hard at such a moment for a man of his position, a man struggling with a growing dilemma, not to be in two minds.

Even if Napoleon's quest for stature hadn't diverted his sights from the invasion enterprise at Boulogne, the length of the preparations for a surprise assault on England diminished its chances of success. Boulogne's closeness to England made it all the easier for the Royal Navy to keep watch. The three thousand swift troop transport vessels needed for the invasion proved hard to assemble: several months after Napoleon crowned himself emperor they still numbered little more than two thousand. A violent storm destroyed key embarkation points, showing how dependent the enterprise was on the Channel's least dependable element – fair weather. Napoleon was no seaman, but it became fairly obvious to him that his chances of circumventing the King's Navy or of taking it by surprise were so low that it would be better to take it on head-to-head, at sea. Accordingly, he began ordering out the remnants of French fleets hiding at anchor in Mediterranean, Atlantic and Caribbean ports for an ocean rendezvous with the fleet of Spain, his submissive ally. The Royal Navy responded by concentrating its strength at the Atlantic mouth of the Channel, convinced that if ever the enemy became master of the Channel, England was lost. English mettle stiffened, Talleyrand observed. As he saw it, the first results of Napoleon's invasion threat were to boost popular support for the war within England and – this astonished him – to create a large permanent army there. He considered it 'unheard of' for England to have a standing home army. It went against all tradition: Britannia's funds supported an invincible navy. Furthermore, William Pitt was back at the reins to maintain pressure on France.

Even so, French war worries took second place to Napoleon's passion for imperial aggrandisement. On 17 March 1805, three months after his coronation, he had himself proclaimed King of Italy. There followed a second coronation in Milan, celebrated with equal pomp and a still heavier dose of self-indulgence. Once more placing the crown on his own head, he declared, 'Heaven gave it to me, woe become he who touches it.' This was tantamount to annexing Italy, merging it with France. It was quite different from holding rich, sprawling Lombardy and much of the rest of the peninsula in independent statehood under French sway, and was in any case a violation of peace agreements signed three years earlier.

Talleyrand was alarmed. Now that France was no longer a republic, there was no stopping Napoleon from turning the Italian republic into a kingdom, nor much interest in trying to stop him. The fine medieval cities along the Po had been besieged, attacked and ravaged for centuries by one power or another and Napoleon's coming didn't much put them out. He was in fact quite popular. That wasn't the issue. For Napoleon to make himself sovereign ruler of both France and Italy was a dire provocation to the other European monarchies. As Talleyrand saw it, common prudence demanded that France do nothing to excite them into joining a fresh alliance with England, at present the one power at war with Napoleon. A saving solution he pressed on the emperor was to enthrone one of his brothers in Italy, either the older Joseph or the rambunctious Lucien. The proposal wasn't entirely a shot in the dark, for Napoleon indeed contemplated covering Europe with subject thrones to seat members of his family (and very soon set about doing so). But appeals to common prudence seldom dissuaded Napoleon. In Italy, he decided, a brother wouldn't do. He himself had liberated Italy from Austria's grasp, and he believed that an emperor of his calibre had to be a king as well – a dual pinnacle of power matching him with the head of the ancient House of Habsburg in Vienna, Franz II.

It was no comfort to Talleyrand that his predictions at once came true. At this point he moved decisively against Napoleon, though only in his heart. In reality he stayed with him. He saw it as the start of their divorce only in his memoirs, penned twenty years later, for it required hindsight to abandon the strange, insistent affection he felt for the emperor. At the time the warrior's extraordinary gall held him to his side, even when it sent events hurtling in precisely the opposite direction to the one he favoured. He did keep his judgement free, but the affection he felt did its best to cloud it. Just as he foresaw, Austria now armed for hostilities and was joined by Russia under its new young tsar, Alexander, in reviving the war alliance with England. Alexander was still smarting over the Duc d'Enghien episode. St Petersburg, his capital, was bursting with Anglomania, a trend encouraged by England's promise to co-finance Russian military engagement. Continental war loomed. Only Prussia of the large powers stayed temporarily on the sidelines, thanks to strenuous efforts by Talleyrand to keep it there. The Prussians, whom Napoleon regarded as a whipped nation despite their growing military potential, knew where Talleyrand stood perhaps more clearly than Napoleon himself did. The Prussian ambassador in Paris informed his masters in Berlin: 'M. de Talleyrand is in despair, and if he had been able, or were still able, to prevent the outbreak of war or halt its course before victories or defeats forced ambition or lost honour to continue it, he would count it the most glorious feat of his career.' Talleyrand clearly wasn't holding his tongue among the host of foreign diplomats who hung on his words in Paris.

Austria thought it best to catch Napoleon unawares while he was glowering at England from Boulogne, still pondering an invasion but wagering more and more on a high-seas naval showdown to clear the way for it.

Without waiting for Tsar Alexander's army to join them, Austrian forces seized the opportunity to pour through supposedly independent Bavaria in mid-summer 1805 and establish war positions in the Danube basin, hard on France's Rhineland frontier.

Napoleon needed no better encouragement to abandon the invasion of England altogether. Land battles were the theatre of his genius and it was to land battles that he now turned his full attention. In twenty days he force-marched his Grand Army from the Channel to the Rhineland to confront the Austrians – dashing into a continental war from which Talleyrand still hoped to pull him back.

TEN

Austerlitz – and Trafalgar

Talleyrand, under summons, hurried to Strasbourg to meet Napoleon before he engaged the military might of Austria. The emperor seemed particularly pleased to see him, he thought, though he also looked worn and stressed when they dined together on 1 October 1805. He was preparing to leave that same night to join the Grand Army, but the romance of a new campaign seemed far from settling his anxieties. Rising from the table, he embraced first the Empress Josephine then Talleyrand, hugging them to his side. He was close to tears, Talleyrand saw. In a soft voice, he said, 'It's so painful to leave the two people you love best.'

As Josephine went to her quarters, Napoleon collapsed to the floor, groaning and foaming at the mouth. He just had time to ask Talleyrand to close the door before lapsing into convulsions. An imperial first chamberlain who was present tried pouring orange water down his throat while Talleyrand, who hadn't practised first aid since helping his great-grandmother treat sick peasants as a child, peeled away the emperor's cravat and doused him with eau-de-Cologne. Fifteen minutes later, when the convulsions stopped, an overscented Napoleon rose, changed into his uniform and asked the two men not to breathe a word of what they had seen. Within half an hour he was off to lead his Grand Army in the upper reaches of the Danube.

Talleyrand was moved by Napoleon's expression of affection. To hear the emperor call him one of the two people he loved best gave him much pleasure, however oddly he'd been behaving when he said it. The pleasure made him fret over Napoleon's health. He believed the collapse was an epilepsy fit, though he had never witnessed him having an attack before (nor had Bourrienne, or so he claimed, who was constantly with him). To lose Napoleon now would be a worse blow to order and stability in France than any amount of warmaking he indulged in. From Strasbourg he was soon sending the emperor inquiring private notes. He wrote: 'On learning from Her Majesty the Empress that we shall be four or five days without news of Your Majesty, I suffer feelings I find it impossible to express.' The fondness seemed inexhaustible. What sins would it not survive?

Talleyrand's stay in Strasbourg was not meant to last long. Napoleon wanted his chief diplomat right by his side as he dented Austrian might; he was to put the pieces together for the benefit of the French Empire. Talleyrand did not relish the prospect of having to tidy up in central Europe as Napoleon manoeuvred a rampant Grand Army around its heart. But that was Napoleon's wish. He was to compose armistice treaties on the hoof, impose territorial gains and transfers, provide diplomatic counsel before the blood dried on the battlefield.

He was not to know it on the night Napoleon passed out, but he was to spend much of the next two years in central Europe as the emperor's nego-tiator-cum-quartermaster, camped close behind the lines from Munich to Vienna, Berlin to Warsaw. Napoleon was never happier than when he was in camp preparing for battle, never more morose than when inactive in peacetime. 'Conquest has made me what I am, and conquest alone can main-tain me,' he cheerfully told Bourrienne.

If anyone, on the other hand, was not made for tents, bivouacs, the stench of battlefield corpses and field infirmaries it was Talleyrand. Where possible he billeted himself in ducal dwellings where his servants could operate and he could entertain the aristocratic political grandees of central Europe. But there was no avoiding the horrors of war. While he endured them with a fair grace, much as he had once confronted the virgin forests of America, the contrast with the life he liked to lead was close to intolerable, let alone uncomfortable, for a statesman of his class.

Life in Paris in fact had been treating him better than ever. Napoleon's warrior passions now separated him from an existence of extreme gentle-manly ease. In Paris and Valençay an army of servants pampered him; with Courtiade in command, they dressed and coiffed him with such care that he received his first official visitors of the day while they trousered him. Better still, he had the services of the renowned chef Antonin Carême. He took Carême into his employ from a Paris pastryhouse where he had risen from apprentice tart maker to a virtuoso chef who held Paris society in thrall. With Carême behind him, Talleyrand conclusively proved a theory he had long held: eating was a form of government.

It was Carême who saw to Napoleon's desire that kings and ambassadors vied for a place at his first minister's table. The chef made his meats and pastries a feast for the eyes. Moreover, Talleyrand was a connoisseur in his own right: he conceived lavish table décors to set off the food he served and made himself familiar with prized provincial dishes from Alsace to Provence. People who dined at Talleyrand's home called it the best table in Paris, so that it wasn't much of a stretch to call it the best in the world.

With the inventive Carême he was always on the lookout for new recipes. Soups were Talleyrand's forte. He counted three hundred different soups he knew, two hundred French and a hundred foreign. As host, he indulged his taste for the grand performance by having Carême present him with roast beef on an enormous silver carving tray, then slicing it himself for each guest in turn and having each plateful relayed by a servant accompanied by a word of flattery and respect for its destined recipient, such as, 'Your Highness, I beg you to do me the extreme honour of accepting this piece of beef', or 'Your Excellency, please accept this small tribute to your gracious government'. The meat was the same for everyone but not the commentary. When he got to lesser lights at the end of the table he sent the beef off with a tilt of the head in their direction and a muttered name.

At dinner he kept his own intake simple: soup, cheese, a glass of tangy Madeira (also his requirement at breakfast) and Bordeaux claret were his mainstays. For he was conscious of his health, and not only about making sure he dressed warmly enough to fight off the colds that plagued him. Now fifty, he was aware of having put on weight. His face had assumed a certain waxen look. He took little exercise; his leg with the chafing iron strut at his calf stopped him from walking further than he had to. Going to bed at around four o'clock in the morning after his social rounds, his whist session and all his letter-writing didn't help. But none of that stopped him enjoying his food. Among cheeses, his favourite was the soft Brie from pastures just south of Paris. 'Brie is the king of cheeses,' he enthused to guests, 'it was the best in my youth and it's still the best. I have always remained faithful to it.' He was equally partial to coffee, a taste he developed during his exile in America. He was lyrical about his house blend: 'black as the Devil, hot as Hell, pure as an angel, sweet as love'.

His only grief as an epicure, aside from high society's reaction to his wife Catherine, was that he sensed he would have trouble in holding on to Carême despite their near perfect professional understanding. Napoleon wanted the chef for the Tuileries Palace kitchens and it was difficult to hold the emperor off. Napoleon continued to be fascinated not only by his minister's sense of hospitality but by his whole stance in public, particularly his reputation as a brilliant conversationalist. The emperor had put it to him not long before departing for Austria:

—You are the king of conversation in all Europe! What is your secret?

—Sire, permit me to draw a comparison with your vocation. When you make war you always make sure you choose the field of battle.

—Yes, that is so.

—Well, Sire, I choose the ground for conversation. I accept it only when I have something to say. For the rest I don't reply. At a hunt I only ever fire when I am within six feet, when I have a sure kill. In conversation I let a thousand things run by to which I have only a banal reply. What runs between my legs, though, I never miss.

Talleyrand's mastery of conversation was, however, largely in the ear of his listener. He might have told Napoleon what he told the harem: that there was no better way to make people love one's conversation than to listen carefully to them telling one what one already knew. He was suave, knowledgeable and uniquely courteous, but no quickfire wit. It would have pained him to be regarded as a punster. Much of the time he was taciturn. Silence came top of his list of human qualities, as also of his list of diplomatic weapons. No woman ever professed to be bored by him – charmed more likely, or piqued by the impertinence at the tip of his flattery. But men who found themselves parked next to him sometimes found him so close-mouthed and glacial as to be dull. He himself recognised his talent and its limits. 'They say I'm a wit. What do you think?' he observed to a young politician who questioned him on his conversational arts. 'I have never said a *bon mot* in my life. What I endeavour to find, after much reflection on many things, is the *mot juste*.'

Talleyrand stayed in Strasbourg long enough to hear of Napoleon's first success in his march into central Europe, which occurred with the usual glorious promptitude. In fact he was sufficiently convinced in advance that Napoleon would succeed that he prepared his recommendations on how to handle victory before receiving news of it. Napoleon forced the Austrian army to surrender at Ulm on the Danube in southern Germany on 18 October. After that, there was nothing to stop him marching on to Vienna and occupying the Austrian imperial capital to complete the humiliation of Emperor Franz. Napoleon relished the idea of dating his decrees from Franz's Schönbrunn Palace.

A full week before the triumph at Ulm, Talleyrand wrote to Alexandre d'Hauterive, his like-minded stand-in at the foreign ministry in Paris, setting out his ideas on how Napoleon should treat a defeated Austria. Napoleon, he dearly hoped, would say he did not wish to abuse his victory but felt entitled to make certain conditions for peace. Austria would forfeit control of disputed territories it held dear, including Venice, Tyrol and Swabia, but would gain in compensation lands it cherished to the east — Moldavia, Wallachia, Bessarabia and lower Danube territories which Talleyrand believed could be eased out of tenuous Ottoman control. That agreed, Austria would enter an alliance with France and 'throw to the devil' any plans for an alliance with its Germanic neighbour Prussia. Furthermore — and this was paramount — Napoleon would calm Austrian anxieties by giving up the crown of Italy he had just placed on his head. In other words, he would desist from humiliating Austria and instead make it a grateful ally.

Alas, Talleyrand knew that with a character like Napoleon this was probably pie in the sky. 'This is my dream for tonight,' he conceded.

Nonetheless he persisted with the dream, fought for it. What he outlined to Hauterive was the crux of a broad European peace plan he now presented to Napoleon himself, for he hadn't been whiling away his time in Strasbourg: he had been meditating long and hard on the formulation of his ideas. He sent him the plan as a tightly argued covering note to a draft treaty he hoped he would put to the Austrians. This was his big diplomatic throw with Napoleon; it showed exactly where he stood.

With his usual disarming tact, he prefaced his plan with a tribute to Napoleon's 'desire' for peace:

> Those who know that Your Majesty considers each victory solely as a gauge of the peace he desires, have no doubt that after succeeding in this war with Austria he will yield once more to the noble leanings of his great soul.

This was, of course, a baldfaced misstatement of Napoleon's true leanings, as was obvious to both of them. But the trick was to arouse the warrior's generous sentiments if there was to be the slightest chance of guiding him. Talleyrand continued: 'I have felt it my duty to submit this work to Your Majesty. I regret that it is only an outline, but it suffices to indicate to Your Majesty what it is necessary to develop at length to others and in any case, to expose my theory in full, it would take longer than Your Majesty takes to win battles and to subject entire countries.'

For all the false modesty the plan was simple, thorough and serpentine, the mark of its author. There were at present four great powers in Europe: France shared the honours with England, Austria and Russia. As for Prussia with its stunted population, harsh soil and little industry or capital, it lived on the faded eighteenth-century glory of the warrior-liberal Frederick the Great and was now no more than first among powers of the second order. Of the three powers vying with France, her true rivals and natural enemies

were England and Austria. As long as that was so, the pair would themselves be natural allies. Tsarist Russia, far removed geographically, wasn't at
present a direct enemy of France, only an indirect one. As long as Austria
and Russia weren't at loggerheads, England was able to knit them into
alliances of her choosing. 'It is evident that such a system of great power
relationships will produce causes for war ad infinitum, that periods of peace
will only be truces and that human bloodshed can at best be only suspended,'
Talleyrand argued. 'It is no less evident that in all wars born of this state
of affairs, France will always be involved as principal or accessory.'

It was a state of affairs, then, that had to be replaced. A root solution
was to banish the old-established enmity between France and Austria. That
would separate Austria's interests from England's. But it could only be
achieved if there were no longer troublesome common frontiers to invite
discord between Austria and her possessions and France and hers. Hence
the need for Austria to relinquish lands in the west and centre which abutted
Napoleon's empire and to receive compensatory lands in the east which
didn't. Compensation was essential because Austria couldn't be a viable ally
if her heart bled over lands she gave up. All the better if Austrian expansion into loosely Ottoman-controlled lands to the east aggrieved neighbouring Russia, for that would be a further block to the remaking of the
old alliances against France. To Talleyrand, Russia was in fact the chief
danger to the harmonious Europe he envisaged. To fortify Austria against
Russia was thus the sensible course. The Russians would then turn their
attentions away from Europe towards southern Asia and India where they
would exhaust themselves competing with the English. And the upshot of
it all? England could no longer find ready allies for war on the Continent,
save for useless ones.

Talleyrand hadn't turned against England; rather he sought a balance of
power in Europe to render war impossible. And none of this was feasible
without lasting rapprochement with Austria. This meant being magnanimous and moderate in victory. He applied every weapon in his armoury –
flattery, sagacity, affection, obstinacy – to convincing Napoleon he was right.
Such was his plan; it was a challenge to the emperor bearing a faint but
discernible trace of an ultimatum. Everything in their partnership would
ultimately hang on how Napoleon received it.

But how was a soldier drunk on fresh martial triumph and already thirsting
for more to take heed of such reasoned interference? Talleyrand's wisdom
did not reflect the immediate realities of victory and defeat. Napoleon lived
for the martial moment, Talleyrand for a prosperous civilised future that
excited a conqueror less. Besides, Napoleon hadn't yet finished with Austria.
Though he was now advancing fast on Vienna, the Austrians were by no

means done for. Following the debacle at Ulm, Emperor Franz vacated his capital to take charge of his remaining forces thirty miles or so north of the city, where a Russian army led by Tsar Alexander arrived to join them.

Talleyrand caught up with Napoleon at Munich on the road to Vienna. There they discussed his grand peace plan, but the emperor was generally unresponsive and in any case had his mind on other things. By mid-November he was accompanying the warrior into Vienna where the populace received the French invaders with quite as much fascination as anguish.

From there Napoleon marched his Grand Army north to confront the Austro-Russian armies, carefully selecting his site to do battle. At Austerlitz, on 2 December 1805, he displayed his full military genius, a combination of ruse, daring and innovation. The result was the most glorious and clear-cut of all Napoleonic victories, also the most bloody. His rival emperors, Franz and Alexander, lost 27,000 men between them and most of their weaponry. Napoleon was master of all he surveyed — on land at least. The remnants of the Russian army limped home behind their beaten tsar. The shock waves travelled fast to England where Talleyrand's nemesis, William Pitt, back as prime minister after sitting out the past three years, wilted under the pain of it and died.

From Talleyrand's perspective, however, Austerlitz looked less like the apogee of military greatness than the beginning of the end for Napoleon. For just before that battle was fought he was obliged to inform the warrior of a defeat suffered at sea at the hands of England's Admiral Nelson. Napoleon's chances of neutralising the Royal Navy, and thus of turning his military might one day on England herself, were shattered for good off Cape Trafalgar.

The Trafalgar disaster off the southern Spanish naval base of Cadiz on 21 October had occurred right after the Ulm victory and the news, when it arrived, inevitably took some of the shine off Austerlitz. Talleyrand did his tactful best to deliver it without detracting from Napoleon's glory. His dispatch began: 'It gives me deep pain to send Your Majesty the sad news I have received from Cadiz on the situation of the combined fleet. Our genius and fortune were in Germany.'

Privately Talleyrand was far more deeply disturbed by Trafalgar than he let on. To Hauterive, his deputy, he expressed his full anguish. He wrote: 'What horrible news from Cadiz! Let us hope it won't sabotage any of the political operations I believe are now necessary. The first letters I have received are appalling. I fear that further details we learn will only make it more heart-breaking. I am worried by the destruction of the fleet and the impact this misfortune will have on opinion in our ports and among our sailors.'

Though he hadn't yet heard of Nelson's death at Trafalgar, the English hero's disappearance wouldn't much change things anyway. The significance of the showdown at sea seemed pretty clear to him: Napoleon could march and vanquish at the head of the Grand Army to his conquering heart's content, but final victory could not now be his. Final victory, whenever it came, was England's.

Napoleon was, of course, too dazzled by his successes for such gloomy clairvoyance. Placing Talleyrand's peace plan in a back pocket, he took the position that Austerlitz changed everything and that the conditions for peace could not be the same as they might have been before the battle. From victory flowed new rights, and a victor's rights had to be satisfied. This was his judgement in a battlefield note from Austerlitz addressed to Talleyrand, now camped in comparative comfort in Vienna. Napoleon's meaning seemed clear: he was rejecting the plan.

The House of Périgord withstood the blow. Talleyrand's self-belief, veiled as it was by his urge to flatter and compose, was the equal of Napoleon's. He wrote back, by return messenger:

> Sire,
> I delight in the idea that Your Majesty's latest success puts him in a position to ensure repose for Europe and to guarantee the civilised world against the invasions of barbarians.
> Your Majesty can now break the Austrian monarchy or lift it back up. Once broken, it would not be in Your Majesty's power to put back the shattered pieces and make it a single mass once more. Now the existence of this mass is vital. It is indispensable to the future safety of civilised nations. I dare tell Your Majesty that this is what all sincere admirers of his glory expect of his perspicacious policy and magnanimity . . .
> I implore Your Majesty to reread the project I had the honour of sending him from Strasbourg. Today more than ever I dare regard it as the best and the most salutary. Your Majesty's victories now make it easy to implement.

This showed courage on Talleyrand's part. Napoleon hated to be opposed and made people pay for it. He grew particularly agitated over constant carping at his imperial ambitions from the Left Bank salon crowd, the politically aware intelligentsia he disdainfully labelled the *Faubourg Saint Germain* – the Saint Germain district. Criticism from the vociferous Mme de Staël led to her police-enforced exile from Paris, which Napoleon calculated would hurt her most. One day Talleyrand caught the emperor stamping

on his tricorn in rage over some reported slight from a salon hostess, and
again it was all he could do not to laugh, contenting himself instead with
the mild taunt that stamping on a hat was absolutely pointless since the hat
couldn't feel a thing. But Talleyrand's reply this time was a step up on
Faubourg Saint Germain raillery. Here was Napoleon's chief minister telling
him to go back and redo his homework because he hadn't understood it. It
could not have escaped the emperor that Talleyrand was in deadly earnest
about his call for moderation.

In the circumstances, it was a mark of Napoleon's continuing favour for
Talleyrand that he took the warning in good spirit. Although he did not
intend to heed it, he only teasingly put its author in his place after Austerlitz,
telling him, 'M. de Talleyrand, now that I have won the battle, you are a
great minister.' A great minister, naturally enough, did what Napoleon said;
his task was to negotiate the armistice with Austria strictly along lines
Napoleon dictated. The fact that he entrusted this treaty to Talleyrand at all,
knowing his strong leanings, showed how disinclined he was to alienate him.

For his part, Talleyrand was indeed immutable over his policy but allowed
himself to fall back on his old conviction that if he couldn't make it stick
now he would do so further down the line. His was an ultimatum to the
extent that he was telling Napoleon that, if he didn't heed it, things would
go wrong – not to the extent that he would leave him should he fail to heed
it at once. If he thought of resigning at this point, there was no evidence
for it except perhaps in the glum tone of his correspondence. To stand down
from high office in the Napoleonic age was so rare as to beggar the thought.
When power was so absolute, ministers abandoned it only when dismissed.
Moreover, there was likely to be a high penalty to be paid for deserting
Napoleon.

There were other reasons for Talleyrand's sombre tone. Work on the
armistice took him to Austerlitz to consult with Napoleon. The scene tested
to the limit his belief in the civilisation he cared for. Several days after the
battle he witnessed 15,000 rotting corpses strewn over the ground or half
immersed in putrid ponds. In the zone he rode through he passed two thousand dead horses, their flanks torn by gunfire. Nothing, neither men nor
horses, had been cleared. He asked himself what he was doing amid such
carnage. 'What a day for the Foreign Minister of France!' he wrote to
Hauterive. His deputy sensed what he was getting at. He wrote back that
it would be a good thing if God were to take all the statesmen of the civilised
world by the hair and drag them through the Austerlitz corpses 'to teach
them the result of their vanity, ambition and folly'. This was seditious material coming from the heart of Napoleon's foreign ministry, but Hauterive
was sufficiently familiar with his superior to know that he wouldn't disagree.

In Brno, the Moravian town which Napoleon made his field headquarters, Talleyrand found his circumstances equally gruesome. The wounded from Austerlitz arrived there. Many thousands of them filled the town with their cries and the stench of their gangrenous wounds, dying in their tents. There was no food to sustain them. 'Yesterday the smell was unbearable,' he wrote to Hauterive. Fortunately it was winter. 'Today it is freezing, which is good news for everyone.'

None of this seemed to faze Napoleon. Talleyrand was astonished, and fascinated, to observe how well the warrior bore the misery around him. 'He is in marvellous form,' he wrote. 'The latest actions have made him a man of fable. There isn't a general in the army, not a single soldier who doesn't think and say that the Emperor won the great victory of Austerlitz all on his own. He ordered everything down to the last detail, and every order succeeded.' His observation, far from expressing horror for an ogre, was aglow with admiration for the man himself.

All the same, Talleyrand's visits to the front could not but further sour his views on the emperor's militarist vocation. What he saw was enough to make him seek a little more comfort than usual in his field wine cellar. From Brno he bade Hauterive send him a consignment of strong Spanish wine, urgently. His servants, he reported, had informed him that his travelling supplies were running low. This time he wasn't thirsting for Madeira; he wanted a vintage from Malaga, something 'very dry, the least sweet possible'.

Moving around on Napoleon's heels was both physically and emotionally demanding, especially in the depths of winter. Though Talleyrand's life wasn't conspicuously in danger, the violence around him was such that gossipmongers in Paris decided it was. A rumour in Paris that he had been killed by the tsar's Cossacks soon became firm news, causing shock and a certain amount of glee. Hearing of the mixed popular reaction, he asked Napoleon's brother Joseph to assure his wife Catherine that he was alive and well, noting, 'I have just learned of my death. My resurrection arrived in the same post.' In truth he spent as much time as he could in the calm of Vienna socialising with what was left of its beau monde, most of whose members had temporarily vacated the capital with Emperor Franz to evade the occupiers.

From Vienna he went to Pressburg (latterly Bratislava) further down the Danube to draw up the armistice with the defeated Habsburgs. Reaching Pressburg on 22 December was hard going, though the adventure gave him something of an explorer's lift. To enter the city he had to cross the river, which was half frozen over and full of treacherously running ice blocks. The Slovak boatmen to whom he entrusted himself and his precious armistice papers were reluctant to try the crossing; it looked too dangerous for their oars. Talleyrand persuaded them of the importance of his mission, arguing heroically: 'A negotiation for me is the day of battle for an army.' Then there was the harshness of Napoleon's armistice instructions to contend with. The emperor wanted a treaty that indeed humiliated Austria: Emperor Franz had to cede Venice to his Italian kingdom and yield substantial Habsburg domains to the lesser German states of Bavaria and Württemberg whose ducal rulers, in an additional poke at Franz, were to be elevated to the rank of kings under French protection. What was more, the instructions contained nothing about territorial compensation for Austria to the east. To stiffen the punishment further, Napoleon demanded heavy war indemnities.

Talleyrand was conscious of his powerlessness. Tucked into the initial treaty draft he had put to Napoleon with his peace plan were two articles in particular that drew an imperial scowl. Both resonated far beyond the treatment of the Habsburg monarchy. The first set the permanent continental frontier of France as the river Rhine, running from its mouth on the North Sea to Basel, then roughly the line of the Alps running south to the Mediterranean. Under this article, Napoleon was to pledge on behalf of himself and his successors never to expand France by acquiring territory lying beyond this 'natural frontier'. The second separated the crowns of France and Italy forever, stipulating that Napoleon would name a successor in Italy to be ratified by the rest of Europe. Little wonder that Talleyrand used such tact in first presenting this scheme to Napoleon: together, the two articles were meant to kill his dreams, to halt any ambition he had to recreate Charlemagne's Western Empire. This was what Talleyrand aimed to achieve in the name of a general European peace. That Napoleon rejected it, or simply ignored it, was hardly unexpected. If it acted as a subconscious brake, that was something. There was no longer much point in deluding himself that he could control Napoleon.

Needless to say, neither article appeared in the finished Pressburg treaty, which Talleyrand nonetheless contrived to sweeten up in Austria's favour. He reduced Napoleon's 100-million-franc demand for reparations by a good 10 per cent and made sure he clarified the text of the treaty to a point where there were no vagaries left for Napoleon to be able to interpret to his further advantage. The Austrians appreciated the favourable nuances insinuated into the text, and the government in Vienna released from state funds at that very moment the sum of 60,000 florins payable to 'a person whose name His Majesty [Franz] alone knows'. The intended destination was no doubt Talleyrand, though the Austrian foreign minister let it be known that his grand French counterpart refused to accept a sweetener on this occasion because he did not feel it right to do so. Some months later, when an astute young statesman by the name of Count Klemens von Metternich arrived in Paris as Austrian ambassador and delved into where its governing class stood with respect to Napoleon, he informed his masters in Vienna:

> From the campaign of 1805 [Austerlitz] onwards, M. de Talleyrand conceived a plan to oppose with all his influence as Foreign Minister the destructive projects undertaken by Napoleon. His influence has been secondary as regards the Emperor's policy but powerful as regards its day-to-day execution. We are positively in his debt for the more or less favourable nuances in the Pressburg negotiation.

Metternich, who knew Talleyrand from Pressburg and came to share confidences with him, was soon able to make out a split in France between two camps: the military camp, whose fortunes lay entirely with Napoleon, and a fretful civil camp – a burgeoning resistance – which sensed that the emperor was leading it down the road to ruin. At the head of this mute national camp Metternich placed both Talleyrand and the watchful Fouché, who was back in action as police minister after falling from grace and losing his post for a while prior to the dismal Enghien affair.

Napoleon was well aware of what transpired at Pressburg. Although he had virtually dictated the wording of the armistice, he didn't like its final tone. It seemed to him subverted somehow by Talleyrand's deftly placed commas. He chided him: 'You made me a treaty at Pressburg that displeases me greatly.' The rebuke sounded menacing, but the minister decided not to take it seriously. He accepted it, rather, as a tribute to his negotiating skills. He was never afraid of Napoleon, though he avoided provoking him deliberately; rather than take his lance in the midriff his habit was to step aside to let the point pass by.

Besides, Talleyrand was the one who felt the more affronted by the ratification of the armistice on New Year's Day 1806. It wasn't just what he regarded as the folly of keeping Austria down and out, and thus hostile, that dismayed him; it was Napoleon's growing propensity for operating diplomacy on his personal whim. His diplomatic freelancing, like his sword, was putting all Europe on edge. He tossed states around like so many stray marbles. While Pressburg was still in negotiation, he handed the German state of Hanover to Prussia. This was done to retain King Friedrich Wilhelm's sympathies, but since Hanover was actually an English possession occupied by the French the main effect of its handover was to sharpen England's belligerence. At the same time he summarily dispossessed minor rulers in the south of Italy, which by now his forces had overrun, papal states included, and enthroned his older brother Joseph as King of Naples. Louis, a younger brother, he made King of Holland. Napoleon's dynastic urge as emperor was to convert the states in his grasp into kingdoms under his brothers or under his sisters' husbands. Talleyrand was aghast, he later recalled, at 'everything that was impolitic and destructive in this manner of overthrowing governments to create others which he wasn't long in toppling once more, and that in every corner of Europe'.

For the time being, however, he was amused if not delighted with a bauble which Napoleon lofted his way. He was made sovereign prince of the papal statelet of Benevento, a rugged domain near Rome which Napoleonic forces had aimlessly taken in charge. Whether Napoleon's first purpose was to reward Talleyrand for his sterling services, as he professed, or to tie him to his side in Ruritanian fealty wasn't clear. No doubt it was both. The comic opera side of it all wasn't lost on Talleyrand. Life in impoverished Benevento hadn't changed much since medieval times. Besides landing in his lap as a result of imperial larceny, it had a population of barely forty thousand and promised him an income only a fraction of that brought in by Valençay. Also it fell upon him to tell the pope he must relinquish it with good grace, which poor Pius was palpably unable to muster. Still, prince was a nice title – as long as people didn't think he needed it to be grand. Indeed, the pride of the Périgords soon grew impatient and a little stiff with those who relentlessly called him Highness in public and overdid it. The memory of the ridicule he'd felt for Cambacérès over just such a matter still lingered. 'Don't call me Highness,' he chided an overweening official in his company. 'I am less and perhaps more than that. Call me quite simply M. de Talleyrand.'

Whatever humour might be attached to Benevento, the title of prince was the most precious gift he was able to make to his abandoned wife Catherine, and the last of note. To be addressed as Princess – or better still as Serene Highness, which was now her formal due in the tossed velvet of the Napoleonic order – caused her no qualms. It was all she sought. She stepped up her hostessing activities in Paris even when Talleyrand wasn't present, signing her invitations 'Sovereign Princess de Talleyrand' or, when in still loftier mood, 'Reigning Princess of Benevento'. It delivered a good flow of guests, though not always an added hunger for her company. A princess of the old school she now felt en-titled to claim as a friend wrote in her diary: 'There she was, seeking some dire friendship between us, for friendship with Mme de Talleyrand was a calamity. She regularly came visiting twice a week, in the morning to see me alone and in the evening out of courtesy, she said, and always succeeded in annoying me, though I couldn't tell her so and she didn't see it. I escaped her when I could by running to M. de Talleyrand where I was sure she wouldn't pursue me because she was afraid of him and no longer loved him.' The latter feeling, the diarist might have added, was mutual. But it did not bother Talleyrand enough to make him do anything about it.

Up to a point he took his princely charge seriously. A first move was to install his own civil administrator in place of a French military commander who had stepped in as governor of Benevento. He instructed his man: 'Assure the inhabitants of all the pains I shall take for their wellbeing. If my sovereignty is of value to me, it is in the hope and desire that my power shall be beloved of its citizens.' Talleyrand showed his interest by making Benevento a mini-laboratory for his liberal social outlook. He instituted free primary education for the boys and girls of the principality in line with a project he had pressed at the start of the French Revolution but failed to push through. Benevento became perhaps the sole spot in Europe with universal free education. The schooling of girls, he held, was the surest way to provide society with decent manners at all levels. The meagre princely revenues that came his way he reinvested in his state's upkeep. For although it was a mere enclave in the kingdom of Naples, the throne now occupied by Napoleon's brother Joseph, there were practical needs to cater to. In its one township he provided a new public water fountain and had a disabled existing fountain repaired along with an ancient triumphal arch built by the Emperor Trajan; he also created a botanical gardens and a public library. To the citizens, though, he remained a phantom sovereign. His attachment was real but distant. Never once in his life did he set foot in Benevento.

Part of the problem during 1806 was that Talleyrand had dozens, scores even, of similarly tiny states to attend to on Napoleon's account. This was the time that the Confederation of the Rhine took more or less final form under Napoleon's protection and there was nothing for it but to join him in tossing the marbles around. The south German union was that centre-board of the empire conceived as a buffer against those larger powers – Prussia, Austria and ultimately Russia – which Napoleon could bully or defeat but not in all sanity seek to bring under his personal rule. Talleyrand worked on adding bits here and subtracting bits there, down to the minutest detail. He threw the marbles with an accountant's twist, specifying where they landed for the emperor. Thus his balance sheet for the month of August 1806:

Prussia to cede (souls):
Neuchâtel (47,000)
Cleves, with Essen (75,000)
Anspach (240,000)

Prussia to obtain (souls):
Anhalt (152,000)
Lippe (95,000)
Waldeck (82,000)
Pyrmont (6000)
Rottberg (18,000)
Hohenlimberg-Rheda (13,000)
Scharen (1000)

Total souls lost: 362,000

Total souls gained: 367,000

While the emphasis on souls maintained something of the human touch, the accountant's approach wasn't inappropriate, for this was too good an occasion to miss to take further *douceurs* from princes, dukes and bishops anxious to hold on to their lands or at least to obtain proper compensation. Moreover, he was able to do the sums in good diplomatic faith. The confederation coincided with his overall view: it made some sense of middle Europe's hopeless crazy paving.

It was a sideshow, however, when set against the new opportunity to break the deadlock of conflict with England that appeared to present itself with the untimely death of William Pitt. The man who took charge of English policy in his place was none other than Talleyrand's liberal acquaintance from his exile in London, the Whig statesman Charles James Fox. While Pitt could never have contemplated coming to terms with Napoleon, the good-natured Fox, who had supported the French Revolution and opposed English intervention, held more conciliatory views. Though he too was shocked by Napoleon's imperialist swagger, he wrote to Talleyrand soon after taking office in the early spring of 1806 to inform him of a fresh assassination plot against Napoleon just uncovered in London. Seeing an opening, Talleyrand seized on Fox's gesture to propose a new round of discussions with the English government and rallied Napoleon, as he thought, behind the initiative. Fox, five years Talleyrand's senior, helped him in this by maintaining a flexible stance and designating a pair of lords with known French sympathies to negotiate – the first of them, Lord Yarmouth, as keen a card player and dauntless a night owl as Talleyrand. To bowl things along, Fox told Talleyrand he was the one man in Europe he would personally want to partner in 'so fine and great a cause'. For his part, Talleyrand whispered in the ear of every ambassador he met that, in the absence of peace with England, Napoleon was headed for a series of military victories that were likely to add up to nothing in the end.

For a time the emperor seemed to enter the spirit of their endeavour, deciding to pander to the English by revoking his promise to give Hanover to Prussia's king. 'Prussia received Hanover out of fear and will yield it out of fear,' he declared publicly, not bothering to mask his disdain for the king whose support he supposedly wanted. In reality, though, Napoleon never had much faith in the negotiations. Talleyrand's constant urgings perhaps encouraged his hesitation. He suspected his chief minister of deceiving him as regards England – or of being quite ready to do so – and he did not intend to fall for it. In his eyes, Talleyrand was perched on his familiar hobbyhorse, preaching the need for a trade pact with England to underpin peace. Napoleon wasn't about to abandon his continental designs to that vision.

On the contrary, he was on the point of hitting England with a trade blockade to punish her for raising foreign armies against him. This was a secret about which he had barely informed Talleyrand, knowing his feelings on such matters. The blockade he was about to activate wasn't a classic one: it would have been absurd to declare a blockade of the British Isles now that the disaster at Trafalgar had robbed him of the remnants of a navy, for the reverse was only too evident: the English navy was already blockading his French ports unhindered. His answer was to block the sale of English goods throughout the European continent and the sale of all European goods to England. The dual boycott enforced by this 'Continental System' would starve England of oxygen and leave it for dead; its success was ensured, he believed, by the reach of his military dominance in Europe.

The contradictions that infested Talleyrand's peace initiative were therefore pointing to an unsuccessful outcome even before a second famous English death effectively closed the bargaining which the first made possible. After Pitt, Fox too died. With Fox's passing in September the negotiations petered out in failure. The Hanover issue was left hanging, though it so rankled with Prussia that Friedrich Wilhelm understood that war with France was imminent. At heart the English showed no deeper a desire for accommodation with Napoleon than he with them.

England, Talleyrand saw, was somehow fearful of peace. In peacetime she had no leverage over Napoleon; in time of war she could look to all other continental powers as potential allies against him.

ELEVEN

The Quartermaster's Two-step

Talleyrand was walking an increasingly thin line between the pursuit of his principles and the desire to hold on to the munificent blessings that fell to him from Napoleon's rule. The blessings weren't only material. Due to his intimacy with Napoleon, he was the queen bee around whom Europe's statesmen bumped and fluttered. Foreign sovereigns and envoys fought at his door for the chance of a brief interview. Access to his office became well-nigh impossible, not because he was averse to seeing people – his invitations to discussions during his morning toilette showed that he was more than ready to share his thoughts – but because there were simply too many seekers. At receptions he only had to linger with an ambassador a moment longer than courtesy required for the joyful recipient of his attentions to consider he'd received an important political favour worth writing an encoded report home about. To be the centre of such pressing interest was, of course, gratifying. Everyone wanted hints on what the emperor was preparing next.

The line Napoleon walked with Talleyrand was no less thin. While continuing to nourish his minister with imperial benefits, spending hours talking things over with him in private and employing his negotiating skills, he also turned increasingly suspicious and at times nasty. His notes to Talleyrand betrayed the change. No sooner had the dalliance with Fox begun than the emperor called him to task, criticising his work as 'irregular'. From now on he wanted to read each day all the letters Talleyrand received from ambassadors and French agents abroad himself. Talleyrand's personal daily rundown on such things would not suffice. That went for translations of the English and foreign press too. 'I shall send you a portfolio for this purpose and hold the key myself. This arrangement will commence tomorrow,' Napoleon wrote. Soon after, he followed that up with another stinging rebuke: 'In truth I cannot understand your working method. You want to do things on your own and you don't bother to read things and weigh the words. Bring me your explanation this evening.' Coming from

Napoleon this was hard to swallow. If anyone made a habit of weighing his words it was Talleyrand. Wasn't his speciality the *mot juste*?

Napoleon's harsh tone also betrayed his suspicions that Talleyrand was too close to some of the foreign ambassadors who knocked at his door. Metternich's predecessor as envoy of the Habsburg court, who happened to be an old schoolfriend of Talleyrand from Harcourt, was adjudged by the emperor to be an odious man who sent hateful reports home. Napoleon warned Talleyrand: 'I believe it necessary to keep a watch on you so that you remain careful in your communications with him and are no longer duped by his false bonhomie.' With the Prussian ambassador he was warned to be more careful still: 'I have long made my mind up about this wretch. He has constantly deceived you, because I have long known that there is nothing easier than to deceive you.' What was more, it hadn't escaped Talleyrand that the emperor was tracking his private correspondence. He had as good as told him so. Napoleon's postal authorities, assisted by Fouché's police, routinely opened mail to and from political figures the emperor distrusted, and Talleyrand was high on the list. To amuse himself, the victim took to tweaking the postal spies' noses, inserting wry warnings to his private addressees that they might not be the first to read his words.

The relationship between Napoleon and his chief minister was becoming a very peculiar tangle indeed. The emperor's way of showing Talleyrand he was one of the two people he loved most could scarcely have been more contradictory. He seemed intent on spoiling him only for the perverse satisfaction of cutting him down to size. The interests of France that Talleyrand thought he carried within him and the goals of Napoleon's conduct were diverging by the day.

During the testing times of 1806, which culminated in Napoleon marching on Prussia and thence against Tsar Alexander's Russian armies, something in Talleyrand snapped: he decided he had to resign as foreign minister. Not at once, but when the time was right. His personal rule – never to do in a hurry today what was done to better purpose tomorrow – continued to guide him. Besides, he still wasn't underestimating the risks involved in resignation. He was in danger of losing everything if Napoleon regarded his departure as betrayal. That and plain regard for personal safety dissuaded all those of high imperial rank from attempting it. 'It was not as easy as one might think to cease active functions with him,' Talleyrand wrote.

Nonetheless, his decision crystallised in the autumn of that year when, under imperial summons, he was once more called upon to accompany Napoleon on the path of war, this time to Berlin and Warsaw. 'I swore inwardly,' he later recalled, 'that whatever the price there was to pay, I would cease to be his minister – and that, as soon as we returned to France.' For it was hard to maintain much optimism over the worth of his office: his peace plan was ignored, his hopes for accommodation with England dashed. On top of that Napoleon's adventurism was unstoppable. The emperor and his valorous marshals looked invincible.

Considering his frame of mind, Talleyrand attended to Napoleon with something apparently approaching his old goodwill during the devastating campaign against Prussia. The reason that Prussia came off the fence and into England's alliance against Napoleon lay in the calculation that the Emperor of the French was intent on crushing her however she conducted herself. Purportedly for the sake of economy, he had left the Grand Army grazing on German soil after defeating the Austrians. His humiliating game with Hanover and the completion of the south German confederation, an extreme annoyance for Prussia, further combined to convince King Friedrich Wilhelm in Berlin he had better re-arm quickly. The country retained some of the pride instilled by Frederick the Great's bygone martial successes and it certainly still held itself in higher esteem than Napoleon did. This led Prussia to issue him with a rash ultimatum to pull French troops back to their side of the Rhine by the autumn, with 8 October set as the deadline.

Within six days of that ignored deadline, Napoleon, with a larger army at his disposal, obliterated Prussian forces at Jena. Friedrich Wilhelm fled to the tsar's side in St Petersburg for safety, pursued by punishing decrees issued by Napoleon: Prussia would forfeit all her territory lying between the Rhine and the Elbe and pay indemnities that dwarfed even those recently demanded of the Habsburgs. The lands taken from Prussia were moulded with part of Hanover to form the new kingdom of Westphalia, the throne of which Napoleon gave to another younger brother, Jerome. Talleyrand took a sardonic view of the gathering number of Bonaparte kingdoms: since becoming an emperor, he noted, Napoleon evidently wanted no republics around him. The whole of Germanic Europe apart from the rump of Prussia and diminished Austria now entered the Napoleonic empire.

To keep up with the emperor, as he was obliged to do, Talleyrand at first installed himself at Mainz on the Rhine. It was here that he received news of the victory to the east at Jena. He wrote to the conqueror:

Sire,
While Your Majesty has long since accustomed us to prodigies and while the successes that signalled the opening of the campaign assuredly prom-ised greater successes, I would not have dared hope that they could promptly result in so great and complete a victory. I feared – this was

the opinion on this side of Germany – that the enemy would contrive to avoid a general engagement and force Your Majesty to pursue it to the furthest extremes of Germany. If that was their purpose, then Your Majesty's spirit and genius spoiled it. Your Majesty has long since exhausted all admiration; our love and gratitude alone are inexhaustible. Today our deepest wishes are to see an end to dangers which Your Majesty's faithful servants find all the more alarming in that Your Majesty himself treats them as nothing.

For all their arch flattery, these congratulations barely registered his familiar call for a halt to warring. He was tired of tiring Napoleon with his imprecations. Instead, the tribute sighed with irony. From Paris his deputy Hauterive read his real thoughts. In confidential correspondence with his chief, Hauterive concluded that Napoleon was condemned to wage battle after battle without end, for to stop was as good as to step back, and once the coalition made him step back his empire was finished.

It was just as well that Talleyrand's ministry correspondence came by house courier, dodging postal spies. He had a phrase for what Hauterive was trying to tell him: 'You can do everything with bayonets except sit on them.'

From Mainz Talleyrand continued to Berlin, the Prussian capital, now occupied by French troops. He saw little of Napoleon who was driving deep into Polish lands to engage with Tsar Alexander's forces and bring Russia to heel. They kept in touch through messengers. In Berlin, life for Talleyrand was easier than it had been during most of his first field trip. He had a large entourage this time: four diplomatic underlings, his translator, his copyist, the indispensable Courtiade, a pair of chefs and a platoon of servants. He moved into the grand home on Unter den Linden of a prominent Prussian statesman who left town before the Grand Army marched through. There he held court, the queen bee flown from Paris to Berlin. The sovereign princes and dukes of Germany crowded at his door to verify where the victory at Jena left them, and he played his part with grave interest.

Holding constant court was physically wearing. The representative of Weimar, who waited for five hours in a high state of nerves to see him, reported: 'The door at last opened on an old gentleman of medium size, rather well set, dressed in a French embroidered habit, with powdered hair and a pronounced limp. His pale countenance, immobile with no distinctive feature, struck me as being a thick veil stretched over his soul. His small grey eyes showed not the slightest expression, but a light smile, half serious, half ironic, played at his mouth.' At fifty-two, the last signs of youth seemed to have deserted Talleyrand. He rested his bad leg across a chair when listening, occasionally bending it with some effort as if to hold off numbness.

There was nothing to invigorate him in Napoleon's formal promulgation from Berlin in November of his Continental System. Talleyrand lent it tortured support in spite of the fact that it went against all his economic preferences. His backing, contained in a report to the emperor, was based purely on the proposition that England, through dominance of the seas, had been blockading enemies long enough to deserve a vigorous response that might just make her mend her ways. He took this position 'with regret', and he knew, he added obliquely, that Napoleon too was acting with regret.

Regret was in fact the last thing to intrude on the emperor's thinking: he aimed to protect French industry from English competition; if he couldn't beat the 'oceanocrats' at sea he would beat them on land. He would close off England to trade with all of Europe. His Continental System would make his entire empire the commercial preserve of French industry, and other parts of his realm would supply French industry with the materials it required.

The extreme awkwardness Talleyrand experienced in arguing for such a system showed in his lame logic. Worse, he was pretty sure it would back-fire, which it did, though not without bothering England greatly. For a time English exports plunged, hitting the wool and cotton industries partic-ularly hard, and the crisis was deepened by a new split with the United States. Napoleon was soon crowing: 'England has fallen victim to her own cruel cause. Her goods are repelled by the whole of Europe, her vessels loaded with useless riches wander the vast seas they presumed to rule, seeking in vain an open port from the straits of Sund to the Hellespont.' His colourful canvas of an England thwarted from the Baltic to the caressing Ionian was no little overpainted. For the blockade bothered the French nation fully as much as it did the English. Desirable everyday items that came from afar found no easy way through to the French: coffee, tea and sugar went off their menu. The main beneficiaries of the blockade were French profiteers. Aside from putting familiar merchandise out of the average Frenchman's price range, it forced Napoleon's own quartermasters to find ways to circumvent it. It was soon apparent that the Grand Army couldn't take the field in winter without heavy woollen overcoats and leather boots of the kind English factories alone fabricated in volume. In sum the blockade leaked like a sieve, often at the behest of Napoleon's intimates. His brother Louis, King of Holland, was driven by his trade-hungry subjects to grant special licences to Dutch cargo vessels to ply to London with Dutch goods, and his army commander in Portugal gave similar dispensa-tion to Portuguese vessels.

There was a further dire result of the Continental System, no less far-reaching for being indirect. Spain, though beholden to Napoleon under its cringing Bourbon monarchy, at first elected not to join in. To Spain the blockade looked like economic madness promising hunger and ruin. Napoleon was livid at Spain's unforeseen effrontery, which threatened to leave a hole in his scheme. All of continental Europe was lined up to squeeze the life out of England except for Spain. Receiving news of the defection while in Berlin, Napoleon added a country to his list of targets for conquest: he vowed there and then to destroy the Spanish Bourbons. Talleyrand shuddered. Once Napoleon made a vow like that he had an unfortunate habit of keeping it, and it made no difference that the government in Madrid at length submitted to joining the blockade.

Life gained in appeal for Talleyrand, however, when he caught up with Napoleon in Warsaw during Christmas 1806. Elegant women swayed back into his orbit. The Polish aristocracy continued to live in grand style and was none too unhappy to receive the conquering army. For wasn't Napoleon now teaching a lesson to the same three autocratic powers – Prussia, Russia and Austria – which had carved up their country between them thirty years earlier, erasing it in progressive treaties from the map? At this stage Poland was a phantom country, but Napoleon seemed to want to restore it to life, announcing: 'It is in the interests of France and in the interests of Europe that Poland should exist.'

The Polish welcome was such that Talleyrand was able to take up residence in a palace belonging to the Radziwill family, the cream of Warsaw society. It was his home for the next four months; its comforts helped compensate for his not wanting to be in muddy, ill lit Warsaw at all. Though the Polish capital was an incoherent mix of grand mansions and squalid shanties, its stylish parts were as stylish as anywhere in Europe. The Radziwills were the most prominent family in Poland, or certainly regarded themselves as such, and furnished their nation with high-calibre statesmen, soldiers and churchmen as routinely as the Périgords did in France.

Since the biting cold of January was a bad time to make war in Europe's eastern reaches, Napoleon called a brief seasonal break, bidding Talleyrand change out of his itinerant diplomat's attire into the festive velvet of Imperial Grand Chamberlain. He wanted to be introduced to Warsaw society, which he heard was in awe of him and saw him as a liberator. It seemed the right moment to capitalise on his minister's talents for entertaining. Talleyrand was just the man to organise a grand ball. As requested, the Grand Chamberlain went about it with his usual keen regard for the guest list, inviting the noble beauties of Warsaw to parade before the expectant emperor.

To assemble them, he was able to count on a redoubtable local hostess, Maria-Theresa Tiskiewicz, a niece of Poland's last king. Talleyrand couldn't help noticing that Princess Tiskiewicz, in the short time he'd been in Warsaw, appeared to have become besotted by him – 'enslaved', her family observed. For a socialite from the east he had much allure despite his increasingly painful limp: calm, superior, self-assured, wearing the far-off elegance of Paris, he came as guide to the liberator. He had met the princess previously in the Paris salon world and was struck, as many were, by her glass eye, a sharpish accoutrement to her wit. She was far from beautiful herself in her middle years but she knew whom to trot before Napoleon.

It had often occurred to Talleyrand that the emperor was 'unamusable', which led him to think that a love interest, a mistress say, might make him a little more human and take his mind off war. Who could tell? It might give him an altogether more tranquil outlook. He was now a long way from his marital bed in the Tuileries Palace and the Empress Josephine had already proved that she wasn't beyond flaunting herself in his absence. It was a pity, Talleyrand thought, that the warrior didn't seem to need love or even find it a pleasure. In that respect the glittering mid-January ball held at Talleyrand's residence in the Radziwill palace was encouraging. The Grand Chamberlain gave it a theatrical sendoff. Once the hundreds of guests were gathered in the ballroom he had servants rattle and bang its doors for quiet, then stepped slowly into their tremulous midst uttering the magic words 'The Emperor'.

Napoleon's gaze fastened on a pretty young countess named Maria Walewska. He asked her to dance, then danced with her again, an uncommon exercise for Napoleon who had small confidence in his ballroom graces. Talleyrand, with the aid of Princess Tiskiewicz, had made sure that Maria Walewska was present because he'd heard that the emperor had noticed her some days before in her carriage in the street and had asked after her. She was twenty, the daughter of a Polish noble who died in battle trying to save the country from being devoured by Russian and Prussian forces. She also had a seventy-year-old husband who never went out. Napoleon left the ball exclaiming, 'What pretty women they are!' The very next day he wrote Maria Walewska a panting love note and took her as his mistress. He was enchanted by her girlish nationalism and the gratitude she showed him for being her country's liberator. The affair endured through the campaign against Russia and long beyond, though the physical pleasure did little for his gallantry. He told an imperial courtier, 'Talleyrand procured her for me. She did not put up a fight.' He knew from the past he could rely on Talleyrand to fill a ballroom with comely women, noting appreciatively: 'He always had his pockets full of women.'

Talleyrand's own partnership with Princess Tiskiewicz also prospered. She followed him back to Paris and became a fixture in his ageing harem of salon countesses, with a room permanently reserved for her at Valençay. The appeal of Warsaw stretched to Talleyrand's own family ties. Charles, his son with Adelaïde de Flahaut, turned up in Poland with the Grand Army, as did his two nephews Louis and Edmond de Périgord, his brother Archambaud's sons. The three of them were cavalry officers, stripling veterans of Austerlitz and of Jena. Talleyrand looked out for them, seeking to advance their military careers and their prospects for good marriages. Charles de Flahaut, now twenty-two, was in line to become deputy to one of Napoleon's most successful marshals, Prince Murat, and his attentive father intervened with Murat to promote him.

Charles was never far from Talleyrand's mind, though fate – partly in the shape of Adelaïde's marriage to her Portuguese diplomat – had often kept them apart. He had stayed on at boarding school in England long after Talleyrand's expulsion by Pitt, suffered the incessant jibes of his English classmates, brooded over the guillotining of his legal father, the Comte de Flahaut, then joined his mother as an émigré in Germany before entering the French army. In the age of Napoleon a young officer spent very little time on home soil. Talleyrand saw him when he could. He loved his bastard son, and the physical risks Charles now faced with the Grand Army in the war against the Russians only increased the affection. 'You are one of the first interests in my life, and when I say that, I'm talking of just two or three,' he told him in an emotional little note from Warsaw. 'I embrace you and press you to my heart.' He added, not wishing to burden him, 'If you can put your hands on a scrap of paper please write to tell me how you are getting on and if there is anything you want.'

Charles had dash and charm. He was well introduced and his father was confident he would succeed without the added advantage of the Talleyrand-Périgord name. For his nephews Louis and Edmond, less impressive characters both, marriage prospects were the priority. After all, theirs was the responsibility to continue the Périgord line. Phantom Poland hardly seemed the place to promote such concerns, yet now it made an impromptu intervention.

Talleyrand's presence in Warsaw gave him *de facto* charge of a reborn Poland Napoleon was intent on creating from Polish lands belonging to defeated Prussia. A Polish aristocrat involved in setting up the new state, the Duchy of Warsaw, dined with him each evening to move things along, taking time off over wine from Talleyrand's field cellar to rake over the marriage field in this part of Europe. The Pole's excellent rundown made it look more fertile than a Parisian grandee could have imagined. He told

Talleyrand in his prime, lord of statesmen.

(*Above*) Talleyrand aged sixteen,
a reluctant seminarian.

(*Above right*) A lifelong pain:
Talleyrand's corrective shoe.

Talleyrand the courtier,
a wry participant (*bottom right*)
at Napoleon's coronation.

Napoleon in his imperial best.

Napoleon with invasion sights
on England (1803).

Napoleon in full
command, a man
not to fool with.

Joseph Fouché,
the bloodhound;
Talleyrand's
rival, sometime
partner.

Mme de Flahaut, Talleyrand's difficult
mistress, with baby Charles, their son.

Gouverneur Morris, Talleyrand's
fellow hobbler and rival in love.

Valençay, a country home fit for kings.

Authoress Mme de Staël,
his busybody saviour.

Wife-to-be Catherine Grand,
a costly *coup de foudre*.

Duchess Dorothea of Kurland,
soulmate of impeccable pedigree.

Dorothy, Duchesse de Dino,
his muse and adoring companion.

The Congress of Vienna: Talleyrand *(sitting, second from right)* reshapes Europe.

Napoleon in the jaws of defeat (1814).

Louis XVIII, a king shakily restored.

Prince Metternich,
ingenious fellow schemer.

Tsar Alexander I,
monarch absolute.

The Duke of Wellington,
the sword that slew Napoleon.

Lord Castlereagh,
a heavy-hearted English accomplice.

National grouch: Talleyrand nearing eighty.

of a beautiful ex-mistress of his, the Duchess of Kurland, one of the richest landowners in the east, and the mention of her four daughters caught Talleyrand's fancy.

Kurland was a small Baltic state bordering Latvia which seemed to share the sovereign traditions of the Périgords in France; its ruling family was descended from medieval lords, in this case the Teutonic Knights. Though her land was now under the Russian tsar's protection, the widowed duchess, who was approaching fifty, retained her properties and sovereign revenues. She also owned castle estates to the west, in Germany and Bohemia. The youngest of the four daughters, Dorothy, was just approaching marriageable age. The contract that began to take shape in Talleyrand's mind proved agreeably skewed: it changed the life of the uncle who arranged it far more than the career of the nephew whose name appeared on it.

Back-stopping Napoleon on his lightning military campaigns involved more than social entertainment. The warrior chose not to wait for the worst of winter to pass before engaging the Russian army at Eylau, near the Baltic coast in the Prussian north of Poland. The battle of Eylau on 8 February 1807 was fought in a blinding snowstorm which served to obscure its appalling bloodshed, for the result was a standoff recognised by both sides. This was a definite setback for Napoleon, nicely recorded by Talleyrand as a battle that was 'won a little'. The emperor decided there was nothing for it but to pursue the tsar's forces for a rematch as they pulled back further east, though this time he was content to wait for the spring.

The demands placed on Talleyrand at his seat in Warsaw were as exacting as any made on a quartermaster general. Out in the frozen field, Napoleon was continually frustrated by shortages of supplies. His men were hungry and cold and in desperation he put Talleyrand in charge of getting food and warm clothes to the Grand Army. Without shedding his diplomat's attire, he contrived to beat impassable Polish roads and waterways with steady shipments of brandy, beer, flower and fur to the front. 'Do miracles!' Napoleon exhorted him a week or so after Eylau. 'If I have bread, beating the Russians is child's play. What I am asking for is more important than all the negotiations in the world.' The Grand Chamberlain rushed the required foodstuffs in from more bountiful spots far west and south of Warsaw. The emperor was thankful, and impressed. Soon after he wrote: 'I have seen all your exploits to procure food supplies. It is very well done.'

Supplies were not all he had to commend him for. Talleyrand sent him contingents of Polish troops under the command of Polish noblemen to replenish Grand Army ranks. It was not to Talleyrand's taste to be quite so close to war, but he acquitted himself as though it were. He made it his duty to do the rounds of Warsaw hospitals to distribute the usual imperial gratuities to Grand Army wounded: one gold napoleon piece to ordinary soldiers, five gold pieces to officers. He listened to their grouses and personal requests and tried to satisfy them, though it was hard on such missions to live up to Napoleon who had a real bond with his men and addressed lowly soldiers by the matey *tu*. Still, he was rather pleased with the way he handled the mercy chore and reported to Napoleon that he left the wounded happy in their hospital cots.

By early summer a refreshed Napoleon engaged the tsar's army again and on 14 June scored a decisive victory at Friedland, close to the Baltic redoubt of Königsberg. Defeat forced the exhausted Tsar Alexander to sue for negotiations. Thus in mid-1807, with Russia giving up the fight, the entire continent of Europe was under Napoleon's sway, either incorporated into his empire or as subject ally or vassal. Only England on her island lay outside his control. It was the apogee of his power, a time that Frenchmen, dazed by glory, saw as a golden age – an age to breed nostalgia for decades to come.

Why Talleyrand went to such lengths to assist Napoleon in his famous victory at Friedland was a question that surely ate at the minister himself. He wasn't good at shrugging off the emperor's demands; he was quite ready to sit on them, but not to ignore them. His courage was all in putting a brake on Napoleon, not in direct confrontation. Then there was the situation of those scores of thousands of hard-driven Frenchmen at the front line to think of. Conscripts from Italy, Germany and now Poland swelled the Grand Army's ranks, but the French were still its core. All the same his sterling work as quartermaster and as *de facto* governor of 'liberated' Poland earned him the right, he felt, to make Napoleon dwell on where his endless passion for battle was leading. He was in Danzig, inspecting the Baltic port for supply purposes, when he received hard news of the outcome at Friedland. It had the oddest effect, steeling him more than it cheered him. He sat down and wrote to the emperor:

Sire,
I am at last learning some details of the battle at Friedland, and I know enough at present to see that it counts among those famous victories whose memory will live forever in history. But it is not only in terms of glory that I like to regard it; I like to see it as a forerunner and guarantee of peace, as a turning that grants Your Majesty the repose he offers his peoples at the cost of such struggles, privations and dangers. I wish to see it as the last he is forced to win. That is why it is so dear to me, for beautiful as it is I must confess it would

lose more than I can say in my eyes if Your Majesty were to march on to new battles and expose himself to new perils, the prospect of which particularly alarms me in light of Your Majesty's very disdain for them.

This was as straight as he could possibly be with the emperor without abandoning his unshakeable courtesy and deference. Coming from the chief minister, it showed spunk and no little gall. Talleyrand was telling him, through only the thinnest veil of irony: in the name of God, stop. It wasn't the sort of recommendation to please a man drunk once more on martial triumph. Certainly he was tired of tiring Napoleon with advice that never penetrated, but at this stage, with the whole of Europe in submission, Talleyrand had good reason to hark back to his starting position on imperial warmongering: to take 'freedom' to other countries by conquest was the surest way to make freedom hated and to prevent it from taking hold.

It wasn't Russia he was concerned about. His idiosyncratic view of Russia was that it was inherently barbaric; Russia needed keeping away from *his* Europe, out on the eastern fringe tussling with the Ottomans. Russia was outside his orbit of civilisation, which turned on Paris, London and Vienna. So the tsar's defeat was nothing tragic in itself. It was the culture of war carried to new excess by Napoleon that ruined everything for Europe. It was true that the emperor wasn't a cruel man and that he vaguely wished to free nations he conquered, to endow them with equality and justice. But that wasn't the effect his bellicose adventures had. Even as Talleyrand sealed his barbed congratulations on Friedland, he lamented to a diplomatic accomplice, 'Hasn't Europe been through enough misfortune! Where has common sense gone?'

Throughout his stay in Warsaw he led a double life, mixing his urgent responsibilities towards the emperor with secret efforts to refloat the Austrian Empire as the power in central Europe. Alliance with Austria remained the fundament of his own strategy: it was where peace with England had to begin. An opening in this direction came with the assignment to Warsaw of a special ambassador from the subdued Emperor Franz in Vienna. Franz, after all, had a direct interest in Napoleon's plans for Poland since its southern arc was part of the Austrian Empire. He wanted someone permanently at Talleyrand's side to watch over his vulnerable domain. Who better to nurture than the man effectively in charge of the newborn Duchy of Warsaw!

Franz's special envoy, Baron Alexander Vincent, a Habsburg general of partly French background and a veteran of the Austrian embassy in Paris, was well received by Talleyrand. He discussed in confidence with Vincent how to promote Austria's interests and, astonishingly, soon let him into a plan he proposed to activate in the event of Napoleon's death. For caring as his letters were, he could also be very clear-sighted about Napoleon. Yes, he would grieve if the emperor were killed in battle. Through everything, however dangerous and foolish he found his adventurism, his personal bond with the impetuous warrior survived, scarred but intact. But more important, there was the problem of what France would become if he died. Napoleon believed he was protected by good luck. Yet for a commander who prided himself on always being in the thick of the action, trust in luck was thin insurance against cannon fire or the slash of a loose sabre.

Talleyrand now made sure the Austrians knew precisely what he would do if the luck changed. He would have Napoleon's pliable older brother Joseph enthroned as emperor, secure his recognition by the Austrians, at once conclude an alliance with them and together launch negotiations for a Europe-wide peace including England. To promote such negotiations, imperial France would withdraw to its 'natural frontiers' of the Rhine and the southern Alps. Between outlining such a scenario and willing it to happen there was, in Austrian eyes, only the shortest of steps. So from the time of his stay in Warsaw Talleyrand was seen by the defensive Habsburg court as something more than a helping hand: he was a bona fide accomplice against Napoleon.

No doubt Talleyrand did not see himself, at this stage, as an enemy of the emperor he served. It was easier for others, though, to see him as he was. A metamorphosis had occurred. He assured Napoleon that he was always on his guard when dealing with Vincent and that while he received many confidences he gave none away. Vincent reported things otherwise. He portrayed Talleyrand to Vienna as a man struggling to promote an alliance with Austria against 'the violent, irascible character of the emperor'.

By now the shrewd Metternich was installed in Paris, eager to do business with Talleyrand as soon as he returned from Warsaw. While cautious, Metternich offered a similar portrayal: 'Men such as M. de Talleyrand are like sharp instruments it is dangerous to play with. But great wounds require great remedies. He who treats them must not fear to use the instrument that cuts the best.'

It was time for Talleyrand to carry out his decision to resign. He had spent ten years in a post that grew more invidious with every battle Napoleon won.

TWELVE

Disgrace

Talleyrand resigned as foreign minister on 9 August 1807, having informed Napoleon of his decision on their return to Paris from the bounds of Russia. The trick was to carry off the resignation in such a way as to leave his imperial rank and stipends untouched as well as to retain leverage over affairs of state, and it appeared to work better than he'd expected.

In a brief but fond confirmation of his departure addressed to the emperor, he wrote: 'My life's first and last sentiment will be gratitude and devotion.' Flowery deference to the last. He made health his official reason for going and encouraged his salon harem to chatter about how tired he looked, a mission the countesses accomplished to the point where Napoleon grew almost convinced of it, and at any rate felt unable to react in anger. His true reason for going was, of course, the shame and indignation he felt over Napoleon's warmaking, coupled with the wear of having to conceal it. 'I do not wish to be Europe's executioner,' he said when clearing his desk. Later he recalled:

> During all the years I was responsible for directing foreign affairs I served Napoleon with loyalty and zeal. For a long time he listened to the views I made it my duty to present to him. They were based on two considerations: to establish for France the monarchic institutions that guaranteed the authority of the sovereign, holding it within just limits; and to treat with Europe in such a way as to have France pardoned for her successes and her glory. In 1807 Napoleon had long strayed, I recognise, from the path I did everything to hold him on, but I was unable to leave the post I held until the occasion which then presented itself.

So he wasn't whitewashing himself, not entirely at least. And no one could accuse him of deserting the emperor when he was down, for he left him at the pinnacle of his power.

Napoleon himself swung between a vague sense that he had dismissed him and distress at the wilful departure of a man he couldn't do without. He was used to criticising Talleyrand. He even muttered about getting rid of him because of his rapacity, though his poor view of Talleyrand's *douceurs* had long since lost focus. Other courtiers reported him 'very upset' at his minister's leaving, but that he was too pleased with his performance all round to be able to obstruct him. If he rued it at the time, he rued it more in years to come, when all was lost. 'Things went well for me all the time Talleyrand was there,' the emperor lamented, about to be cast from his throne. 'It was his fault that he went down in my esteem. Why did he want to leave the ministry? He's the man who knows France and Europe best. He would still be minister if he had wanted.'

The actual break occurred with a minimum of bad grace. For a time those who felt Talleyrand's departure most were fellow diplomats and government functionaries who lacked his art of calming the emperor's sharp temper and impetuousness. Perniciously, Metternich reported home that those who had surrounded Talleyrand in government were in despair because they too had made small fortunes from sweeteners which they now feared would dry up. Talleyrand himself, though, was not out of pocket, for the emperor intended to keep him in his. The sharp wit, the old-world charm, the knowledge, perhaps just the familiar presence, were all too valuable to lose at a stroke. He was used to sitting up into the early hours with his minister, just the two of them, chewing things over. Only weeks before, in Poland, they had both fallen asleep in front of a crackling fire at 4 a.m. while conferring on that nation's future. Napoleon woke up with a start to see his minister dozing. He shook him. 'What's this, you blighter! Dropping off in front of me!' Then they had worked on until dawn. Now Napoleon wanted to keep him in close range.

To his titles of Prince of Benevento and Grand Chamberlain, the emperor added that of Vice Grand Elector, a richly endowed sinecure providing a high perch in the benefactor's court. Talleyrand's combined imperial emoluments grew by almost half to 500,000 francs, though he was now required to do very little to earn them. The office of Vice Grand Elector, one of three imperial ranks immediately below the emperor, was a Napoleonic fantasy inspired by the grand sounding Habsburg Electors who were sovereigns in the defunct Holy Roman Empire (the Grand Elector title, the sinecure of Joseph Bonaparte, lapsed when he was made King of Naples). A first task of its occupant was to supervise elections to legislative bodies, which made it splendidly redundant under Napoleon's concept of government. Also, on state occasions, to wear a luxurious red velvet cloak as a uniform spotted with golden bees from the emperor's own hive. It was fortunate that the remuneration was high, for to be Vice Grand Elector was no defence against mockery. 'It's the only vice he lacked,' snorted Fouché, ever ready to cut his rival.

Napoleon, having coddled him, also cut him by placing a nonentity at the foreign ministry in his place without consulting him. Talleyrand had trouble in viewing the selection of Comte Jean-Baptiste de Champagny as anything other than a signal of disregard for the post he had filled so long. He had no time for Champagny; he'd known him from the days of the first revolutionary parliaments and remembered him making a mess of reorganising the French navy to take on the bullying English. To Talleyrand, he was the duke of dullards, a spineless yes-man.

He made himself feel a little better by ribbing his successor when introducing him to ministry personnel at an informal farewell ceremony: 'Sir, these are commendable people whom you will be happy with. You will find them loyal, able and precise but also, thanks to my care, in no way zealous.' He added, pleased to notice Champagny's bafflement, 'Yes, Sir, apart from a few busybodies who prepare their envelopes with, I believe, a little precipitation, everyone here is extremely calm and averse to haste. When you have spent a little time treating the interests of Europe with the emperor, you will see how important it is not to rush into sealing his orders and sending them too quickly.' In the weeks that followed he continued to rail at Champagny's unsuitability, a near obsession that amused Napoleon, who nonetheless advised the new man to sit on his letters for a day or so before sending them.

It was the start of a perplexing new round in Talleyrand's joust with the emperor. He appeared to be freer than ever before to try to make his view of the world prevail, but the close-in, professional part of their contest – the daily discussions, the joint letter writing, the phrasing of treaties, the all-night wrangling on policy – was over. The emperor too was even freer to do as he wished.

If there was an ultimate trigger for Talleyrand's long-contemplated resignation it was the course Napoleon took straight after his victory over Tsar Alexander's army at Friedland. Alexander's request for an armistice had led to a hastily arranged mid-summer meeting between the two emperors at the Latvian town of Tilsit. It was a droll affair considering how much carnage they'd produced between them. They met in late June on a raft moored in the middle of the river Niemen dividing Prussian Poland from Russian territory. The raft, topped by a beflagged tent, was meant to suggest neutral ground. Talleyrand was virtually ignored at Tilsit and he felt the slight. For more than a week Alexander, a boyish thirty-year-old with liberal ideas for reform in his vast country, and Napoleon, aged thirty-eight, bargained in private. In the course of their mid-river bonding, the young tsar discovered that he 'hated' the English, his financial sponsors in war, as much as the Frenchman did. Or so he owned to Napoleon. He in turn was charmed by the tsar's curly-headed innocence and his requests for tips on how to win battles. Talleyrand's only diplomatic role, if it could be called that, was to sign the treaty they completed on 7 July; he was deliberately excluded from the tent and only met Alexander in riverside social settings where conversation was impossible. It was small comfort that Alexander asked to see him on these superficial occasions, for they already knew each other. Every statesman in Europe was familiar with Talleyrand and his aura from the days of the universal peace interlude back in 1801 when Napoleon was First Consul. Alexander had awarded him a portrait of himself in a diamond-studded frame to thank him for his efforts and the two men had exchanged chivalrous letters. Now Talleyrand was permitted only to pass the time of day with him.

The Tilsit experience brought home to Talleyrand his powerlessness. In place of the alliance with Austria that he was urging, Napoleon made one with Russia designed primarily to vanquish England. It brought Russia into the Continental System. Exceptionally, the tsar escaped without paying indemnities or ceding territory. In Napoleon's judgement an alliance with Russia put more pressure on England than an alliance with Austria would. Moreover, he envisaged Russia, as an ally, pressing down into southern Asia and tormenting England in its domination of India, which got him dreaming once more of ousting the English from India by his own hand. Now the prospects for war indeed looked endless. And what further disturbed Talleyrand was that Russia had gained a place in overseeing Europe, one he believed it shouldn't have. This was bound to alarm Austria, now pincered between the French and Russian empires. The Tilsit treaty confirmed the emasculation of Prussia: its population shrank by more than half, from nine to four million; its lands between the Elbe and the Rhine entered the Napoleonic empire, as did its large swathe of Poland, the newly named Duchy of Warsaw. Napoleon's brother Jerome was enthroned to rule the first of these new realms, the kingdom of Westphalia, while another vassal, the King of Saxony, was made overlord of the new, reduced Poland. Napoleon declared Tilsit the happiest time of his life. His domination of Europe was complete, though Alexander had fashioned himself a side seat.

Talleyrand was still exasperated over Tilsit as he stumped into the new phase of the relationship with Napoleon. It was not his way to display his anger, but it roiled within him. All he could find in Napoleon's favour was that the monarchy he had helped him create was holding France together.

Calm reigned at home. The economy was picking up despite the costs of continual war, and a revitalised bourgeoisie was picking up with it. Talleyrand also observed that the Paris to which he returned from his labours in the field in 1807 was assuming a definite Napoleonic look. This was a mildly contradictory development since Napoleon had been talking quite seriously of transferring the seat of his empire to Lyons in the south to be nearer his kingdom of Italy. Though the mooted transfer turned out to be a passing fancy, Paris recognised the emperor's change of heart by building to his glory: a triumphal arch at the Carrousel parade ground in front of the Tuileries was near completion; the foundations of a much bigger arch, the biggest that existed anywhere in the world, were in place at the Etoile at the head of the Champs-Elysées; a new colonnaded street, the Rue de Rivoli, was cut alongside the Tuileries and Louvre palaces; and the Madeleine church with its great Doric pillars which the emperor saw as a temple to his exploits was under construction at an impressive open site just off the Place de la Concorde. All this was a tribute to the conqueror, financed by the man it honoured. The city received still further reassurance of its imperial rank as road gangs paved the busiest sections of the fourteen highways spoking out from its heart to the chief provincial cities of France and those of the empire beyond. Now everything would always converge on Paris.

Talleyrand, an icon of imperial grandeur with no department of government to run, fell back on the Paris high-society life of salons, lavish entertaining and gaming he'd known before anyone had heard of Napoleon Bonaparte. He couldn't be sure, but he sensed that the emperor was behaving coldly towards him. Indeed, the word went round behind his back that he was in disgrace. People saw that Napoleon wasn't asking him so often for advice and actually appeared to be shunning his company. The leverage on power he'd counted on keeping was looking flimsier than he first envisaged. It dawned on him that Napoleon felt so strong after Tilsit that he decided he no longer needed advisers and deputies, only people to execute his orders. It looked to be a new imperial mindset into which his resignation fitted very nicely, to his own cost. Still, no one knew better than Talleyrand that Napoleon's moods changed quickly, that he enjoyed deceiving those around him, keeping them guessing about their position. Fooling the enemy on the field of battle was his speciality; fooling his own camp at home also gave him satisfaction.

The emperor's coolness failed to discourage the statesmen of Europe from making a beeline for the latest Talleyrand residence on the Rue d'Anjou where his wife Catherine was installed. Though its master was out of office, the Right Bank mansion at once became open house for those from home and abroad who represented power or meddled in it, starting with the inevitable German princes. Old friends like Narbonne and Choiseul from the Left Bank breakfast crowd of pre-revolutionary days were also regulars, as were financiers with shady reputations whom the Talleyrand harem of countesses, lately strengthened by the leechlike Princess Tiskiewicz, enjoyed themselves whispering about. Carême ruled the kitchens and was never busier. Talleyrand clearly wasn't short of funds to finance it all. Catherine, now matronly, her beauty on the turn, resumed her part as a difficult hostess, making little effort to mix. Her platitudes and mood changes unnerved Talleyrand, his intimates observed, but he let her be, fearful of setting her off, as if she were explosive material.

Metternich made himself a frequent guest. For ambassadors from the cowed courts of Europe it was a fair bet that Talleyrand would let more slip from his ironic lips now that he was unburdened of his official charge of foreign affairs. Metternich, polished, perceptive, always listening out for information that could change the course of events, appointed himself attending psychologist to the shifting intrigue between Napoleon and Talleyrand. He was rigorous in sending his analyses to the court in Vienna, also in keeping track of Talleyrand's income from sweeteners so as to keep Vienna abreast of the rate for potential new calls on its treasury. The handsome Austrian, almost twenty years Talleyrand's junior, seemed to have decided that his generous host was an adversary of Napoleon before he himself knew it. They fell into complicity without having to declare it, entering a state of constant unspoken negotiation. They shared much in noble lineage, education, natural guile and taste for seduction, though the Austrian's way with women was entirely more physical and Talleyrand's political spirit was entirely more liberal than the conservative Austrian's with his absolute horror for revolution.

Prince Klemens von Metternich was born in the German Rhineland, a Habsburg domain part run by his family before Napoleon swept it into his empire; he came into huge estates and wealth through a perfect Habsburg marriage, to an Austrian chancellor's daughter. He was assigned to Paris at Napoleon's request, not because of any overt sympathy he had for imperial France but because the emperor was impressed by the account he gave of himself in his previous post as Austrian ambassador to humbled Prussia when the Grand Army occupied Berlin. Not to be put in an eternally difficult spot in Paris, Metternich aimed to temporise with Napoleon, to go along with him in seeming acquiescence until the occasion looked ripe to resist him to practical effect and to disrupt his alliance with Russia.

All this put Metternich on the same wavelength as Talleyrand, or so he inferred from the Vice Grand Elector's first confidences delivered at the

Rue d'Anjou. 'My small mind,' Talleyrand told him, 'has a very hard time persuading itself that what we are doing beyond the Rhine will endure any longer than the great man ordering it.' The forecast of collapse sounded reasonable – and treasonable. Metternich felt privileged to hear it from the imperial horse's mouth. In a year or two he was to take charge of foreign affairs for the Austro-Hungarian Empire, a perch which one day was to make him political architect of continental Europe.

Talleyrand's 'disgrace' did not last long, though the police surveillance of him that Napoleon ordered did continue. By October, two months or so after the emperor began holding him at arm's length, he drew him back in. Napoleon's warrior mind was on Spain and he wanted to discuss his thinking with those who were most familiar with the peculiar situation there. Spain was a new obsession with him. Her support in the war against England was crucial, yet he was unsure of her; the one way to make certain, he concluded, was to conquer the country. The trouble was that Spain was neither an enemy nor a proven menace; she was a large neighbour with a large history ruled by a submissive Bourbon monarchy – a cousin monarchy, in fact, which France's proudest Bourbon, the Sun King, Louis XIV, had installed in Madrid a century before, reducing the nation to a second-rank power in the process.

These were the elements of the problem Napoleon wrestled with as he moved his court for the autumn season from the Tuileries to the old royal chateau at Fontainebleau forty miles south. The sojourn in Fontainebleau's glorious hunting country, following the marriage there of Napoleon's youngest brother Jerome, the King of Westphalia, was supposed to offer a relaxing break from the Paris round and the cares of the world. As usual, though, the emperor's plans to relax fell rather flat. It wasn't for lack of entertainment. There were hunting parties each morning and balls at night, with performances most evenings by the Comédie Française – classical tragedies mostly from Corneille or Racine, Napoleon's favourite playwrights – or by an Italian opera troupe. But the emperor was unable to put people around him at their ease; he seemed afraid of being remotely familiar with them, which in turn made them afraid of saying the wrong thing. The atmosphere was strained. They were bored in his presence and so was he. The whole thing was disobliging for him, considering the pains he'd taken to ensure that people were kept amused. At last he vented his feelings, 'It's the strangest thing! I've brought a lot of people here to Fontainebleau and wanted everyone to have fun. I've arranged every conceivable pleasure and all I see are long faces, everyone looks tired and sad.' Only Talleyrand dared explain to him why, seasoning his impudence with deference to avoid causing unpardonable offence. 'Sire, pleasure does not march to the beat of a drum!' he said. 'This isn't the Grand Army! People will never enjoy themselves if the monarch seems to be forever ordering them, "Now then, ladies and gentlemen, forward march."'

Talleyrand seemed sure enough of his touch to believe he was back in Napoleon's good graces.

His imprint on policy towards Spain showed him in slippery form, however. The peculiarity of the situation in Madrid was that, although Spain was ruled in name by its Bourbon sovereign Charles IV, it was in practice ruled solely by his queen's lover, Manuel Godoy, a resourceful strongman to whom Charles sheepishly bowed. The usurper was unpopular with the Spanish people and openly opposed by the king's son and heir, Prince Ferdinand of Asturias, so that the monarchy was fatally split. Godoy had an awkward habit, what was more, of crossing Napoleon; among the unhelpful stands he had taken was Spain's initial reluctance to join the Continental System against England. Napoleon's fury had by now burned to the point at which he was resolved not only to dethrone the entire Bourbon family but to replace it with a Bonaparte. The numerous Bonaparte clan were avid for sovereign rank and though the emperor was often pained at the way his brothers and sisters grasped for it – and at the less than perfect way they obeyed him when they had it – he wanted to satisfy each of them. The vision was his, not theirs: to implant the Napoleonic dynasty far and wide across Europe was, he believed, a guarantee that it would endure.

For his part, Talleyrand was a hive of contradictions over Spain. As far back as his stay in Berlin, when he was in full ministerial harness, he'd been talking it over with the emperor. He felt in his marrow that to try to conquer Spain would be both ruinous and wrong. Yet he it was who provided an intellectual rationale for doing so that inspired Napoleon to act, which was no doubt why Napoleon wanted him at Fontainebleau to close the discussions. Talleyrand's elliptical argument for getting rid of Spain's Bourbons was that they were put on their throne in 1700 by the proudest of the French line, Louis XIV. Thus Spain was a rich part of the French monarchy's heritage and, since Napoleon had assumed that heritage, he was bound to assume it in full; he had no right to abandon a scrap of it, let alone as hefty a slab as the kingdom of Spain.

The argument nourished Napoleon's fantasies – and Talleyrand could not seriously have thought it would do otherwise when he first presented it in Berlin. So it wasn't lust for conquest alone that prompted the emperor to conclude at Fontainebleau on 27 October 1807 an elastic treaty with an envoy dispatched by a now thoroughly intimidated Godoy. The declared target of the treaty was Portugal, an obstinate standout still allied with England. The undeclared target was Spain, since the agreement permitted Napoleon's forces to move through it in order to occupy Portugal. This amounted to a licence to occupy all they wanted of Spain as well. Talleyrand swore he had no part in drawing up the treaty; Napoleon claimed he was the 'soul' of the negotiation. There was clearly some misunderstanding as to where their discussions had led.

In Talleyrand's favour, he never argued for the military conquest of Spain. He implored Napoleon, in writing, not to cross the Pyrenees; it was both a plea and a warning. Nor was he wedded to the case he'd made in Berlin. He believed in a courtly way that marrying the Spanish heir to the throne to a Bonaparte princess was the simplest device to ensure Spain's dependability as a neighbour. At Fontainebleau, prior to the treaty signing, he told Mme de Rémusat, his young court confidante, that Napoleon was 'trapped in a pitiful intrigue'. Ambition, anger, pride and 'a few imbeciles he listens to' had blinded him, he told her, adding:

> He suspects me the moment I talk of *moderation*, and if he stops believing me you will soon see what reckless follies he will get us all into. But I shall keep watch to the end. I committed myself to the creation of his empire, I wanted it to stand as my last work, and as long as I see the slightest ray of hope for my plan to succeed I shall not give up.

This fragment of self-analysis with its dauntless conclusion provided the most worthy motive he had for staying with an adventurer who he'd firmly decided was leading France to ruin. How much of it was principle? How much self-serving compromise? How much self-delusion? Talleyrand was never transparent; Spain found him at his most opaque.

Only afterwards did he claim outright: 'I fought the enterprise with all my force, exposing its immorality and its dangers.' More than that, he avowed that the duplicity Napoleon brought to his assault on Spain caused a breach between them that was different from earlier ruptures: it was irreparable. An added effect, more fateful still, was to entice England off the waves she ruled into a land war on the European continent at the side of her junior ally Portugal, where an equally junior general by the name of Sir Arthur Wellesley, later the Duke of Wellington, disembarked to pursue his commander's trade. All Wellington knew of fighting the French was his success in colonial India in putting down a revolt against the Raj by the Sultan of Mysore, a stout ally of the French who was trained to fight in the French fashion, tactically quite different from the English.

Talleyrand's own tactics were in fact thrust upon him. The operational focus was clear: neither disagreement with Napoleon, however fundamental, nor fresh military challenges from abroad, would stop him from maintaining a position somewhere close to the emperor – somewhere he could make good his vow to keep watch.

By the end of November 1807, two months after the strange Fontainebleau idyll began, Napoleon's forces marched across Spain and into Portugal, occupying Lisbon. Inevitably – and as Napoleon intended – the march through Spain also became a military occupation. By early 1808 Napoleon's marshals, with 150,000 men under their command, were taking up positions at the approaches to Madrid, a focus conspicuously removed from the line of march to Portugal. The emperor believed Spain was waiting to be conquered with open arms. Talleyrand had listened to him regaling the court with his optimism in Fontainebleau. 'I shall be received as I was in Italy,' the emperor predicted, 'and all truly national classes will be with me. I shall save this once great and generous nation from its inertia, I shall develop industries to increase its wealth, and, you will see, I shall be viewed as liberator of Spain.'

He was quite wrong. The Spanish people balked at the French invasion, first turning their wrath on Godoy who was already deeply unpopular. Street crowds in Madrid sacked the strongman's residence and he narrowly escaped with his life to find refuge in prison. With a popular insurrection against the French now well and truly ignited, King Charles abdicated on 19 March in favour of his estranged son Prince Ferdinand, who scarcely had time to try on the crown before Charles thought better of it and rescinded his abdication. On 2 May French forces in Madrid earned further popular hatred by slaughtering demonstrators en masse in the streets of the capital. The royal mess in Madrid suited Napoleon, who informed his older brother Joseph, the King of Naples, that he was to exchange his Italian throne for the throne of Spain. To remove the feuding Iberian Bourbons from their capital, he tricked the entire cast of Spanish royals into leaving their country – temporarily, they were told – to meet him on the French side of the Pyrenees in the Basque city of Bayonne. Napoleon fed word to them that he merely wanted to reach an arrangement ensuring him of Spain's lasting friendship and ensuring them that their country's integrity would in that case be guaranteed. He led them to believe he would recognise Ferdinand as king and – picking up Talleyrand's quaint device – give him a Bonaparte princess as his bride. None of this was true. The deception was total. Bayonne was a trap Napoleon set to give himself charge of Spain. He arrived in the Basque city from Paris on 14 April and, once all the quarrelling royals were regrouped there, helpless in their finery and grand carriages, he told them the truth: he was installing his Bonaparte dynasty in their place in Madrid and none of them would return. Under shock, fearing Napoleon's might, King Charles and Prince Ferdinand renounced their rights to the throne.

Talleyrand was left behind in Paris for the Bayonne encounter, which irked him, but he took the full blast of it anyway. Perhaps he had, after all, made clear to Napoleon how deeply he opposed the Spanish enterprise, otherwise the emperor would have had little motive to strike back at him the way he now did: he made Talleyrand the jailer of Prince Ferdinand. The Prince of Benevento's instructions were to hold Ferdinand, his brother Don Carlos and his uncle Don Antonio at Valençay, his estate in the Berri region. Informing him of the three princes' arrival date at Valençay, the emperor wrote from Bayonne on 9 May to the statesman whose diplomatic prowess had borne him across Europe:

Be there by Monday night . . . Make sure they have table and bed linen and pots and pans for the kitchen. They will have ten or so courtiers with them and maybe twice as many servants. I am giving orders for their coming to the general in charge of the gendarmerie. I want these princes received without obvious show, but honestly and with care, and you should do everything possible to entertain them. If you have a theatre at Valençay and you brought in some actors, that would be all right. You could bring Mme Talleyrand with four or five women. If the Prince of Asturias grew fond of a pretty woman, one we were sure of, that would be no inconvenience, since it would be a further means of keeping watch on him. It is most important to me that he makes no false move, so I want him to be kept amused and busy . . . Since he threw himself into my arms and promised he would do nothing without my orders, and since everything is going as I wish in Spain, I have decided to send him to the country and surround him with pleasures and surveillance. This should last through May and part of June, by which time my affairs in Spain will be clearer and I shall see what decisions are needed.

As for yourself, your mission is rather honourable. To host three illustrious figures and entertain them befits the character of our nation and of your rank. The ten days or so you spend with them will tell you what they are thinking and help me decide what to do with them. The gendarmerie brigades will be strengthened, so you will have forty gendarmes to be sure the prince isn't abducted and to prevent his escape. You will discuss it with Fouché who will place his agents roundabout, and among the servants, for it would be most unfortunate if this prince were to make a false move some way or another.

The letter had to be read more than once to measure its full desire to belittle. This was Napoleon at his most spiteful and perverse, and the burlesque tone couldn't disguise it. To call the mission 'rather honourable' only crowned the insult to Talleyrand's wife, whom Napoleon insisted on thinking a slut.

Talleyrand affected to take it like a lamb, as if to draw attention to Napoleon's rudeness. What else could he do? Napoleon had gifted the purchase of Valençay for the purpose of receiving foreign dignitaries. He hurried down to the splendid seclusion of his estate in time to greet the princely prisoners, replying to the emperor that his wife Catherine would indeed be present as hostess and that there was more than enough kitchen help, china, linen and so forth to cater to them. 'The princes will enjoy all the pleasures permitted by the weather, which at present is not good,' he wrote. 'I shall give them mass every day, a park to walk in, a forest with many paths if rather too little game, horses to ride, plentiful meals and music. There is no theatre, and it would moreover be difficult to find actors. Otherwise there will be enough young people present for the princes to be able to dance, should that amuse them.'

Talleyrand's sense of history made him a more gracious captor than he, or certainly Napoleon, first intended. He was deeply moved on their arrival at the sight of their royal garments, their livery and their carriages which to him reeked of charmed centuries past. He communed with their class. The idea that they had been deceived and manipulated grieved him. It occurred to him that he felt their plight more than they did, and he at once sent packing a police colonel whom Fouché assigned to live with them. Napoleon, he stoutly assured the princes, did not reign in Valençay's apartments or its park.

He made sure that everyone at Valençay, starting with himself, was formally dressed in their presence as a mark of respect, he taught them how to shoot and to ride – activities they were barred from in Spain, for safety reasons, he assumed – and did his best to interest them in books. Their yawns were a disappointment to him since his own passion for reading was as strong as ever and he hoped to inject them with it in view of the fact that their stay was likely to be a long one. Most people who caught him in his library were infected by his enthusiasm, for he'd developed from his youth before the Revolution a library routine he fondly kept to: on entering his library, wherever it was, he'd take two or three volumes from the shelves at a time, look over their opening pages, argue with them as if they were living persons, walk away, come back to them, then argue with them further. To anyone present, the performance could make the books seem more compelling than their authors deserved. But the princes weren't to be had. When he saw they weren't interested in texts, he tried them on the beauty of bindings, the engravings inside, plain drawings even. It was a lost cause. Don Antonio, the uncle, had been reared by the Madrid court to regard books as dangerous, and was always ready with an excuse to shepherd Ferdinand and his brother Carlos out of the library.

Talleyrand was better able to assist his charges with letters. They were in the dark about their future, as was Talleyrand, who personally penned their inquiring letters to Napoleon. Ferdinand was anxious to know how long it would be before he was given a Bonaparte princess to marry. While prevaricating on nuptials, Napoleon seemed more interested in putting him right on his terms of address. In a rebuke channelled through Talleyrand, the emperor noted stiffly: 'Prince Ferdinand when writing to me addresses me as *my cousin*. Try to make him understand that this is absurd and he should simply call me *Sire*.' The emperor's note, Talleyrand mused with a thin smile, was one for the imperial archives.

When he next came face to face with Napoleon it was mid-August 1808, and Spanish resistance to the invasion was growing by the day, seriously obstructing the emperor's plans. One of his generals, charged with taking control of the south, capitulated with 18,000 men at Bailen in Andalusia. This was a singular humiliation for Napoleon's empire which cast doubt on his end prospects in Spain. It wasn't like the Napoleonic ventures in Italy and middle Europe where his Grand Army had the habit of scoring decisive successes in pitched battles and taking control of countries at a stroke, unharried by an awed and often admiring population. Now the Grand Army was garrisoned back in Germany and the emperor wasn't on his black charger at the head of his troops: for the moment he was leaving the Spanish campaign to his marshals, and the popular reception was anything but admiring. What was more the junta heading the revolt switched Spanish support to England and her ally Portugal, where the inexperienced Sir Arthur Wellesley had landed with a well-equipped little English army in mid-July to start moving against the French occupiers.

Despite all the bad news – made worse by Joseph Bonaparte's failure to sit on the Madrid throne longer than a fortnight before having to retreat from the capital – Napoleon greeted Talleyrand in crowing mood, mocking his predictions of woe. Talleyrand felt a rush of anger but managed to stay calm. The duplicity employed to remove the Spanish royals had left him with a bitter taste. Expressionless, he suggested the emperor might discover he had lost more than he'd gained in Bayonne. Their exchange, as Talleyrand recorded, turned uncommonly sharp:

Emperor – What do you mean by that?
Talleyrand – Good Lord, Sire, it is simple, I'll give you an example of what I mean. Let a man make mistakes, let him have mistresses, let him behave badly with his wife, let him even do grave wrong by his friends, and no doubt he'll run into trouble. All the same, as long as he has wealth, power and brains, society may still treat him indulgently. But let that man cheat at the gaming table, and he is at once banished from polite company, never to be forgiven.

The reconstruction of the exchange in his memoirs made him sound far bolder than he had in fact been acting at the time. While he wasn't afraid of Napoleon, such blunt effrontery was out of character. Hindsight no doubt stoked his wrath – and his valour. It was evidence nonetheless that the irreparable break with Napoleon took root at this time. Again the break took place in his head, not yet with anywhere near the same finality in his conduct towards the emperor.

The princes were held in their golden cage at Valençay for close to six years, during which time they grew as bored as Talleyrand feared. After the settling-in period he was scarcely ever there to entertain them, though his wife Catherine continued to spend a fair amount of time there as hostess. She was attracted to the princes' listless high chamberlain, the Duke of San Carlos, and began treading a back staircase to his room at night. Rumours of the liaison soon reached the ears of Napoleon, who made a point, when he was in a temper, of bringing it up with Talleyrand, though this gave him little satisfaction. The Vice Grand Elector was immune to injury on his wife's account.

THIRTEEN

Tea with the Tsar

It came as an agreeable surprise to Talleyrand that Napoleon by all appearances shrugged off their dispute over Spain. For no sooner had their respective hackles fallen than the emperor asked Talleyrand to accompany him once more to middle Europe – to Erfurt in Saxony this time – for a fresh encounter with Tsar Alexander in late September 1808.

The prince of diplomats was exhilarated to be back in business. Considering the current level of trust between the emperor and himself, it was more than he could have hoped for. How else should he take it but as proof that Napoleon still depended on his experience and counsel? He grasped at the opportunity to show his paces. Furthermore, the servile Champagny was evidently being removed for the occasion to the diplomatic sidelines where he belonged, an added satisfaction.

Napoleon's aim in meeting the tsar was to make sure he faced no threat from the heart of Europe as he concentrated on bringing the Iberian peninsula to heel. For all his crowing about having things under control in Spain, it was vital to demonstrate beyond dispute that this was so. He was obliged to assure his enemies that he was invincible, for his empire stood on this very thing. Besides, he'd learned that vanquished Austria was secretly re-arming and the best way to keep the Austrians down was to have their Russian neighbours glowering at them. The treaty he signed with the tsar on the raft at Tilsit was only fourteen months old and holding, but the youthful Alexander was showing signs of discomfort with his mooring, complaining about the damaging effects of the Continental System he'd joined to strangle England, and hankering as ever after extending his power down into the Ottoman lands of the Levant. In asking Talleyrand to draft a new convention to constrain the tsar and guarantee his continuing support, Napoleon was vague on the formulation but explicit on his goals:

We are going to Erfurt. I wish to come back free to do as I want in Spain. I want to be sure that Austria is fearful and restrained, and I do not want to be involved with Russia in any precise manner as regards the Levant. Prepare me a convention which pleases Tsar Alexander, which is directed above all against England and which leaves me altogether unhindered as to the rest.

From this terse outline, Talleyrand recognised how high the stakes were for Napoleon; if enemies were to come at him from all sides his empire was at grave risk. The returning statesman thus felt all the more pivotal in his role at Erfurt, a medieval German centre of learning where he arrived three days ahead of Napoleon on 24 September and installed himself in an ornate merchant's mansion, a stone's throw from the palatial lodgings prepared for the tsar. The proximity to the tsar was pre-arranged: Napoleon asked Talleyrand to see all he could of Alexander during the trip and to talk freely with him, especially since he already knew him and was able to 'talk the same language'. Clearly Napoleon wanted him to soften up Alexander for the formal bargaining.

The grand old city played its part. Erfurt was a promising setting for informal talk and social carousing since the upper crust of middle Europe, led by bowing and scraping German princes, wasn't going to miss this chance to mingle with two emperors. The city was teeming with petty sovereigns, all seeking invitations to the residence of Princess von Thurn und Taxis, the sister of the Prussian queen and a distinguished hostess in her own right whose elegant, convivial salon at once became an informal meeting place for Talleyrand and Tsar Alexander. They took tea there together each evening after the theatre where the stars of the Comédie Française, imported on Napoleon's orders for a two-week run, played his favourite tragedies for the Russian monarch.

How did Napoleon so miscalculate as to push the tsar into Talleyrand's arms? It wasn't through lack of natural cunning; he himself enjoyed deceiving people and was adept at it. Perhaps his confidence in his ability to control things blinded him to the reality that not everything was controllable. The confounded Talleyrand was always his own master, particularly of his tongue which he knew better than most how to hold.

Napoleon knew from years past that Talleyrand, despite his deference and that honeyed tongue, did not see things his way in Europe. What he didn't know was that his Vice Grand Elector was amply prepared in advance for Erfurt – for *his* Erfurt – so that he had no need for a last-minute scramble to put things in place. He was in frequent contact by letter with his liberal-minded young friend Armand de Caulaincourt, Napoleon's ambassador to

St Petersburg, who was on close terms with the tsar. It made no difference that Talleyrand was no longer foreign minister; his relations with Caulaincourt remained intimate and confidential. Before accompanying the tsar to Erfurt, Caulaincourt had gently massaged his amenable head with Talleyrand's latest thinking. None of this was easy for the upright young ambassador: as a veteran of the Grand Army, he maintained his loyalty to Napoleon to the last, yet he suffered inwardly from an urge he shared with Talleyrand to question the sense of it. He feared that he knew the aspirations and the war weariness of most Frenchmen better than his master did. And how could he disagree with what Talleyrand, who was no populist, kept telling him: 'There is someone more intelligent than Voltaire, more powerful than the emperor – and that is the people.' If Grand Army soldiers were ready to lay down their lives for their heroic commander, most Frenchmen weren't. Scores of thousands of youths liable for military service had taken to the forests across France to avoid it.

A second valuable instrument in Talleyrand's preparation was Metternich. He knew the handsome Austrian well enough by now to rechristen him 'His Paleness', his Habsburg pallor being a match for his own Périgord hue. He was sharing not only his private judgements with His Paleness but running confidential diplomatic papers before him in Paris, not without the prospect of financial reward. From such information the Austrian was able to judge with increasing clarity where Talleyrand stood, and he so informed Vienna: 'According to Talleyrand, the interests of France herself demand that the powers able to stand up to Napoleon should unite to form a dyke against his insatiable ambition. Also that Napoleon's cause should not be seen as France's cause. And that Europe can only be saved by the closest union between Austria and Russia.'

Metternich's conclusions inevitably reached Tsar Alexander's ears, so he was well primed for his informal side meetings with Talleyrand. France's diplomatic champion seemed to have metamorphosed into an all-purpose performer at Erfurt: representative of France, protector of Austria and mentor of Russia. Alexander, though something of a butterball who was easy to influence, had in any event become extremely wary of Napoleon, and the news of French setbacks in Spain further affected his calculations. His intention, he assured his mother on leaving St Petersburg, was to do no more than temporise with the warrior in these new negotiations. (The dowager tsarina was worried for him because she feared he might end up as Napoleon's prisoner, like the Spanish royals at Bayonne.)

All the same, Alexander wasn't ready for Talleyrand's opening thrust as they met over their first tea, served in an alcove at the crowded von Thurn und Taxis residence. Talleyrand's mood may well have been fortified in advance by a glass or two of his choice Madeira, for his greeting, as over-heard in their corner, was an extraordinary harangue, shocking in its candour:

> Sire, what is your purpose here? It is up to you to save Europe and you will only succeed by standing up to Napoleon. The French people are civilised, their sovereign is not. The sovereign of Russia is civilised, his people are not. The sovereign of Russia must therefore be the ally of the French people.

Alexander was naturally astonished, still more so when Talleyrand volunteered his view on the boundaries to which he wanted Napoleon pinned back. The Rhine, the Alps, the Pyrenees were lines drawn by France's history and geography. 'All the rest is the emperor's conquest. France cares nothing for it.' This was Talleyrand talking from his marrow.

Thereafter the negotiations on the convention which Napoleon asked Talleyrand to draft were a comedy of duplicity with a cast of three. Talleyrand presented his copy to Napoleon who indeed appreciated the looseness of it, especially the start laying down certain *principles*. 'Principles, yes, that's good,' he enthused, 'they don't commit me.' But he was only half satisfied with the whole and wrote in two important articles to alter it to his taste: the first made him the judge of what would cause Russia to declare war on Austria; the second, the heart of the matter for Napoleon, required the immediate dispatch of a Russian army corps to camp on Austria's frontiers. Napoleon inserted the additions by his own hand and personally gave the amended treaty to Alexander, making him promise not to show it to any of his ministers. The first thing the tsar did was to show it to his teatime colleague Talleyrand, who advised him to cross out the new articles and anything involving military pressure on Austria; he could tell Napoleon such concerns were implicit anyway in the Tilsit treaty.

Each morning Talleyrand discussed the course of the negotiations with Napoleon, and each evening he went over the same ground with Alexander. With Caulaincourt at his side, he had Alexander under his spell at Erfurt. He coached him on how to answer Napoleon during their negotiations, offering him the precise phrases that would work best, and observed with satisfaction that Alexander made notes of what he was telling him, then took his words away to learn by heart overnight for his meeting with Napoleon the next day.

The Emperor of France was at a loss to explain the tsar's obduracy. He found every reason but the obvious one, at length convincing himself of the most labyrinthine – that a devious Grand Army marshal of his was to blame. He'd been counting on his personal charm and his military magician's aura to enchant Alexander as they had at Tilsit. He tried him again and again on his two articles. In vain. The net result – a convention signed on 12 October – was for him a failure since it took him no further than Tilsit. He could hail it as a triumph as much as he liked, but Russia did not agree to contain the re-arming Austrians, who indeed were back at war with him by the following spring.

Talleyrand had more solid cause to congratulate himself and he did so generously. 'You know,' he told his salon circle, 'everyone has saved France, it happens three or four times a year. But at Erfurt, I saved Europe.'

This was a large boast, inspired by his self-imposed task of halting Napoleon's 'insatiable ambition'. On later reflection, he saw his perform-ance at Erfurt as the last service he was able to do Europe while Napoleon held power – and also as a service to Napoleon himself, had the emperor only known it. But ambition of the magnitude Talleyrand aimed to halt wasn't quelled simply by dickering with treaties, and it grew harder for Talleyrand to talk with pride about what he achieved at Erfurt when detrac-tors within the French military caste – people disinclined to believe that he was serving France's interests ahead of his own – began linking his name with treason. Treason! Betrayal! He was impervious to such loose talk, treating it with disdain. It was hard, though, to stop it adhering to his statesman's persona.

The complicity with the tsar born at Erfurt had the odd result of tilting Talleyrand's private life quite as much as it did his career as a statesman. Beyond political alliances, personal ones too were up for negotiation. Marriage was in Saxony's autumnal air. For all the changes in social mores brought in by the Revolution, marriage was still the first maid of states-manship, and vice versa, a fact which Talleyrand himself in a rasher moment had chosen to ignore. But now the maid returned, holding out fresh prospects.

First in line as likely bridegroom was Napoleon himself. The Empress Josephine's failure to bear him an heir had made up his mind: he was resolved to divorce her and find a fertile replacement, a bride of the right rank and lineage to enhance his imperial power. This was of paramount importance to Napoleon. Though smitten by Josephine and her sugar plan-tation sensuality, he had grown tired of her infidelities, her extravagance with money and her caprices which included her dog Fortuné (Lucky), a whippet-sized creature which nipped at his calves when he sank into her bed. Pride in status persuaded the Corsican squire's son to ask for the hand of one of Tsar Alexander's two younger sisters, the Grand Duchess Catherine, who had just reached marriageable age. Forward as he was in his selection, he was coy in broaching the subject with the tsar. His desire to divorce

Josephine was by now common knowledge at the Tuileries and was sure to have reached Alexander's ears, but he was reluctant to put his imperial pride to the test of a direct refusal. So again he turned to Talleyrand, the man who 'spoke the tsar's language', asking him to discuss the matter with Alexander and to impress upon him how important a new marriage was for the Napoleonic dynasty. If Alexander reacted at all favourably, he would then discuss it with him directly.

This put Talleyrand on the spot. He hadn't changed his view that Russia was a barbarous nation and, much as he had come to appreciate its young tsar, he saw him as a tactical partner and had really been making up to him out of political necessity. To Talleyrand, the prospect of monarchic fusion between Russia and his beloved France was preposterous. But the matter had to be handled with the utmost sensitivity if Napoleon's pride was to escape grave injury. In his approach to Alexander he played on their newfound complicity to propose a solution: the prospect of marriage should be left open just enough to satisfy Napoleon, but should be surrounded with just enough reservations to make it more than a little difficult to achieve. Though he sensed that Alexander would in any case be against the marriage at heart, he struggled with himself for hours about how to present the yes-but-no formula to him. Having found the right note, he realised that he needn't have tortured himself. The tsar grasped exactly what he meant before he was halfway through his pitch and the next day took it upon himself to make vague but obliging noises about a marriage to Napoleon, assuring him that his interest in marrying his sister was a great honour for Russia.

Napoleon's quest ended there, despite a subsequent exchange of court notes and well-wishing that kept his interest alive for a while. Three months later the Grand Duchess Catherine was safely married to a German prince of the oldest stock and word was relayed from St Petersburg to Paris that the tsar's remaining unwed sister, the Archduchess Anne, was, at fourteen, unfortunately not of a ripe age to marry. Napoleon fooled himself twice over at Erfurt. His naïvety in thinking he could break into the family of the Tsar of all the Russias was of the same cast as his turning to Talleyrand to soften up the tsar against Austria. And where he met disappointment on both politics and marriage, Talleyrand obtained satisfaction.

Ever since his stay in Warsaw and his impromptu conversations there with the Polish nobleman he dealt with in designing a new Poland, Talleyrand had kept in mind the prospect of marrying one of his nephews into the sovereign family of Kurland on the Baltic borders of east Prussia. The House of Kurland had family links with all the courts of Europe, an asset the House of Périgord was these days able to match only through the renown brought it by Talleyrand's imperial rank. But if there was any mismatch in standing involved, it struck him as manageable. His main consideration wasn't the depth of blue in the blood: Duchess Dorothea of Kurland was one of Europe's wealthiest landowners, which made the youngest of her four daughters, the unmarried Dorothy, a rare prize. He'd wanted to put forward Louis, the older and more promising of his brother Archambaud's two sons and his own favourite, as prospective prizewinner, but Louis died of typhoid on his way back to Paris from the victory at Friedland. Talleyrand was devastated by Louis' sudden death. He'd seen him as the future head of the Talleyrand-Périgord family – the family he himself now headed, no thanks to his parents, by virtue of his imperial rank and renown – and he felt the loss as a grave setback for the Périgord line. It left Edmond, the younger nephew, likewise a captain in the Grand Army and a good soldier, though a plodder beside his brother, to be suitably placed.

Talleyrand used Erfurt for this purpose. It was a perfect opportunity. The Duchy of Kurland had not long since come under Russian steward-ship, so that Alexander was in effect its ruler. As a friend of Duchess Dorothea, a beautiful, strong-minded widow in her late forties, he had felt obliged to compensate her handsomely for Kurland's loss of independence, endowing her and her daughters with rich additional incomes to go with their castle estates dotted across Prussia, Saxony and Bohemia. Talleyrand once more put Caulaincourt to work on the tsar, who wasn't entirely igno-rant of what was expected of him since Caulaincourt had touched on the matter of Dorothy's marriage before they left for Erfurt.

Once reminded, Alexander was quick to reward his new accomplice. Talleyrand weighed in with a brief exposé on the difficulties involved in obtaining a fitting marriage for a Périgord heir in France: Napoleon, he explained, reserved all the wealthiest heiresses from the noblest French fami-lies for his aides-de-camp, the young men who rode at his side in battle. Alas, Edmond was not at this stage an aide-de-camp. 'Your Majesty has as his subject a family with which I dearly wish to be allied,' he appealed to Alexander. 'The hand of Princess Dorothy of Kurland is all that my nephew could desire.' On his way back to St Petersburg the tsar made a point of staying the first night at the Duchess of Kurland's estate in Saxony, Löbichau castle, with Caulaincourt and Edmond in his train. Alexander had seignior-ial rights when it came to deciding who married whom within the titled houses of his realm and Duchess Dorothea, a well-travelled woman partial to French culture, accepted his choice of a husband for Dorothy without protest, indeed with enthusiasm. While the duchess was well acquainted with Alexander and his family, her French leanings made Napoleon a saviour of sorts in her eyes as he bestrode her Europe and, furthermore, she was a little dazzled by the lights of Paris she saw in a family link with the famous Talleyrand.

Her lastborn daughter was of another mind. Dorothy was fifteen years old, Edmond twenty-one. With adolescent fervour she had her heart set on a man almost twice his age, the heir to the dismantled throne of Poland, and she pretended not to notice Edmond when the tsar paraded the young French hussar before the Löbichau household. What was more, Dorothy, unlike her mother, hated the very name of Napoleon. By background and sympathy she and her married sisters were more Prussian than their cosmopolitan mother, and Napoleon had humiliated Prussia. Dorothy was particularly conscious of the humiliation since she spent most of the year living in downcast Berlin, away from her travelling mother, in a Kurland family residence on Unter den Linden.

The duchess had doubts about her youngest daughter – not about her intellect or her looks but about her character, which she worried was a little waspish and unfeminine. Even after Dorothy bowed to the inevitable and fell in with the duchess's wishes, as she tearfully did, she was hard on Edmond when they were first left alone. 'I trust, Sir, you will be happy in the marriage arranged for us,' she said, adding that she was simply obeying her mother. Edmond was also at his most wooden, replying, 'I too am marrying because my uncle wishes it. Men of my age prefer the bachelor life.' It was a shaky start. Talleyrand was clearly more conscious of the great good fortune befalling the Périgords than the placid Edmond was, for Dorothy's wealth ensured a comfortable life from then on for the new heir to the House of Périgord.

The marriage took place with all pomp the following spring on 23 April 1809 in Frankfurt, the German nexus of Napoleon's empire in the Confederation of the Rhine. Talleyrand's intense personal interest in the match bordered on clairvoyance. For although he hadn't set eyes on either the Duchess Dorothea or her adolescent daughter prior to the marriage he arranged, the two Kurland women filled his sentimental life from that day on. Now fifty-five and distinctly pudgy, in ever more pain when obliged to walk, he was the most willing of victims of their charms. The duchess moved with Edmond's bride to Paris, effortlessly joining the salon world that intrigued her and marking her entry into it by giving a grand ball to celebrate the marriage. Her style enchanted Talleyrand. He fell in love with her and she – intrigued by his status, intellectually curious, politically aware, free for a moment from the many suitors who pestered her, a slim, dark-haired equestrian goddess at ease in all the courts of continental Europe – with him. While he conversed and gamed the night away, she was more than ready to dance it away. The physical contrast between them further warmed his admiration for her, as did the private channel of communication she offered to her patron, the tsar of Russia.

Talleyrand did not, of course, miss the opportunity to build on his relations with Alexander, sending him syrupy thanks for making the marriage happen. 'All has succeeded, Sire, as it was bound to succeed when two forces as powerful as Yours and love combine.' In the same letter of thanks he struck a grave note, cataclysmic even. It was his fervent hope that Alexander's friendship with Napoleon wouldn't break down. 'A collision between two such colossuses would leave both wounded and whatever the outcome it would ruin humanity.' But if he saw tragedy on the horizon, it was love that took first place in Talleyrand's thoughts at this moment. As usual, it was the delight of having such an alluring woman as the duchess enter his orbit that fired him most. He made her the target of intimate little 'morning notes', an engaging habit he'd salvaged from the *ancien régime* which entailed passing on tidbits of news and amorous thoughts in three or four brief lines sent each day before lunch, even when it was certain the author and the recipient would see each other later the same day. Talleyrand modulated their intensity by affixing, or not, the postscript 'Burn this note'. At first he addressed her in writing as 'Your Highness' but soon loosened the tone, using the signoff: 'I love you and embrace you with all my heart.'

If his sentiments towards his new niece were more avuncular, they led to a still stronger bond. In years to come Dorothy became his guardian angel, his minder in affairs of state and affairs of the home. On turning sixteen, though, Dorothy was less self-confident than her mother imagined. She confided as much to her adolescent diary: 'Small, yellow, excessively thin, sick since my birth, I had sombre eyes that were so big that they were out of proportion with my face and left room for nothing else. I should really have been very ugly if I hadn't had what they call a lot of character.' To other eyes, though, she looked distinctly better. At the ball the duchess threw for her arrival in Paris, she struck one seasoned society hostess as 'extremely pretty, lively and gracious, her wit already shining brilliantly, possessing all possible appeal except that of being natural'.

Dorothy was, then, a little stiff, as Edmond had learned. This didn't disturb Talleyrand who enjoyed having a princess of peerless European pedigree in his entourage and looked after her closely. At his table one night he caught his old friend Narbonne paying her compliments in the suggestive Paris salon spirit, and saw that she was flummoxed. She seemed to have no idea what the greying gentleman sitting next to her was talking about. 'Be quiet, Narbonne!' Talleyrand cut in. 'Madame de Périgord is too young to understand – and too German to appreciate you.' He was amused also to find her so thirsty for knowledge about her new surroundings. With him as teacher, she forgot how much she detested Napoleon. Her sympathy grew for the civilisation and the language her famous step-uncle introduced to her. The indoctrination went unimpeded, for Edmond was back on foreign duty with the Grand Army, leading the bachelor life he thought was his due, before he had time to get to know his child wife.

Despite the festivities and the dawning of tender sentiments, the year 1809 began badly for Talleyrand. He had the worst run-in ever with Napoleon, a clash so terrible that it left those who were present trembling. Straight after Erfurt, the previous autumn, Napoleon had rushed to Spain to take personal charge of his failing military campaign on the Iberian peninsula, transferring the bulk of the Grand Army and his best marshals from Germany to retrieve the situation. With Austria re-arming unhindered in the east, he was like a ship's captain running from one end to the other of his holed vessel, repairing the bow only to find worse damage developing in the stern, then a renewed breach back in the bow. It was the fate of a conqueror who wanted his empire to cover all Europe.

Nonetheless, while he had cause for concern, he remained resourceful, his ambition unblunted. Within weeks of arriving in Spain with the Grand Army he turned the military situation back in his favour and entered Madrid where his brother Joseph gingerly returned to the throne. His success was marred by an incipient mutiny within the Grand Army, an unheard-of event whose significance he chose not to contemplate: French troops being marched across harsh sierra in the north downed their weapons in appalling winter conditions and refused to move further, yielding only when Napoleon jumped from his horse and resumed the advance at their head on foot. A combination of the same bad weather and thin information prevented more than a wintry skirmish in the north with the English army which otherwise kept out of his way and retreated to the coast, more or less intact; it was, though, temporarily deprived of General Wellesley who was recalled to London to face disciplinary charges (on which he was cleared) for unnecessary gentlemanliness in allowing a beaten French force in Portugal to embark for France scot-free the previous summer. Still, the first glimpse Napoleon had of the English army was the satisfactory one of its tail in full, if orderly, flight.

The instructions the emperor gave Talleyrand before leaving for Spain were of the domestic kind, betraying his all-round unease. He asked him to give dinners practically every day – 'at least four times a week with thirty-six places' – for government ministers and members of those neutered legislative bodies that remained in being. That way, Napoleon indicated, the servants of the empire would be able to stay in contact while he was away and their generous host would keep abreast of what they were saying and thinking.

In short, he wished to be informed by Talleyrand of what was brewing behind his back. It was an ungracious request, which Talleyrand met only as far as he indeed held the countless dinners prescribed.

The entertainment fell within what might be expected of him as Imperial Grand Chamberlain, the rank he retained beside those of Vice Grand Elector and Prince of Benevento and one which called upon him to cater to the emperor's domestic wishes. Moreover, he currently had room to put on dinners of any size Napoleon required, having just moved from the compact mansion on the Rue d'Anjou, where his wife Catherine had felt most at home, to a stately residence on the Rue de Varenne – back on the Left Bank with the liberal Faubourg Saint Germain folk whose subversive chatter infuriated the emperor and whom he selectively banished to distant provinces for their impertinence. Talleyrand bought the Rue de Varenne property, the Hôtel de Monaco, for the very purpose of holding larger dinners and receptions. His compulsion to act the lavish host grew with his means, so that by the New Year of 1809 Carême's talents were taxed as never before in the kitchens of the Hôtel Monaco (later renamed Hotel Matignon, the official residence of French prime ministers).

The feasting chez Talleyrand did Napoleon little good, however. The emperor had gone to the wrong man to ascertain what was happening behind his back in Paris, and he surely knew it. No doubt his more opaque aim was for Talleyrand's many guests to keep track of what their host was saying. Neither man seemed to recognise, or want to recognise, the nature of the battle they'd joined: it was a fight to the political death, but one that remained eerily undeclared. Past fondness and the mysteries of pride on both sides stood in the way of a declaration.

Talleyrand made use of Napoleon's absence in Spain to pursue his own campaign in Paris, aided by a curious new accomplice, someone whose company he normally shunned, whose partnership he would not previously have dreamed of enlisting, so outlandish it now appeared to all who perceived its flowering. That person was Fouché, the stealthy police minister, who, as it happened, shared Talleyrand's fears on the dangers facing France from the emperor's endless warring and who had already begun taking his own action in response to intelligence he was supposed to be presenting to his master.

People knew enough of the fierce rivalry between Talleyrand and Fouché – a contest it had suited Napoleon to encourage until now – to know that something consequential was afoot when the two of them quite deliberately began parading together in public. These were the two most careful operators in the imperial entourage. What were they doing side by side? Their overt connivance could only be some kind of masterful ploy. Perhaps they believed cooperation made them stronger. Or were they betting that Napoleon was on the way out? Talleyrand had always held the joyless workhorse of a police minister in contempt. He amused the harem by saying of Fouché, 'They say he hates humanity – I fear he has spent too long studying himself.' But the disdainful jibes seemed for the moment forgotten.

It was at one of the large dinners imposed on him by Napoleon that Talleyrand first displayed the reconciliation with Fouché. As the police minister entered, a hush came over the astonished assembly of ambassadors, jaded senators and salon priestesses. The host hobbled up to him, took him by the arm and threaded him back and forth through the reception rooms of the Hôtel Monaco in rapt conversation until the evening was half over. Clearly, two such men did not spend their time discussing the weather. If what they were scheming was a secret, the fact that they were colluding no longer was. The arm-in-arm dinner performance resulted from discreet earlier meetings organised by Talleyrand's old foreign ministry deputy Hauterive, who was still highly placed at the ministry and aware of the direction Fouché's calculations were taking. The issue that most occupied them was the succession to Napoleon in the event he was killed in Spain, an old Talleyrand concern kept simmering by the emperor's reluctance to name his heir and his fruitless efforts thus far to produce a direct one. The former rivals, sensing that things might be coming to a head, now fixed on one of Napoleon's marshals, Joachim Murat, as their choice of successor. Murat, they calculated, had the advantages of being well-known, brave, exceptionally ambitious and, best of all, easy to influence. With a malleable figure like him as emperor they could move France in the right direction. What was more, Murat already possessed a regal touch through marriage to Napoleon's sister Caroline, a family link that only months earlier had obliged the emperor to crown him King of Naples in place of Joseph, now occupying the shaky throne in Madrid. Having established that Murat indeed aspired to succeed Napoleon when the time came, Talleyrand and Fouché between them sent word to him in Naples that he should be ready to return to Paris as soon as they sounded the alert.

All the while Talleyrand's relations with Metternich continued to ripen. There was indeed a lot happening behind the emperor's back. In mid-January, after one of his frequent rendezvous with the Vice Grand Elector, the Austrian sent a coded message home laying out the position: Talleyrand would not instigate 'a catastrophe' but would jump on any that might occur. Also, Talleyrand believed Austria was taking the right course in re-arming and preparing for war – the coming spring was the time favoured by Vienna for a renewal of hostilities – and advised it to stick by that position. In his coded messages, Metternich even stopped referring to Talleyrand or Fouché by name: they became 'X' and 'his friend'.

According to the Austrian, 'X' was warning Emperor Franz not to allow Napoleon to take the initiative in making war on Austria. Better for Franz to strike first. It could hardly have been clearer where Talleyrand's hopes now lay. They were not with the man he had helped become emperor of France. None of this, despite its gravity, would necessarily have brought a shuddering frontal collision between Talleyrand and Napoleon had not the letter addressed to Murat in Naples been intercepted by someone close to the emperor – the Empress Josephine's son Eugene de Beauharnais who commanded French troops in Italy. The mishap ensured that Napoleon was at once informed. He was likewise informed by his mother of scurrilous talk of his decline which she said she overheard at a Talleyrand reception. The Corsican matriarch didn't let much pass without warning her son.

These two fortuitous pieces of intelligence sent Napoleon into a blind rage at his military headquarters in the Basque Country. Though the Spanish insurrection was thus far only curbed and the persistent General Wellesley was on his way back to the peninsula to lead English forces, he returned to Paris at the gallop. A five-day ride over treacherous January roads, stopping only to change mounts, did little to temper his fury.

His intention was to have Talleyrand executed.

FOURTEEN

A Stockingful of Mistrust

28 January 1809: Talleyrand waited patiently in the emperor's study at the Tuileries, listening to a chill wind from the Seine tapping at the windows. He was not alone. He was one of five imperial dignitaries summoned at short notice to a meeting with Napoleon on this wintry Saturday afternoon. They were the highest office-holders in the land, led in rank if not in influence by the enduring Cambacérès, the Imperial Arch-Chancellor. Fouché's presence did not augur well, Talleyrand thought, though at least the police minister had given him some forewarning of the emperor's mood, sharing with him the information that fresh horses had been laid on all along the road from Bayonne in the Basque Country for a mystery army general in a great hurry to reach Paris. Talleyrand had no doubt who that horseman was. He propped himself against the fireplace, standing, to avoid putting his leg to the test of bobbing up and down when the emperor appeared. It occurred to him that he'd seen Napoleon acting up often enough at this same fireplace; his habit when upset was to kick at the burning embers, singeing his boots. Replacing burnt boots was a recurring cost to the imperial household budget.

This time, when he descended to the study from his private quarters, Napoleon appeared calm. Unnaturally calm. He began talking of public opinion, what people thought of his campaign in Spain. They seemed to have the wrong idea. The campaign was going to plan. Each day brought successes. He'd heard, though, that people in Paris were saying the opposite. People in high places. They were even speculating on his succession. Where they got such ideas puzzled him. The first duty of those who held high imperial office, he reminded them, was obedience and absolute self-discipline. They owed him everything; they were what they were thanks to him alone.

Napoleon paused, looked around the faces in the small room and paced between them, silent.

Had he finished? Talleyrand, who had put on weight himself, couldn't help noticing the emperor's protruding belly. In place of the slim young officer with long, lustrous black hair of old he saw a tubby forty-year-old with short hair betraying incipient baldness. Recently he'd reverted to simple military looking dress with a dark green habit, having learned that people smiled at the resplendent emperor's costume he had devised for himself with its profusion of white satin, gold rosettes, diamonds and feathers. Talleyrand's whist crowd had christened him 'King of Diamonds'. The emperor loved to dress up but hadn't quite the physique to carry if off, still less so these days. The statesman held a smiling memory of the day he saw him covered in golden bees, bootless, before his coronation in Notre Dame, though the present moment seemed no time for amusement.

As Talleyrand pondered Napoleon pacing to and fro, the object of his observations suddenly transformed itself into a ball of fury bounding his way, as if he were the only other person in the room. Napoleon was almost choking on his wrath: 'Thief . . . liar . . . coward . . . heretic . . .' He bunched a fist in front of Talleyrand's unmoving face. 'Trickster . . . traitor . . . you would sell your own father! I've given you everything and there's nothing you won't do against me. You think things are going badly for me in Spain and you tell everyone who wants to listen that you've always been against it. But you're the one who gave me the idea! You're the one who kept pushing me. And that wretched man, Enghien! Who told me where he was living? Who got me to move against him? What do you want? What are you hoping for? Tell me, I dare you! I should smash you like a glass; you deserve it. I have the power, but I despise you too much to bother.'

Napoleon's fist was momentarily unclenched. His quarry's expression remained unchanged. Not a muscle in the Vice Grand Elector's face had moved during the onslaught, nor did it now. It was inhuman. His skin was smooth, like putty, its life ironed out by the ravages of age. The self-control he showed stung Napoleon into a final assault: 'Why haven't I had you hanged from the Carrousel railings? There's still time. You're a . . . a shit in a silk stocking.'

Talleyrand's fellow dignitaries looked on aghast. It was painful to see Napoleon in this state, a ranting wine-tavern sergeant. His dignity was gone, with it the imperial decorum he laboured to maintain. It was he who lost face, not the target of his abuse. But still it wasn't over. Striding from the room, Napoleon threw a last gratuitous insult. 'And your wife! You hadn't told me San Carlos was your wife's lover!' Talleyrand, an elbow perched on the mantelpiece for balance, turned a baleful eye on the departing emperor: 'I had not imagined, Sire, that such reports could concern Your Majesty's glory or mine.'

Taking up his cane, he too left the room, observing to his imperial colleagues in a grave, unruffled tone, 'What a pity, such a great man and so ill-mannered.'

In truth he felt anything but unruffled. His heart was pumping fast. Before he left the Tuileries a palace bailiff asked him to surrender the key he held as Imperial Grand Chamberlain. So Napoleon was relieving him of the post! That would deprive him of the instant personal access he'd always enjoyed. That night he felt faint and his servants summoned his doctor who was disturbed by his rapid heartbeat, which most times was exceptionally slow, the pulse of his calm temperament. Now he was expecting to be arrested at any moment, though he had kept his nerve long enough on leaving the Tuileries to call in at the Vicomtesse de Laval's home to recount the experience. His circle of countess friends was horrified.

'What! He said that to your face!' Mme de Laval shrieked. 'You didn't pick up a chair? Or a poker? You didn't throw yourself at him?'

'Oh, I thought about it all right,' said Talleyrand. 'But I'm too lazy for that.' It especially irked him that Napoleon appeared to believe he'd driven him to kill the Duc d'Enghien. And to make war on Spain! Wherever the emperor got those ideas, he was deluded. Talleyrand was convinced that invading Spain was the greatest mistake Napoleon had ever made; it had turned into a war against the Spanish people and it was unforgivable to make war against another country's people.

Later, thinking back on the scene at the Tuileries, Talleyrand said he never for one moment felt afraid, either then or in subsequent bust-ups of similar violence. 'I might almost say that the hatred the emperor displayed did him greater harm than it did me,' he concluded. He regarded Napoleon's behaviour as proof that he had left the rails.

Yet what seemed most extraordinary about the emperor's explosions was what he did not accuse Talleyrand of. Nowhere in the venomous cascade of charges did he accuse him of scheming with his enemies – of treason, an offence payable by the ultimate penalty with which Napoleon threatened him before otherwise exhausting his fury in his barrage of insults. Though he kept him under surveillance and intercepted his mail, Napoleon remained oddly unaware of just how far Talleyrand's relations with Metternich and the tsar's representatives went. Fouché surely had a hand in maintaining his ignorance.

In the immediate aftermath of the Tuileries scene, Talleyrand's first concern was not to lose touch with the man he now regarded as the greatest danger to France herself. If the convenient inside track provided by the post of Grand Chamberlain was closed, together, alas, with the income it carried, he still held the handsomely paid rank of Vice Grand Elector in which Napoleon retained him, wittingly it seemed, for it wasn't his habit to keep anyone at the summit of the state through negligence. There was still no point, then, in publicly declaring his opposition to the emperor, for that would merely make it all the more difficult to lay the ground for his fall. At the very least he would risk exile from Paris, where everything happened and where his presence was most useful. No, whatever lay in store on the foreign field of battle, the preparations had to be made from the inside. The nation faced a catastrophe in the making. Of the weapons he possessed to counter it, intrigue and subterfuge looked to him the most potent. Since he was to some extent independent now, he would pretend indifference to Napoleon's actions, act the perfect courtier. That would avoid aggravating the emperor's maddened suspicions and at the same time give himself a chance to keep abreast of where things were heading. He did not lack support. Besides Fouché, whom he still found it hard to like, he had the connivance of powerful men from the foreign courts which Napoleon was racing back and forth across Europe to hold in permanent submission.

If keeping in touch with Napoleon this time required more than the usual dose of flattery, a degree of self-abasement even, so be it. To Napoleon's formal notice of his removal as Grand Chamberlain, he replied:

Sire
I have obeyed Your Majesty's orders in surrendering my key . . . But if Your Majesty will permit me to say so, for the first time it pained me to obey you. Of all the dignities with which you have deigned to honour me, the one that placed me in your personal service was dearest to me. A benefit Your Majesty bestowed on me thus becomes the subject of my deepest regret. My consolation is to be bound to Your Majesty by two sentiments that no pain could stifle or weaken – by my gratitude and devotion that will last as long as I live.

Up to a point, the hurt tone worked. And perhaps it wasn't all artifice. Was it possible to want to destroy Napoleon and at the same time feel attached to him through some helpless, undying admiration? It wasn't the rarest of human conditions and despite the mask he wore Talleyrand was only human. Furthermore, Napoleon seemed to have worked off the worst of his fury, though he pointedly ignored him when he had the temerity to present himself not a week later in the Tuileries Palace throne room at a routine reception for courtiers and government figures. The emperor stopped for a word with the person standing on Talleyrand's right, then had a word with the person on his left, passing his former Grand Chamberlain by as though he didn't exist. At a Tuileries diplomatic reception some days later Talleyrand, unblushing, was there again, which took some fortitude because Napoleon had meanwhile importuned him further by barring his wife Catherine from court as punishment for her affair with the noble Spanish detainee, a petty vengeance that entertained Paris society no end. This time too Napoleon ignored him, addressing a question to a diplomat standing next to him. But seeing the envoy stuck for a reply, Talleyrand took a step forward and answered for him. The emperor stopped in his tracks, astonished, which gave Talleyrand an opening to bow and kiss his hand.

The ice wasn't broken, but it began to melt. Talleyrand was tenacious in his feigned humility. Trusting to his principle that 'politics is women', he put his diarist friend Mme de Rémusat on his case and she in turn, as a lady-in-waiting at court, prevailed on the Empress Josephine's daughter Hortense, Queen of Holland and a favourite of Napoleon, to assist. Hortense, by her own admission, so overdid her assurances of Talleyrand's sincerity when intervening with the emperor that he burst out laughing. A little humour helped too.

'I shall do him no harm,' Napoleon told Hortense. 'Only I no longer wish him to run my affairs.'

In the end Talleyrand always received clemency from Napoleon: respect for the Périgord pedigree, memories of what they had been through together, the countless hours in private discussion, Talleyrand's coaching in the social graces, and perhaps most of all the strange mutual attachment that plagued them both, all played their part. What Napoleon told Hortense he repeated to imperial officials he trusted: he still felt warmly enough towards Talleyrand – who could keep his other high posts – only he no longer had the right to walk into his study for a private talk whenever he chose. That, Napoleon told himself, would prevent Talleyrand from going around claiming to have advised or dissuaded him on the fateful course he now took.

Napoleon's course pointed east, back to war with a newly menacing Austria. Leaving Spain to fester, its people still in revolt and England's General Wellesley intent on moving in after first securing Portugal, he returned to middle Europe in April 1809 to meet an Austrian thrust into Bavaria. This was part of a broad offensive the Habsburgs planned against Napoleon's empire: emboldened by English government subsidies, they also envisaged striking south into Italy and north at the Duchy of Warsaw, hoping to induce downhearted Prussia to join battle at their side.

The image of the ship's captain racing from damaged stern to holed bow was ever more an imperial reality. The extent to which Talleyrand dealt in encouraging the Austrians to keep him running was recorded by Metternich's busy coded traffic that spring. Following the painful scene at the Tuileries, Talleyrand had made a second call after stopping at Mme de Laval's: he went straight to see Metternich. Their meeting led the Austrian ambassador to fire off a coded dispatch to his foreign minister in Vienna, Johann von Stadion, saying that 'X' had discarded his mask entirely and was convinced it was now his duty to enter direct relations with Austria.

In sum, Talleyrand felt free to make common cause with the Habsburgs. For that, Metternich reported, he was prepared to accept suitable remuneration – 'a few hundred thousand francs, say', since Napoleon had severely reduced his means by taking away the Grand Chamberlain post and leaving him to foot the hefty bill for the upkeep of the Spanish princes at Valençay. Metternich advised Emperor Franz to accept the proposition and to advance him 400,000 francs in bills of exchange drawn on a Dutch bank. In a pressing follow-up dispatch, he added: 'However large this sum may seem, it is far smaller than the sacrifices to which we are accustomed and the results can be immense. Moreover I cannot tell you how useful X has been to me since our relations assumed this new character. I beg Your Excellency to make your calculations on the high side.'

Before a figure was settled upon, Metternich was able to tell the anxious Habsburg court that he had learned from X that one of Napoleon's best generals in Germany, Marshal Nicolas Oudinot, had received orders in February to march with his army corps for Bavaria. Austria should keep a very close eye on the movements of this corps, Metternich wrote, because Napoleon held it in highest esteem. 'X believes that we should use Oudinot's movements as a *casus belli*. We should waste no time. It would be criminal to nurse illusions about Napoleon: he definitely wants war.' Von Stadion's grateful response to this information was to give Metternich *carte blanche* in dealing with Talleyrand, saying he could promise him anything he reasonably asked once he was absolutely sure he was able to provide useful and important services. When it came to opening the till, however, von Stadion grew less generous. He sent 100,000 francs as an instalment and specified that further sums would depend on the value of services rendered, a proviso designed to help Talleyrand provide precise information and draw him out on what he himself aimed to achieve.

Talleyrand apparently felt he was being short-changed, for by mid-March Metternich was signalling his minister: 'My relations with X are most active. It is largely through him that I learn from one moment to the next what interests us. I beg Your Excellency to go as high as the sum I have asked.' As a titillation, he said he'd been able to procure two memos of 'immense interest' from Napoleon's office which he was loath even to trust to the diplomatic pouch; they showed that Napoleon's lust for war extended to

Russia as well as Austria. In a nutshell, Metternich concluded, Napoleon's policy was to destroy anything not under his dynasty's thumb.

An endless supply of intelligence on the emperor's activities now seemed to be falling into Metternich's ready hands. Later in March he sent Vienna detailed tables specifying the state of readiness of all French armies, copied from Napoleon's war office. With them he sent word that Napoleon had received a letter from Tsar Alexander asking him to send Talleyrand himself to St Petersburg to work with Russia on suing for peace with England, a proposal Napoleon rejected. It wasn't Talleyrand's fault, then, that Austria once more took a beating from Napoleon when the actual fighting began.

As a military tactician, the emperor remained masterful and resolute. He reached Bavaria to take charge of his troops on 17 April 1809, a week after the Austrian army launched hostilities, and in a five-day blitzkrieg during which he was lucky not to lose a foot he had the more numerous enemy in retreat. Making light of a nasty leg wound that had military doctors fussing for a time over the possible need for amputation – his first injury since becoming emperor – he told his men they would be in Vienna within a month. And so they were, though only at its gates. It wasn't the Grand Army he was leading (that peerless force was attempting to hold Spain), it was his new Army of Germany made up mainly of foreigners and local conscripts, and the retreating Austrians not only held it at bay on the Danube beside their capital for weeks but came within an ace of routing it. Summer was well underway before Napoleon, helped by reinforcements from his Army of Italy, finally had his way at the battle of Wagram on 6 July at a cost of eighty thousand dead and wounded on both sides. An armistice called by the luckless Emperor Franz led in mid-October to the Peace of Vienna which handed to France southern Austria and Austrian territories stretching far down into the Balkans, plus heavy war indemnities.

On paper, despite some ugly rips and whorls, Napoleon's empire at the close of the first decade of the nineteenth century was bigger than ever.

Talleyrand was kept well away from the Peace of Vienna negotiating table. Having to leave his old place to Champagny was galling, though it was nice to hear that Napoleon chided his successor for being slow to conclude the negotiations. Referring to a 100-million-franc indemnity he was demanding from Austria, the emperor complained to Champagny: 'In Talleyrand's time we would have taken perhaps 60 million, and he would have had 10 million, but it would all have been finished two weeks ago. Now do it.'

Even a backhanded compliment was welcome. It told Talleyrand he was still very much in Napoleon's thoughts. The renewed war was both a busy time and a frustrating layoff for him. Busy because he had a demanding

Metternich to deal with and the Périgord merger with the House of Kurland to see through. The marriage mission assumed an added tingle of tension because Edmond and Dorothy were wed in Frankfurt precisely as Napoleon locked horns on German soil – within marching distance of the altar and with an Austrian foe for which Talleyrand was acting as backroom intelligence officer.

Cultivating Fouché also required time and patience, and besides grew trickier when England landed an army on the coast of Holland in midsummer to increase the military pressure on Napoleon. In Napoleon's absence in Vienna, the English landing, which didn't come to much, galvanised the police minister into taking independent action to secure the situation at home in the event of the need to replace the emperor, a scenario he thought through with Talleyrand. Fouché, moving a little too precipitately for his own good – certainly in Napoleon's eyes, who thought he saw a grab for power – lost no time in organising a national guard of thirty thousand men in Paris, with Talleyrand's brother Archambaud among its commanders.

Talleyrand himself was more careful. His credibility with foreign courts was at stake and it was vital to maintain it. Although his disgrace was with any luck again on the mend, it was nonetheless a fact. If he were seen to be altogether out of the imperial loop he would have no role; foreign courts would lose interest in him. Regaining contact with Napoleon was thus an urgent concern. As soon as he learned of Napoleon's battlefield injury, which was not limb-threatening as it turned out, he wrote him a letter from Paris that reeked of his past winning ways as foreign minister:

Sire,
Your Majesty has been gone for thirteen days and already added six victories to the marvellous history of previous campaigns. While we thought no triumph however great could still surprise us, you continue to astonish us. None of us shall ever understand how a campaign can be so near its end when we had hardly grasped that it was about to start. I do not know whether you will permit me, Sire, to speak of the dangers Your Majesty has consented to face, for few people here realise them, but I dare assure you that when the frightening news is made public, despite all the efforts that are rightly made to hide it, all hearts will be broken with grief and I'm not afraid to add that the gratitude and admiration that moves all your subjects may falter, for your life is our existence.

There is nothing left for me to do here for I am unable to serve Your Majesty. Everything that reminds me of the time when I was happy to think I was useful in your service makes my life in Paris the

sadder . . . Removed as I am from the scene of Your Majesty's glorious
enterprises, all my feelings, all my thoughts, nonetheless place me in
the first rank of your servants who base their hopes for esteem, glory
and happiness on the accomplishment of Your Majesty's great plans.

The two elements of sincerity in this grovel were no doubt the fact that he
was fed up with not being in the thick of imperial affairs and the fact that
he cared in his own way about Napoleon's person. It was a bond he attempted
to explain to Caulaincourt, who enjoyed his confidence in most matters,
though not in the full reach of his connivance with Austria. He told
Caulaincourt that Napoleon's current severity towards him would never
shake his gratitude for the generosity he'd shown him. There was a lot of
good in Napoleon along with the bad. 'Good grows and takes root in a
discerning heart; evil slides away and vanishes. There are bonds that last a
lifetime and those I have contracted with the Emperor will last to my dying
day.' This may have struck Caulaincourt as a strategic confidence that
Talleyrand hoped would reach the emperor's ear, but it clearly went a lot
deeper than that.

All the same Talleyrand's powerlessness allowed him to stand back and
take stock of what Napoleon was bringing on France and on all Europe.
The perspective relit his indignation and his will to stop the emperor. It
wasn't just monarchs Napoleon outraged, it was entire peoples. The campaign
against Spain was the limit; it was shameless, with no pretence to be useful
or to bring good. That was something a people would never forgive. And
his Continental System? It aggravated every country that Napoleon forced
to join, not least his own, garrotting industry and trade across the Continent.
It was a state of affairs that couldn't and shouldn't last since it held out no
prospect of repose for anyone. 'All peoples were suffering,' he recalled later.
'All sovereigns were anguished and perplexed. Napoleon everywhere stirred
hatred and invented difficulties which in the end were bound to be insurmountable.' Why, he even ousted the pope from Rome. He'd been bullying
the miserable Pius for years, ever since concluding the Concordat in 1801,
and now, while he was busy humiliating Emperor Franz once more in Vienna,
his forces arrested the pontiff in Rome and annexed to France outright the
papal realm which he had refused simply to place in Napoleon's keeping.

Talleyrand, a former prince of the Church who, despite his own transgressions, never lost respect for its mysteries, was mortified by the hounding
of the pope during 1809. To be sure, he was personally somewhat compro-
mised in this matter, having accepted the title of Prince of Benevento, a
domain filched from the Vatican. But Napoleon's pretensions in this instance
struck him as particularly ludicrous. Having commandeered Rome, he

dislodged the pope on the grounds that Charlemagne – 'the Emperor of the French, my predecessor' – had merely made over the papal domains to the Vatican in medieval times, without ever ceding them. He took the parallel with Charlemagne seriously, oblivious to the historical impertinence of his actions. His plan was to turn the pope's Roman lands into a brace of French administrative departments, as he did with old city states such as Hamburg. This was to plant the new machinery of Napoleonic organisation in places with their own ancient rights and customs; it was like clamping a round imperial frame on an old woodcut manifestly square in shape. Pius's only comeback to this arrogance was to excommunicate Napoleon, which of course enraged him further. The pope's fate was to be carted off in captivity to various stopping points in Italy and France, forced to disguise himself in ordinary clothes so that no one recognised him en route. He ended up at Fontainebleau close to Paris, which Napoleon deemed a convenient place for the papal seat.

Every victory Napoleon won, including the latest at Wagram, Talleyrand saw as an obstacle to better times, to the civilised world he believed to be the one defensible goal of national ambition. Everything told him that Napoleon had long since stopped working for France; he was working for himself. He had no thought for preserving anything, merely for extending his power out of 'puerile vanity'. And his dynastic pretensions? To Talleyrand they looked doomed. Every throne he created for his family and his marshals helped undermine his empire, not only because they lacked legitimacy but because the sovereigns he made, whether blood brothers, brothers-in-law or fellow soldiers, were soon driven by ambitions of their own, conflicting with his.

The entire imperial setup had become a mockery in Talleyrand's eyes. He saw the luxury of the various Bonaparte courts as an absurd mixture of Austrian gravity, St Petersburg tyranny and Rome of the Caesars. There was precious little of the dignified charm of France's old court. 'What this kind of luxury lacked above all was good taste,' Talleyrand decided, 'and in France, when good taste is lacking, ridicule is never far away.' To tap into Talleyrand's mind on Napoleon at this time was to listen in to a long story, bizarre and alarming, of a naïve madman at work.

Caught between the need to be close to Napoleon and the greater desire to bring him down, Talleyrand often found himself at a loose end during his disgrace in 1809. He took a long break in early summer at the family spa of Bourbon l'Archambault to soothe his bad leg and his latest chest wheeze, but otherwise fell back into the salon life of which he was deemed the ultimate master. He was not the sort to feel sorry for himself, though he did at times feel twinges of regret over the way he led his life – not over his conduct towards Napoleon but over the way he conducted himself. With the young Mme de Rémusat, who scolded him for not showing his emotions, he waxed penitent, rummaging back into his childhood with her and blaming his parents' coldness and indifference for his own elusive character:

> You see, in that situation, I had the choice of dying from grief or numbing myself so as not to feel what I was missing. Well, I preferred to numb myself – and I must agree with you that I was wrong. I have often felt disgusted by insouciance of my soul. I haven't loved others enough, but I have hardly loved myself either.

His young confidante was startled, and moved, by his rare show of candour. 'If only you would be more *you*,' she told him. More often, though, she was dissatisfied by his habitual tactic of resorting to pleasantries to avoid expressing his feelings. He was worth so much more, she decided, than the Talleyrand he displayed. 'He pleases a lot, but satisfies never.'

His harem of society hostesses was faithful to him all the same. The forced layoff from the imperial court did him no discredit in Faubourg Saint Germain eyes, nor in those of foreign ambassadors and passing dignitaries who knew of his situation but still flocked to evenings at the Hôtel de Monaco for the chance of a word with the great man.

Once Napoleon had again imposed armistice terms on Austria, Metternich was pulled back to Vienna to take over the foreign ministry and the chief receptacle for Talleyrand's leaks was gone. But both Emperor Franz and Tsar Alexander paid him the extraordinary honour of accrediting special 'ambassadors' to the Hôtel de Monaco as well as formal ones to Napoleon's court, a secret ploy by the two monarchs to make optimum use of the information and interpretations which Talleyrand dispensed quite liberally late in the evening. Frequent guests related that he was as tight as a steel safe at the start of an evening, but by midnight, left with half a dozen friends, he let loose and chattered with the best of them – a fact which had reached Napoleon's ears. In fonder moods the emperor called him an 'old gossip'.

An evening at Talleyrand's or at Mme de Laval's, where he had his own corner to perform in, was a long, many-layered affair. It began at around 5 p.m., with dinner – the one full daily meal Talleyrand and his kind took – served with a luxurious spread of fine meats and wines. There followed at 11 p.m. a reception and often dancing for non-dinner guests, after which, around midnight, came refreshments and conversation, then, punctually at 1 a.m., the moment Talleyrand always looked forward to, came whist. He drew the Duchess of Kurland into his social routine as soon as she settled in Paris with Dorothy. It wasn't long before the duchess's admiration for Napoleon changed under Talleyrand's tutelage to scepticism, then dislike, after which she became 'my angel' in his morning notes and had to put up with a certain coolness from Mme de Laval and other members of the harem. They were right to feel jealous; at the age of forty-eight, the newcomer from the Baltic lands had kept a sinuous figure and a roguish smile she'd successfully turned on the titled heads of Europe, from the tsar down, and she was richer than they were.

Talleyrand enjoyed further moral support from his one-eyed Polish admirer Princess Tiskiewicz, the second eastern newcomer to his salon circle; she sat at her idol's table, shuffling the cards for him and fixing opponents with her glass gaze. It was well that his most devoted admirers were on their guard, for outsiders, as ever, judged him severely. To them he was intimidating; for all the outward charm and supreme courtliness, the way he masked all emotion repelled them. Mme de Rémusat found that whenever she as much as suggested that he possessed emotions like everyone else, she was obliged to nod vigorously and defend her revelation to their disbelieving ears.

All the time, Talleyrand's separation from Napoleon had him fretting. He jumped upon the slightest sign that the emperor's attitude might just be softening. There were precious few of them. He kept Caulaincourt abreast of any shift. 'The anger so crudely expressed has turned to politeness, and that's where things stand,' he reported in March. A little later: 'The Emperor is very polite but very cold.' Later still: 'By all appearances the esteem is there, but not the trust. In fact there is no trust whatsoever.' This was frustrating because he was sure Napoleon gained something from having him close by to talk things over with in private, to open his heart to from time to time. 'What I find the most painful,' he lamented to Caulaincourt, 'is no longer being able to chat informally with Napoleon on behalf of my friends. I daresay he loses something there too because there are certainly many occasions, as in the past, when I could give him all my thoughts on subjects which others couldn't raise and which I was able to discuss because of the great familiarity he allowed me.'

The irony was that at the very time he was looking for chinks of sympathy in Napoleon's heart, he was helping the Austrians in their new battle – futile as it turned out – to destroy him. He did not confront the morality of his position, or the seemliness of those secret meetings with Metternich and the income they brought him. Common morality did not concern him. Wasn't it something that slipped this way and that, with the changing seasons? 'Man was given the power of speech to conceal his thoughts,' he liked to say, in respect of straight talk. If he contemplated the concept of morality at all, he put himself above it. He had liberal regard for ordinary men, but his breeding somehow elevated him above their rules of conduct. He was different – his birth made him different. The latest panting suitor of his old flame Mme de Staël, the German philosopher Friedrich von Schelling, encapsulated his code for him: 'The secret of morality is to be at one with oneself.'

If there was an ethic to which he subscribed, it was a broad one: it consisted of any non-violent conduct that would save France. This was understood by the special envoy Tsar Alexander placed at his side, Count Karl von Nesselrode, who defined the position of both Talleyrand and Fouché for the St Petersburg court: 'These men believed they were not betraying their master but saving him from the madness of his passions by preventing him from pursuing perpetual wars that depopulated and impoverished France and risked ending in horrible catastrophe.'

Talleyrand could have put it no better.

A first promising chance to move back into imperial favour came in December 1809 with the announcement of Napoleon's divorce, for which he had mercifully prepared the Empress Josephine well in advance, telling her he loved her but had to move on. The great question was, who would the new empress be? Napoleon hadn't given up on Tsar Alexander's younger sister but there was also the intriguing prospect of marrying into the Habsburg family now that Austria was back under the conqueror's thumb. The supposed blessing of either match was that it would place Napoleon within Europe's ancient establishment of kings whose legitimacy was rather more widely acknowledged than his own. Under pressure, Emperor Franz agreed to make his eighteen-year-old daughter, the Archduchess Marie Louise, available, though there was something a little sinister, indeed historically perverse, in the proposition: Marie Louise was the niece of Queen Marie Antoinette, the Habsburg princess whom France's Louis XVI took as his bride and whose head fell with his at the guillotine.

Napoleon summoned a private council of state to determine his choice on 21 January 1810, which Talleyrand attended as Vice Grand Elector, already marginally buoyed at having been asked by Napoleon to do the honours for him in greeting the vassal King of Saxony on a visit just before Christmas. Furthermore, it was he who had done the spadework on Napoleon's confidential request to secure Emperor Franz's offer of his daughter. The council of state was the chance he'd been waiting for and he was determined to shine. Napoleon launched the proceedings with a pious statement that if it were up to him personally he would take the daughter of one of his brave soldiers as his wife, except that the needs of his empire dictated otherwise.

Sham governed the meeting from the start, which suited Talleyrand, for perhaps more clearly than his fellow privy counsellors he recognised that the coming marriage was designed more to satisfy Napoleon's vanity than to ensure the stability of his empire. Fouché was among several dignitaries to counsel the Russian match. Talleyrand, of course, came out for Marie Louise. He was on firm ground here because the Habsburg link ostensibly fell in with his universal peace plan based on friendship between France and Austria, and because he was quite sure in any case – even if Napoleon refused for the sake of form and pride to acknowledge it – that Alexander wasn't going to deliver his underage sister to his French nemesis. Tackling the Marie Antoinette issue, Talleyrand argued that to bring her niece to France in her unfortunate footsteps would absolve the French nation in the eyes of all Europe of a crime which Robespierre's fanatics had committed. What was more, he said, it would assist 'European reconciliation', repeating the term several times over to make sure Napoleon took it in.

Several others strongly backed Talleyrand's view, which encouraged Napoleon to fire off a dispatch to Vienna that same evening asking Emperor Franz for his daughter's hand. In March, to show the Austrian monarch who was who and to rub it in, he sent to Vienna the army marshal who had starred in Austria's final defeat at the battle of Wagram to take Marie Louise's hand and fetch her back to Paris. Viennese society was stupefied. Amid gasps and sobs, its members greeted the match between Europe's first princess and its 'most infamous usurper' as a heinous abduction. Sensitive souls said Marie Louise would die of shame before such profanity was consummated. All Napoleon knew was that she wasn't beautiful but that she was said to possess a maidenly charm, and his curiosity drove him out to Compiègne, a half day's ride north of Paris, at the end of the month to take a peek at her before she reached his capital. The marriage took place two days later on 1 April 1810. Within a year Marie Louise bore him the son and heir he wanted. He crowned his infant offspring King of Rome.

Talleyrand did seem to rise in Napoleon's favour with the settlement of the imperial marriage question, though others were more convinced of it than he professed to be. The Austrian diplomat secretly accredited to his side after Metternich's return to Vienna reported that he was again having almost daily discussions with the emperor and appeared to have regained the privilege of being able to visit him at will. Shortly afterwards, however, the Austrian rowed back to say that, though Talleyrand had his foot in the door, he wasn't quite yet sitting by the emperor's desk. All Talleyrand himself ventured was that he felt happier with the emperor's attitude towards him than he'd felt for some time.

That he enjoyed some measure of improved access to Napoleon was clear from his simultaneous dealings with Nesselrode, his Russian minder. From the spring of 1810 onwards Nesselrode, more imaginative with code names than Metternich, identified Talleyrand as 'Cousin Henry' (Napoleon was 'Ladykiller' – *Joli Coeur*) in his secret correspondence with St Petersburg. Cousin Henry was full of foreboding about Napoleon's plans for dealing next with Russia, the thrust of which he most likely gleaned from *Joli Coeur* himself. The background to this was that Napoleon's desire to re-establish Poland in its entirety as a vassal kingdom was bound to drag Russia into war to prevent it, and Napoleon was already contemplating such a war. His army staff had been asking French representatives in St Petersburg for a confidential rundown on Russian army positions, strongholds and recruitment as well as the state of Russian rivers and bridges.

Talleyrand was convinced that Napoleon was only waiting to complete the subjection of Spain before striking out with the Grand Army for Russia. The only way he saw of forestalling this was for Russia and Austria to drop their traditional wariness of each other and make a joint stand against Napoleon. Furthermore, Russia needed to end her age-old scuffling with the Ottoman Empire so as to concentrate on what really mattered for her security. This was Talleyrand at Erfurt all over again, only the context had shifted. Summarising Talleyrand's concerns, Nesselrode informed the tsar that Napoleon intended to keep relations with Russia on hold 'until he judges the moment ripe to discard his mask'. The basis for these warnings, Nesselrode threw in, was a series of secret imperial memos drawn up for Napoleon and communicated to him, Nesselrode, by Cousin Henry.

The best personal terms Talleyrand was able to establish with Napoleon resembled, alas, a pendulum swinging between favour and disfavour with perverse regularity. And it was now England's turn to give the pendulum a nasty tilt, albeit not by design.

Beyond his running concerns over Russia and Austria, Talleyrand still made peace with England his end goal. At present the stifling Continental System placed that goal as far off as it had ever been. By 1810, however, the emperor's huge leaky scheme to cut England off from trade with Europe found a fervent opponent in his own brother Louis, King of Holland, who was dismayed over his kingdom's battered commercial prospects. Louis' determination to ease the blockade led to an illicit peace mission to London by the powerful Paris banker Gabriel-Julien Ouvrard, a sufficiently astute operator to be both a close associate of Talleyrand and a financial sponsor of the Grand Army. The addresses at which Ouvrard called in London were supplied by Talleyrand, though the latter's direct part in the peace-feeler operation was restrained compared with that of Fouché. Shrugging off Napoleon's extreme irritation over his recent high-handedness in organising a national guard in Paris in his absence, the police minister personally directed the unauthorised peace initiative which, partly due to its paternity, only half interested London.

When Napoleon got wind of it in early June from his own spies he at once sacked Fouché, who burned compromising papers connected with the mission and decided to make himself scarce for a while, taking refuge in Tuscany. In the imperial dressing down Fouché received before his departure, Napoleon threatened to put him to death, telling him scornfully, 'You think you're very clever but you really aren't. It's Talleyrand who is clever and this time he has played you like a child.' While this could again be taken as a compliment, it made matters delicate for Talleyrand. And unfortunately, on the very day that Fouché was removed, Talleyrand found himself in an inconvenient spot. He was present at a small private gathering to welcome Ouvrard back from London and could only watch, startled, as police under the orders of Fouché's replacement, the robust army general Anne-Jean Savary, burst into the party and arrested the itinerant banker.

It seemed a miracle that Talleyrand escaped this time with no more than an unkind swing of the pendulum. Though the emperor asked him to account for his presence at Ouvrard's arrest and found his explanations 'painful', it was lucky for Talleyrand that Napoleon chose Hauterive, his old friend at the foreign ministry, to conduct an inquiry into the unauthorised contacts with London. The obliging Hauterive found no evil intention in what Fouché had been up to and no indication that Talleyrand worked with him, which were unsurprising findings in view of Hauterive's original role in bringing the two distinguished suspects together. The emperor even summoned Talleyrand to a meeting of imperial dignitaries to settle on a punishment for Fouché, who was eventually let off with mere disgrace. Talleyrand spoke up for him: 'No doubt M. Fouché was very much in the wrong and I believe he should be replaced. But by one man alone, by M. Fouché himself.' The emperor made as if not to hear and closed the meeting.

Whatever his disfavour, Talleyrand continued to act unafraid of Napoleon. It marked him out from other imperial courtiers, which was no doubt the reason why the emperor treated him differently. The courage it required had a simple, constant source: bow and flatter, perform and dissemble as he would, he never in his heart of hearts felt anything but superior to Napoleon. It was this innate sense of superiority that provided his protection. It extended to just about everyone he knew, and he was so sure of it that he joked about it to the harem: 'When I examine myself I worry, but when I compare myself I am reassured.'

Though Talleyrand spoke up for Fouché, the minister's reinstatement was of course out of the question and his departure much disappointed the foreign courts that were coming to rely on the Vice Grand Elector and his partner in government for inside intelligence on Napoleon's plans. The tsar's man, Nesselrode, was despondent. It was from Fouché, he said, that Cousin Henry got much of the information he was able to transmit to the tsar. 'I fear my correspondence will suffer and I would ask your indulgence in this regard from now on.'

By this time, however, Talleyrand's warnings had already had their effect on Alexander. In August 1810 he began contemplating a first blow against the Napoleonic empire rather than wait to receive one. It was a hard decision to reach but he had plenty of information to support it. In fact, Talleyrand now seemed to think he had been of sufficient service to Alexander to ask for a service for himself.

His need was suddenly urgent. The renewed disfavour with Napoleon once more imperilled his overall income, which was worrying. But there was worse. A Brussels bank in which he was heavily invested had just gone bankrupt and he was obliged to take a ruinous four-million-franc loss that he now urgently needed to cover. With Ouvrard out of reach in prison, he decided to turn humbly and in all candour to the monarch he'd befriended over a teapot at Erfurt. No doubt he was emboldened by the rising warmth of his friendship with the Duchess of Kurland, who was on near family terms with Alexander. There was no need to mention the duchess by name; to have her shimmering behind his inquiry ought to be enough. So in his own scribbled hand, in a letter dated 15 September 1810, he felt able to appeal to the Tsar of all the Russias:

> Sire,
> Your Majesty has shown an interest in me that in adverse times has been my pride and consolation, and I count on both your goodness and fairness to dare speak to you as I do now. Since Erfurt I have been continually beset by accusations, problems and inner torments that have made my position here difficult, and with it my financial affairs. Any action of mine that would have been thought simple in other times was likely to be wrongly interpreted. I decided that time alone would resolve the Emperor's suspicions, which were bound to disappear since I have always been devoted to him. I do believe my objective was more or less attained, but I have had to absent myself from the business scene and keep my name out of things as far as possible, and the result is that my financial affairs, though basically sound, have

taken an increasingly bad turn. After much thought and effort I see no way out that does not present grave inconvenience.

My need is for fifteen hundred thousand [1.5 million] francs, and it would be important to have this sum in November. While this is simple enough in itself, I must take considerable precautions over the means I choose to procure it and over how I repay it as soon as my circumstances change. This painful situation has come about abruptly without my realising it due to my forced absence from affairs, which has not reduced the expenditures I am honourbound to make. The matter should not come to public notice and for this reason I must address myself to someone sensitive and prescient enough, should they wish to do me a service, to take the indispensable precautions I here indicate. [There follow precise instructions concerning a Frankfurt bank to be used.] The malice of those void of trust, generosity and straight motives compels me to ask Your Majesty to burn this letter. My heart, in writing to you, is full of gratitude, affection, devotion and respect.

I am, Sire, with deep respect Your Majesty's most humble and obedient servant.

Charles-Maurice, Prince of Benevento.

Alexander did not burn the letter. Who could tell, it might be useful ammunition one day. But nor did he meet the colossal demand. The refusal was couched more elegantly than the request, which, for all its touching frankness, was a little brash by Talleyrand's standards. Alexander told him he certainly understood the size of his problem and thanked him for the great trust he showed in making the request. But wouldn't it be doing Talleyrand a disservice to agree to it? He did not wish to compromise him. It would be impossible to keep such a matter secret. 'Consequently, my Prince, it would only expose you to suspicion, while I myself would be straying from the pure and simple rule to which I hold in relations with foreign powers and those in their service. It is therefore with regret, Prince, that I refuse myself the pleasure I shall always find in obliging you.'

This was more than disappointing for Talleyrand. It was only the second time, after the experience with the prim Americans a dozen years back, that a request of his for financial consideration fell absolutely flat. His present position, though, was quite as serious as he made out. He was hugely in debt. Apart from the bank loss, the expense of running Valençay with half of Spain's royal house inside was crippling. The trouble was that his opulent living style couldn't be halted even if he tried: it was a very large vessel

with a large crew that wasn't to be turned around in the short time creditors wanted.

He didn't give up on Alexander. He tried a different tack, as Cousin
Henry. Since the tsar was opting out of the Napoleon's Continental System,
Talleyrand leaned on Nesselrode to get the tsar to grant him licences to run
goods from Russian ports to England, a reviving trade that could swing a
man's fortunes in no time. He wanted the licences left blank so that he could
pass them to an American financial associate of his in Paris who had author-
isation to visit England on business. Cousin Henry and his American friend
would fill in the blank documents with the names of ships and shipmasters
'with all necessary circumspection'. This enterprise too ran adrift, for by
April 1811 he was compelled to start selling off his worldly possessions,
first the Rue d'Anjou mansion which he'd kept on for his wife Catherine
after moving to the Hôtel de Monaco, then, once more, his library, including
a precious original edition of the encyclopaedia and its printing plates created
by the *philosophes* of the Enlightenment. For a book fancier like Talleyrand
this was a terrible wrench. It was the third time he'd sold a lovingly collected
library to help tide himself over, though judging by the inevitably modest
receipts the book sale may have been designed not so much to satisfy creditors as to make Napoleon aware of the jam his Vice Grand Elector was in.

Still, experience had made him an adept survivor. The present situation
was all very inconvenient, but not as bad as consorting with revolutionary
fanatics in search of an elusive passport to save his head from the guillotine, or being expelled from England with nowhere else in Europe to go.
Something always turned up to save a man of his rank. 'One must let time
take charge and bow to circumstances,' he now told himself. He was ever
the betting man awaiting better luck. The saving stratagem was to place
himself at the disposal of events.

It was, to be sure, the wrong emperor who saved him this time. While
Alexander demurred, Napoleon stepped in. But there were unspoken conditions. To have a bankrupt among the leading dignitaries of the empire would
clearly spoil its image, so the choice before Napoleon was either to dismiss
him or refloat him. That he chose not to remove him was further proof of
his desire to keep Talleyrand close at hand for his wisdom and experience.
More than once he'd thought of arresting him, or worse, but in the end his
need for him was too great to permit the sacrifice.

From the summer of 1811, as Talleyrand retired for a long stay at Bourbon
l'Archambault to tend his foot, his spreading rheumatism and his wheezy
chest, Napoleon called on the imperial treasury to tend his financial ailments.
Before the year was out the treasury disbursed some five million francs in

all for the backdated upkeep of the Spanish princes at Valençay, the purchase of minor Talleyrand properties and furnishings – and finally for the purchase at an inflated price of the Hôtel de Monaco itself. Talleyrand would have come in for more had Napoleon not fussily docked him 680,000 francs for a notable *douceur* he was said to have received from the Baltic ports of the Hanseatic League for services they now complained he never rendered. He would have received more still if, as he proposed, he'd been able to sell back to Napoleon his principality of Benevento, a transaction the prospective buyer balked at since it was anyway part of the empire he had made and owned.

There was a double purpose to Napoleon's generosity: to maintain the image of his regime and to hold his old antagonist ever more tightly in his grasp. As he saw it, Talleyrand was caught over a barrel. He told courtiers, 'My wish is that Talleyrand should be reduced to living on what my generosity provides.' He aimed to keep his Vice Grand Elector in humble subjection. That should blunt his cursed superiority! He rammed the point home, cruelly, to Talleyrand's new niece Dorothy, taking the intimidated girl aside at court one day to tell her he was 'totally indifferent to your poor Périgords'. The remark left her in tears. She wasn't yet used to the recriminations Napoleon bandied around at court, having just set up home with the soldiering Edmond de Périgord.

As for Talleyrand, he played the pendulum game according to his own designs. Still the important thing was to remain close to Napoleon. This required a certain amount of acting, which wasn't difficult: he was an actor so used to his part that he was at his most natural when playing it. Humbled was an easy role. In that part he was now glad to be asked by the emperor to walk with him and talk over political developments in the park at Versailles and else-where, which happened on several occasions. He took it as a sign of favour that Napoleon appointed Dorothy as lady-in-waiting to Empress Marie Louise, a fellow German speaker; also that the emperor agreed to be godfather to the first son Dorothy bore that year, the new heir to the House of Périgord.

When he looked back on this trying time, though, what stayed in his mind was how Napoleon enjoyed 'humiliating and torturing those he elevated'. He was thinking mainly of the Bonaparte brothers and of the marshals Napoleon enthroned as sovereigns, and he concluded that the emperor's desire to humiliate not only failed in its purpose, but that it was his downfall. 'They were placed in a perpetual state of distrust and irritation, and as they fought doggedly to counter the power that elevated them they soon regarded it as their prime enemy.'

Talleyrand was surely also thinking of his own position. The perverse standoff with Napoleon was nearing its denouement.

FIFTEEN

1812

Talleyrand's first purpose was to stop Napoleon making war, not to assist his enemies in making war against him. By 1812, though, the two issues grew a little blurred. This was inevitable once Napoleon was set in his stirrups for war on Russia. He was not about to dismount for anyone. To his fellow schemer Metternich in Vienna, Talleyrand forecast 'a very stormy year'.

Even so he was not altogether without success in his increasingly shadowy role as peacemaker. Through Nesselrode, he cajoled Tsar Alexander into abandoning plans to strike the first blow against Napoleon. The tsar had by now formally broken free of the Continental System. As a result he would do best, Talleyrand advised him, to take up a defensive position which would give him time to end his perennial hostilities with the Ottoman Empire, enter a firm alliance with Austria and repair the old tactical partnership with England. Talleyrand had in fact been labouring to slow Alexander down since the previous summer. Let Napoleon take responsibility for launching a new war! Again via Nesselrode, Talleyrand devised a fresh defence policy for Russia which was put to the tsar. In partnership with the Austrians, the Russians should draw a defensive line against Napoleon's empire. The line would say: French domination stops here. Starting on the Baltic and following the eastern boundaries of Prussia and the Duchy of Warsaw, it would curve down the frontiers of the Austrian Empire southwards. Any military violation of the line would be taken as a declaration of war.

Alexander liked the idea enough to postpone his original war plans. Indeed, it was likely that Talleyrand at least broached it with Napoleon too since the warrior was bound in any event to learn about it from Caulaincourt in St Petersburg, who was obliged to inform him of Alexander's latest intentions. Napoleon mulled it over, intrigued. It offered a framework in which Austria would mediate a peace between the French and Russian empires. The emperor couldn't mistake its parentage, which made him smile. 'You're the devil of a fellow,' he told Talleyrand at the close of an hour-long private talk that summer. 'I can't stop talking to you of my affairs and I can't help loving you.'

The bout of good humour was brief. Within days he reverted to his most menacing mood against Russia. Raging at the tsar's official ambassador – a colleague of Nesselrode, who himself remained 'accredited' to Talleyrand – he told him that even if Russian armies were camped in Paris on the heights of Montmartre he wouldn't yield an inch of the Warsaw duchy he'd created. This was fighting talk which Alexander took to be Napoleon's true position. Besides, Talleyrand's defensive line didn't really satisfy the tsar any more than it did Napoleon. All Alexander could see in the creation of the Duchy of Warsaw was a move towards restoring the old kingdom of Poland and as current master of a large part of that realm he couldn't tolerate it.

The war clouds gathered fast in the spring of 1812. Before striking out east on 11 May to join a huge if somewhat ragtag Grand Army – 600,000-strong and reinforced by the transfer of the crack Imperial Guard from Spain but nonetheless composed more of Germans, Poles and sundry middle European recruits than native Frenchmen – Napoleon conceived the idea of taking Talleyrand with him. If there was going to be a struggle over Poland, he wanted the right man at the helm of his Duchy of Warsaw, a demanding job for which no one was better experienced than Talleyrand. His ex-minister's personal relations with the tsar might also prove an advantage as hostilities progressed. The emperor's secondary motive for having Talleyrand with him was to prevent him from causing serious mischief at home. When asked, in strict confidentiality, to take the post, Talleyrand agreed, though with evident mixed feelings. While the 500,000 francs remuneration that went with the Warsaw position looked extremely tempting in his delicate financial state, the prospect of becoming a central figure in the belligerent enterprise against Russia ran against his own European designs. To him, the war on Russia was doomed anyway. He wasn't the only one to regard it as insane. No less a military insider than Marshal Auguste Marmont of the Grand Army shared his view, delighting the Faubourg Saint Germain with a judgement he preferred to put in the mouth of a government minister but which was more than likely his own: 'If you want to know the truth, to know where we're heading, the Emperor is mad, completely mad. He'll send us all flying arse over head, and it will all end in appalling catastrophe.'

Nonetheless, Napoleon's offer posed a dilemma which Talleyrand couldn't resist mentioning to the harem, for even though it put him on the spot he could brandish it as proof that he was once more back in the emperor's favour. Once he let the secret out, things went wrong. Napoleon's latest foreign minister, the successor to the ejected Champagny, saw Talleyrand's pending return to foreign affairs in central Europe as a threat to his own powers and spread word around Paris through his talkative wife that all Talleyrand intended to do was scuttle the emperor's campaign against Russia. Napoleon, furious both at the damaging gossip and at Talleyrand's unusually loose tongue, reacted by cancelling the appointment altogether. This was an outcome Talleyrand would have settled for, except that the emperor also ordered his police to expel him from Paris and keep him somewhere out of harm's way while he waged what he was promoting as the 'greatest and most difficult' campaign of his conqueror's career.

Typically, Napoleon left without insisting on having the banishment order enforced. The spirit of clemency Talleyrand aroused in him once more prevailed. He made do with telling Fouché's successor, General Savary, to keep Talleyrand and his friends under the tightest surveillance. At the same time he told Empress Marie Louise to do nothing that could possibly be seen as a favour to him, above all not to invite him to play whist at court. The location of Talleyrand's whist games appeared to cause Napoleon as much concern as his plans for battle.

So Talleyrand stayed in Paris, by all appearances able to get by without the large supplementary income briefly dangled in front of him. Thanks to the emperor and the inflated purchase price the imperial treasury paid for the Hôtel de Monaco, Talleyrand's financial affairs were once again looking at least manageable.

The change of home forced on him was anything but a comedown. He rehoused the large Talleyrand-Périgord retinue in an imposing mansion on a corner of the Place de la Concorde, back across the river in the Right Bank financial world. After all the home-moving brought on by rising rank, the threat of the guillotine, exile, ministerial grandeur, imperial favour, bountiful wealth and sudden financial crisis, the large stone mansion on the Rue Saint Florentin – at the corner of the Tuileries Palace gardens and the Place de la Concorde – was to remain his Paris home for the rest of his life. Not twenty years before it had provided a balcony seat at Louis XVI's execution, an appointment with the guillotine Talleyrand himself had barely managed to avoid.

In attacking Russia, Napoleon was driven by more than a blind passion for conquest. His ambition was to cripple England in the process. Once he got to Moscow he had the idea, a recurring dream, of using it as a base for moving on to India and knocking his worst enemy out of power in Asia's commercial heart. To be sure, the tsar's outright defection from the Continental System was a comfort to England, which she celebrated by once more renewing the continental alliance against Napoleon, this time with Russia alone as partner.

The London government, in which Lord Castlereagh, as foreign secretary, took charge of countering Napoleon, would have liked to bring Austria and Prussia into the coalition too, and they would certainly have agreed had they not been too far under Napoleon's domination to show the necessary independence. Castlereagh it was who planned the Peninsular War to drive Napoleon out of Spain and gave the dogged Arthur Wellesley command of the campaign. Castlereagh was an experienced head in war. All the same, it looked clear to Napoleon that England, in 1812, was just about as tight-stretched militarily as he himself was, so there seemed a good chance that once he crushed her lone coalition partner she would want to come to terms with him and stop insisting that he evacuate Spain as a first condition for compromise. Moreover, if Napoleon was rated mad by some, the crowned head of England was certified so. It was less than a year since George III's insanity had forced him off the throne to make way for a regency under his son, the future George IV. The regency was so far untested, hence, Napoleon thought, vulnerable.

And now, in June 1812 – precisely the moment Napoleon began his march on Moscow – England found herself not only engaged on land in the Peninsular War, she was pitched abruptly into a new land war across the Atlantic, against the United States. This seemed a godsend to Napoleon; it tied England down at the propitious time.

Like Talleyrand, who considered the United States a gawky power of small weight after his exile there, Napoleon had lost interest in the distant new republic once he'd settled his most pressing American affairs back in the days when he was First Consul. The world was Europe. Power was Europe. Beyond Europe little really mattered – except for colonisation possibilities. Besides, Napoleon now had his huge European empire to concentrate on. What interest was there in catering to this far off 'sister' republic? The imperial monarchy into which he'd transformed revolutionary France retained scarcely a shred of republicanism. Moreover, but for the new outbreak of hostilities with the mother country, the Americans weren't much interested in the world outside either; they were too busy testing the structures of the democracy they'd just created, and would be caught up in that for some time to come.

All the same Talleyrand's view that the US wasn't worth France's close attentions was a little off the mark. It grew from his conviction that the Americans, having taken their independence, were bound to remain in league with their colonial mother country. But now here was a sign that the US had more muscle to flex than Talleyrand allowed it. The new war with England in 1812 resulted from dire trading frictions aggravated by Napoleon's Continental System. For years now both the English and the

French had gone back to harassing and seizing neutral shipping, much of it American, as they struggled for the upper hand in blockading each other. The Royal Navy acted the toughest; English warships became progressively entangled with American vessels off the US coast and in American ports, infuriating Americans by impressing their sailors into England's service. Naval gunbattles sent ships of both sides to the bottom. Though England, by 1812, was finding this ugly sideshow to the war in Europe a luxury it could do without and decided to make concessions, mixed diplomatic signals and long delays in transatlantic communications brought the American president, James Madison, to declare war on England on 1 June – the same day Napoleon boasted in a letter to Empress Marie Louise, from a battle tent in eastern Europe, that his war on Russia would be over so quickly that he'd be back in Paris at her side within three months.

England was in no position to forecast so rapid an end to the war with the US. Though Castlereagh was at first set on a speedy compromise, once President Madison had declared war there was no escaping it. English and American forces went at each other from the Great Lakes and New England down to the mouth of the Mississippi, with fortunes swinging wildly. The fighting was to continue for more than two years. In August 1814 English troops marched unopposed on Washington and burned down Madison's White House and the Capitol, a retaliation against the torching by American troops of their Great Lakes stronghold of York, later to become Toronto. Neither side came out conspicuously victorious in the end and the peace they signed at Christmas 1814 did little else but secure the release of prisoners and confirm the US boundary with English Canada.

Still, a war that was bound to deplete his enemy on the other side of the Atlantic seemed a benediction to Napoleon on his march to Moscow. Indeed, certain of his adversaries in Europe complained that America was fighting Napoleon's war for him, a charge which riled Madison and brought the White House to call a plague on both the French and English houses.

Whatever help Napoleon ultimately derived from American belligerence, the outbreak of war between England and the United States was infinitely better tidings than he received in mid-1812 concerning England's prior military enterprise, the war against his own forces in Spain. General Wellesley, risen to Viscount Wellington, two years shy of his dukedom, had by now thrust from Portugal into Spain with the troops of those two countries fighting at his side and Napoleon's own commanders found their English opponent impossible to deal with. He refused to make war as they did, head on, with devil-may-care dash. Instead he concealed his forces behind slopes and had them lie down so as not to offer themselves as targets. He was irritatingly cautious, ready to retreat even after a victory so as not to outreach himself. Once he accepted to do battle, he stood his infantrymen in lines of fire instead of moving them forward in columns to engage the enemy in the French manner.

On his march to Moscow Napoleon was therefore beset by dark thoughts that he was losing control of Spain. Wellington's defeat of Marshal Marmont at Salamanca in July 1812 – an event which the courts of Europe happily seized upon as a turning point in Napoleon's fortunes – reached him just as he entered Russian territory. The unfortunate Marmont's crude forecast that so entertained the Faubourg Saint Germain had caught up with its author, landing him too on his rump. For Napoleon, the sole consolation was that Wellington once more celebrated victory by retreating to Portugal.

Talleyrand was obliged to settle back in Paris and turn these momentous events round in his diplomat's brain. He dwelt continually on the prospects for making peace with England. But all he could reasonably do now was to wait and see what became of Napoleon. The point at which trying to stop him made the slightest sense had long since passed, and 'Cousin Henry' couldn't help much either. The French nation was exhausted and demoralised by the emperor's endless lust for conquest, yet by and large remained so convinced of his military genius that it never doubted he would emerge victorious. Talleyrand was of a different mind. This was, he sighed, 'the beginning of the end'. The mission he gave himself now was to make sure he was adequately positioned to pick up France's pieces.

He missed the Duchess of Kurland. He was truly attached to her and his 'morning notes' showed it. She stirred hidden feelings in him, a fervour calling forth a tender flow of words. In the Talleyrand way, he was, his visitors noted, head over heels in love. But the duchess left Paris in early June, in Napoleon's tracks, intent on protecting her estates in the lands the Grand Army was likely to pass through and also on protecting her generous pension from Tsar Alexander. She had felt the tsar wouldn't take kindly to her residing in the enemy's capital in time of war; she was, after all, a Russian subject.

In the Talleyrand harem, the spirited duchess was already known as the 'Sultana' although she was its newest member. Mme de Laval and the rest of the countesses couldn't help but admire her dresses, her make-up, her slenderness, her inborn haughtiness and her facility with languages which produced a charming little foreign accent in French. The old-guard harem's sole consolation was her nose, which, like her daughter Dorothy's, was rather long. But she would turn up in the best salons at midnight flashing a new ballgown and jewels like a twenty-year-old and Talleyrand couldn't take his eyes off her. That spring Talleyrand spent days on end at a grand villa the

Duchess Dorothea had bought at Saint Germain in the country, a short carriage ride west of Paris. He rode on horseback in the forest there with her, trying to keep up; he helped her compose a stream of letters to Tsar Alexander, and in his morning notes to 'my angel' he told her, a touch sadly, how he felt about Napoleon's disfavour: 'One must try not to become too bitter. The thing is to be there in one piece for the times ahead, which won't be easy.'

He was seldom inactive. To amuse himself and the countesses he penned rude poems about Napoleon and recited them with his best impassive face. He finished writing a tart biographical work on the Duc de Choiseul, the *ancien régime* foreign minister and uncle of his schooldays companion at Harcourt College. While glad to finish it, he wasn't pleased with it, at least not with his handwriting. He told the Duchess Dorothea it was so illegible that he'd have to copy it out again himself, which was going to be a huge bore considering it ran to eighty pages.

There were also more serious matters to attend to. Even while taking his regular summer cure at the family spa, he was busy thinking up ways to ensure he was well placed to shape events in a post-Napoleon crisis. He hadn't quite made up his mind what form of government would serve France best, but no one who cared strongly about legitimacy, as he did, could exclude some constitutional role for the exiled Bourbon dynasty. No doubt the French people were still too marked by their Revolution to want a Bourbon restoration, but the mood could quickly change. While it wasn't easy to communicate with the portly prince who styled himself Louis XVIII at his English retreat in Kent – and less than likely that the man would want to hear from him anyway, given his part in the Revolution – Talleyrand gave it a try.

It was no more than a feeler. And there was the eagle-eyed Savary, the police minister, to slip it past. But he had two promising lines of communication: his young diarist protégée Mme de Coigny had a prominent royalist uncle who lived at the court in Kent, and his own uncle, the Archbishop of Reims, his amiable mentor as a youth, was the court's Grand Almoner. By one means or the other, Talleyrand managed to get a letter through to his uncle who handed it to Louis XVIII.

What it said was never published, but it amused the would-be monarch. A letter from Talleyrand was bound to have a motive. 'Good God,' he said, with an ironic smile, 'Bonaparte must be finished . . . Tell him I accept the omen his greetings carry.'

The family retinue Talleyrand took to the spa included his half-abandoned wife Catherine, who was content to be Princess of Benevento if nothing else; his penniless brother Boson, whom he supported with a monthly allowance; and, more entertainingly, the Princess Dorothy, only eighteen but a girl of precocious intelligence with a good head for politics. Her recent position as lady-in-waiting to the Empress Marie Louise was an ideal learning bench. Talleyrand enjoyed her company. In her mother's absence in the east, he was getting to know her well. Most of the time she lived in his mansion on the Place de la Concorde since her husband Edmond, now a cavalry colonel, was constantly away. He was in effect her guardian. He noticed that she breezed through the social receptions he held there – and not because of her conspicuous beauty. 'At this stage she was what women vulgarly call a prune,' Charles de Rémusat, the court chamberlain observed. 'Excessively thin and restless. Her face was small, tight, chiselled and full of grimaces, so that her sole allure was her big eyes and beautiful teeth.' Still, he forecast even then that she was going to become one of the most beautiful women of her time.

Dorothy was in awe of her 'uncle'. It amounted to adoration, which flattered him. Her young spectacles were tinted deepest rose:

What made him so impressive was a trait that showed through his natural indolence. It was his courage, a courage full of sang-froid and presence of mind, a bold temperament, an instinctive bravado that inspires an irresistible taste for danger in all its forms, that makes peril seductive and lends so much charm to chance. Beneath his noble features, his slow movements and sybaritic habits was a rash audacity that sparkled and revealed all his talents. The very contrast made him one of the most original and appealing of creatures.

Dorothy's wasn't a standard view of Talleyrand. The countesses with their liberal views and love of sharp political banter of course remained forever admiring. But many who crossed his path saw only coldness in the 'sang-froid' and straight laziness in the 'natural indolence'. Still, what the girl saw in him was also one of the things that most impressed Napoleon: Talleyrand the audacious, Talleyrand the chancer. It was a trait that no doubt made him want to keep Talleyrand near and stopped him from ever breaking off their relations altogether.

All the same, the closest Talleyrand was able to keep to Napoleon during the assault on Russia was through an intermediary, his longtime confidant Caulaincourt, now serving as the emperor's aide-de-camp. Caulaincourt slipped into that demanding post because as ambassador to St Petersburg he had unrivalled knowledge of Russia and the tsar's likely tactics. His and Talleyrand's views on the bleak future facing the Napoleonic empire were very similar, yet they carried on a curiously upbeat correspondence during this time. From Talleyrand's end came praise for the Grand Army's early progress and the old bouquets to Napoleon's glory. Opinion at home, Talleyrand wrote, was that the Russians would fight to save their honour but after a first battle they wouldn't try to prolong the resistance. He added that he wasn't receiving much mail from the Duchess of Kurland in her eastern domains. 'If you can be of any assistance to her in her difficult situation, I commend you to her and her family.' His letters were extremely prudent, masking his true feelings, since he knew Savary would intercept them, make copies and forward them to Napoleon.

This game continued through October when an extraordinary episode, a half successful *coup d'état* against Napoleon, set Paris on edge. Talleyrand wasn't part of it. Those involved were not of his rank, his class or persuasion. The leader was an eccentric ex-general by the name of Claude François de Malet, a recent asylum inmate, who bluffed his way into taking over the government by announcing to the commander of a Paris army barracks that Napoleon was dead and securing his support in the emergency. Having killed the military governor of Paris, Malet's next move was to arrest Savary, neutralising Napoleon's police power. The life of Malet's provisional government was brief. Less credulous army officers swiftly halted the plot, executing its leader and eleven fellow conspirators, an odd mix of royalist and republican crusaders. But news of the near successful putsch came as a grave shock to Napoleon, who was wary of even the merest threat to his power.

As Vice Grand Elector, Talleyrand was called in by Arch-Chancellor Cambacérès to help calm things down, but he couldn't take the plot itself seriously beyond pointing out that if halfway credible parliamentary institutions were in place – the kind, that is, that Napoleon had throttled – the plotters would never have succeeded as far as they did. His letters to Caulaincourt sounded as though his first concern was to make sure that Napoleon didn't impute the slightest blame to him. It just showed, he wrote, that the troops in Paris were a poor lot to have been taken in so easily. Paris needed a reliable garrison of well-trained soldiers. 'All that remains of the whole affair is public astonishment at how easily troops can be led astray.'

Behind the anodyne views on the emperor penned for prying police eyes, Talleyrand was growing increasingly blunt when talking face to face with friends. People like Malet were fools, but action was urgently needed to save France. What action? asked Mme de Coigny in one of their frequent discussions. 'Napoleon must be destroyed, no matter how,' Talleyrand told her:

> The man has nothing more to do of any use. His time of strength against the Revolution is past. The ideas he alone was able to confront

have lost their force and are no longer a danger. They were bound to go away. He has destroyed equality, so be it – but we must keep liberty. We must have laws. With him it's impossible. Now is the time to get rid of him.

But this was mere sounding off. Talleyrand had already decided that the emperor was about to destroy himself, and his own role was to lubricate the process. The trick was to prevent Napoleon's defeat from being a defeat for France. It was a challenge that tested the very logic of war.

Until October the campaign in Russia appeared to go tolerably well for Napoleon, except that the foe kept melting away in front of him before he could deliver his customary decisive blow. The result was that a quarter of the Grand Army was wiped out through disease, desertion and exhaustion from forced marches before a serious engagement occurred. This was Tsar Alexander's plan. Time and space were on his side. He would keep withdrawing to the extremes of the Russian Empire if need be, but never lay down his arms or sign an armistice with Napoleon. Aside from a pair of brutal head-on encounters at Smolensk and then Borodino on the approaches to Moscow, neither of which entirely went Napoleon's way, the Grand Army was still pursuing an elusive foe and warding off perpetual harassment by Cossacks when it entered Moscow itself on 14 September.

Alexander wasn't there to meet Napoleon, nor was any Russian peace negotiator. The tsar was holding to his plan, sucking the Grand Army into Russia's heartland. The day after Napoleon dismounted, Moscow caught fire and became a smouldering ruin within three days. The blaze was started by the Russians themselves, as Napoleon at once wrote to inform the tsar in St Petersburg, though the news of it inevitably struck Europe as symbolising his craze to destroy. He stayed in Moscow's charred husk for a month, undecided on further action, as Russian forces massed in his rear. He wanted to dictate an armistice but there was no one to dictate it to. His situation was bleak and also pointless. Cut off from supplies and with a Russian winter almost upon him, the conqueror opted to retreat, leading the Grand Army out of Moscow on 19 October. He headed back west the way he had come, through country devastated twice over by Russian scorched-earth tactics and the ravaging passage of his own troops, so that the stink of rotting corpses was everywhere in his soldiers' nostrils until the first snow fell and the thermometer dropped to minus 25 degrees at the turn of November. The ill-equipped remnants of the Grand Army froze, yet still had to give battle to maintain the retreat. Those who couldn't keep up or became separated by marauding Cossacks were clubbed to death by Russian peasants.

It was the worst military disaster to befall France in her entire history: by the time the Grand Army recrossed Russia's confines on the river Niemen fewer than 20,000 men remained of the 600,000 who had set out in the other direction. Napoleon himself narrowly escaped capture by Cossacks and ordered a strong poison from his doctor to keep in his pocket in case of need; he wasn't going to be dragged through the snow to St Petersburg at the end of a Cossack rope.

Napoleon abandoned his forces in Lithuania on 5 December, some two weeks before they reached the Niemen. He'd abandoned an army once before, in Egypt, in order to have his way in Paris. Now he was twisting with fury and foreboding at the news that had not long since reached him of the Malet putsch. He had to be in Paris to restore his power. There was no smoke without fire in such plots. Who had put Malet up to it? He would find out. The emperor left the tragic campaign at night in secret with only Caulaincourt and a pair of orderlies for company, leaving his surviving marshals to discover his departure on receiving his last orders in the morning. 'In the current state of things I can only have my way in Europe from the Tuileries Palace,' he told his aide-de-camp, cursing himself for having stayed in Moscow for more than a month and allowing the weather to close in on him.

Back in Paris, Talleyrand's ears burned. He seemed to haunt Napoleon on his journey home.

In his solitary carriage bumping over the snowbound tracks of Lithuania, wrapped in a bearskin, his fur hat pulled far down over his ears, his breath freezing on his lips, the emperor mused endlessly on his Vice Grand Elector. He regretted not taking him on the campaign. That was a mistake, he told Caulaincourt. 'I was wrong to get angry with Talleyrand. He would have given a real sense of direction to things in Poland.' But he blew both hot and cold at his old antagonist. It annoyed him that Talleyrand attributed his disgrace to his opposition to the war in Spain. No one was more convinced than Talleyrand, the emperor groused, that cooperation between Spain and Portugal against England was the only way to force the London government to the negotiating table. 'Now he's the apostle of the malcontents! I'm not holding it against him. He's a good judge of things. He's the most capable minister I've had.' In the next breath, though, he accused Talleyrand of being against the war in Spain for the pettiest of reasons – because he was riled at not being made Imperial Arch-Chancellor as he'd hoped. 'He threw stones at me, like all cowards, when he thought I was beaten.'

The carriage was getting nowhere on the blocked roads. Caulaincourt swapped it for a farmer's sled which whistled over the iced tracks into east

Prussia. The faster going lifted Napoleon's spirits, though he kept his fur hat well down to make sure no one recognised him. At times his situation pulled at his sense of humour. It was a matter of days, he realised, before Prussia took stock of his retreat and rose against him. What if the Prussians arrested him and handed him over to the English to be paraded through London in an iron cage! He couldn't allow that. Then back he came to Talleyrand, aware that Caulaincourt was in regular contact with him. 'He is a man of intrigue, of great immorality, but of high intellect. He is certainly the most capable minister I ever had. I kept him out of affairs for a long time, but I'm no longer angry. He would still be minister if he'd wanted.' But then again, why placate Paris salon society? The Faubourg Saint Germain crowd that Talleyrand personified always criticised, never praised. All the fuss they made when he removed troublemakers like Mme de Staël from Paris for intriguing against him! 'They call that tyranny! They say I'm a tyrant because I won't let a few mad women get themselves talked about.'

Napoleon's thoughts were running wild in the farm sled. The root of his trouble was England, always England! 'It is England that drove me, forced me to do everything I've done. If England hadn't broken the Amiens treaty, I would have stayed at home quietly.' England wanted a monopoly on trade. If England was of good faith she wouldn't constantly refuse to negotiate with him. 'If we negotiated she would be forced to show her ambitions for what they are. Then we'd see which side has the good faith!' As they crunched into Warsaw, where Napoleon felt safer, Caulaincourt thought he seemed disappointed that people on the street didn't recognise the man who held out the promise of an independent Poland. But it was too cold for passers-by to stop and stare, and too cold for the emperor to remove the hat hiding his face. Nevertheless in Warsaw, his old self began to re-emerge, masterful, self-deluding: 'The sole difference between me and other sovereigns is that they let difficulties stand in their way. I like to overcome them, when I can see the goal is grand and noble, worthy of me and the nation I govern.'

Within fourteen days of leaving the Grand Army to fend for itself he was back at the Tuileries Palace. By chance, Talleyrand was among the first to know of his return. As lady-in-waiting to Empress Marie Louise, Dorothy was present in the Tuileries Palace late on 18 December when two shabby men in furs came to the empress's quarters. Recognising the emperor and his aide-de-camp, Dorothy scribbled a note to Talleyrand and sped it to him by messenger. Talleyrand, woken from a doze, was astonished. He thought Napoleon was still somewhere in Russia.

SIXTEEN

A Conqueror's Fall

Napoleon never seemed at a loss, not even now. Nonetheless on 3 January 1813 he summoned an emergency council of state, which Talleyrand attended as Vice Grand Chancellor, to field suggestions from imperial dignitaries on how to meet the crisis facing his empire. News was just in that Prussia was indeed joining forces with Russia, which meant that the rest of Germany in the Confederation of the Rhine could soon start peeling away from the empire, with the skeleton Grand Army powerless to resist. 'Negotiate,' insisted Talleyrand. 'Today you still have pieces to play that you can afford to give up. Tomorrow you may have lost them and you will have lost any negotiating advantage too.' What Talleyrand wanted was what he had always wanted: a retraction of the empire to France's 'natural frontiers' of the Rhine and the western Alps. He believed no foreign power would quarrel with that. It would leave France whole and in peace to mend herself.

But Napoleon would still have none of it. He chided Talleyrand for harping on about peace without knowing how to achieve it. He had a fresh troop levy in the pipeline for 350,000 recruits. His surviving marshals, he openly acknowledged, were dispirited and longed for rest, but there were always more bodies to be found. He was determined to pursue continental war to prevent his empire unravelling.

All the same he accepted that his position was fragile. In February he created a Regency Council to plan for his eventual succession by his infant son, the King of Rome. Marie Louise was titular head of the putative regency, a choice which suited Talleyrand, also a member of this council by virtue of his imperial rank.

For years now Talleyrand had been dwelling on the prospect of Napoleon being killed or abdicating – this was a statesman's responsibility whatever his inclinations in the matter – and he rather preferred at this stage a regency to the return of the Bourbons and their archaic obsessions. The polite contact he'd managed to make with 'Louis XVIII' didn't alter his preference. The trouble with the Bourbons was that they would need to be shaken and retrained into accepting the new liberties that Napoleon had inherited from the Revolution and then discarded. In a regency, things would be easier. Also, Talleyrand could be fairly confident of taking charge. Who else but he could both square things at home and obtain the support of foreign powers now closing in on Napoleon? It wasn't power he sought; it was the chance to resettle France safely within her natural frontiers and restore lost liberties.

Thus decided, he set out to hasten Napoleon's fall, to bring on the inevitable sooner than fate might be proposing. He reappeared as 'X' in renewed secret contacts with the Austrians. In coded diplomatic dispatches addressed to Metternich in Vienna, X was quoted as saying that Austria couldn't begin to influence Napoleon unless it strengthened its army to at least 200,000 men – and it should 'exaggerate' the size if it hoped to impose itself as mediator between the emperor and his immediate Russian–Prussian foes. Quite so, Metternich responded, Austria would do just that.

By May 1813 Napoleon was off at war once more, this time flashing his sword at the reawakened Prussians who now threatened his empire at its heart. With a patched-up army of Grand Army survivors and new conscripts, devoid of cavalry, he struck at combined Prussian–Russian forces ranged against him from Saxony to the Baltic, winning a series of partial victories but nothing conclusive. He was surprised by the venom of the Prussians, whom he'd regarded as a wheedling folk since he first took power. 'Those animals have learned something,' he muttered, signing a truce in June, merely by way of brief respite to replace further cruel French troop losses. During the truce he went to Dresden to meet Metternich who proposed Austrian mediation on condition he lifted his imperial yoke from Prussia and the Confederation of the Rhine. The effect of Metternich's demands on Napoleon was that of a mind-doctor probing his torments. 'What do you want of me! Dishonour myself? Never! I shall die before yielding an inch of territory. Your monarchs are born on their thrones. They can afford to be defeated twenty times over and still return to their capitals. Me, I cannot, I'm an upstart soldier! My domination won't last beyond the day I cease to be strong and people fear me.'

Napoleon's self-analysis sounded sufficiently interesting to Metternich to induce him, with a push from England, to enter forthwith a secret pact with the Russians and Prussians. By mid-August, as the truce expired, Austria's Emperor Franz too was at war with his despised new son-in-law. Now Napoleon was gravely outnumbered and outgunned. His last hopes vanished at the battle of Leipzig in October 1813, his final engagement of the war outside French soil. His routed forces, again depleted by tens of thousands of losses, fell back on Frankfurt, then to the Rhine, that 'natural frontier' beyond which Talleyrand had warned French arms, be they revolutionary or imperial, never to venture in the first place.

If Napoleon himself wasn't finished, his empire was. The kingdom of Westphalia collapsed; the German princes in the Confederation of the Rhine rushed into Austria's arms; a national uprising liberated Holland; Italy too dropped away, though the freelancing pretensions of Napoleon's brother-in-law, Marshal Joachim Murat, to take charge of all Italy for himself delayed its release. To queer the ambitions of Murat – King of Naples, husband of his sister Caroline, the knight who had led the Grand Army cavalry into Moscow – Napoleon freed Pope Pius from captivity in Fontainebleau and sent him back to Rome to reclaim the papal lands.

Things were no different in Spain. Wellington's stubborn campaign forced Joseph Bonaparte off the throne in Madrid and put Napoleon's forces to flight in a decisive engagement at Vitoria in the Basque Country, allowing English troops to march round the Pyrenees and enter France for the first time on 8 October.

Talleyrand could hardly help welcoming Wellington's unremitting progress. First there was the part it played in undoing Napoleon, then the fact that it prompted the emperor to free the Spanish princes from his estate at Valençay where their gracious upkeep had been straining his resources for the past five years. Prince Ferdinand, the house guest slapped down by 'Cousin' Napoleon for overfamiliarity, regained Spain's throne as Ferdinand VII. Napoleon's impulse to liberate Spain by conquest ended after years of war and turmoil by restoring the Spanish Bourbons he had overthrown.

As Napoleon's reign crumbled, Talleyrand's old sympathies for him briefly resurfaced, competing with his revulsion. It wasn't easy to convince himself that he hated Napoleon and he battled to square his conscience. He recollected:

> It is not without bitter pain, I confess, that I assisted at such a spectacle. I loved Napoleon. I had attached myself to his person, despite his faults. At the start I was drawn towards him by the irresistible attraction a great genius carries within him. The benefits he brought me earned my sincere gratitude. Why deny it? I partook of his glory and the reflection that glowed on those who helped him in his noble task. I can thus bear witness that, as far as it was within my power, I served him with enlightened devotion. As long as he knew how to hear the truth, I told it to him loyally. I told it to him even later, when one had to employ certain manoeuvres to reach him. The disgrace that my

candour brought me is justification, before my conscience, for having first separated myself from his policy, then from his person when he reached the point of imperilling my country's destiny.

That emphasis on 'my' country showed how deep their split went. Talleyrand couldn't recognise *his* France in Napoleon's France.

His disdain soon regained the ascendancy as the emperor ensconced himself at the old royal palace of Saint Cloud on the wooded western side of the capital on returning from Leipzig on 9 November 1813, complaining bitterly about being let down by all the ingrates on whom he'd heaped honours and privileges. Talleyrand was present at his return and no doubt took the diatribe to heart. As he reached home that evening he ran into a countess friend who was curious to hear of the emperor's condition. 'Oh, please! Let me be,' he said. 'The man is finished.' She begged him to explain. 'What I mean is this, he's a man who will hide under his bed.'

Similar venom poured from Napoleon when his Vice Grand Elector attended an open-court reception the very next morning. The emperor was in darkest mood. Talleyrand hadn't entirely kept to himself his particular interest in the advantages of a regency, and the emperor evidently had wind of it. Seeing his former minister, he called: 'What are you doing here? I know you imagine that if I was no longer around you'd be the head of the regency council. Be careful, sir. You gain nothing by fighting against my power. Let me tell you, if I was dangerously ill, you would die before me!'

Talleyrand, imperturbable, observed: 'Sire, I did not require such a warning to pray to high heaven for Your Majesty's enduring good health.'

With Napoleon's military back against the wall and the continental powers preparing to cross the Rhine, invade France and take the fight to him, Talleyrand's quick irony, the bravado of it, reflected a change in their long-running duel. The balance had shifted. All at once Napoleon's need for Talleyrand seemed stronger than Talleyrand's need to stay close. Not a week after Napoleon threatened to kill him, he called him in for private consultations on the mess in Spain.

'Well now, Sire! You consult me as though we were not at odds!' Talleyrand half objected.

'Circumstances! Circumstances!' said the emperor. 'Let's leave the past and the future and have your view on the present.'

'Well, you have only one solution. You have made a mistake. You must say so, and try to say it graciously.'

Talleyrand indeed felt stronger now. He bade the emperor tell the Spanish people he had never intended to make war on them as a nation; he could now see that they were attached to their Bourbon monarchy, for all its past faults, and he was giving it back to them so that no one could say he opposed the national will. 'A lofty admission of this kind when foreigners are still considering their course of action on your frontiers can only do you honour, and you are still too strong for anyone to take it as cowardice.'

Events moved very quickly now. Prior to an attack on France by the continental allies, Napoleon tentatively agreed to armistice talks. Neither he nor they believed such negotiations held out any real chance of success; they were too far apart for that. But Napoleon thought formal talks might buy him time to regroup militarily, and the allies thought it worth the semblance of a try to achieve what they wanted without having to march on the emperor's home territory. At the very least they insisted on France retreating behind her pre-revolutionary frontiers, which largely fell a good way short of the Rhine. So Napoleon thought it worth having in his corner as foreign minister at this critical stage a man the allies knew. Grudgingly, he turned to Talleyrand, who was backed by Caulaincourt and also by Savary, no friend of Talleyrand but better placed than most to judge how desperate Napoleon's plight was. Caulaincourt was to represent the emperor at the armistice talks and it was he who pushed him into restoring Talleyrand at the head of foreign affairs. At first the warrior only played with the idea. 'After all, I'm not entirely opposed to it. He has a great mind. He has never been anyone's fool. Only he has kept vile company . . .'

It was strange, given the drastic situation, that the vile company started in Napoleon's eyes not with the ogre-ish financiers who inhabited Talleyrand's world but with his wife Catherine. No matter that she was by now a background figure in the Talleyrand household. Here was the emperor seeking to hold off an alarming coalition of foreign armies stamping at his doorstep, and all the while fussing obsessively over the sort of impression 'that trollop' was likely to create if he reinstated her husband to face them. For several days in mid-November he wrestled with himself over the nomination, his views lunging back and forth. 'I don't want Talleyrand,' he told Caulaincourt. 'Not that I don't value his talents. He's the man with the most opinions, the most skills. But what a mixture! Gold and shit in one!' The old epithet stuck.

If he did take Talleyrand, though, he wanted him to divorce himself from his ring of feminine 'intrigue', in which he counted not only his salon soulmate Mme de Laval, a true mistress of the art, but also the Duchess of Kurland, now back in Paris, who he thought was much too close to the tsar. Furthermore, Talleyrand would have to give up his Vice Grand Elector rank since a high imperial dignitary couldn't rightly double as a government minister. The wall of conditions grew high.

Talleyrand was disinclined to scale it. He found the emperor's approach bizarre. The two of them could never see eye to eye on how to extract France from the mess Napoleon had landed her in. Why put himself in the position of trying to save the man he wished France to be rid of? It was, of course, the wrong time for *douceurs*. No one would be requiring favours of France, not even the German princes. Granting favours meant holding the whip hand; it would be France that sought favours now. Moreover, Napoleon's conditions stung. The rank of elector was precious insurance for Talleyrand: along with the opulent salary, it promised him control of a future regency despite Napoleon's dark threat. 'The emperor asks me to discredit myself, to abandon my friends,' he told Caulaincourt. 'That ill equips me to serve him. For himself and myself, I refuse.'

While it was recognition of his singular talents and certainly better than disgrace, to be called back into Napoleon's close service was a most uncomfortable experience for Talleyrand. He knew that Napoleon didn't stand for being refused. And now came proof of it. The emperor fumed at his 'ingratitude'. Talleyrand was on his high horse because he believed he was indispensable! Very well, the emperor allowed, he needn't drive out his scheming feminine entourage from one day to the next; he could do so gradually. And surely he would find a way to move his wife to some place where she was no kind of political embarrassment! Caught in the middle, Caulaincourt had orders to force Talleyrand's hand. Three times he arrived at his door with the same demand, the conditions marginally softened but never lifted. The emperor's instructions grew more pressing. 'Remind him he is a Frenchman and his emperor has the right to command him! No one defies the emperor!' And sterner still: 'He who refuses me his services today is necessarily my enemy.'

The threat of punishment, imprisonment, exile again rang through the emperor's words, though as usual, when addressed to Talleyrand, the threat proved empty. By the end of November Napoleon saw that his blandishments were in vain; he ordered Caulaincourt instead to take the foreign ministry, which was no doubt his true preference and one he would have imposed from the start but for Talleyrand's larger reputation with the vengeful European powers.

Once he was off the hook, Talleyrand sensed that the tussle over the foreign ministry was perhaps an ultimate encounter in his long duel of wills with the emperor. He felt relieved. Now he could plan for what lay in store after Napoleon and induce France's enemies to be magnanimous. All the same a last shred of his old sympathy lingered in the damning reflection: 'The emperor's greatest misfortune, a misfortune without remedy, is his isolation. He is alone, as he wanted it, alone in Europe. But that's nothing – he is alone in France.'

*   *   *

In late December 1813 the combined forces of Prussia, Russia and Austria, joined by Sweden – their monarchs at their head – crossed the Rhine to invade France. The battle for the Napoleonic empire's homeland was engaged. In the south the assault was already proceeding apace with Wellington's army moving up through Aquitaine towards Bordeaux. Against 250,000 allied troops marching on Paris from the east Napoleon could now muster a force of no more than eighty thousand. French youths who hadn't melted into the forests were pulling their teeth and burning their limbs with acid to avoid the call to arms. The nation was listless in face of the invasion; people in the east largely displayed apathy towards the attack, even support. But Napoleon wasn't giving up. He would continue to fight. Vanquish or perish, that was all he knew.

Talleyrand attended, not unmoved, an emotional ceremony at the Tuileries Palace on 23 January which Napoleon called to make his farewell to the National Guard, the mainstay of his Paris garrison. This was the signal for his imminent departure to join the meagre field army awaiting him in eastern France. He also attended the next day a 'lugubrious' final meeting of imperial dignitaries and ministers at Fontainebleau, at which the emperor formalised his appointment of Marie Louise as regent in case of his death. Talleyrand, still a member of the Regency Council, observed Napoleon looking daggers at him and heard him fuming about leaving behind enemies in Paris as real as those he was about to meet in the field. And now his absence gave them a free hand! Aware, like everyone present, that he was a particular target of Napoleon's discontent, he sought to deflect it by starting a conversation in a corner with Joseph Bonaparte, the dethroned King of Spain, who wasn't on the best terms with his brother either since he was suspected of having a flirtation, and maybe more, with Marie Louise. Predictably, the diversion only inflamed Napoleon further.

Talleyrand wouldn't forget the emperor's sour face. It was the last time he ever saw him.

It was not, though, the end of their contest. Taking stock, Talleyrand peered at the grave challenges ahead and the part he intended to play in meeting them. He recalled:

> Once invaded, France had so much piled against her. What could be done to hold off the ills that threatened her? What form of government did she need if she came through this terrible catastrophe? Those were grave matters for all good Frenchmen to meditate upon. To do so was a duty for those whom circumstances, or, if you will, ambition, had already summoned in other times to exercise influence over the fate of their country . . . The closer I saw the frightful denouement

coming, the more closely and carefully I examined the resources that remained to us.

This was neither to betray Napoleon nor to plot against him, though he more than once told me it was. I have only conspired in my life at times when I had the majority of France as my accomplice, or when I sought with that majority the security of our country. The mistrust and insults Napoleon directed at me cannot change the truth. I repeat it at the top of my voice: there was never more dangerous a conspirator against Napoleon than Napoleon himself.

This was looking back, with a good measure of self-justification, but it has the ring of truth.

Napoleon's fall had its peculiar excitement. Gloom was threaded with exultation. At the outset of 1814 Paris tensed – and feasted on rumour. There was the unpredictability of it all. The odds never seemed to matter to Napoleon. What size of rabbit would the conqueror pull from the hat this time? Talleyrand, turning sixty, downed by a heavy cold, lived the finale from the capital, which he had no intention of leaving. The daily tension stirred his sexagenarian ardour for the Duchess of Kurland, increasing his stream of morning notes to three a day, according to the war news.

He was concerned for her safety now that she was back in Paris, and for Dorothy's. As long as Empress Marie Louise stayed in the capital, he advised the duchess in a heady little note sent on 25 January, Paris was a better place to be than most. 'If she were to leave, you should make sure there is nothing to stop you leaving immediately. That is my advice, dear friend. I find all is bearable when I am near you. You! You! You! The one I love most in the world.'

He poured his heart into these notes, a curious blend of high politics and love that echoed the incredible events taking place. 'We are close to what may be a terrible crisis. God protect us,' he wrote, purveying news of a bad setback for Napoleon in early February not 150 miles from Paris at the hands of the Prussian commander, Gebhard von Blücher. Three days later he had convinced the duchess to leave with Dorothy for Rosny, a country chateau which Dorothy and Edmond owned on the safe road to Normandy. 'Take with you when you travel the little picture I have sent you and place it in your bed. It is a guard against ill fortune,' he tenderly advised. Next he was reporting that Napoleon had sent four hundred cannons to the capital. 'That means the emperor wants to defend Paris, which frightens everyone. I am delighted you have left. It puts what I love most in all the world in a safe place.' He showed smaller concern for the woman who was still formally his wife. Catherine, no doubt hoping to retrieve a little of her old stature from Dorothy's absence, stayed on throughout the dangers at the Place de la Concorde residence where her young rival had by now overtaken her as social hostess.

For some weeks Napoleon's fortunes swung back and forth. One day he was holding his ground, the next he was in the jaws of defeat. The Austrians and Prussians made the mistake of separating their forces and sending them on different routes to Paris, which allowed Napoleon to strike at each with less risk. One day the guns of Paris boomed to celebrate news of a half-victory, the next they fell silent. 'Uncertainty is sheer horror,' Talleyrand wrote to the duchess. 'We are four days away from I don't know what!' It was official now: the allies would no longer accept the 'natural frontiers' he counted on preserving; a defeated France had to squeeze back to her pre-revolutionary borders shorn of Belgium, a slice of Germany and the Italian flank of the Alps. By late February, for all Napoleon's never-say-die bravado, bloody battles were indeed being fought within earshot of the capital. 'If the war continues, our beautiful France will be in a deplorable state,' Talleyrand reported, sending to Rosny a trunk packed with shirts and underwear linens. Were he to be forced, come what may, to leave Paris in a hurry, he wanted to travel light and have what was needed at his destination.

The trunk of linens was no doubt dispatched on a good day for Napoleon: it wasn't the victory of the allies that would drive Talleyrand out of Paris. His health took his attention too. In winter he seemed to have a constant cold, though he spent much time and ingenuity in fighting it. The daily intake of water through the nose and subsequent snort, though spectacular, wasn't the only remedy he tried. 'I am taking rhubarb, like children do,' he informed the duchess. 'I am amazed to be drugging myself, it is absolutely not my normal method.' His statesman's nerves he cared for otherwise. With Caulaincourt, who stayed close to Napoleon, he devised a coded message system to keep the edge off surprises; it enabled him to keep track of the emperor's propensity to fight on or to surrender.

Talleyrand was careful to maintain contact with the Empress Marie Louise during this frenzied time. His regency interest demanded it. But was a regency leading to the eventual succession of Napoleon's infant son a viable proposition any longer? On the one hand it suited him – and he'd openly favoured it – but he recognised there was something grotesque in the prospect. Moreover, the populace seemed unenthusiastic, if not hostile. When Wellington's English army entered Bordeaux on 12 March, it was to the roar of townsfolk chanting the name of Louis XVIII. The spectacle moved

Wellington, whose report to London confirmed the government in its support for a Bourbon restoration in France.

For Talleyrand, the overriding issue was legitimacy. Who – or what – best represented the legitimacy at the top of the state that could save France from the abyss? He had a harsh view of the Bourbons, and they of him. Yet increasingly he felt his favour swerving back towards the old monarchy. In part this was practical politics: England and her allies – except perhaps for Austria, which had Marie Louise to think of – appeared decided on the Bourbon restoration. But it was impossible simply to revert to old times. The Revolution had changed France too much to allow that. A return to the *ancien régime*, Talleyrand was sure, was not the road to recovery. If the Bourbons were to return, it could only be as a constitutional monarchy subject to parliamentary control along the lines of the English system.

On a personal level, Talleyrand had reason to feel uneasy even at that prospect. A Bourbon restoration in whatever form posed difficulties he couldn't yet see his way through. 'You have to know how things are in my relations with that family,' he told Mme de Coigny as the allies bore down on Paris. 'I confess I do not wish to expose myself to a pardon in place of thanks, or to have to justify myself.' He'd had some gambling-table relations in the past with Louis XVIII's brother, the Comte d'Artois, and allowed that there was 'something between him and me'. But the man who wanted to regain the throne really didn't know him at all. Louis would be aware, he thought, only of his part in the Revolution and his sharp condemnations of past attempts by royalist extremists to shoot their way back into power. A closed royal mind did not augur well for him.

Nevertheless, Talleyrand now concentrated his thoughts on the nub of the succession problem. He had to have things clear in his head before the invaders were in the streets of Paris. Above all, there could be no smell of the usurper about the regime that replaced Napoleon. It was his usurpation of power that brought France to ruin. The new regime had to be legitimate beyond challenge. Because the French saw their country was strong and relatively calm at first under Napoleon, its prosperity on the rise, they convinced themselves that the rights on which the government of the nation were based didn't much matter. That was the terrible mistake. If only he and others had sniffed hard enough from the start to realise that the nation's strength under Napoleon was never anything but precarious, that its calm had no solid foundation, its prosperity no chance to endure. Why? Because it largely derived from the devastation of other countries' wealth! Legitimacy alone granted the right to power: the right to take power without usurping it, without being seen as usurping it or even raising the slightest suspicion of usurping it.

Talleyrand wrestled long and hard with the legitimacy issue. It did not necessarily mean preserving the power of kings. As he came to define it: 'It is above all the necessary ingredient in the peace and happiness of peoples, the strongest guarantee, indeed the sole guarantee, that these benefits will last. The legitimacy of kings, or to put it better, of governments, is the safeguard of nations. That is why it is sacred.' Talleyrand clearly wasn't contemplating a revival of the republic, though his legitimacy principle did not rule it out. But to avoid all odour of usurpation, legitimate government did need a bit of history to its credit – what he called 'a long succession of years behind it'. It was those years, history rubbed into the people, that granted possession of sovereignty.

So there was nothing for it in the end. A Napoleonic regency was impossible. The Bourbons had to be returned to the throne, albeit cured of their absolutist fantasies.

By mid-March the allied monarchs had Napoleon all but beaten, but held off from taking Paris, unsure of the situation in the capital. Their hesitation perturbed Talleyrand, who for once wasn't looking for peace. The last thing he wanted was some last-ditch arrangement that might maintain Napoleon in power in France.

For a day or so he held his frustration in check, ascribing the allied delay to the plodding character the French accorded Austrians, among others. 'It's really inconceivable! The proverbial Austrian slowness never better deserved its name,' he wrote in a sardonic note to the duchess, asking her as usual to burn it. Then, with Napoleon still resisting, his tone grew edgier. 'As long as he lives, everything remains uncertain and no one can foresee what will happen.'

Something had to be done to get the allies moving. To end the suspense he looked for a way to get advice through to the allied forces halted twenty miles from Paris. A curious feature of war in Napoleon's time was that emissaries and agents from all sides moved about fairly freely, though not without peril, between opposing camps to secure a hearing or deliver a request. Now a message of encouragement to Tsar Alexander and his fellow monarchs was urgently needed, a message they could trust because they would recognise the source. Recruited for the task was a restless southern nobleman with royalist leanings, Baron Eugène de Vitrolles, whose post under Napoleon as Inspector of Imperial Sheep-Pens if anything nourished his desire to see the Bourbons back on the throne. Vitrolles had to be careful, and so did Talleyrand. There was a strong risk that Napoleon's forces would waylay this kind of enterprise.

All went well for Vitrolles, however. On reaching the allied side, he talked his way into seeing Talleyrand's old diplomatic partners, Metternich and Nesselrode, even Tsar Alexander, imploring them to move fast. Since no one knew him he handed them a crumpled note from his pocket. The unsigned message said: 'The person I send you has all my confidence, listen to him and hear me. It is time to be quite clear. You are walking on crutches. Use your legs. You can do all you want.' It wasn't in Talleyrand's own handwriting, which all of them knew, but the allied statesmen had spent enough time questioning Vitrolles to be sure who it came from and what it meant. The way to Paris was open.

It was unlikely that Talleyrand's anonymous exhortation alone drove the invaders into Paris, though Nesselrode for one said it did. It was not something Talleyrand boasted of; he thought better than to mention it in his memoirs. Perhaps he thought it stretched the idea of patriotism a little further than many genuine patriots would care to comprehend. Still, Vitrolles' additional assurance to the allies that a free provisional government was ready to replace Napoleon helped square his conscience on that. Talleyrand's logic was that if a provisional government was known to be in place, overseen by him, the invading monarchs might reasonably decide to forego a military occupation government of their own. That would spare the nation unnecessary hardship and humiliation.

The closet boost to the invaders nonetheless put Talleyrand on the spot. When Tsar Alexander and Prussia's King Friedrich Wilhelm at last led allied forces to the gates of the capital at the end of March – Austria's Emperor Franz indeed lagged behind, living up to the poor expectations of him – it was imperative for him to be on hand to receive them. Here Napoleon unwittingly intervened. Continuing to put up a fight south of the capital, the emperor ordered Marie Louise, the imperial dignitaries and the government ministers to leave for safe quarters at Blois on the river Loire before they fell into enemy hands. The imperial court's departure took place in a frantic clatter of gilded carriages on 30 March, closely observed both by Talleyrand, who was instructed to be part of it, and by Savary, whose police were enforcing it. Talleyrand had long argued, in vain, that Empress Marie Louise should stay in Paris, whatever happened, to represent the regency. But now that she was going, he was bound, as a Regency Council member, to accompany her. Napoleon had in fact ordered the entire court's departure so that no one with authority – he had Talleyrand in mind specifically – remained in Paris to negotiate with the enemy.

The situation called for the performer in Talleyrand. He rose to the call out of sheer anxiety. He wasn't afraid of Napoleon the man, though the emperor was in a corner which made him and his apparatus more than usually unpredictable, so that even now it wasn't worth needlessly testing his wrath. Talleyrand's real fear, though, was of seeing things botched at this last tantalising moment when they were otherwise falling into place. Having purposefully missed the hectic departure of the court by an hour or so, he therefore made a show of having himself driven in a convoy of carriages accompanied by Courtiade, a troupe of under-valets and numerous trunks that same evening to the city gate at Passy, an exit for the Loire region. Savary's police watched him go. At Passy, however, the National Guard commander turned him back, ruling that his papers weren't in order and that travel was anyway too perilous. Talleyrand didn't argue. Being refused passage by the guard gave him formal leave to stay in Paris. He headed his carriage straight home. Before he had his trunks unpacked an emissary from Tsar Alexander was at his door to discuss the capital's capitulation.

This was a satisfactory conclusion to a difficult day, part of which he'd spent dickering with the National Guard to make sure it would turn him back. In charge of the guard at Passy was Charles de Rémusat, the husband of his diarist friend, who agreed without much fuss, knowing that Napoleon's marshals, helpless to defend the city, were on the point of surrendering it. In his morning note to Duchess Dorothea the next day, Talleyrand was nonetheless curiously guarded about his escapade. Giving news of his continued presence in Paris, he noted: 'I found the gate closed, dear friend. Impossible to continue my journey,' and signed off with, 'I fear you were tired from staying up. What are your plans today? I love you with all my soul. Adieu.'

Talleyrand was now at the centre of events, controlling them. He was up early on 31 March being oiled, perfumed and powdered by his valets as Alexander and Friedrich Wilhelm, accompanied by a stand-in for Emperor Franz, rode abreast at the head of their troops through the boulevards of Paris past huge supine crowds of onlookers.

Nesselrode came ahead, aiming to settle arrangements with Talleyrand who was still in his dressing chair as he arrived at his residence on the Place de la Concorde. At the sight of his old diplomatic partner, Talleyrand rose from the armchair and threw himself into his arms, choking him in a cloud of powder. Where was Alexander to install himself? Nesselrode had heard a rumour that the Elysée Palace where he intended to go was mined. They agreed the tsar must stay at Talleyrand's mansion to be safe. This suited its owner, who wasn't past having spread the rumour of the perils at the Elysée himself to make sure he had total access to the principal invader. He made his first floor over to Alexander and his servants, the second to Nesselrode and his foreign ministry staff and kept the mezzanine floor for himself. The tsar's Cossack guards roamed the corridors and the kitchens, where Carême flew between his ovens performing for the royal guests.

Alexander's first question of his host was what was to be done: 'Well, here we are in your famous Paris! You are the one who brought us here, Monsieur Talleyrand. There are three options now – bargain with Napoleon, establish a regency or restore the Bourbons.' Talleyrand swiftly corrected him. There were not three options, there was only one – the last one. The tsar looked flummoxed by his assurance. Seizing his opportunity, Talleyrand squeezed a formal promise from him that neither he nor his fellow monarchs would in fact bargain with Napoleon, or with his family. At this point, deciding what to do with the emperor seemed to Talleyrand more urgent than selecting the form of government to replace him. For he was holed up at Fontainebleau, suicidal – two attempts to poison himself left him retching and hiccuping violently before doctors got to him – reluctant to abdicate, and still commanding a weary force of fifty thousand men.

Out on the streets, though, allied military posters shouted for the change of regime. From walls and lampposts, the invaders proclaimed to Parisians:

For twenty years Europe has been flooded with blood and tears. All efforts to put an end to such misery have proved useless because the power which has oppressed you is itself an insurmountable obstacle to peace . . . The allied sovereigns faithfully seek a GOVERNMENT OF SALVATION in France that can seal the union of all nations and governments.

England was quite sure she wanted that salvation to come from a Bourbon restoration, and Lord Castlereagh, as foreign secretary, had now arrived in France from London to press for it.

Alexander, however, wasn't so sure. Despite Talleyrand's quickfire response, he remained unconvinced. Still flirting with liberalism in Russia, he looked with disfavour on a return to the old regime in France, however liberally dressed up. To turn the tsar, Talleyrand insisted on his principle of legitimacy: ignore it, he warned, and civil war would surely follow. He added for good measure that the return of the king was a popular desire 'beating in the hearts of all'.

This was a large claim, given the absence of conspicuous royal fervour on the streets of Paris, and Alexander challenged him on it. Talleyrand undertook to prove it through a vote in the French Senate, Napoleon's legislative echo chamber. Alexander knew as well as Talleyrand how low a place the Senate had in public esteem, but it did have one merit that now seemed a critical one: it was really all that subsisted of institutional authority outside Napoleon's court. Furthermore, Talleyrand, as Vice Grand Elector, was empowered to call it into session, which he did on 1 April.

Its first act was to proclaim a provisional government with Talleyrand at its head. He was master of France for the first time since he held the slippery reins of the Revolution. Of the government's four other members, two were close political associates of his – François de Jaucourt, a blueblood veteran of the Rue de Bellechasse breakfasts and companion-in-exile in England, and Emmerich de Dalberg, a statesman of Rhenish origin who loathed Napoleon and had insider connections at all the courts of Europe. The remaining two were moderate Bourbon supporters he also knew well. It looked a cosy administration to the Faubourg Saint Germain which baptised it 'Talleyrand's whist table'. Yet there could hardly have been a less cosy moment for Talleyrand to take power. Paris was full of foreign soldiers, encamped from the Champs-Elysées to the Bastille. In manpower and in riches the blessed land of France was bled white. Who knew what toll the victorious allied monarchs would exact for two decades of humiliation? A Bourbon king was edging home, trapped on England's shore by an attack of gout. And an embittered Napoleon, camped not fifty miles from Paris, remained Emperor of the French by his own brooding lights.

The priority was to resolve the succession problem. On 3 April, at Talleyrand's urging, the Senate voted the dethronement of Napoleon, absolving French soldiers of loyalty to him. It found him guilty of having 'violated his oath and transgressed the rights of the people by levying men and taxes contrary to the constitutions'. These were tame indictments compared with charges being hurled at Napoleon in the streets, but long servility had killed political furies in the Senate. All the same, Talleyrand put the proclamation of Napoleon's overthrow to Tsar Alexander as evidence of popular support for the return of the Bourbons, which the Senate duly approved three days later. If it wasn't strictly the popular will, Alexander bowed to it. Talleyrand's legitimacy principle prevailed, much to the satisfaction of Castlereagh. His alignment with English policy didn't end there. During the time now given him in power he aimed to saddle Louis XVIII with the same constitutional constraints the English imposed on their monarch. His respect for English practice was stronger than he sometimes liked to acknowledge. The English might plausibly have thought he was doing Castlereagh's work for him.

Back in Fontainebleau, Napoleon could no longer ignore reality. Nor could the three marshals he had with him. Faced with the trio's ultimate refusal to pursue the fight, he abdicated. He did so on 4 April – in favour of his infant son. But it was too late for Napoleon to make conditions. The regency was a dead duck. The allies forestalled any serious bargaining with

Napoleon's negotiators by demanding unconditional abdication, in which case he would not be harmed, he would be sent into exile. Brooding over the indignity, still suicidal, contemplating back-tracking on his abdication from one day to the next, the fallen conqueror nonetheless took the news of Talleyrand's rise to head of government with surprising equanimity. He told Caulaincourt, 'I forgive Talleyrand, because I treated him badly . . . The Bourbons will do well to employ him. He likes money and intrigue, but he is capable. I've always had a soft spot for him.' Old thoughts came rolling back, thoughts he'd had in the farm sled on the frozen return from Moscow: 'My affairs went well all the time Talleyrand ran them . . . He's the man who best knows France and Europe.'

The nostalgia was no longer reciprocated. Talleyrand's patience with the emperor had altogether burned out, and with it any lingering ember of fondness. At this point he felt nothing but contempt for him. He viewed him as a 'highway robber' who had to be treated as such. Indeed, Talleyrand's first act as head of government was to induce bewildered French fighting men to see the emperor as a destructive monster. A proclamation published in the official newspaper *Moniteur Universel* told soldiers they owed no loyalty to a man who had ravaged France, left her defenceless and made her name odious to other nations – a man, the notice added, 'who is not even French'. In light of the Corsican warrior's fifteen years at France's helm, this was a low blow. It certainly lacked Talleyrand's usual polished touch; the lapse translated the rawness of his contempt and the urgency of the moment. The proclamation ended: 'You are no longer the soldiers of Napoleon. The Senate and all France relieve you of your vows.'

Had Talleyrand had time to stand back, he would have seen what was happening around him for the outlandish tableau it was: a powerful monarch from the bounds of Asia come to overthrow one of the greatest conquerors of all ages, his throne sought by a dusty monarch of old crawling forth from the grave dug for his dynasty by the most convulsive revolution Europe ever witnessed. Giving sense to it all was urgent work and, owing to circumstances, exceedingly cramped, since most of it was done in the salon room on the mezzanine floor of the Talleyrand residence into which Tsar Alexander's presence now squeezed the seat of France's provisional government.

It was there that Talleyrand and his partners created the broad lines of a constitutional monarchy, a concept entirely new to France. As observed by Vitrolles, they did so in the best Talleyrand salon manner – to all appearances casual, unlaboured, entertaining. 'M de Talleyrand presided in his salon, the theatre in which this grand performer excelled, raising conversation to the height of great affairs, or rather bringing great affairs down to the level of conversation, admitting only what could be translated into that simple tongue. His work was to talk, and it was through talk that he produced ideas.' The drift was liberal, designed to undo Napoleonic despotism. Within no time the provisional government curbed imperial police powers, sent Napoleon's last terrified levy of army conscripts back to their families, freed his political prisoners, lifted press censorship and halted official snooping on the postal services. A practical precaution was to maintain imperial prefects and civil servants in their posts, which stopped a bureaucratic vacuum from slowing the new broom's sweep.

His mezzanine ran with emissaries and supplicants night and day, delaying his bedtime from the customary 4 a.m. to dawn and beyond. Then he was up at 9 a.m., taking callers during his elaborate morning toilette, a luxury he did not allow his busy agenda to foreshorten. All the same, the casual performance that impressed Vitrolles was just that – a performance. Talleyrand burned with anguish inside. It was hard to maintain peace of mind when foreign armies occupied the country, pillaging, acting rough with the population, and when an armistice wasn't yet in sight. France in effect was still at war, especially in the south where Wellington – a hero in his homeland, a general who had done England proud – continued to trounce imperial forces whose commanders somehow hadn't received notice of Napoleon's abdication.

The uncertainty of it all, coupled with lack of sleep, had a cost in Talleyrand's relations with the Duchess of Kurland, who was peeved by a sudden falloff in his morning notes. He had no time to dispense political tidbits and sweet nothings now, though she was close at hand once more, having returned with Dorothy to Paris from Rosny on learning that her sovereign was installed at Talleyrand's house. Moreover, urgent affairs of state obliged him to dine alone each night with the tsar, which she no doubt understood but which annoyed her anyway because she would have liked a seat at her friend Alexander's table. The duchess acted up, making difficulties over catching a spare moment with him. Talleyrand was both irritated and strangely pleased. 'Do as you wish, dear friend,' he wrote to her on completing his constitution blueprint. 'I don't much wish to go out this evening because I am going to the Senate and shall be tired from the busy session we have in store.' And a day or so later: 'You were angry with me yesterday. I didn't really deserve it, but it pleased me. I love a little touchiness in the woman I love. I shall dine with you.'

After nine days the situation eased. The tsar moved with his retinue to his original destination, the Elysée Palace, though Carême had so spoiled him that he returned to Talleyrand's each evening for dinner. When the duchess duly received her invitation to dine with the tsar, the prevailing order had changed in the Talleyrand household. Her daughter Dorothy was hostess. The master of the house, taken by his aristocratic young ward's grace and political awareness, had envisaged her running his social affairs from the start. Now it was done, thanks to a certain estrangement already evident in her girlish relations with her husband Edmond. 'It is Dorothy who receives at my house,' Talleyrand advised the duchess in a curiously terse morning note the day after the tsar moved out. Had mother and daughter talked the girl's role over together? It didn't sound like it.

Dorothy's rise to prominence in the Talleyrand household in fact had no noticeable effect on his feelings for her sensitive mother, who remained his 'angel' and whose letterbox stayed full of his daily attentions. But her daughter did come to absorb him more and more. Gradually Dorothy took charge of his heart along with his household.

The constitutional model which Talleyrand pushed through the Senate – a work completed in less than a week – was generally well received, except by hardline royalists. Some of his erstwhile critics applauded in astonishment. One was the liberal politician and writer Benjamin Constant, the browbeaten lover of Mme de Staël who herself had long since turned against Talleyrand, complaining bitterly that her old intellectual heartthrob had done nothing to discourage Napoleon from banishing her from Paris as a political nuisance.

As a rule Constant knew better than not to share his mistress's umbrage, but now in a fulsome change of heart he wrote to Talleyrand: 'I cannot resist thanking you for both bringing down tyranny and laying the foundations of liberty. Without the one, I could not have rendered all grace to the other. 1789 and 1814 stand nobly in your life. It is sweet to express admiration when one feels it for a man who is at the same time the saviour and the most likeable of Frenchmen. I write these words having read the basis of the decreed constitution.'

Metternich too was impressed. 'The success surpasses all we could have hoped,' he told Emperor Franz. With so much going on and so many problems to resolve, it may at first have escaped Metternich that Talleyrand's constitutional model was meant above all as a safeguard against the excesses of a restored monarchy whose autocratic outlook, on past experience, much resembled that of the Habsburgs. It created a two-chamber parliament in the English manner: an elected commons and a hereditary house of lords. To guarantee rights trampled on by Napoleon, it gave parliament control over taxes and established the independence of the judiciary, freedom of the press and freedom of religion and conscience. In sum, it established the rule of law.

Talleyrand knew the charter was a frail creature. Time pressures made it so. It was inevitably subject to modification by Louis XVIII once his gout allowed him to mount the throne. But he wasn't dissatisfied. 'This constitution is not good,' he told Dalberg, his fellow framer, 'but after all there's something there to govern by.'

Unfortunately he had less say in deciding the fate of Napoleon. His recent house guest, Tsar Alexander, who was enjoying himself as monarch-in-charge in occupied Paris, chose to send him to the Mediterranean island of Elba off the coast of Tuscany, a short boat crossing from his native Corsica. Elba, attached to France during Napoleon's reign, was essentially a unilateral choice by Alexander, though the allies in general agreed that Napoleon shouldn't be guillotined, hanged, shot or otherwise harmed, nor yet judged, but dispatched into peaceful exile still bearing the rank of emperor. The victors wanted to appear magnanimous, to capitalise on *their* peace. Besides, a legend such as Napoleon wasn't to be erased from history. Alexander grew quite mawkish in discussing the conqueror's future during abdication negotiations, particularly since Emperor Franz made sure that neither Marie Louise nor his son would be accompanying him in exile. 'Napoleon is miserable. Today I become his friend once more,' the tsar told Caulaincourt when deciding on Elba as his sovereign sanctuary. There he was to enjoy a personal budget of two million francs, with a further three million for his mother, brothers and sisters, the entire outlay to be borne as long as he lived by the French treasury; he would have his own four-hundred-man army (as it turned out, one thousand men of the disbanded Imperial Guard went with him); and control of Elba would be his down to the new flag of the midget realm – Medici red and silver, dotted with golden bees.

Napoleon wasn't alone in holding misgivings about Elba, an unpretty outcrop of iron mines and vines a dozen or so miles long and half that across. Alexander had heard that it had prospects, unrealised over the centuries, for becoming a hub of Mediterranean commerce. Despite the tsar's innocent goodwill, it was a ludicrous comedown for Napoleon. Talleyrand disapproved for quite a different reason, though on behalf of the provisional government he agreed at Alexander's insistence to foot the exile bill. To him, Elba was too close for comfort to the European mainland which its sorry incoming sovereign had so recently overrun. Castlereagh and Metternich shared his concern, but bickered about it only after the decision was announced by Alexander, who was convinced that Russian arms alone had liberated Europe from odious tyranny and that he therefore had the call. Metternich argued for a Caribbean island. England's spokesman wanted some home redoubt, somewhere that a bulldog eye would be kept on his activities, but his cause was undermined by an editorial in *The Times* which snorted: 'We would be unhappy if British territory were to be polluted by such a bandit.'

Like Metternich, Talleyrand wanted transatlantic exile, though he preferred the United States. Failing that, the Portuguese Azores in mid-Atlantic looked the right sort of place. He couldn't change the tsar's mind, but perhaps he could influence Napoleon to put an ocean between himself and his fallen empire. Through Fouché, ever the opportunist in times of chaos and thus back in the political swing, he sought to dissuade Napoleon from going to Elba. The Mediterranean rock was not only below his dignity, he would always be under suspicion there, Fouché cautioned the warrior in a letter penned with Talleyrand at his shoulder. Everyone would think he saw it as a place to escape from to restore his fortunes. 'You would find more glory and consolation in living as a simple citizen, and the safest and most fitting exile for a man like yourself is the United States of America. There you will have the protection of laws that are equal and inviolable for all that breathes. You will prove to its people that if you had been born among them you would have preferred their virtues and liberties to any mastery of the earth.'

It was a glowing tribute to an America of which Talleyrand hadn't always spoken so well when he himself lived in exile there – and it didn't work. Elba it was. Napoleon left for his island prison on 20 April. A fresh whirl-wind of the kind only he could sow already loomed on the horizon.

SEVENTEEN

'One More Frenchman'

Talleyrand was master of France for seventeen days. It was a curious time, near unique in national indignity. Paris had last fallen four hundred years before when England's Henry V entered the capital straight from his long-bowmen's triumph at Agincourt.

Talleyrand paid due heed to the strangeness of the hour. Mindful perhaps of his financial opportunism at the head of foreign affairs, he prided himself on being an inexpensive leader. By his calculation the work of the provisional government cost the budget 200,000 francs – a fraction, he might have added, of a decent *douceur*. And he rather congratulated himself on failing to settle the travel expenses of the army officers he sent hither and thither around France to stop Napoleon's troops fighting.

From the moment Louis XVIII's brother, the Comte d'Artois, arrived in Paris on 12 April, 1814, in the advance guard of the returning Bourbons, Talleyrand's task as head of government became more complicated. Strains were inevitable; the problem was how to limit them. One urgent precaution he took was to head off the surefire embarrassment that lay in the imperial archives in the Louvre. No sooner had he arranged Napoleon's formal dethronement than he sent an emissary on a clandestine mission to the archives to pull out all his letters to the emperor, formal and private. The emissary's instructions were to bag them and burn them, which he did (though some copies survived and floated around mischievously for decades). Now the Bourbons had little to pin on him except his record during the Revolution. That he could cope with.

There remained his own attitude to the Bourbons: his desire for legitimacy could not alter his personal feelings. He was, in Caulaincourt's eyes, like a man obliged out of necessity to marry a woman he neither loved nor much esteemed. He wasn't at all sure that Louis was the right stuff for the task facing him. The Bourbons exemplified the 'emigration' – the numerous members of the aristocracy who fled at the time of the Revolution. Talleyrand saw the term in narrower focus: to him it stood for reactionary émigrés, a doggedly illiberal tribe setting themselves apart from any number of more open-minded bluebloods who'd seen that change was necessary in France and came back to breathe it as soon as they could be sure of keeping their heads.

Talleyrand detested the die-hard 'emigration'; he blamed their constant conspiracies to regain their former powers and privileges by the sword for upsetting social peace in France, making Napoleon, he thought, still more dictatorial than nature made him. His scathing verdict on the 'emigration' was salon lore: 'They have learned nothing and forgotten nothing.' In turn, arch-royalists loathed Talleyrand. Of course he'd had to make distinctions in his feelings towards them. His mother, since dead, and his uncle, the arch-bishop, were among their number, monarchists to the core. And he had to temper his distaste for the Bourbons themselves now that his own principle of legitimacy dictated a certain level of respect for them as an institution.

He passed word to the Comte d'Artois, whom he'd known from salon gaming tables in pre-revolutionary times, that it would be fitting to re-enter Paris flying the red-white-and-blue tricolour rather than the white flag with the fleur-de-lis of the Bourbon dynasty. The king's brother found the advice disobliging and wasn't in the best of moods when Talleyrand drove out to meet him at the city gate of Pantin on 12 April to escort him to the Tuileries Palace. But it was a glorious spring day and the man in charge of France was at his flattering best, hobbling to the royal steed, steadying himself by the halter and calling up to its rider, 'Sire, today is a day of regeneration that melts our hearts, and the happiness we feel will be beyond all words if by the heavenly grace of your august house you will accept the homage of our most respectful affection and devotion.' The effusive greeting left Artois tongue-tied – he hadn't expected anything quite so fanciful – and all he found in reply before riding into the city past cheering crowds was 'Thank you! Thank you! You make me too happy! Thank you.' This wouldn't do for the morning papers, which Talleyrand wanted filled with the grandeur of the Bourbon homecoming. That evening he had an inventive aide write a report on the event for the *Moniteur Universel*, telling him to put something more compelling into the royal mouth. 'Give him a response! Make it good, something that fits the person and the moment, and I promise you Monsieur will not only accept it, after two days he will believe he said it, and indeed he will have said it.' As reported the next morning, the moving speech made by the Comte d'Artois at the Pantin gate concluded: 'No more divisions. Peace and France. At last I see her again. Nothing has changed – except that there is one more Frenchman.'

Paris loved the modesty of it, the simple grandeur. The 'one more Frenchman' line – fruit of a third draft approved by Talleyrand – was the talk of the capital from the Faubourg Saint Germain to the working class in the Faubourg Saint Antoine. Talleyrand allowed it was felicitous; Artois said he was proud to have said it. Napoleon's eviction from the Tuileries was accomplished for all to see. It was a good start for the Bourbons. But it did no more than reduce the strains between their dynasty and the man who contributed most to its resurrection.

The portly personage seeking to make his title of king official was still on his tentative way back to Paris when Talleyrand went out to meet him at Compiègne just north of the capital on 29 April. By this time authority was in theory transferred to the Bourbon throne, which Louis' brother was commissioned to re-warm for him. But power was a hazy item and Talleyrand was still the man the allies did business with to conclude an armistice. The slowness of Louis' return had much to do with the situation in Paris where the Russian tsar, a lukewarm convert to his cause, was still in residence and foreign troops continued to occupy the streets.

Louis received Talleyrand at the old royal chateau of Compiègne, making him wait three hours in an ante-chamber before inviting him into his suite. Talleyrand, aware of his exalted sense of dignity, was expecting him to assert himself, though this was a little much. He did not underestimate the Bourbon heir despite the guileless and sometimes boorish reputation he earned for himself in exile in England. In drawing up the new constitution, Talleyrand had warned his government colleagues that Louis, a Latin buff who quoted Horace at will, was sufficiently erudite and perceptive to be able to pick the work to pieces unless it were historically and intellectually sound. In fact the two of them had much in common: they were the same age, sixty; both had bad legs, though gout, unlike Talleyrand's deformity, crippled only when it chose; they dressed, coiffed and powdered themselves like the holdovers from the *ancien régime* they were; they suspected they had once, before the Revolution, shared a mistress; certainly they shared a quick, sardonic sense of humour to put lesser mortals down.

There was more than a trace of that humour in Louis' opening observation as he waved Talleyrand to an armchair. They hadn't set eyes on each other for twenty-three years and in any case scarcely knew each other. The king said, 'I am most pleased to see you. Much has happened since we last met. Our houses date back to the same epoch, only my ancestors have been cleverer. If yours had been more so, you would be telling me today, "Take a chair, come closer, tell me of your affairs." Instead it is I saying, Sit down, let us talk.'

Talleyrand elected to hear only the agreeable side of the remark, for it was gratifying to have the Périgord pedigree compared with that of the

Bourbons – especially by a Bourbon. They talked for two hours or so on the military occupation, the scene in Paris and Napoleon's situation, and by Talleyrand's account got on well together, Louis throwing out a stream of caustic comments, his visitor remaining highly respectful. The king wasn't all impishness; he was curious about Talleyrand. He told him he much admired the influence he'd exerted on everything that had happened in France, asking: 'How did you bring down the Directory, and now the colossal power of Bonaparte?'

'My God, Sire, I really did nothing like that!' his visitor shrugged. 'There is just something inexplicable about me that brings misfortune on governments that neglect me.'

Talleyrand's half-smiling retort may have sounded to Louis like a threat, but it went to the heart of his statesman's career. The king was implying that he had defeated Napoleon. This was a large question, one on which his place in history would surely turn. Had he, Talleyrand, won? Had he conquered the conqueror? He wasn't inclined to see it quite that way. In his view Napoleon defeated himself. He had, though, placed himself all along in a position to make his fall possible. To make it, at length, inevitable.

Louis' tribute fell pointedly short of royal gratitude. He *was* grateful, but not to Talleyrand. He couldn't afford to feel grateful to a man such as Talleyrand who held too many levers and whom he mistrusted. Accordingly he reserved his public gratitude for England, having proclaimed on leaving his residence-in-exile and shipping out from Dover that he owed his return to the throne of his ancestors to 'this glorious country and the steadfastness of its inhabitants'. Still, to be congratulated by the king on bringing down Napoleon wasn't faint praise either, and it raised Talleyrand's expectations that he would be asked to continue in office as head of the king's government.

Louis avoided the subject in this first interview, inquiring only whether the title Prince of Benevento didn't sound somewhat empty in view of Napoleon's fall and whether the French title Prince Talleyrand wasn't more fitting, since of course he would remain a prince under the restored monarchy. Their relations weren't meant to sweeten, however. Talleyrand was bound to the constitution he'd drawn up not only by personal conviction but by commitment to Tsar Alexander, who liked its liberal form and wanted Louis trussed by it. Two days later, as Russian, Prussian, Austrian and English troops paraded through Paris in a less than sensitive welcome to Louis, Talleyrand endeavoured to tighten the truss. In a speech presenting the Senate to the king, he reminded Louis that it would require prodigious efforts to cure the wounds of the *patrie*, and his constitutional model was a vital start:

You know better than we do, Sire, that the institutions that have been
so well tested by a neighbouring people are buttresses and not obstacles for monarchs who befriend laws and are fathers of their nations.
Indeed, Sire, fully confident in Your Majesty's enlightenment and
magnanimity, our nation and senate wish France to be free for our
king to be powerful.

His greeting was a straight challenge to Louis, who liked England well
enough and was most grateful to her but nonetheless thought sovereignty
had passed too far to the side of the people there. He was already smarting
over Talleyrand's insistence on striking out references in Bourbon homecoming posters to his being in the nineteenth year of his reign. Such claims
struck Talleyrand as vainglorious delusion, not to say provocative. Louis
was dating his reign from the death in childhood in 1795 of Louis XVI's
son (the boy hadn't reigned but assumed the title Louis XVII on his father's
execution as a comfort for shocked émigrés).

Louis turned out to be as cantankerous as Talleyrand feared about his
Bourbon 'rights'. Side-stepping a coronation, he became Louis XVIII by
the grace of God through a Te Deum mass at Notre Dame and the indis-
putable fact that he was sleeping in the Tuileries. He also chiselled at
Talleyrand's constitutional model until the emphasis on parliamentary power
was scraped thin. Not only that, he excluded him from the commission he
named to draw up the finished charter by which the nation was to be
governed.

Talleyrand fumed over his exclusion. The final constitution, he
complained, mildly in the circumstances, was created by the 'intrigue and
incapacity' surrounding Louis. Still, it bore enough of his own imprimatur
to make it a conspicuous advance on the *ancien régime*. To be sure, it
contained much he didn't like, and which Tsar Alexander didn't like either.
The king reinstated the Catholic Church as the state religion, giving short
shrift to freedom of conscience. Sovereignty lay with the king, not with
parliament or the people. Executive power was in the king's hands as of
old. And Louis XVIII, immune to mockery from the Faubourg Saint
Germain, stuck to his guns to have the constitution place him in the nineteenth year of his reign.

On the other hand absolutism of the old kind was gone, giving way to a
certain tolerance. The charter's chief novelty was the two-chamber parliament that Talleyrand proposed – house of commons and house of lords –
with responsibility for voting taxes, formerly an untouchable royal prerog-
ative. The parliament, in which Talleyrand and his uncle the archbishop
were to sit in the upper house as peers, was also empowered to initiate laws.

And the king's plan to have members of the commons, the Chamber of Deputies, provide their democratic services free, for the honour of it, was put aside on Talleyrand's objection. 'Yes, Sire . . . but free! free! That will be most expensive,' he warned Louis. He could guess what would happen if the commons were to become a den of rich royal cronies who didn't need paying. All in all a good deal of respect for fundamental human liberties brought in by the Revolution ran through the government charter that Talleyrand managed to save from Louis' corrections.

Despite this bow to liberty, the tsar was disappointed. He'd wanted Louis to receive his crown from the people. Besides, he disliked Louis. He felt the Bourbon king hadn't shown him the deference and gratitude that was his due. His dissatisfaction outran Talleyrand's, causing a rift between them as well. In light of the autocratic history of his own Romanov regime, the young tsar wasn't on the firmest ground here. But he somehow managed to blame Talleyrand for the shift of emphasis away from the genuine constitutional monarchy they'd talked over together. The Russian monarch underestimated Louis' stubbornness; he seemed to think Talleyrand had waved his liberal model before him simply to win his approval for the return of the Bourbons. He felt he had been fooled and made his feelings known by acting short with Talleyrand, holding him at a social arm's length while making ready to return to St Petersburg.

Talleyrand tried hard to defrost him, with little success. He stroked his ego, assuring him in a thank-you note, 'You have saved France, and by entering Paris you put an end to despotism.' He also tried explaining that the French weren't used to freedom after fifteen years of Napoleon: they needed institutions that accustomed them to liberty little by little, otherwise they would rush into excesses. To Alexander, though, the Bourbons were 'incorrigible' and Talleyrand was responsible for pushing them back on to the throne.

This was poor payment, it seemed to Talleyrand, for his work in coming to terms with the victorious allies in settlement of Napoleon's legacy. Here he was bargaining for France's existence. Never in all his life had he worked such long hours, so intensely. It was now that he had to draw on the credit he'd built up over the years in his defiant contacts with the allies. They intended to conclude an armistice with him, not with the Bourbons. More than the wrestling match with Louis over the constitution, it was haggling over armistice terms that dominated his twenty-hour days.

He was a night owl by nature, but now he was dog-tired. The fatigue was aggravated by outbreaks of violence among occupation forces that only he seemed in a position to smooth away. 'My life exhausts me and displeases me for a thousand and one reasons, but it's no use worrying about them, or about oneself,' he lamented to Duchess Dorothea in a morning note in mid-May. And a day or so later: 'My poor head is done for. The worse thing is, I'm not seeing anything of you.'

The weak hand he held with the allies further strained his energies. The France whose very shape he had to bargain for was in a precarious state, which he described with painful clarity:

> Exhausted of men, finances and resources, she lay invaded on all fronts at once – the Pyrenees, the Alps, the Rhine, Belgium – by innumerable armies composed in general not of mercenaries but of entire peoples fired by the spirit of hatred and vengeance. For twenty years these peoples had seen their lands occupied and laid waste by French armies. They had been held to ransom in every way, their governments insulted and treated with profound scorn. There was no outrage, one could say, that they did not have to avenge. If they were resolved to satisfy such hostile passions, what means did France have to resist?

The answer was, none. To be sure, there was always the lure of the Talleyrand dinner table. Through his fatigue he kept the monarchs and statesman he needed on his side well supped. The Duke of Wellington, having reached Paris from the south, spread his napkin there most nights. He and Talleyrand exerted their charms on each other. 'Wellington is the most curious character of our time,' his host wrote to the Duchess Dorothea, who attended a dinner with him. 'I'm glad you were able to meet him. You must have enjoyed it, you who like the tall, handsome kind.' Fortunately Alexander, despite his antipathy for Louis and his autocratic instincts, was also personally well disposed as to armistice arrangements. So were Metternich and Castlereagh. Their mood was merciful. Establishing peace promised greater benefits than revenge. Rather than carve France up and bleed her drier still with massive war reparations, they concentrated on bringing Napoleon's gargantuan realm down to size.

Talleyrand was more than happy to oblige in theory, since downsizing the empire was something he'd sought for years as his prescription for peace in Europe. But though the allies aimed to respect France's territorial integrity, they weren't benign enough to settle for the 'natural frontiers' that Talleyrand argued made most sense. The trouble was that those frontiers included territorial gains from the revolutionary wars before Napoleon's time. Instead the allies insisted on France returning to her *ancien régime* borders, those of 1792, which essentially excluded Belgium – Flanders, as the English generally called it – and German provinces west of the Rhine. It was less than likely, Talleyrand accepted, that England would agree to France keeping all Flanders when control of the port of Antwerp, England's time-honoured trading gateway to the Continent, had so long inflamed hostilities between England and Napoleon.

Before Louis XVIII stepped into the Tuileries, Talleyrand therefore signed up for the 1792 borders. He likewise agreed to evacuate fifty-four French military fortresses which studded middle Europe from the Rhine to the Vistula and which remained fully manned and equipped despite Napoleon's fall.

What he agreed to annulled at a stroke the gains from Napoleon's entire run of military triumphs over fifteen years. Though he had no alternative, it was nonetheless a staggering outcome to the pair's long personal struggle, one that deeply aggrieved those many Frenchmen who saw more glory in imperial aggrandisement than Talleyrand did. He came under bitter criticism for not using the fortresses as leverage to bargain harder for the 'natural frontiers', particularly from royalists who aimed to regain control of the army and were distressed at the loss of its foreign strongholds. And wasn't he putting Prussia on France's doorstep by relinquishing the German provinces on the left bank of the Rhine?

The criticism ignored all reality. Napoleon had torn Europe apart, made reckless sport of its map and broken lands he conquered under the crushing weight of war indemnities. Though the boot was now firmly on the other foot, Talleyrand's armistice strategy still worked wonders: he managed to hold France in the familiar shape that history and geography made for her, the largest nation in Europe with twenty-nine million souls. It also saved her from paying a franc in indemnities. To loud English and Prussian cries that it cost them dear over the years to defeat Napoleon – 700 million pounds was an estimate thrown out in an aroused London parliament – he replied that King Louis would 'rather be arrested and held prisoner in his palace' than meet their financial demands. For wasn't every nation more secure with France starting a blank page in her balance book? The safe thing was to encourage Louis, not humiliate him. All Europe would gain by it.

Castlereagh, a perceptive diplomatist but no financier, bought the argument. In the end Talleyrand also retrieved numerous overseas French colonies taken by the Royal Navy during the Napoleonic Wars on the grounds that they were important to French trade and that a peaceful, thriving France was vital to European prosperity. Furthermore, Talleyrand had the military occupation end there and then, a noble concession from allies whose lands Napoleon had made permanent prey for Grand Army occupying forces. Typically, too, he talked Alexander and allied leaders into letting France keep the 'marvellous art works' which the Grand Army had plundered from the museums of Europe. (Castlereagh pliantly agreed it might harm the paintings to send them on long journeys back to their owners.)

The day the Treaty of Paris containing the armistice accords was signed, 30 May 1814, was one of profound relief for Talleyrand. He believed he had saved France. A proud little note to the duchess said:

> I have finished my peace with the four great powers . . . At four o'clock it was signed. It is very good, made on the basis of the greatest equality and rather noble, though France is still full of foreigners. My friends can be pleased with me, especially you, whom I love with all my soul.

He especially liked the notion that the treaty was made among equals and approved by all. Knowing Metternich and his taste for putting his personal stamp on things, he slipped him a private note imploring him not to try to modify it. 'Leave it as it is. Don't meddle with it, you would spoil it. A good thing well done can only be productive. This one will be.' Moreover, he believed it settled things between France and England: the prosperity of one went with the prosperity of the other – they grew together. He was ready to hang his reputation on the treaty and allowed himself a little burst of vanity: 'I await the judgement of posterity with confidence.'

Posterity did not disappoint him. After the Treaty of Paris, Europe was spared a general war for all of a hundred years, while England and France stopped fighting each other forever more – as soon, that is, as they came through an unprogrammed encounter at Waterloo.

King Louis made Talleyrand foreign minister for his pains, which should not have come as a surprise. He was in full charge of foreign affairs anyway, and he was altogether too great a handful for the king to place in charge of his government. He was dangerous. His political vision and experience promised something other than the level of servitude Louis required. Indeed, the new king preferred to rule without a head of government than to name Talleyrand.

Nor was Talleyrand a popular hero. He could never aspire to that. Louis himself, victor over futility and loss of heart in his moth-eaten struggle against oblivion, had rather more of the hero about him. Guile, intelligence and genius for survival, even when backed by courage and a taste for risk, were not the stuff of heroism. For the French there was one true hero of the age and that, love him or hate him, worship or curse him, was Napoleon. Besting a legend did not win popularity. Talleyrand's unerring presence in the eye of every storm that battered France instead made him a choice target for the frustrated – royalists, Catholics, Jacobins and now Bonapartists. From the day of Louis' accession Talleyrand was bombarded with anonymous letters spitting hatred. There wasn't much that immoderate people – the 'small minds' he called them – didn't hold against him. Now his name was further dragged through the mud, falsely and by pure hearsay, over the curious disappearance of part of Napoleon's crown jewels. Anything pertaining to largesse rebounded against him. When would the small minds exhaust their venom?

'People need teaching how to forget,' he wrote to Mme de Staël, who was back in intellectual action in Paris and reconciled with him, though a little stiffly, now that her imperial persecutor was gone. He asked her: 'Remind those around you what a German author says: to forget is so important that even when you find it impossible to do so you must still hope to do it.'

Still exhausted, Talleyrand returned to his old desk at the foreign ministry on the Left Bank. It was seven years since he'd resigned to show his displeasure with Napoleon, but it was a field he'd never left, except in title. Resuming his former office meant swearing an oath to Louis XVIII. This amused him. After their first meeting at Compiègne, where he thought they got on quite well, he'd had time to reconsider. A little familiarity bred a fresh judgement. Now he saw the ponderous Louis as a complete egotist, insensitive and ungrateful, and a shameless liar. This darker view didn't entirely grow out of disappointment at not being made head of the definitive government. There was Louis' recooking of the constitution to digest. Furthermore he was bringing back royalist extremists, the class of émigrés Talleyrand loathed, to head the army in place of imperial officers. Talleyrand was flexible with oaths, however, which was the very reason that those who took them seriously hated him. In taking formal charge of the ministry, he observed to Louis with sardonic pleasure, 'Sire, this is my thirteenth oath. I hope it will be the last.'

June 1814 was a busy time. Foreign troops pulled out of Paris on the 3rd, the day Tsar Alexander also left, still peeved. He left without receiving Talleyrand to say a personal farewell, despite the week or so he'd spent as a guest at his house on the Place de la Concorde. But there was more than Russia and the moody tsar to think about. The Treaty of Paris settled Europe's war with France. But what about the huge problems affecting the rest of Europe thrown up by the rise and fall of Napoleon's empire? Not only France but all Europe needed putting back together. An international congress to reorganise the Continent and keep it at peace was scheduled to convene in Vienna in the autumn, with the four victorious allies calling the shots. It promised to be the most fundamental overhaul of the Continent ever undertaken, given that Napoleon had made the grandest mess of it.

Talleyrand's worry was that defeated France would have little or no voice at the congress, for all her history and size. To avoid that, he had to start reconciling the other great powers to Bourbon France. It came down to preserving his country's rank as a great power; without that, there could never be the stabilising balance of power he was looking for.

England, he at once decided, was the vital power to rally to his cause – the intractable enemy, the power most hostile to Napoleon, the power Napoleon hated most. Wellington, his palate well satisfied, was sympathetic, and so to a degree was Castlereagh. But the Prince Regent and the rest of the London government had to be turned and there wasn't much time. He wrote to his ambassador in London with instructions on how to satisfy them: 'Our sense is that the security of France is inseparable from the security of Europe. Our situation will be that of a state which has nothing to fear for itself, and which, since it threatens no one, will have many friends – a situation that seems much preferable to one of domination.'

Yes, indeed. Talleyrand portrayed France as determined to make the present peace a sincere end to warfare. The grounds for her stand were neither exhaustion nor the defeat of French arms, which were real enough, but her desire for moderation and, above all, reason. Talleyrand's post-imperial tips to his ambassador in London resumed the position he'd held all along: France's best interests were Europe's best interests, and vice versa. *Sotto voce*, it would behove England and her allies to think the same way. It was an eccentric idea, approximately a century and a half ahead of its time.

Since Talleyrand appeared to be on a different European wavelength from the victors, great tact was required in drawing up negotiating tactics for the Congress of Vienna. King Louis had old-fashioned views on world affairs but he couldn't be left in the dark, nor would he accept it. Talleyrand therefore conferred with him assiduously in the royal chamber at the Tuileries. The prime objective was to preserve France's rank as a great power in light of disturbing signs reaching Paris that the allied signatories to the Treaty of Paris suspected they had let France off too lightly and left her too powerful.

Talleyrand particularly wanted an amenable set of royal instructions to work from, so having gone over the ground at length with the king he wrote them himself. Louis was sage enough to let him do so, asking him to present a proposal for the instructions. Talleyrand shared the charade with Duchess Dorothea. 'I'm doing my damnedest for the congress,' he notified her skittishly, 'for I must arrive with my instructions to myself.' What he came up with was an extraordinarily detailed and logically argued blueprint to achieve his objectives, with an emphasis on conference procedure which he was pretty sure opposing delegates would find too dull to turn their minds to in advance. His negotiating plan wasn't set in stone; it gave him more than a little of the flexibility in which he traded.

Talleyrand's team for Vienna was, like the king's instructions, his own work. Aside from Carême, his sub-chefs and a heaving caravan of pots and pans, he chose four principal associates, each with useful talents to add to his negotiating skills. His three assisting plenipotentiaries were Dalberg, the Rhineland aristocrat and fellow provisional government member who knew every crowned head and his dog in Europe, Alexis de Noailles, an able young Bourbon courtier he'd befriended, and Frédéric de La Tour du Pin, a very old friend from exile in America since become an imperial administrator well grounded in European frontier-shifting. The way Talleyrand ran through his team for the benefit of the harem, these three had the most excellent skills: Dalberg would let out all the secrets he wanted everyone to know, Noailles would spy on him, a task better met by a Bourbon agent he knew than by one he didn't, and La Tour du Pin would 'sign passports'.

The fourth principal member of the team was young Dorothy, a flower of the European aristocracy that gravitated around Vienna. Just turned twenty-one, Dorothy had come through her hostess test at the Talleyrand residence with such bright-eyed grace and poise that he couldn't afford not to take her. He'd watched her catering with equal dexterity for one so young to monarchs, statesmen and Wellington's military caste. What was more, she found it perfectly to her taste. Guests responded with bubbling praise. A French admirer enthused: 'Her gay shining wit nicely tempered the gravity of political matters . . . her presence, her gestures, her attitude, the sound of her voice made a whole that was extraordinarily enchanting.'

As an eminent salon performer himself, Talleyrand judged that if he was to defuse the hostility Napoleon had aroused among those great men who were about to inhabit Vienna's high society, he would best start by making his legation an agreeable place to be. Who better than Dorothy to help him achieve it? A more hot-blooded nephew than Edmond might have accused Talleyrand of sealing the marital breach with his young wife. But their estrangement anyway looked more or less irreversible, especially since Edmond had just received promotion to brigade general from King Louis – at his uncle's bidding – and consequently was still away from Dorothy's side most of the time.

Talleyrand's departure for the largest international conference ever staged was a trip into the unknown, starting with matters personal. If Duchess Dorothea charmed, stirred and piqued him, her daughter was now set to rule him. As a statesman, he approached his finest hour.

EIGHTEEN

The Congress of Vienna

Talleyrand got to Vienna on 23 September 1814 holding the new title of Prince Talleyrand. This was the gift of King Louis, who wished among other things to mark his disapproval of the imperial title Prince of Benevento. The opening of the great congress was a week away and emperors, kings, sovereign princes and grand dukes, accompanied by their ladies, were already assembling by the score.

He installed his legation at a splendid old Habsburg pile, the Kaunitz Palace, which was so moth-eaten as to force an immediate change of bedding, carpets and upholstery throughout. However, its aura of grandeur more than compensated for its insect life. The congress was likely to last weeks, maybe months. Talleyrand always moved in style, this time bringing with him from Paris not only Carême and the kitchen crew but a celebrated miniaturist artist, Jean-Baptiste Isabey, and a pianist, Sigismund Neukomm (a talented young musician he employed to play for him as he worked on his papers) – the first to paint flattering portraits of the numerous potentates he was about to do business with, the second to provide ambiance for his Vienna salon, to which he counted on drawing the assembled sovereigns.

He had spent endless time and thought clearing up the pieces after each of Napoleon's victories; now he was engaged in clearing up the colossal end mess. The trouble was that England, Russia, Austria and Prussia had agreed among themselves, as major powers and victorious allies, that they alone were to take all major decisions on redrawing the map of Europe. Indeed, as Talleyrand settled into the Kaunitz Palace, they spent the week in Vienna before the official opening of the congress in secret conclave, nodding heads over the wisdom of their fundamental agreement. Pettier princes from Denmark to Parma could shout all they wished; it was the Big Four who would decide things.

Talleyrand, of course, had wind of this, though he wasn't officially informed since it was meant to be secret. It ran straight up against his balance-of-power theory on which he believed durable peace stood. He was more than ever inclined to regard Europe as a whole, its interests inseparable from those of the countries of which it was made. To leave the largest nation in Europe out of the reckoning was, in his view, asking for trouble. France was down but would never be out; to exclude France out of spite was folly, an invitation to future hostilities. Only Castlereagh, aloof, glacially well-mannered and not much given to explaining himself, had any real notion of the benefits of the balance of power Talleyrand sought. This was because early nineteenth-century England was sufficiently strong and sure of herself to prize 'a just equilibrium', as Castlereagh put it, as an ideal way to keep her rich possessions and enjoy her ease. Castlereagh tended towards Talleyrand's thinking that an even distribution of strength made aggression a futile risk for any one country. Other great powers less self-assured than England preferred to think that only by making themselves stronger than large neighbours, and feared by them, could they achieve security and the chance of lasting prosperity. These powers miscast balance-of-power politics as more likely the cause of war than of peace, and it took them around a century and a half after the Congress of Vienna to adjust their vision.

On the eve of the scheduled opening of the conference on 1 October, Metternich, the host negotiator, invited Talleyrand to attend a private meeting of the Big Four to brief him as to how they intended to run things. Here was the Frenchman's chance to unleash on his antagonists the instructions he'd drawn up for himself regarding procedure. With Metternich were Castlereagh, Nesselrode for Russia and Chancellor Karl August Hardenberg for Prussia, who was almost stone deaf. Apart from Hardenburg, the principal delegates were all old associates of Talleyrand whose strengths and weaknesses he well knew. When they casually referred to themselves in opening remarks as the 'allied powers', Talleyrand leapt on the term:

Allies? Against whom? No longer against Napoleon, for he is on the island of Elba. No longer against France, for peace is made. And surely not against the king of France, for he is the guarantee that the peace will last. Gentlemen, let us speak frankly. If there are still allied powers, then this is no place for me! And yet if I weren't here you would badly miss me. Gentlemen, I am perhaps the only one who asks for nothing. All I want for France is your high regard . . . I repeat, I ask for nothing. And I bring you a very great deal. The presence here of a minister of Louis XVIII consecrates the principle that underpins all social order. Europe's first need is to ban forever the idea that rights can be acquired by conquest alone and to revive the sacred principle of legitimacy on which order and stability stand. To show here today that France stands in the way of your deliberations would be to say that true principles no longer lead you and that you do not wish to be just.

It was a measured outburst, yet it rang with indignation and it had the Big Four writhing in their seats. For two hours he went on, driving home the need to settle things according to 'public law'. White-faced, they had no reply to this furious logic save to offer stammering excuses, now denying, now attempting to explain away what they had agreed together beforehand.

Talleyrand's intervention changed the tenor of the entire congress. The Austrian conference secretary noted: 'It hopelessly upset all our plans. It was a scene I shall never forget.' For Talleyrand also reminded Metternich, Castlereagh and company that the Treaty of Paris which preceded the Vienna congress specified that *all* powers engaged in the Napoleonic Wars would send plenipotentiaries to the Austrian capital to settle things in Europe. It so happened that Spain, Portugal and Sweden, like France, had also signed the Paris treaty. Stunned, the Big Four at once discarded the protocol they'd drawn up to decide things between themselves and replaced it with one reflecting the sense of Talleyrand's intervention. It was the tamest of come-downs for proud victors.

They were now the Big Five. France had an equal part in driving the congress. A certain amount of cavilling went on to make it Six, or even Eight, but for practical purposes this failed, not least because the gushing Spanish representative was out of his depth and bored leading participants to distraction, Talleyrand included.

It was a pity that Tsar Alexander was less receptive to Talleyrand's 'public law' summons than Nesselrode, his man at the bargaining table, and the other principal negotiators. The ministers met in the mornings, their royal masters in the afternoons. Of the monarchs whose armies defeated Napoleon only England's Prince Regent, the future George IV, his royal muscle limited by his constitutional position, was absent from Vienna. As soon as Alexander heard of the Talleyrand performance on the conference eve, he called him to an interview. It was their first private meeting since Alexander had left Paris in a huff four months earlier, angry with both King Louis and his minister. Predictably, it was awkward. The Frenchman stuck to his rule-of-law and legitimacy principles, determined that they should govern the congress. The tsar, who aimed to leave Vienna with all Poland brought under his sway, assumed he was the law.

The fates of Poland and of Saxony, Prussia's vulnerable neighbour, were the largest issues confronting the congress, together with how far Austria and Prussia were to extend their frontiers into the deceased Napoleonic empire. After a wary greeting, Alexander observed to Talleyrand that he had no qualms about disposing of Saxony since its king had 'betrayed Europe' by siding with Napoleon all along. Talleyrand, who aimed to save Saxony, stared at him, hooded eyes unblinking: 'That, Sire, is a question of dates!' He was recollecting the scene of two emperors embracing years before on a raft at Tilsit. Hadn't Alexander himself betrayed Europe by making up to Napoleon when it suited him?

Saxony, then, was put aside. But Alexander was adamant about the sense of the congress:

'Everyone must have his just deserts.'

'And his rights,' said Talleyrand.

'I shall keep what I occupy.'

'Your Majesty will surely only wish to keep what is legitimately his.'

'I am in agreement with the great powers.'

'I do not know whether Your Majesty counts France among them.'

'Yes, to be sure. But if you do not wish everyone to have their just deserts, what is it you want?'

'I put law first, deserts after.'

'In Europe deserts are the law.'

The rat-a-tat exchange between emperor and statesman was a measure of their long familiarity but even so it was developing an unpleasant edge. Talleyrand, propped against a carved wooden screen for support, objected, 'This language, Sire, is not yours. It is alien to you and your heart rejects it.'

'No, I repeat, in Europe just deserts are the law.'

Talleyrand was exasperated. He leaned his head on the screen and beat the wood panelling with his hand, sighing, 'Europe, Europe, poor Europe! Will you let it be said you destroyed her?'

Alexander ignored his antagonist's show of emotion, though it was the first time he had heard more than high politics and flattery coming from those controlled lips. He stamped, 'Rather war than give up what I occupy! Yes, rather war!' At that he turned his head to the door, indicating he had other things to do. He had to go to the theatre. Emperor Franz, his host, was waiting for him. As he left, though, he suddenly turned back and hugged Talleyrand, saying in a strained voice, 'Goodbye, goodbye, we shall see each other again.' It occurred to the minister what a peculiar character Alexander was, a split personality, now the bullying autocrat, now a large-hearted, liberal do-gooder. Too unstable to count upon, Talleyrand decided, even if he wished to do so, which at present he did not. His aim at the congress, and King Louis', was to keep Russia as far away as possible from Europe's heart.

Prussia's Hardenberg had little time for public law either. The day Talleyrand insisted on making it a governing principle of the congress, Hardenberg rose from his seat, pounded the negotiating table and shouted, at a decibel level only the deaf reach when wanting to make sure of being heard, 'No, Sir. Absolutely not! Why say we are acting according to public law? That goes without saying.'

If it went without saying, Talleyrand replied, it would go still better if it were said.

But containing Russian and Prussian demands wasn't easily done. Talleyrand's negotiating hand looked empty. For once, King Friedrich Wilhelm's Prussia had a fuller hand, added to which the king held Alexander in awe. It seemed to be almost taken for granted by the four victors that Russia would obtain all of Poland – nominally recreated as an independent kingdom to satisfy public opinion, but in fact a tsarist satrapy – while Prussia, in return for giving up its part of Poland, would obtain all Saxony. Talleyrand opposed both of these major shifts, and he thought it a reasonable bet that England and Austria could be brought to share his view. It was true that France asked for nothing for herself, and was in no position to do so, but Talleyrand did ask that victors shouldn't get what they demanded merely because they occupied it or had the military strength to take it. To condone this, he said, was to condone Napoleon's 'horrible principles which must forever be rejected in Europe'. What was more, the dual prospect of Russia swelling into middle Europe and Prussia becoming master of all Germany – the inevitable outcome, he judged, of a Prussian takeover of Saxony – would do nothing for just equilibrium.

Time, then, for some diplomatic creativity. It seemed to him that the best way to hold back Russia and Prussia was to divide the four victors and he began to concentrate all his negotiating skill and logic on devising a united front between France, England and Austria to halt the tsar's and king's designs. But this wasn't to be done in the Council of Five. It was behind-the-scenes work, the work of persuasion best done in salon alcoves and opera boxes. Or during a Carême meal at the Kaunitz Palace.

In the advancing autumn of 1814 there was no place like Vienna for the sovereign cream of Europe to let loose. Everyone gathered there wanted something from the congress, but the congress kept putting off the plenary sessions that were likely to give them something to do. No one knew when their stay was going to end. The five chief negotiators were extremely busy in spurts, but even they had time on their hands. The leading monarchs, bowed down with invitations, looked for amusement. The heads of 215 princely houses looked for it with them, less sure of their invitations. Legions of chamberlains and equerries crowded the city to keep their masters and mistresses in the social swim. At the centre of the web of jollity and distraction was the Habsburg host, Emperor Franz, who by nature was unsociable but was now an overstretched impresario; his Hofburg Palace provided liveries and carriages for each and every princely guest, kept 1400 horses saddled for them and laid out forty grand tables each night for their dinner. For their musical delight, he brought in the celebrated Ludwig van Beethoven who, though deafer than Hardenberg, took the baton to conduct a piece he had just composed to celebrate the Duke of Wellington's campaign in Spain.

As for off-Hofburg entertainment, Talleyrand was not the only one providing it. The congress participants vied with each other to stop the fun fizzling out. Through October, November and into December each day brought theatricals, charades, tombolas, sleigh rides, banquets, masked balls, operas, hunts, secret love affairs and balloon ascents. As summed up by a visiting French aristocrat, 'The Congress of Vienna doesn't work. It dances.'

Talleyrand couldn't dance. Mornings, he received princes and statesmen while Courtiade and his dressers finished attending to his silver curls, pushed his white cravat ever higher on his spreading chin and oiled his bad foot. Most evenings he gave a reception at the gilded Kaunitz Palace with Dorothy as hostess. With guests able to skip from one event to another, the Talleyrand receptions were always crowded. Europe's *beau monde* seemed utterly fascinated by a man who was so intimately involved in Napoleon's downfall. What was it like in Paris at that time? What did he do? He fielded the questions courteously, answering with an ironic shrug: 'I limped.'

He wasn't a lovable figure. His expressionless, putty mask of a face shocked as much as it impressed. The awe he aroused was close to horror for some spectators who were ill-disposed towards him from the start, Russians in particular. Alexander's mistress said he had 'the eyes of a dead fish and heavy lids that he kept lowered like a shop blind'. At conference sessions he mostly lay doggo; it was a performance that demanded astonishing body control. A fascinated Austrian delegate who watched him said: 'If I hadn't seen his eyes I would have thought he was a waxwork. He never moved. He stayed in the same position for three hours. The sovereigns all spoke to him, but he stayed in the same position, the exact same place.' Alexander's political adviser Carlo Pozzo di Borgo, an acid-tongued Corsican who was assisting Nesselrode at the congress, likened his supreme courtesy to 'a moneylender's investment' which recipients found they had to pay back with interest before the day was out.

Pozzo di Borgo was no doubt behind rumours that Talleyrand was netting millions in *douceurs* offered by the King of Saxony, Italian princes and unfortunate margraves who saw their lands slipping away from them unless they took preventive action. The unique circumstances of the congress and Talleyrand's intrusion into the Big Four made the rumours particularly credible for those who wanted to believe them.

His table, though, received unanimous acclaim. When Louis sent him a message from Paris inquiring whether he needed further diplomatic assistance, he wrote back that he didn't need more diplomats, he needed more cooks. The shy Castlereagh caught Wellington's addiction. For Talleyrand, it was good to have Castlereagh at his table as often as possible: the Englishman was the one negotiator, besides Metternich, he most needed to pull to his side. At dinner one evening his guests began a well-fed little competition, comparing the merits of their national cheeses. There was nothing to beat Stilton, said Castlereagh. Since the Kaunitz kitchens were out of Brie, Talleyrand's favourite, he kept quiet at first as others talked up Gorgonzola, Edam and such. But just then a valet came to announce the arrival of a messenger from Paris bearing letters from King Louis and pantry supplies for Carême. Talleyrand, who placed the pantry orders, was fairly sure the supplies would contain a delivery of Brie. 'Have the letters taken to my office and the cheese brought straight here,' he instructed the valet. 'There, gentlemen!' he said as his creamy Brie reached the table. 'You may judge the winner for yourselves.'

Dorothy looked after the wider salon ambiance. She danced. She led the dance. Within no time, with her dark curls, her big black eyes, her quick spirit and agile form, she became the darling of Vienna. She was a beautiful, slender young woman now, confident in herself. Potentates smiled at her, princes were besotted by her – and she by more than one of them. Each morning she came to sit at the end of Talleyrand's bed to discuss the house activities she was to attend to and talk over the progress of the congress. She had sharp observations on most things and, far from treating them as girlish chatter, Talleyrand appreciated them. 'Our child is a great success,' he wrote to the duchess, who seemed to be showing no jealousy over her daughter's rise, or masked it if she felt it. 'She is a success with all ages. I wish I could say the same, for I'm quarrelling with all the potentates of the earth.' Then, a day or so later: 'Dorothy is having a wonderful time. Her success is total. To be so pretty does no harm and she is at her very best.'

A curious pair they made. The congress seemed drawn to their door by a mysterious scent of scandal. He almost sixty-one, she twenty-one. He thick of line, wobbly on his feet, cheeks puffed, elegant to an *ancien régime* fault in his salon wear – pale mauve topcoat, frilled white cravat, black silk stockings, black slippers with red heels and diamond buckles. She dazzling in her youth, her intelligence, her Paris fashions and Kurland family jewels her mother gave her to impress Vienna. Her life seemed back to front, though. It was as if she reached the peak of her triumph as a woman before reaching the fullness of her womanhood. 'Vienna! My whole destiny is in that word,' she later recalled. 'It is here that my life devoted to M de Talleyrand began, here that this extraordinary, no, unique, association took form, one that death alone could break.' The success she knew as his hostess in Vienna made this beautiful, dominating slip of a girl his confidante, his companion, his guru in matters of state and matters of the heart.

And that was where it ended – an intimate, confidential, mutually admiring companionship. Despite the age difference, they shared a love of politics and statecraft. His deformity gave her the shudders. She it was who likened his club foot in her diary to 'a horse's hoof made of flesh ending in a claw'. Even in Vienna she wanted more than devoted companionship from love, and since she had outgrown Edmond entirely she indulged it with a handsome Austrian count, Karl von Clam, who had been making brooding eyes at her. Clam was a twenty-three-year-old cavalry officer attached to Emperor Franz's negotiating team – a young man on the rise – and she began making brief sorties of a day or so at a time from the Kaunitz Palace to be alone with him, which displeased Talleyrand, especially since she had another Austrian suitor in line to take her on sleigh rides. Was his hurt a guardian's concern? Or a jealous heart? He was certainly under her spell. It was hard to face the thought of losing her. What jealousy he felt, he managed as usual to bury. On her return from one of her short absences at the end of the year, he reported in a dexterous and wounded little note to the duchess: 'Dorothy has a heavy cold of the kind you catch on staircases in Vienna when you leave a ball.'

As Talleyrand manoeuvred among the great of the earth, Napoleon, only a few days' carriage ride and an isthmus away on the sparse island of Elba, struggled to adapt to his derisory new status. He employed the thousand guardsmen he'd brought with him to plant olive orchards, pave the streets of the rude little port, Portoferraio, erect lampposts, lay out grass borders around its fort, put benches along the quays and devise a decent sanitation system.

Since arriving in May aboard an English man-of-war he'd conceived a project to turn the scrappy island into a market garden to make it economically self-sufficient, discarding Tsar Alexander's woolly notion that it had the makings of a Mediterranean trading hub. His palace was an old three-storey house by the fort called I Mulini (The Mills), to which he added a storey. He set up a royal court with something of the decorum of the Tuileries Palace: a sovereign household of four chamberlains, a protocol guard of seven officers in sky-blue uniforms, punctual morning receptions and a social side run by his extravagant sister Pauline whom he encouraged to hold regular masked balls for worthier Elbans provided the cost didn't run to more than 1000 francs per event. To keep in military trim he rode on horseback for three hours a day, an activity in which his warder, a watchful English commissioner named Neil Campbell, likewise encouraged him, though he noticed he was growing increasingly broad in the beam despite the exercise.

By the time the Congress of Vienna was in its slow stride Napoleon abandoned hope that Marie Louise and his three-year-old son, the ex-King of Rome, would ever be allowed to join him. Emperor Franz's intransigence depressed him deeply, adding to his grief over the recent death of his first empress, Josephine, who was stricken in early summer by a sudden attack of diphtheria. He began taking his daily rides in the back of his carriage instead of mounting his horse, which Campbell reported to London in the autumn as a sign of something. Life had gone flat. He was bored as well as depressed. After less than six months on Elba he began taking to his bed at 9 p.m., morose and restless.

Back in Vienna Talleyrand was aware of Napoleon's evolving mood. As foreign minister he'd taken the elementary precaution of placing agents on Elba to inform him on the fallen warrior's activities. Aware he was spied upon, Napoleon, reverting to quaint island subterfuges, asked mainland correspondents to address their letters to Signor Senno, who ran a local tunny fishery, so as to thwart both Talleyrand's agents and curious English eyes. He wanted to hear more of what stray visitors from France were obligingly telling him: that the population was already disenchanted with the fusty, reactionary Bourbons and were clamouring for his return.

So although Napoleon was manifestly done for, a prisoner of the English, reduced to pettifogging ritual on a paltry rock, he somehow re-emerged as a phantom power at the congress. Talleyrand kept Castlereagh and Metternich alive to the danger, holding it like a lit fuse before the Big Five. He advised King Louis: 'Quite a strong body of opinion is developing to remove Bonaparte from Elba. Nobody has a fixed idea on just where. I have proposed the Azores. It is five hundred leagues from any land. Lord Castlereagh rather seems to believe the Portuguese would accept this, though the question then arises of who finances it.' Louis was all for it, urging his minister to press the proposal. By Christmas, Talleyrand was able to inform the king his idea was 'bearing fruit'. He concocted some scheme with Castlereagh to have England pay for Napoleon's upkeep in exchange for France's agreement to join England at once in abolishing the slave trade, another issue on the table at Vienna. His optimism, though, proved to be merely wishful thinking because Tsar Alexander in particular wasn't ready to go back on abdication conditions agreed with the Emperor of the French.

The cost of Napoleon's upkeep on Elba was no light matter. Family grief and boredom apart, it was a cause of his restlessness. His Bourbon successor balked at paying the stipulated four million francs annuity to the upstart Bonapartes who had kept him off his throne. Although Louis, for diplomatic reasons, couldn't make this a formal refusal, the royal exchequer never disbursed a sou to the sovereign ruler of Elba. Accordingly, Napoleon could no longer afford to pay his thousand-man army, which anyway was a meaningless luxury as long as it was stranded on a barren island. Elba clearly had no need of a defence force.

Talleyrand's concern mounted. Like himself, Napoleon was a risk taker.

Logic had won the opening match at Vienna. Talleyrand's choice weapon had found a gap and cut through it. Could he now mobilise logic to create the gap leading to a stable Europe? Despite the broad initial assumption among participants that Russia was going to have Poland and Prussia was going to take Saxony plus, no doubt, much of the Rhineland, recriminations among the Five soon got in the way of so stark a distribution of the northern spoils. Talleyrand hardly needed to arouse Metternich against Tsar Alexander, since the two were already exasperated with each other. The clash between Metternich's mysterious intrigues and Alexander's dogmatic demands to obtain all of Poland brought the congress to a deadlock envenomed by intemperate words on both sides. Austria wasn't going to yield Galicia, her southern slice of Poland, said Metternich, only for the entire land to become a tsarist puppet. The tsar, beside himself, threatened the noble Austrian with a duel and though this theatrical solution to the deadlock was averted he refused to speak to him for weeks.

Here was an opening for Talleyrand to exploit. He was fairly sure of being able to line himself up with Austria, whose cause he had endlessly supported through the heat of the Napoleonic Wars. Though Metternich darted this way and that in pursuit of his shifting objectives, Talleyrand dogged him with reminders that he couldn't possibly wish for a wholly reconstituted Poland since it would never manage to stay independent of Russia: it would simply be placing a Russian belt around an already thinned Habsburg Empire. The same went for next-door Saxony. 'How can you allow the patrimony of an old and worthy neighbour like Saxony to be handed to your natural enemy, Prussia?' he probed Metternich in a private note. It was true that as the congress went on he felt increasingly irritated by the grand Austrian negotiator whom he found to be 'tortuous' and a vain wordsmith. But Metternich understood his aims.

The phlegmatic Castlereagh, whose country faced no obvious physical threats, was in every way a different proposition for Talleyrand. To start with, each appeared to the other to be a caricature of his race. The English lord lacked a devious, slippery side for Talleyrand to appeal to. 'It is extraordinary how much the English don't know,' the Frenchman reflected on his partner's grasp of Europe. The Englishman's stiffness might loosen at times – as a series of dancing lessons he booked with Lady Castlereagh to master the frisky polonaise attested – but Talleyrand saw he was always thinking of how the English parliament would take his actions, which made him timid and indecisive.

As it was, opinion in London was largely sympathetic to the prospect of a reborn, entirely independent Polish nation, and English concerns that it would inevitably fall into Russian hands were slight. Moreover, while Castlereagh very much favoured a 'just equilibrium' to safeguard peace on the Continent, his vision of it struck Talleyrand as patently unrealistic: it focused on equalising population numbers, troops and cannons. To keep the large French nation in check in future, for example, he thought it might actually be a good thing to enlarge Prussia by feeding her the Rhineland on France's receded border.

Talleyrand, in the careful Vienna instructions he wrote for himself, took a far more pragmatic view of the balance of power than Castlereagh. To his mind the balance was bound to be relative:

> It can only be a system of partial balance. An absolute equality of power between all states not only cannot exist, it is not necessary to political equilibrium and would in some respects be harmful. Such equilibrium lies in the relation between the power to resist and the power to attack. If Europe were made up of states related in such a way that the minimum resistance capacity of the smallest equalled the maximum aggression capacity of the largest, then there would be true balance. But that is not and never will be the situation in Europe. The actual situation only admits an artificial and precarious balance that can last just as long as certain large states are driven by a spirit of moderation and justice to preserve it.

Moderation. The rule of law. This was the stuff of just equilibrium. Castlereagh eventually came to appreciate it, though perhaps less due to Talleyrand's relentless badgering than to his distaste for Tsar Alexander's arrogance. For despite home opinion on the Polish question, he realised that if there was going to be an agreement at Vienna the Russian monarch would need to moderate his position. When he put this straight to Alexander, however, all it did was to push the tsar's hand back to his duelling pistol. Russian troops now occupied Poland, Alexander declared, and they were a large force: if England didn't like them there, she would have to turn them out.

By the New Year of 1815 the congress seemed to be veering beyond dead-lock towards a fresh bout of war. It was then that Talleyrand's peripheral operations paid off. He proposed to Metternich and Castlereagh that they sign a secret treaty of alliance against Russia and Prussia – and on 3 January they did so. The three contracted to give each other military support if any one of them was attacked because of its stance at the congress. Talleyrand was cock-a-hoop over his unexpected coup. Without waiting to see what effect it would have on unblocking the congress, he wrote to King Louis, hardly able to contain his self-satisfaction:

> In my best hopes I never flattered myself on being able to obtain such complete success. Now, Sire, the coalition is dissolved, once and for all. Not only is France no longer isolated in Europe, but Your Majesty already has a federative system such as fifty years of negotiations seemed unlikely to give her. She walks hand in hand with two of the great powers . . . and soon with all those states that pursue principles and maxims other than revolution. France will truly be the heart and soul of this union, formed for the defence of principles she has been first to proclaim. So great and fortunate a change can only be attributed to the hand of Providence so visibly reflected in the return of Your Majesty.

The jubilant letter ran to fairly wild exaggeration for a man as careful with his words as Talleyrand, and not only in its cute ending. To anticipate some kind of European federation bound by the rule of law at this stage was to let those 'best hopes' of his play tricks with him. But there was much to be said for his diplomatic agility in bonding France, England and Austria at so difficult a time in Vienna. In reality it was a huge bluff. Its effect, once Tsar Alexander and King Friedrich Wilhelm got to hear of it, was to call their bluff. For they weren't in fact prepared to provoke more war to satisfy their demands on Poland and Saxony.

Thanks to Talleyrand's manoeuvring, the way suddenly opened to compro-mise. Within a month agreement was reached on Poland: it would remain divided with Prussia keeping a reduced western chunk, Austria holding Galicia and Russia adding Napoleon's Duchy of Warsaw to its Polish lands further east. On paper the duchy was formed into an independent kingdom of Poland with Warsaw as its capital but this was a fiction: the kingdom was bound to fall under Russia's sway, and it soon did. Alexander failed to obtain all he wanted but had enough of Poland to satisfy him without whetting the fears of people like Talleyrand and Metternich that he was about to become master of middle Europe.

Prussia acquired less than half of Saxony, whose monarch, King Friedrich August, remained at the head of an independent realm that included the great middle European trading and cultural centres of Leipzig and Dresden. But where Prussia failed to annexe Saxony, she profited in the west, gaining much of the Rhineland that lay within the 'natural frontiers' that Talleyrand had originally aimed to preserve for France. Little Luxembourg became independent, escaping French control. Prussian dominance in northern Germany was assured. This didn't please Talleyrand, still less so the truculent back-seat negotiators and popular press in Paris. But neither Castlereagh nor Metternich appeared much concerned by it.

As for Austria, the Habsburg Empire swallowed up the Tyrol and the Slav lands of Illyria on the Adriatic while restoring its hegemony over Lombardy and most of the rest of northern Italy. Austrian influence in southern Italy also grew, for the congress reached a secret agreement by which an Austrian army was to head south and depose Napoleon's marshal, Joachim Murat, as King of Naples, returning the throne to the Italian Bourbons whom Napoleon had evicted. The long-suffering pope would also get his lands back, including the Talleyrand fiefdom of Benevento.

On the North Sea the Kingdom of Holland took in Belgium, a fusion of the Low Countries that secured Antwerp for England's continental trade – free of interference by France or other great powers. This was a Castlereagh priority. Indeed, it was the one issue he pursued with any passion. Once it was laced into the spider's web of Vienna accords he returned to London, handing over his negotiating seat to the Duke of Wellington. The switch was welcome news to Talleyrand who endured Castlereagh but positively liked Wellington for his love of discussion and the tactical breadth he brought to it.

In early February 1815 these were the outlines of the continental compromise which in broad terms endured for the next hundred years. All in all it was the finest performance of Talleyrand's long career. From the tone of his dispatches to King Louis, he rather felt he came out as the leading statesman in Europe, that is, the world. The effect he had on Europe's most powerful monarchs certainly impressed his colleagues. 'Alexander pipes down before him, Emperor Franz slips out of the door and the King stares at his boots,' a high-born French admirer observed.

At this point he and his fellow chief negotiators settled down to what they assumed would be a serene period of crossing t's on a final treaty and of further indulgence in the social amusements of the Habsburg capital.

How wrong they were.

*   *   *

At dawn on 7 March Talleyrand was awoken by an urgent message from Metternich inviting him to his ministry. He had been up late as usual and was fast asleep when the messenger arrived. He dragged himself to the ministry to hear the Austrian read him a dispatch just in from the Austrian consul in Genoa. It reported that Neil Campbell, England's commissioner on Elba, had sailed into Genoa in his Royal Navy frigate wanting to know if anyone had spotted Napoleon there; he had disappeared from the island. When Genoa shook its head, Campbell had raced back to sea.

So Napoleon had escaped! Where to? Talleyrand calmly inquired of Metternich. The Austrian said the report didn't say. 'He will land somewhere in Italy and throw himself upon Switzerland,' Talleyrand forecast. 'No, he will go straight to Paris!' Metternich said.

As they conferred, Napoleon was in fact already well on the road to Paris heading north through the Alps from his Provençal landing place at Golfe Juan, his island exile troops swelling in numbers all the while as he rode through cheering French towns and villages. Regular French troops refused to fire on him, then began joining him. His objective was to regain power and his imperial bed at the Tuileries. He had sailed from Elba with his small army on 26 February aboard a French vessel left at his sovereign disposal, taking advantage of Campbell's brief absence in Florence for appointments with a dentist and a mistress. He escaped because he was bored, his name was Napoleon and he was still only forty-five-years old. Yet with all the security worries over his place of exile, it seemed a miracle – or a setup – that he'd been able to leave unhindered, without being stopped by Royal Navy men-of-war patrolling the Mediterranean. There was inevitable speculation that someone – perhaps Castlereagh, Talleyrand and Metternich between them, so the stories flew – had eased the departure from Elba as a means of trapping Napoleon into a fruitless comeback that would make it possible to rid Europe of him for good. But the prosecution here ignored these statesmen's deep puzzlement and indignation over the conqueror's return to France, and the harm it was bound to do them if he succeeded in seizing power. For Talleyrand, it would undo all his labours in Vienna, all his efforts for peace in Europe, so he had more cause than most to feel distressed. Straight after hearing the news from Metternich, he wrote with unsuppressed anger to King Louis that Napoleon must be considered a common outlaw. 'That is how he must be treated and all measures permitted against outlaws must be employed against him.'

Vienna was in uproar, its amusements curtly halted. Talleyrand was besieged by questioners anxious to hear his thoughts on the outcome. Imperturbable, he told everyone, 'It will be a matter of a few weeks; he will soon be worn out.' Inside he seethed. Napoleon was 'a monster', 'a madman', he told the Kaunitz Palace team, a man who could never be despised enough for playing with the fate of the country which had given him everything. He liaised on military counter-measures with the Big Four, who began mobilising English, Prussian and Austrian forces in the Rhineland and the Low Countries and turned round the Russian army which was on its way home. In his flurry of advice to Louis he permitted himself to name those marshals he thought best suited to confront Napoleon. In reply Louis feigned confidence, telling him that Napoleon's enterprise would shake neither the tranquillity of Europe nor of his royal soul.

This was hardly reassuring. Talleyrand wanted something stronger than airy Bourbon platitudes as a defence against Napoleon. On 14 March he convinced the great powers gathered in Vienna to sign a declaration, penned by himself, committing them to halt the warrior's return and save Europe from his depredations. It thundered: 'Napoleon Bonaparte has placed himself beyond the pale of civil and social relations and delivered himself to public judgement as the enemy and destroyer of world peace.' While expressing the certitude that all France would reject his 'criminal delirium' and rally behind Louis XVIII, the solemn declaration committed the sovereigns of Europe to use all means and combine all efforts to stop the peace being destroyed anew.

Again, Talleyrand was pleased with his work. In a note to the duchess in Paris, where she was in fact packing her bags to leave in face of Napoleon's seemingly unstoppable advance on the capital, he said he had never seen an international document like it: 'History has no example of such revulsion expressed by the whole human race.' To another member of the Paris harem he wrote: 'In Paris you place Bonaparte outside the law of France. Here we place him outside the law of mankind.'

There wasn't a trace of hesitation in Talleyrand's reactions to Napoleon's return. Not for a moment did he start sizing up the situation to see which way to jump, which many of his peers now did. So often it was said of him that he served whichever regime landed in power simply because he had to be there, and the facts did seem to bear out the reproach. But in all cases – the Revolution, the Directory, Napoleon as Consul, Napoleon as Emperor, Louis XVIII – he'd done so not only to put himself forward but to shape things in the way he thought best for France and the civilised life, the two of which he regarded as much the same thing. In this case no such shaping was possible; Napoleon was the enemy of civilisation, the enemy of France. He had no high opinion of King Louis the man, but he was bound to stand by him. To Kaunitz Palace colleagues he argued: 'Regimes come and go. France stays. Sometimes by serving a regime with ardour you may betray your country's interests, but by serving your country you are sure to betray only the passing regimes.'

From his landing at Golfe Juan on 1 March, Napoleon took just twenty days to regain his bed at the Tuileries. It was still warm from the corpulence of King Louis, who had fled north the night before to the coast of Belgium, there to wait things out in the city of Ghent. Napoleon hadn't got halfway to Paris before his march became a triumphal popular procession spurred on by roadside hurrahs of 'Vive l'Empereur'. His progress through the mountains, Lyons and the plains of *France profonde* was indeed unstoppable, a sentimental phenomenon inexplicable in terms of the suffering the people had known before the close of his rule. He retook Paris with scarcely a drop of blood shed. Louis' forces, commanded by former imperial marshals, caved in without a fight.

Prince Talleyrand was disappointed in Louis. No doubt it was easy, from the safety of Vienna, to be contemptuous of the king's flight, but he had counted on sterner royal backbone. Louis' departure ruptured his legitimacy. Right up to the moment he slipped out of the Tuileries at dead of night on 19 March he had been making noble noises about being ready to die for throne and country. With the time it took news and mail to travel, Talleyrand was only belatedly aware of events in Paris, but he kept urging Louis to stay put until he discovered he hadn't. Tsar Alexander too, evidently feeling guilty over Napoleon's escape, urged Louis to stay in Paris 'to defend the interests of Europe'. As soon as Talleyrand heard he was established in Ghent next to the port of Ostend, he pressed him with all courtesy to move inland to Liège where at least he wouldn't be seen as ready to flee overseas by the next boat – and where he could put on a show of involving himself in military resistance to Napoleon, since the allied forces were congregating close by.

Talleyrand was nonetheless in an invidious position. He was now out on a diplomatic limb in Vienna, representing a government which had clearly stopped functioning and been replaced by an outlaw. Like a bunged tap, the funds he received from the royal treasury in Paris to keep the Kaunitz Palace a centre of attraction suddenly ceased to flow. Fortunately he had his reputation to stand on; to most of those present at the congress he *was* France.

His reward for steadfastness in opposing Napoleon's return came promptly. One of the warrior's first actions was to sequester all Talleyrand's property, from the Place de la Concorde to Valençay, pointedly excluding him from a general amnesty accorded to those in the king's service. This was depressing news, the second time in twenty years that everything he owned was ordered confiscated. He tried to make light of it. 'What a joke!' he wrote in a morning note on 5 April to his 'dear friend' the Duchess of Kurland, who had just reached Vienna to keep out of Napoleon's way and was staying with him and Dorothy at the Kaunitz Palace. In fact, he felt unutterably sour. There was no telling how long Napoleon's absurd new hold on power would last. He was disgusted by the fickleness of his compatriots. All those in France who were bowing to Louis a week ago, he told her, were now bowing to Bonaparte. People had often accused Talleyrand himself of fickleness, but this was different! 'What poor creatures men are. The heart and the mind they pride themselves on don't match the intelligence of farmyard animals.'

Knowing Napoleon as he did, he wasn't entirely surprised, however, when the warrior changed his tune and began soliciting his help. It was obvious why. The Paris in which Napoleon sought to refloat his reign was off-limits to the world, the entire diplomatic corps departed. If he was to make his return work, he had to gain a minimum of international understanding. He couldn't expect it from England. There was one man, though, who might be able to make his case with leaders like Tsar Alexander and Metternich. He needed Talleyrand!

As the difficulties involved in re-establishing control in France and in facing allied armies regathering on his borders piled up, Napoleon stalked the Tuileries, frequently raising his old antagonist's name in conversation: 'Talleyrand is still the man who best knows the world and our century. He knows the governments, the peoples. He left me. And I left him, I was harsh with him. He won't have forgotten my farewell last year.' Little more than a month after re-entering Paris, Napoleon moved to get him back. He pledged to return his confiscated property 'if he conducts himself as a Frenchman and renders me some services'. The warrior believed the financial bait might yet hook Talleyrand. He thought a financial proposition might likewise hook Metternich, for an emissary he sent to make contact in Vienna with Talleyrand was also authorised to offer the Austrian foreign minister 'from one to ten million francs' to pull out of the coalition. They were sorry offers, cynical as well as desperate. In the case of Metternich, the sole reason Napoleon had for thinking he might sell himself was his personal conviction that he was in England's pay.

The response Talleyrand sent to Caulaincourt, who was again at Napoleon's side, dog loyal, was a model of unspoken disdain. He had seen the emissary, he wrote, adding: 'He will tell you I am well and that I am doing what I think you would do in my place . . .' By way of postscript he couldn't resist asking Caulaincourt to protect his confiscated property as far as he was able. His position, though, could not have been clearer: the allied military offensive now in the offing was not a war against France; it was solely against the fugitive from Elba.

The Duchess of Kurland's stay in Vienna revived Talleyrand's ardour in her direction, without changing his sentiments towards Dorothy. It was an odd situation that would have been odder still had he at present been carrying on more than an affair of the soul with either. At fifty-two, the duchess passed for forty. He gave an April dinner in her honour to which Wellington and Metternich came at a trot, one of the last amusements the Peninsular War victor attended before leaving Vienna to take command of English forces in the Low Countries. The duchess spent time with Dorothy discussing her marriage to Edmond and the two infant children she'd left behind in Paris, but she had little to say on her daughter's affair with the Austrian officer, Karl von Clam, which was now an open secret. The duchess was a woman of the world who expected the youngest of her four daughters to be no different. Moreover, she had no cause to question Dorothy's taste (the winsome Clam was later to follow Metternich as the Habsburg foreign minister).

The duchess stayed for two months at the Kaunitz Palace before moving on to visit her properties in Bohemia and Prussia. Dorothy took the opportunity to follow close behind, planning to meet Clam in Berlin. The congress was running down and with it her hostess responsibilities, and, since neither she nor the duchess could return to Paris as long as Napoleon was there, she judged it a convenient moment to desert Talleyrand for a while. For his part, he trusted it wouldn't be for long. Besides, it looked as though he would soon have to rejoin King Louis in Ghent, a thankless journey he had no desire to undertake: it promised to be a voyage into embarrassment and malice with detestable émigrés massed at its end. What was more, King Louis, as he had just discovered to his extreme annoyance, had been trying to second-guess him right through the congress, using back channels to reach both the London government and Emperor Franz. So Ghent was no place for Dorothy.

The duchess's departure actually pained him the more. He had no idea when he would see her again. For him their relationship carried a special mystique: it was a splicing of two exquisite pedigrees – they were Europe united, Europe enchanted. 'These partings are so much sadder than those one feels in ordinary life,' he told her in a last morning note. 'The memory of you, your tenderness, will help me through my troubles, dear friend. I love you with all my soul for as long as I live. Adieu.' Dorothy's mother, too, was upset, though not too upset to leave on schedule at the beginning of June. She confided to her diary that no parting from 'friend Talleyrand' was ever more painful.

The Congress of Vienna dragged to its end with a Final Act signed on 9 June – seven weeks after Napoleon's return to France made its decisions moot. Talleyrand could only hope a second crushing defeat for Napoleon would restore the treaty's force. He dallied two further days before leaving the Austrian capital, stashing away private conference documents and correspondence for later. He preferred not to take such material with him; it wouldn't do to be relieved of it by Napoleon's agents on the perilous road to Ghent. There was no alternative to putting Louis back on his throne, but he feared the king's faint-hearted run for the border had damaged the legitimacy of his crown – and with it the status of France he had managed to regain in Vienna.

NINETEEN

Waterloo

Napoleon's freakish new escapade lasted one hundred days. It was a time of peculiar elation for the French nation, joyous yet baleful; popular loyalties had butterfly wings. Progressively, while marching on Paris, the *Bonaparte* who landed in the south had become *General Bonaparte* in the popular press by the time he reached Grenoble, then *Napoleon* in Lyons and finally *His Majesty the Emperor* on regaining his suite at the Tuileries. Marshal Ney, hitherto one of his favourite commanders, at first vowed to roll him through Paris in an iron cage, then turned round and joined him. The liberal leader Benjamin Constant, Mme de Staël's principled friend, denounced him as Attila the Hun, then became his political adviser.

These were somersaults of a kind Talleyrand never thought of emulating, even though Napoleon came back pronouncing himself a changed man. Liberty would reign! He was a 'convert' to liberty, he declared, and to show it he freed book publishers and newspapers to print what they wished, within limits. His police – under the unsinkable Fouché, a holdover from King Louis' government who all the same was betting that Napoleon couldn't last more than four months – were instructed to stop tormenting the people and to act as a 'liberal, positive force' committed to protecting them. Though the emperor's snap decision to revive military conscription somewhat spoiled the penitent effect he sought, he desperately wanted to believe his own words that he was a different man. 'I am no longer a conqueror, I cannot be,' he told Constant, who was oddly prepared to believe it. 'I know what is possible and what isn't. I have but one mission – to lift France and give her a government that suits her.' Why, he was ready to be a constitutional monarch if that was what France wanted. Indeed, it seemed a prudent offer, given that Louis XVIII had refused to squeeze himself into so modest a role and had thereby lost no time in reigniting the popular dissatisfaction that permitted Napoleon to try his luck once more.

The Hundred Days palpably stirred France. Peasants and workers thumped their chests, the bourgeois crossed them. All the same the pathos of it all was evident even to Napoleon's most credulous well-wishers. For while he strove to give his return a political meaning on the home front, he knew that nothing could happen unless he squared things with the allied armies that were assembling to attack him in the Low Countries, a few days' march to the north. Since negotiations with Wellington, now Field Marshal Wellington, weren't feasible, he himself crossed into Belgium in mid-June at the head of 110,000 men in hopes of obliging the English commander and his Prussian co-enforcer Blücher to review the orders they carried. One more sharp, decisive victory and he might yet be left unpestered on his throne in Paris.

Having taken his time to leave Vienna, Talleyrand preferred not to hurry over the journey to Ghent either. Not rushing things was a method adapted to both his infirmity and his temperament. 'I have never hurried, yet I have always arrived in time' was his old boast to the harem. By now he had heard through unimpeachable sources that Louis intended to make him head of government once Napoleon was out of the way again, and he rather thought the king's intentions would harden if he himself were hard to obtain.

Since one of his heavier colds was upon him, he spent a day or so resting up in Frankfurt, the family seat of his Vienna understudy Dalberg. On 19 June, on reaching another old family seat, that of Charlemagne at Aix-la-Chapelle, he received some staggering news – Wellington had defeated Napoleon the day before at a village named Waterloo. The defeat was bloody and decisive, among the worst ever sustained by French arms. Blücher's Prussian forces had linked up with the Iron Duke just when needed to ensure the allied victory. Napoleon was finished for good.

The terrible ending to the Hundred Days left Talleyrand blank at the time. As an epitaph to his life with Napoleon, it seemed both fitting and unimaginably stark. If only the warrior had listened to him in the early days! It was of course no time to be feeling grateful to Napoleon (though that would come). But Napoleon quite unwittingly had given him his statesman's ethos. It was the emperor who made clear to him what he perceived to be a principle fundamental to the wellbeing of all nations: that true progress never came from conquest, only from a nation's own internal efforts to reform and prosper. Though its confirmation had come the hard way, he could thank Napoleon for that insight. And it was Napoleon who, equally unwittingly, confirmed his belief that Europe was one and a whole, not a collection of adversaries condemned to best one another. As Talleyrand vouched to his private diplomatic notebook: 'All the nations of Europe together form a general system from whose influence none can abstract itself. All share therefore in the blame or the praise that one or other may merit.' If this was peering a century and a half ahead and seeing a union of all Europe, it was Napoleon's finale at Waterloo that gave it focus in Talleyrand's eyes.

All the same, Waterloo caused Talleyrand to concern himself more with King Louis' situation than with the meaning of Napoleon's destruction. This was surely the occasion to make the king toe a constitutional line, to pull him clear of the ultra-royalist émigrés who ran his court. Moreover, Louis' acceptance of a return trip to his throne in Wellington's baggage struck Talleyrand as an insult to national pride. French kings made their own travel arrangements; they did not ride home upon English gun carriages. Talleyrand felt strongly on this. Indeed, he sent word to Louis advising him to install himself for a while in a French city such as Lyons to avoid returning to Paris under the protection of foreign occupants. It wasn't that the man of Vienna had remotely lost respect for his friend Wellington. From Brussels he sent the Duchess of Kurland a note praising the English soldier to the skies: 'Our admirable duke has won by talent, by tenacity, by genius, using thoroughly new manoeuvres.' Indeed the Iron Duke, as the English were calling him, ranked as 'a kind of god' for Talleyrand, and it was naturally going to be of immense advantage to maintain close relations with him from now on. For all that, Louis needed to understand that he lowered his station by returning to his throne beneath England's skirt.

Talleyrand eventually joined the king on 23 June – five days after Waterloo – in the Belgian town of Mons where the Bourbon court pulled in from Ghent in Wellington's rearguard. Napoleon was now effectively at Wellington's disposal, having reabdicated the previous day under pressure from Fouché, who extended his police powers to take overall political charge in Paris.

Nonetheless, Talleyrand was in no hurry even in Mons to see the king. His studied standoffishness offended Louis, who elected to leave for France at dead of night without receiving him, ordering his carriage for three o'clock the next morning. Talleyrand received word that the royal bags were packed only minutes before this challenging departure time, and, sensing that he had overplayed his no-haste doctrine, managed to hobble to his carriage as it departed. The royal coachman lowered his whip, calling down, 'Sire, it is Monsieur Talleyrand!' 'He's asleep,' said the king. 'But here he is, Sire!'

Louis descended slowly from the carriage, motioning to his visitor that he would receive him. Talleyrand launched into an explanation of the imponderables of travel that had prevented him from showing up earlier, at the end of which Louis observed icily: 'Prince, you are leaving us. It will do you good to take the waters. You will send us your news.'

Talleyrand was, in the language of princes, sacked. Instead of leading the government, he was removed from it, bidden to repair to his country spa. How else could he interpret Louis' remarks? He stood agape, propped on his cane in the night, as Louis' carriage rumbled off. 'I didn't much like our first interview,' he wrote of the encounter in a laconic note to the duchess. It was, in its way, worse than being dismissed by Napoleon. After all, hadn't he personally resurrected the Bourbons? Recycled them? Furthermore, his thoughts were even now ripening on how to make them the acceptable ruling house they had done their best to show they weren't.

Thanks largely to Wellington, the dismissal was of short duration. Louis' fit of pique benefited no one, and as the allied armies marched once more on Paris with the routine task of reoccupying the capital, it struck the victor of Waterloo that Talleyrand's presence was indispensable. For the king was already displaying his obtuse side. No sooner was he back on French territory than he signed a proclamation on 24 June that seemed designed to divide the population: he promised to reward 'good Frenchmen' who had spurned the returning Napoleon and to use the full force of the law against the 'guilty' who sided with him. It was a patent sop to hardline royalists. The Paris press, like Wellington, feared it was a recipe for civil war, which wasn't what the allies wanted, not with the capital already disastrously short of food, out of work and awash with political rabble-rousers and street violence. Fouché, holding fast as head of police after Waterloo, was just about managing to keep a lid on things in the capital. The city was in his hands, but there was no telling what might happen before he was able to realise his intention of handing it back to the king. Wellington therefore induced Louis to send word to Talleyrand in Mons, summoning him to his side at a road stop in northern France for a council of ministers that would decide how to proceed. Though the summons did not in so many words rescind his dismissal, Talleyrand recognised it for what it was – his instant recall. After a day of studied hesitation, of which he trusted Louis would be apprised, he accepted. How could such a summons not strengthen his hand?

The royal council met on 27 June at Cambrai, still only fifty miles or so from Belgium. Talleyrand had hurriedly prepared a second proclamation for the king to sign, employing for the task the same wordsmith who had put such memorable homecoming remarks into the mouth of Louis' hesitant brother during the first restoration. Now it was a matter of placating both the French populace and Wellington. The new proclamation was as moderate, humble even, as the first was aggressive. But in its humility it was also frank, intolerably so for some of the Bourbon clan. It said Louis

was placing himself as a buffer between the allied armies and his compatriots in order to save France, adding:

> My government is said to have made mistakes, and perhaps it has done
> so. There are times when the purest of intentions do not suffice to
> rule, or they go wrong. Experience alone teaches. The lesson is not
> lost. My wish now is for everything that can save France . . . I promise
> to pardon those Frenchmen who found themselves lost during all that
> happened between the day I left [French soil], amid so many tears,
> and the day I returned amid such acclamation. However, the blood of
> my subjects has flowed as a result of treason unmatched in world
> annals, and I must exclude from the pardon the instigators and perpe-
> trators of this horrendous betrayal.

This was like swallowing a nail for Louis' court. To be sure, the king wasn't
pardoning ringleaders of the Hundred Days, but the proclamation was a
mea culpa for injudicious rule. His reign had gone wrong and he would have
to do better. The admission particularly offended Louis' brother, the Comte
d'Artois, who had assumed strong influence during the reign. He asked
Talleyrand to omit the talk of 'mistakes'; it was prejudicial to the authority
of the crown. Talleyrand stood his ground:

'Monsieur will forgive me if I differ with him. I find these expressions
necessary, and, I might add, right to the point. The king has made mistakes,
his entourage has led him astray. There is nothing that should be omitted
here.'

'Is it me, Monsieur, whom you wish to criticise indirectly?' Artois asked
angrily.

'Yes. Since Monsieur raises the issue, Monsieur has done much harm.'

'Prince Talleyrand forgets himself!'

'I fear it is so,' Talleyrand replied. 'The truth got the better of me.'

Louis intervened to restrain his brother. The new proclamation was
published virtually untouched. The king needed no further nudging from
Wellington to put Talleyrand at the head of the government installed on 8
July. As prime minister he also held the foreign ministry. In that summer
of 1815, with France rocking perilously in the wake of the Hundred Days,
his power had never been greater – and he could thank Wellington quite as
much as his own positional sense for that.

Talleyrand recognised that to maintain control in such unpredictable conditions Fouché's continued presence in government would be useful, much
as he disliked the idea. None of their past dealings had made him trust

Fouché; they seemed fated to be rivals for power. Fouché was efficient and he could be flexible, liberal-minded even, but he wore his revolutionary deeds – the massacre of thousands in Lyons, his part in the execution of Louis XVI – as the dark uniform of his true self. To royalists he was a criminal. Even now he had gone to Napoleon's side in the Hundred Days, insisting that he did so to organise things for King Louis' return. Again it was Wellington who had the last word. Convinced that the police minister was the key to order in the capital, he wrote to Talleyrand saying that he took it for granted that Fouché wasn't counted among those ringleaders of the Hundred Days whom Louis intended to eliminate, adding his opinion that 'the king cannot at this moment refuse to employ him'.

Still unsure of how the Paris populace would receive him, Louis gave Talleyrand *carte blanche* to ensure it would be without hostility. 'Do everything that you consider useful to my service,' he suggested, meeker now, from a safe distance on the edge of the capital at Saint Denis. Talleyrand's response was to take Fouché with him to the abbey at Saint Denis to have him sworn in before the king as police minister. A strange pair they made: two powdered ogres from a bygone age who couldn't stand the sight of each other – except when they wished to use one another.

The pair's outing to Saint Denis intrigued the Faubourg Saint Germain, and, thanks to a snapshot offered by the literary lion Chateaubriand, who was there seeking the king's favour regarding a plum ambassador's job, the scene entered the album of French statecraft. François René de Chateaubriand, a blueblood veteran like Talleyrand of travel in the American wilds, was seated in a corner of the salon leading to Louis' private chamber when Talleyrand and Fouché appeared arm in arm. He reported: 'All of a sudden the door opens, and without a sound there enters vice leaning on the arm of crime – M de Talleyrand supported by M Fouché, a hellish vision that shuffles slowly before me, enters the king's cabinet and disappears.'

Later that day Vice and Crime were spied getting into their carriage for the return trip to Paris by Tsar Alexander's emissary, the observant Pozzo di Borgo, who was similarly startled. 'I'd love to hear what those two lambs are saying to each other,' he smiled to himself.

Talleyrand took up residence again in his grand townhouse on the Place de la Concorde as though it had never been taken away from him. The seals attached by Napoleon were gone. He poured his efforts as prime minister into trying to persuade the allies not to regard France as an enemy which had to be punished. If what he had achieved at Vienna was allowed to stand, that would suffice. It proved a near impossible task. To argue that the Hundred Days was no fault of the French nation had a logic that only

Talleyrand truly accepted. His logic was weakened by the butchery of Waterloo, where the dead and wounded ran to at least sixty thousand French and some fifty thousand English, German mercenaries and Prussians. The Prussians in particular were in vengeful mood. Blücher's occupying troops decided to blow up the Pont d'Iéna in the heart of Paris, a Seine crossing now named after Napoleon's crushing victory over King Friedrich Wilhelm's troops some years before at Jena. The Prussians decided the bridge was an insult to their military pride. King Louis was as incensed as his prime minister at the prospect of losing the bridge, promising to stand there and go up with it if the Prussians persisted.

Royal spunk was saved the supreme test. Talleyrand raised his cane to Blücher as his men prepared to touch off their dynamite, assuring him that there was no earthly point in destroying a good bridge: he would simply change the name. Overnight it became the Pont de l'Ecole Militaire. Once the Prussians left Paris, Talleyrand sighed, there would no problem in reverting to Pont d'Iéna. He remained appalled by the pillaging and violence of Prussian troops elsewhere in the provinces. He feared they were out of control. 'Their dishonesty is only matched by their barbarity,' he complained to the duchess, herself a native of Prussian parts. Worse, Prussian statesmen were talking about dismembering France and annexing various provinces to Prussia.

Perhaps the most galling thing for Talleyrand about the allied discussions to put a cap on the Hundred Days was that he was barred from taking part. His exclusion irked him more than he could say. Gone was the gain he'd made in Vienna – his breakthrough that made defeated France the equal of her victors. Instead he received strong hints that the new allied peace terms would be harsher than he or King Louis expected. A day or so after Louis re-entered Paris at last on 8 July, Tsar Alexander arrived to join the discussions with Wellington and company and he was brimming with resentment against Talleyrand for his part in dividing the allies against Russia at Vienna.

The tsar and his fellow monarchs were enraged by Napoleon's costly final outing. It was clear that what satisfied them when the conqueror first fell in 1814 would no longer satisfy them in 1815, and they let Talleyrand know it. Even Wellington played up. His insistence on making France surrender all the art booty accumulated from throughout Europe during Napoleon's campaigns shook the head of the king's government. No doubt there was a case to be made for returning this immense treasure trove of foreign monuments and paintings, but hadn't he successfully negotiated to keep them for French museums just one year earlier? His admiration for the Iron Duke dipped. He perceived a certain crudeness in Wellington's admonition that the day of restitution had arrived, and he saw 'the brutality of the soldier' in his deployment of English troops to relieve the Louvre of its foreign treasures. What particularly rankled was the tone of a note from the Englishman saying that the allies no longer intended to miss the chance to teach the French a 'great moral lesson'.

What hopes were to be pinned on the good duke's moderating influence with the allies now? By September they had drawn up their new peace terms. France would cede more territory: not very much, but enough to discourage her from taking the offensive again. A strip in the north would go to the united Netherlands, small bits in the east to German states; Savoy in the Alps region would be lopped off altogether. War reparations would run to a hefty 800 million francs, including monies needed to build new defensive fortresses in countries neighbouring France. To wrap up the punishment, an allied occupation army of 150,000 men would deploy along France's frontiers in the north and the east for the next seven years.

Talleyrand was mortified. He found the terms both insolent and iniquitous. There was not much he could do about it except protest. This he did, bitterly. Why were they punishing his country to this degree when throughout the Hundred Days they had never once stopped recognising Louis XVIII as its crown head? Louis was their ally. You didn't make war against an ally and take territory from him. But Talleyrand never got far with his argument that Napoleon's last fling was none of France's doing. Tsar Alexander in particular wouldn't wear it; he seemed to delight these days in beating down his old mentor. 'My mood could not be darker,' Talleyrand informed the duchess, discussing his campaign to limit allied demands. 'I shall pursue it to the end, but it takes a lot of courage and love of country.'

Though he had tried it before, heading a government was out of character for Talleyrand. He never flinched from hard work, but that was not the impression he gave. He was under the microscope of public opinion now. The nonchalance that so became him as a seer of diplomacy and eminence of the salons – indeed the nonchalance of the whole copyrighted Talleyrand performance – now struck many, Louis included, as misplaced lethargy. It looked unsuited at any rate to the urgent matters of the hour. Who could measure the depth of his involvement from his personal habits? He continued to rise from his bed between 11 a.m. and noon, opening his hour-long toilette to anyone who called by to talk – the countesses, cabinet ministers, even the Wellingtons, Metternichs and Nesselrodes of the allied negotiating circle.

The prime minister's public ablutions, as observed in elaborate detail by

Charles de Rémusat, his old associate at Napoleon's court, were something to make Wellington blink:

> He first appeared as an enormous bundle of flannel, muslin, twill and cottons, a whitish mass that arrived in laborious hops with scarcely a greeting for the company, then sat before the fireplace where three valets awaited him . . . They at once began removing woollen stockings and flannels from his legs, plunging the limbs into a bowl of sulphur water. They gave him a cup of camomile tea, of which he took another cup or so during the toiletry session by way of lunch. The rest of him was swathed in underclothes, waistcoats and dressing gowns with all sorts of loops falling from him, his head covered by a sort of cotton tiara kept in place by a pastel ribbon over a tight bonnet that came down to the eyebrows to show a pale, inanimate face with rush-coloured eyes and a rather short chin hidden by thick neckerchiefs. His coiffure was high, displaying fine, abundant hair which must once have been fair, now perhaps whitened more by age than by powder. He was rather proud of his locks. Two of the valets then began to comb, curl, scent and powder his hair, meanwhile handing him a silver bowl in which he soaked a cloth to wipe his face. Of all these treatments the most remarkable – so bizarre as to stop one feeling too disgusted to watch – was his consumption via the nose of a large beaker or so of warm water which he then snorted forth like an elephant from its trunk. When his hair was done, it was time to wipe his feet and put on woollen understockings, then white silk overstockings, black silk trousers and long buckled shoes. Then he rose somewhat painfully, dropping his two or three dressing gowns for the valets to replace them nimbly with a shirt. The head valet then rolled several white muslin cravats around his neck before putting on his hat, this because it was considered a lapse in elegance to show one's hair straight from the coiffeur's hands. His shirt, instead of being tucked in his black silk trousers, usually fell over them like a smock.

Talleyrand was quite indifferent to visitors viewing his sexagenarian torso as he shed his night gowns and acted oblivious to his bared club foot – the 'claw' which the courtly Rémusat was too polite to mention but which left other morning callers shocked by Talleyrand's complete unconcern in exhibiting it. His visitors gathered that he wore so many clothes to bed to hold off the head and chest colds that plagued him. He had other odd sleeping habits. His bed was so angled as to make him sleep almost sitting up, the object being to stop him falling out of it during the night. Beside the dressing chair at which his valets worked on him lay a stack of French and English newspapers which his morning callers paged through and read out loud from, drawing the odd tart comment from the abluting prince which they gleefully spread around Paris as his latest maxim. To be first out with a Talleyrand zinger was a mark of social distinction.

It was 1 p.m. by the time Talleyrand was ready for serious business as prime minister. He held daily cabinet meetings at his private quarters on the Place de la Concorde, aiming this time to cage King Louis in the liberal constitution designed for him from the first. But for all his craft as a statesman, dispensing power wasn't his strength. Something in his character – his courtly side, his relish for female company, his delight in responding – prevented him from being a natural chief. He was at his best when having a chief to bend. A chief such as Napoleon drew the best from him, which was a running irony of their relationship.

With King Louis, who was no more a natural leader than he, he tended to let things drift. His governing method was to bring hospitable public relations to the task. To him, high politics was personal contact and subtle persuasion: to have Wellington, Metternich and King Louis' courtiers for dinner at 5 p.m. – his regular dining hour – and to grant them the pleasure of his table went a long way towards fulfilling the role of prime minister. However cross he grew with Wellington, that didn't change. It was in that spirit that he continued to press for constitutional reforms that would limit the power of the monarchy. The Hundred Days made new parliamentary elections necessary. To strengthen parliament's hand, he stripped away financial restrictions facing those seeking election to the commons and got Louis to accede, under protest, to his plan for an all-hereditary house of lords. Talleyrand's logic was that hereditary peers were likely to be far more independent-minded than the sitting body of life peers, who were assigned by Louis or held over from Napoleon's empire.

Nonetheless his troubles with the allies and with Louis' court got him down. People who watched him found him suddenly aged, debilitated. He attended with his usual interest to the foreign ministry but let other ministers do as they wished, content to hear the results over his whist table. Fouché excelled himself, revoking press freedoms of his own volition to combat anything that smelt of sedition against the monarchy. This was unacceptable to Talleyrand, yet he let it ride for a while. Perhaps, too, not having Napoleon to deter any longer somehow stilled him. A further factor in his apathy, the harem whispered, was an intensely private matter that ate at him without him quite realising it. Dorothy's continuing passion for Karl von Clam, the young thruster from the Habsburg court, had placed a wedge between 'uncle' and 'niece'. If Talleyrand was below his best, wrote the diarist Mme de Boigne, it was because he had 'lost his head': he was tormented by Dorothy's breakaway passion.

Dorothy in fact returned to Paris to live at his residence a week or so after he took charge of the government, but it was clear that she wasn't present in the way that made him proud and content in Vienna. She wanted to divorce Edmond to marry Clam. His nephew, too, was distraught. Despite his estrangement from his celebrated young wife, the Clam affair wounded his honour. He challenged the Austrian to a duel which ended, not mortally for either, with a sabre slash across the young Périgord cheek. As for Talleyrand, the words of love he still showered on the Duchess of Kurland in his morning notes were no relief for the empty feeling her daughter caused in him. Dorothy's 'absence' was temporary, he told himself. At least he dearly hoped it was. He longed to resume their intimate working partnership. To the duchess, presently back in Paris, he was careful not to allude specifically to Dorothy in his morning notes, in one of which he wrote: 'Everything is going so badly that it can't go on like this. Too much bad can only bring a little good. Sad reasoning, I know.'

The parliamentary election of August 1815 yielded a further unwelcome surprise. It brought a Chamber of Deputies with a sweeping royalist majority clearly not made to curb King Louis' absolutist instincts. Though the reactionary majority did not like Talleyrand, it liked Fouché, the 'regicide', still less. To save a semblance of working order between the new parliament and his government – in sum, to save his government – Talleyrand opted to dismiss the police minister. This wasn't the only reason to be rid of him. Fouché was too much of a lone operator, which made him a threat to Talleyrand's authority. To sack him would no doubt upset Wellington, his backer, but Fouché had completed the job Wellington wanted him for – keeping a lid on unrest in Paris after the Hundred Days.

Talleyrand's urge to be rid of Fouché was further driven by the police minister's perverse desire to spread the punishment net far and wide among those who played a part in Napoleon's second coming. This was typical Fouché, for few had played a larger part than he himself. Talleyrand aimed to keep the punishment list to a minimum; there was no point in fanning more civil war. But Fouché's blood was up. He wanted victims. Talleyrand's son Charles de Flahaut and the good Caulaincourt were among those risking deportation or worse as long as Fouché was around.

Talleyrand dismissed the policeman with off-hand elegance one afternoon in early September during a meeting of ministers at the Place de la Concorde residence. So indirect was his manner that only Fouché with his alert antennae fully grasped what happened. As the meeting drew to a close, Talleyrand began perorating to no discernible purpose on the wonders of foreign travel, foreign capitals, the prestige of ambassadors, and soon he was recalling his years in America. 'Such a wonderful country! I know it, I've been through it, I have lived there. A superb country.' The ministers listened politely, ready to leave, but Talleyrand trilled on. 'It has rivers unlike any we know. There is nothing more beautiful than the Potomac. And the magnificent forests full of those trees we grow in boxes here . . . I forget, what are they called now?' Only at this quizzical point did his gaze fasten on Fouché, who stiffened in his seat. He realised he was being put out to grass – to Washington or some such ambassadorial backfield.

After everyone left, Talleyrand told his aides, 'This time I have wrung his neck for good!'

On 19 September the king named Fouché ambassador – not in fact to America but to the court of Saxony in Dresden. This seemed a first step to banishment for the peerless policeman, and soon the banishment became official when Louis' court had him condemned in his absence for the crime of regicide. (He died five years later in lonely exile in the Habsburg realm, in Trieste.)

Fouché's dismissal was the end of a remarkable pairing: Talleyrand and Fouché, diplomacy and security, the good life and the zealous, civilisation and revolution, 'vice and crime'. The match between the giants of French statecraft always tilted more towards contest than partnership, and on a strictly numerical count they ended fairly even as to who changed allegiances the more. After the Napoleon–Talleyrand duel, theirs was the one that most indelibly marked France's age of revolution, imperial glory and fall. From these two monstrous matches a sole contestant now remained standing, propped on a cane.

The Great Survivor had been head of the king's government for a week when Napoleon again left France, this time for good. It was the English, not King Louis or his first minister, who decided his fate. Louis' more ardent supporters, as well as Blücher, talked of executing him if they could lay hands on him. But the English, like Tsar Alexander, still shrank from sending such a figure to the gallows. Napoleon's aura of legend gave him good protection. On 15 July 1815 the English navy, which the conqueror blamed for wrecking his empire, took him in charge at the Atlantic port of La Rochelle. He was thinking seriously of making for the United States. However, he boarded the Royal Navy frigate *Bellerophon* on the understanding that to tread its deck put him on English territory under the protection of English civil law. Before boarding he handed its captain a letter addressed to the English people seeking the grace of their hospitality.

The *Bellerophon* sailed to Torbay, then Plymouth, waiting to see what

Castlereagh and the Tory prime minister, Lord Liverpool, had in store for its famous passenger. At both Devon ports inquisitive Englishmen assembled in their thousands for a glimpse of him – and Napoleon satisfied them by standing at the gunwhales or strolling on the deck. English liberals who had never quite lost faith in French intentions since 1789 applied to have him put ashore under a writ of habeas corpus, giving him temporary leave to stay in England unmolested. But Castlereagh, harried by the press, decided otherwise. He couldn't have Napoleon taking tea with English ladies. The idea he had promoted, with Talleyrand, the year before of stranding Napoleon in the Azores no longer seemed adequate. There could be no chance of a second escape. On 9 August the ship of the line *Northumberland* embarked with him on a two-month voyage to the island speck of St Helena in the south Atlantic, a Royal Navy watering stop, in order to deposit him there for the rest of his days.

Talleyrand's only contribution to the emperor's final exile was to name a French commissioner to St Helena to liaise with England's governor there. His choice was a twittish nobleman, one Marquis de Montchenu. 'It is the only revenge I seek for Napoleon's conduct towards me, and I might say it is a terrible one,' he told the harem. 'What torture for a man of the likes of Bonaparte to have to live with an ignorant, pompous chatterbox. I know him, he won't survive it. He will fall ill and die a long death.' This was pure Talleyrand, only the sting was crueller than usual. The barb no doubt reached Napoleon's ears. He simply refused to talk to Montchenu.

Before the Royal Navy landed Napoleon on St Helena in mid-October, Talleyrand's tenure as prime minister abruptly ended. His spells in charge of the nation's affairs seemed predestined to be short. In 1815, just under three months did it.

On 24 September he hobbled before the king to ask for his unconditional support against the reactionary new parliament which seemed intent on blocking reform and turning back the clock on most of what had happened since 1789. To the liberal premier, this was dangerous folly. He also wanted stronger royal support against the allies, who weren't budging an inch in their peace demands. Louis took his pitch as an ultimatum, though in truth Talleyrand's objective was not to resign. He thought Louis would implore him to continue. Instead the king treated him to the show of piqued royal indifference he'd employed not long before in the coaching stables at Cambrai. Looking at the ceiling, he decided, 'Well then, I shall take a new government.'

The writing had been on the wall for a week or so. Louis had more than once mentioned the charms of Valençay and how restful life must be at such a peaceful country estate. The monarch disliked Talleyrand's air of superiority. For all his lethargy, his chief minister had been acting with him like a master with his apprentice. Talleyrand, too, realised he was vulnerable. Two days before his approach to Louis, he wrote to the duchess: 'It's impossible to be useful. Within a few days, I think, I shall have a successor and I confess I hope I do. When you cannot do any good, it is time to withdraw.' But he still thought his unique standing with France's foreign occupants would force Louis to beg him to stay on, which in turn would enhance his ability to control the reactionary parliament. And sure enough, once the news of his departure broke, Metternich and Castlereagh, who happened to be in Paris, beseeched him not to go. The English foreign minister thought him too valuable to lose. Perhaps England could find some way to keep him in harness! 'Why not become Minister for Europe with us?' he asked Talleyrand. It was a strange, off-the-cuff offer, plainly made more in sympathy than in Castlereagh's usual seriousness – and a statesman as adept in the arts of flattery as Talleyrand knew how to refuse such a proposition gracefully.

Tsar Alexander remained silent over his departure. This was to be expected since it was in fact he who manipulated it. His late-blooming hostility towards Talleyrand, far from fading, induced him to press upon Louis the services of another Frenchman of equally shining pedigree, one whom St Petersburg could fully count upon to appreciate Russia's views. Owing to the tsar's personal interest, Louis suspected that there was a reasonable chance of obtaining concessions from the allies if he dropped Talleyrand and replaced him with Alexander's candidate, the Duc de Richelieu, a name that rang pleasantly in French ears. Talleyrand barely knew Armand de Richelieu – a direct descendant of Cardinal Richelieu, chief minister to Louis XIII and the very symbol, two centuries before, of brilliance in French statesmanship – mainly because he'd been in the tsar's service for the past two decades, as a young general in the Russian army and latterly as governor of the Crimea. Initially it had occurred to Talleyrand, as prime minister, that it might be useful to take Richelieu into his government in a ministerial capacity close to King Louis, thus tying a knot with the irritable Alexander, but Richelieu, a fugitive from Robespierre's Terror who hadn't returned to France since, had somewhat ingenuously ruled himself out: 'I have been absent from France for twenty-four years and am alien both to men and events,' he'd replied to Talleyrand's offer. 'I do not know how things work . . . Nobody is less well equipped than I to take a place in government, anywhere, let alone in France.' Now the same man, not yet fifty years old, was stepping into his shoes as head of government! It was a little hard for Talleyrand to take.

The king's apparent ingratitude stung. Richelieu was abler than his retiring self-portrait suggested, and also fairly moderate, but it was all Talleyrand could bring himself to do to show him the ropes as prime minister and foreign minister, the same dual responsibility he had held. Moreover, he left office without an official word of thanks from Louis for having sat him on the Bourbon throne, twice. 'We leave without a single compliment,' he lamented to the duchess. 'There was never anything more dry in the official gazette. Not a single word on us; we might as well have never existed.' He felt deeply insulted that Louis hadn't even tried to veil his ingratitude. At least it freed him on his salon rounds to take scornful digs at Louis' selection of his successor. 'A truly excellent choice! The man of France who best knows the Crimea.' Furthermore, the incoming finance minister happened to come from Genoa. 'That does it!' he scoffed. 'A Russian premier and an Italian finance minister. All that to defend France's interests!'

Once he was out, though, he accepted that the circumstances he faced would have made it well nigh impossible for him to govern to any great effect. And in the end, he told himself, it was perhaps a good thing that the peace terms the allies were offering were patently harsh. It proved that the terms were being imposed; no one could think he had negotiated or condoned them. Thank heavens his signature wouldn't appear under 'this lovely work'. All in all he was able to convince himself he went willingly, asserting: 'I can say it is without regret that I retired from public affairs, with the firm resolve never again to direct them.'

Since he finished writing his memoirs only the following year, his sacking featured in those pages as the end of his career. He owned up to 'mistakes' and to 'personal faults' but swore that through it all he had always done what he honestly thought best for France.

The retirement pledge was, however, as deceptive as only Talleyrand knew how to be. It was a pledge as fluid as the state of France on the day he made it.

TWENTY

National Grouch

It was difficult for Talleyrand to take forced retirement lying down. He was the most renowned world statesmen of the age. Louis XVIII's reign, mark two, was a time Talleyrand had been looking forward to, had fought for – and not because it put a blinkered king back on the throne. The autumn of 1815 was a time in which France, rubbing her eyes, recovered from military drunkenness and was able dimly to perceive the social and political changes granted her by the Revolution. It was a time that invited those changes to proceed.

It promised to be hard going all the same. For through it all the nation remained split between those with the Revolution in their veins and royalists who thought the Revolution a crime against mankind. The clash of wills was further aggravated by the drift back to France of sore-headed multitudes of soldiers and petty officials who had manned the ramparts of Napoleon's empire from the Baltic to the Adriatic and who now found no place in their homeland.

With his lust for the civilised life, Talleyrand, turning sixty-two, often found himself nipped between conflicting camps.

Fortunately King Louis' poor thanks were limited to political ingratitude. Though ill feelings flowed in both directions between the Tuileries and the Talleyrand residence facing it across the Rue de Rivoli, the elder statesman did receive royal thanks of a kind. Louis appointed him Grand Chamberlain, the conveniently flexible court rank he held under Napoleon. It was a rank that had proved a rewarding holding position when he was otherwise out of favour. It now gave him open access to Louis' private quarters, with the chance to influence policy if he chose to work at it, plus a generous stipend of 100,000 francs to soothe the chagrin of retirement. This was 'reasonable', Talleyrand conceded. He was a prince of the realm, a hereditary member of the house of lords and a court eminence – and added to that, just as he left government that autumn, came a dukedom with further income attached.

The title Duke of Dino spoke for itself, since no one, Talleyrand included, prior to consulting a Mediterranean marine survey map, knew what or where Dino was. The rank was conferred on him by King Ferdinand of Naples in creative gratitude for his work at the Congress of Vienna in helping him regain his throne from Napoleon's ex-marshal Joachim Murat, lately executed for taking his monarchic fantasies a frontier too far. Dino turned out to be a rock off the coast of Calabria with fewer inhabitants than olive trees, themselves scarce; it was a reward Ferdinand hit upon to compensate Talleyrand for his loss, on Napoleon's fall, of the old papal statelet of Benevento and the princely title that went with it. Pope Pius, not wishing to cross Talleyrand when Benevento returned to Vatican ownership, agreed to inflate the revenues settled on the new Duke of Dino – enough to bring them up to his old income from Benevento. Pius blamed Napoleon, not Talleyrand, for his suffering and incarceration during the French Empire. He wanted to believe that Talleyrand remained a prince of the Church by culture at least.

All the same, Dino was the sort of honour that had Paris tittering, and Talleyrand wasn't in the mood to hear it. The title had a nice Latin ring, elegant even, and he off-handedly played it up as far as the truth allowed. 'It is the name of a royal land situated in Calabria,' he notified the Duchess of Kurland. But he shrank from carrying the title himself. He side-hopped embarrassment by arranging to have it transferred to his nephew Edmond. This kept the title in the family and made Dorothy the Duchess of Dino, despite the estrangement from her husband. Though her grand Teutonic pedigree already made her a bona fide princess, she liked the sound of the new title and, because it was conspicuously Latin and came to her through Talleyrand, she presented herself from then on as Duchess of Dino. Alas, not a month after Talleyrand's dismissal, she made herself scarce again. She felt she had to get out of Paris. She was pregnant, by Clam, her now subsiding Austrian flame. She refused to parade her condition before malicious salon-goers. Both she and Talleyrand were aware that their household arrangements on the Place de la Concorde set tongues wagging. In Paris, people who might spot that she had 'the nine-month sickness', as her mother the duchess diagnosed it, would believe they were right about her and Talleyrand. Would they never drop that gleeful scent? To avert scandal, she left Paris sometime in late autumn to go into hiding at a Kurland family estate in Bohemia. She bore the child, a girl, in early February 1816, delivering it to suitable foster parents. By then the affair with Clam was over.

Talleyrand wasn't advised of the reasons for her absence, though he no doubt guessed. Dorothy was mature, strong-headed, financially independent and efficient; she was also a sensual young woman of twenty-two. Life with the crippled Talleyrand couldn't give her physical satisfaction. His elegance in dress and manners never changed, but his outward appeal was definitely on the wane, victim of the advancing years. Those who now saw him for the first time found him frightening, his putty face eerily pale, his eyes lifeless. A young American visitor thought he resembled 'an old rat'. What drew Dorothy to him was the high politics, the sense of taking part in shaping the world, the sophistication, the wit. But she needed more than that and she took it. Dorothy wasn't shy in these matters. A beguiled Austrian statesman who clerked the Congress of Vienna, whom she probably rejected, decided she was depraved. Talleyrand's agent Vitrolles, who also had a crush on her, received a letter from her in which she avowed she was constantly driven by amorous desires that welled up to fill her empty heart. Clam's child was not the last of her offspring by passing lovers (she bore two more which she also declined to recognise, entrusting them to foster parents). Yet the sensual maid in her battled all along with a convent novice, a gothic combat spurred by the Kurland bloodline.

What developed into a near religious devotion to Talleyrand really began as soon as the Clam affair ended; once his child was out of the way, she returned to Paris in April, took charge of her two infant sons by Edmond – the future heads of the House of Périgord – and left with Talleyrand for a long summer stay at Valençay. Allowing for occasional adventures, she was back at his side for good. Talleyrand was overjoyed. The intellectual fit they made pleased him no end. He wrote to her, unable to resist poking a little French fun: 'With you, one jumps between ideas without having to wait. Your mind is never closed. That's where you have stopped being German. You have stayed German in everything except your mind, where you no longer have the slightest accent.'

The stay at Valençay was Talleyrand's first visit in eight years. His previous one had been to lay out a welcome for Spain's royal princes, on Napoleon's instructions. Now there were major repairs to see to. The bored Spanish royals had laid out an indoor garden in their rooms with a watering system which rotted floorboards and imperilled ceilings; a stairway needed rebuilding. But mostly he used the glorious property to take stock, finish penning the memoirs he'd been working on for some years and, not least, to work up sulphurous hostility towards the Richelieu government. He was a wounded mammoth back in a familiar sanctuary, trumpeting discontent from Valençay's splendid balustrades.

In journeying to and fro between Paris and Valençay throughout 1816, he installed himself as a national scold. His favourite targets were Richelieu, who signed the allied peace terms that he himself found so objectionable, and a new police minister, Elie Decazes, a brilliant young man in a hurry who established himself in King Louis' personal favour without sharing his authoritarian views. Talleyrand was furious to discover that Decazes, a minor nobleman from nowhere in particular, was spying on him at Valençay and intercepting his mail. That the capable Richelieu and Decazes were keeping a lid on royalist extremism did little to temper Talleyrand's scorn. Indeed, his unconcealed griping briefly recommended him to the royalist side in parliament, which was likewise disenchanted with Richelieu because he wouldn't let it do as it wished. Talleyrand, champion of the royalists! It seemed an absurd twist. He had nothing in common with their party and its aims, and though he now briefly flirted with them as a mark of shared opposition to Richelieu, the dalliance was hollow. Yet it was somehow beyond him to recognise that his opposition to his successor was also hollow, rooted in personal rancour. The fact that Richelieu smoked a pipe and dressed like a Russian in black boots and a black cravat was enough to condemn him; he just didn't look the part to head the government of France. Talleyrand couldn't decide whom he abhorred more, Richelieu or the impudent Decazes. He was in the mood to let everyone have it. At his Paris table, a tiresome fellow peer boasted, 'I have done only one truly bad thing in my life.' Talleyrand glared at him: 'And when will it end?'

The mammoth's dyspepsia came to a head during a banquet at England's embassy in Paris soon after Louis, at Richelieu's insistence, dissolved the royalist-packed parliament in September 1815. The dissolution aroused feverish speculation that the government too would fall, and Talleyrand, whose hat was in the ring for a comeback, was feeling especially sour that Louis overlooked him. In fact, Richelieu and Decazes stayed on, stronger than before. At the embassy, Talleyrand buttonholed another re-engaged minister, one who had served in his own government after the Hundred Days. He pitched into the poor man, raising his voice as his prey looked around for a quiet exit. 'Remember well what I say,' Talleyrand rasped, as foreign statesmen and the cream of France's political class looked on, all ears. 'The police ministry is a blot on the country. A mantrap, that's all. A snakepit.' And Decazes himself, he added, was a 'gutter rat'. With such people in charge, France was lost. His rage was compounded by the discovery that Decazes had snared letters of his to Dorothy and the duchess and shown them to the king. For the onlookers, though, the scene tended to confirm Wellington's expressed view that loss of power was driving Talleyrand mad.

Within minutes, reports on the scene at the embassy reached King Louis. Sentence was swift. Royal disgrace. Louis barred his Grand Chamberlain from court until further notice. Sterner courtiers wanted him stripped of his office and exiled, but Richelieu insisted on the more moderate punishment.

Talleyrand had calmed down by the time he received the verdict, responding to Louis in stinging innocence, with a typical Talleyrand dig at the end:

> I shall obey Your Majesty's order with much pain, but without understanding how it is that reports Your Majesty receives concerning me can make any impression on him . . . I would ask his pardon for my bad handwriting if I did not know that Your Majesty has long been familiar with it and reads it with ease.

It was up to Louis, damn him, to interpret the allusion. Let him dwell on his copious handwritten dispatches from the Congress of Vienna. Or on the private correspondence with the Kurland women which Decazes intercepted for him! While the embassy ruckus took its toll on his position at court, it also swelled the numbers of curious callers attending his morning ablutions at his Rue Saint Florentin residence on the corner of the Place de la Concorde. Without really wishing it, he was an opposition icon. Indeed, he bore the dubious honour with some satisfaction, setting his Paris dining table for a hundred places twice a week when he wasn't at Valençay. He took the trouble, though, to write to Wellington playing down the importance of the incident, insisting that people were making something out of nothing. And to the duchess, he shrugged it off entirely: 'I complained about a minister. That's all.'

But there was no ignoring the outcome: for so guileful a statesman he was establishing an unfortunate record for falling into disgrace. First with Napoleon, now with Louis. His taste for risk was much to blame. Through silken folds of courtesy, he spoke his mind. It came from his sense of superiority, but also from a natural courage that even his enemies did not dispute. As for Dorothy, who also took risks, she found it his most enduring appeal. As she had already noted in her diary, she knew it as 'a courage full of sangfroid and presence of mind, a bold temperament, an instinctive bravura that brings an irresistible taste for danger in all its forms'.

Audacity both aided and, on occasion, failed him. Talleyrand was forced to recognise it when he blithely attempted to curtail his disgrace in the new year of 1817. Dressed in Grand Chamberlain finery he presented himself at a grand ceremony in the basilica of Saint Denis commemorating the execution of Louis XVI; once by the altar he limped to a place of highest court rank next to King Louis, as though nothing had occurred to question his right to occupy it. Louis, catching sight of him, had an usher redirect him to the nave where the general run of peers were seated. To try forcing Louis' hand in public was an enormous risk, and this time he paid the price – a day of humiliation and a lot of malicious salon chatter to follow. But he was above feeling foolish; awareness of his superiority was a powerful guard against ridicule. He resumed his sour opposition to Richelieu.

Having nothing much to do provided the chance to clarify his domestic arrangements. His wife Catherine took the precaution of installing herself in London during the Hundred Days and remained there during his debut as head of government. They were separated by geography, which was all right with Talleyrand, but not by agreement, legal or otherwise. From the summer of 1816 she was back in Paris with her malapropisms, officially carrying the title Princess Talleyrand and keen to resume the social life she had resolutely sought to adhere to even as relations with her husband had deteriorated.

Her first thought was to take up the squeezed place on the Place de la Concorde for which she'd settled when Dorothy joined the Talleyrand household. But he couldn't tolerate that now. 'I need to finish with it. I am not afraid of money sacrifices,' he told the duchess. He proposed to Catherine that she return to London or go to live in Switzerland at his expense, adopting 'a simple lifestyle' befitting her changed situation. He had been disturbed by her runaway spending in London earlier. Dorothy was more brutal. She was offended by Catherine on Talleyrand's behalf, which she demonstrated in a waspish letter addressed to him from Valençay when he was staying for a few days in Paris:

> I very much fear that one fine day Mme de Talleyrand will burst into your rooms. She'll begin by saying she is only staying an hour or so, and needs to talk things through with you. All this in hopes of extracting more money from you. Since money is the true motive in all Mme de Talleyrand's actions, you must always see them from this viewpoint. You should give Perrey [Talleyrand's current secretary] some sort of letter of credit and have him tell Mme de Talleyrand that she won't receive another cent of the allowance you give her until she is back in England, otherwise she won't get a penny. Have Perrey accompany her to Calais or Ostend and not return until he has seen her embark. This is very good advice, I swear, and you would be wrong to ignore it.

Catherine, who wasn't a bad businesswoman, managed to resist the pressure, which never quite reached levels outlined in Dorothy's turf war. Lawyers joined the fray. Mme de Talleyrand stayed in Paris. Under their legal separation Talleyrand installed her in a pleasant villa in Auteuil, on the western fringe of Paris, comfortably maintained and out of his way. His outlay on Catherine was far exceeded by expenditures on his kitchen at the Rue Saint Florentin, where he gave his resident chefs *carte blanche* to spoil his innumerable dinner guests. 'Why don't they spend more!' he would mutter, shaking his head on his daily kitchen round.

All the same, riches continued to preoccupy him. While he could well afford the 'sacrifice' made to his wife, it led him to another matter he'd left hanging since he left government. This was a larger enterprise, and infinitely more delicate. It directly concerned Napoleon. When he'd taken charge of the provisional government in 1814 on Napoleon's departure for Elba, he not only retrieved and burned all he could find of his own letters to the emperor, he separately removed from the foreign ministry archives all the correspondence Napoleon addressed to him during his long years as foreign minister. This was a secretive back-up precaution he took at the time against a possible barrage of recriminations from the incoming Bourbon court. Better for the Bourbons not to know what had passed between him and Napoleon.

Now he'd been sitting for two years with his precious trunkload of imperial mail, undecided what to do with it. It also contained Napoleon's letters to his successors at the foreign ministry, so the legal position was clear: the hoard rightly belonged to the state and he had filched it. But with Napoleon gone forever and he himself removed from power, things were different. It would be hard to give it back without causing himself huge embarrassment. Besides, its commercial value was evident; Talleyrand never really stopped considering public life to be a gold mine. Since the precious correspondence couldn't be sold in France, he decided to sell it to the Habsburgs. Metternich, he was sure, would jump at it.

So began one of Talleyrand's shabbier enterprises. His old moneylust took hold of him – only this time it was harder to argue that, whatever his faults, he never did anything that went against the interests of France. His exploratory approach to Metternich, now master of Austria and well on the way to being the diplomatic umpire of Europe, had all the art of a used carriage vendor. In his opening move in January 1817 he concocted a tale according to which a Russian had passed by the foreign ministry archives in Paris to take a look at Napoleon's correspondence and, failing to find it, had come to him asking if he knew where it might be. He'd indicated it was in his possession. The Russian's inquiry set him thinking, though, that the tsar, with his troops still in France and his obvious hold over Louis and Richelieu, might soon try to relieve him of it. Hence his decision to divest himself. 'It is incontestably the finest archive piece one could have.'

Then the hard sell:

I am sure that England and Prussia would be delighted to acquire it and would pay a great deal for it. I mention England and Prussia, because nothing would make me hand it to Russia. It befits you more than anyone, because you Austrians have been the most deeply involved in all actions in Europe for the past twenty years . . . I am and shall always be a Frenchman, and a good Frenchman, whatever injustices I and my family may now face here, but you know that after being a Frenchman I am closest to being an Austrian. My wish is that this precious and often compromising part of our modern history should be in your hands.

I ask you to reply promptly, dear prince, since the security of this little treasure is somewhat at risk. My intention is to conclude something in this regard by March, when I shall be returning to the country. I prefer not to leave such precious things to chance . . . I have reason to believe, as I say, that England would place a high price on the correspondence of which I speak, but its place is with you.

Metternich was no doubt as surprised by Talleyrand's transparent sales patter as he was by the news that Napoleon's diplomatic correspondence was available. The letter read as though it might have been penned by an impostor trying to get Talleyrand into serious trouble. But it was true: it indeed came from the distinguished French statesman. And Metternich was indeed interested. Having advised Emperor Franz, he wrote back in February asking Talleyrand to state his conditions and promising to assign the treasure 'a place worthy of its value' in Vienna. He also set up a secret courier system to work out the details of the transaction. On 6 March – more or less within the time limit he'd laid down – Talleyrand dispatched a crate of twelve fat packages of letters to Vienna and with it a note to Metternich rather more nonchalant in tone than the first. It said: 'If I had dealt with the other powers of Europe on this matter, I would have asked 500,000 francs. If these papers satisfy the Emperor, he will set the price and it will be well with me.'

This was being a little too trusting in Metternich, who clearly recognised from the start that to take Napoleon's papers into his possession was bound to compromise Austria sooner or later. The Austrian played Talleyrand along for a while, having a team of scribes go through the letters and make copies. How much of his airy asking price did Talleyrand receive? Judging by the pinched tone of subsequent exchanges, precious little. In the end Metternich sent the whole crate of originals back to Talleyrand, calculating that he had lost his leverage to complain now that he was out of power. Thanking him, Talleyrand noted dryly, 'Farewell, dear prince, and keep a little friendship for me.'

Despite his earlier sales talk of sure English interest, he knew better than to make a pitch to Wellington to recoup.

Talleyrand's disgrace was lifted just a month after his sorry attempt to lift it himself. Louis was careful not to push him into deeper opposition. From March 1817 he resumed his tasks as Grand Chamberlain, propping himself in full paraphernalia behind Louis' throne at royal mass on Sundays – when he was in Paris, that was. He took the role as an honour to be exercised at his convenience. This worked well, since Louis no more wanted him around all the time than he himself wished to stick any closer to Louis than pragmatism required. Certainly he aimed to find a way back into government: it was, after all, his birthright to take charge of France's fortunes. He might be an elder statesman but that didn't make him too old for power. He was looking for the right moment.

It was slow in coming. Things seemed to be settling down under Richelieu. Talleyrand was bored by Louis' royal council meetings, which he attended sporadically. After one endless meeting, he was asked what had gone on there. He replied: 'What went on? Three hours.' Now and then he took his place in the Chamber of Peers to attack new laws he particularly objected to. He put up a spirited defence of individual liberties, taking his adversaries through his argument that individual freedom was inseparable from press freedom (Louis' attitude to the press, though less crude than Napoleon's, was nonetheless cramping). Despite the relative calm, he couldn't see the king's government lasting – or even doing any good. 'It is truly painful to see an establishment for which one has done so much perish before one's eyes,' he groused. 'That saddens me deeply.'

To console himself, he read Plutarch on slow evenings, finding ancient wisdom more fertile than that of the modern moralists he was obliged to listen to. With Dorothy and a train of servants he set off on a tour of France which took up the entire summer and early autumn of 1817, visiting his childhood haunt of Chalais near Bordeaux and also southern regions he had never seen – the Pyrenees, Languedoc and Provence around the cities of Nîmes and Marseilles.

The chance of a political opening first came late the following year when the allies who had put Napoleon out of the way met in Aix-la-Chapelle to review their peace terms with Bourbon France. Richelieu, who Talleyrand insisted possessed 'neither talent nor guile', returned from the German city in December 1818 showing that he had a good deal of both. He secured the departure of allied occupation armies from France two years ahead of schedule and France regained her place as the equal of the other great powers. His success was an extreme irritation to Talleyrand who was pleased to see the foreign armies leave so early but vexed that Richelieu had brought it off. Diplomatic masterstrokes were a Talleyrand preserve. He was disgruntled that he wasn't asked to take part in the congress. Shouldn't he have been the one to represent France? He was the one who stood up against the original peace terms. He was the one who knew how to talk to Europe's great powers.

As it was, success at the congress spawned a crisis for Richelieu when he got home. During his absence, policy differences with the more populist Decazes became a chasm. The government was hopelessly divided. Parliament's old ultra-royalist bent was tilting left, which disturbed Richelieu but not Decazes, who, despite the spell he cast over Louis, thought the way to run France was to 'nationalise royalty and royalise the nation'.

Talleyrand's sour predictions on a breakdown looked justified. With Richelieu on the point of resigning, he saw his chance. So convinced was he that he would be called upon to bridge the gulf in government that he carried lists of ministers' names with him on his salon rounds noting whom he intended to put here and who would go there. For the Faubourg Saint Honoré the Talleyrand patronage lists were entertaining accompaniment to the heavy strains of crisis. To improve relations with Decazes, whom he had so openly reviled, he proposed finding him a suitable wife – the daughter of a Périgord cousin. Indeed, he was so far along the public road to a comeback at Christmas 1818 that when Richelieu informed King Louis that he planned to resign, the monarch sighed: 'You are reducing me to the deplorable extreme of turning to Talleyrand, whom I neither like nor esteem.'

The extreme was avoided. Perhaps the one thing most firmly set in Louis' uncertain mind was the conviction that he didn't wish to be led by the nose by his old antagonist Talleyrand. He appointed an amenable stopgap as head of government instead, whose rapid fall once more encouraged Talleyrand to circulate his intriguing lists, though with less twinkle of purpose in his eye. This time Decazes took over, still enjoying Louis' high favour. Since Talleyrand's marriage-brokering efforts couldn't compensate in the young premier's eyes for his recent public hostility, he felt no compulsion to put him back in charge of French diplomacy either. Decazes now seemed untouchable. But a shocking event that occurred on 13 February 1820 changed that: King Louis' nephew, the Duc de Berry, an heir to the throne, was stabbed to death by a royal saddler outside the Paris Opera. France and its monarch were horrified. The police were blamed for failing to avert the crime and Decazes, who had formerly run the police, had to resign. Once more Talleyrand's hopes rose. Just as instinctively Louis dashed them. He reappointed Richelieu.

Talleyrand had to accept the obvious: as long as Louis was king, he could never aspire to power. 'Good news only comes to those with a future before them, and mine is closed,' he lamented. He was sixty-six and clearly feeling it. He hadn't seen his 'angel', the Duchess of Kurland, in two years; she was away on an extended tour of her estates in Bohemia and the east and was in no hurry to return to France, despite the continuing flow of fond letters he sent to bring her back. She'd attuned herself to leaving Dorothy as his muse and hostess now.

There came stunning news the next year, 1821 – Napoleon was dead. He expired on St Helena on 5 May after suffering stomach seizures, at the age of fifty-one. For France the news could no longer register as good or bad; it was simply stunning. Talleyrand was dining at an English diplomat's table in Paris when it landed. Lord Holland, a civil rights champion and nephew of the late Whig leader Charles James Fox, was among statesmen present who witnessed its effect on him. Talleyrand's first instinct was to play down its importance. 'It is not an event, it is a news item,' he observed to the thunderstruck company. Indeed, to die in bed of a stomach ache did seem too small a thing for Napoleon to do. How could so great a myth perish thus? (Cancer was later diagnosed as the cause of death.)

Soon, though, Talleyrand launched into an appreciation of the emperor that was by and large so admiring that it puzzled listeners familiar with the vicissitudes of their damned partnership. Holland recorded Talleyrand's words:

> His genius was inconceivable. There was nothing to match his energy, his imagination, his spirit, his capacity for hard work, his will to create. He was sagacious too. His judgement wasn't so strong, but still, when he took the time, he knew how to capitalise on the judgement of others. He was only rarely carried away by poor judgement, and it was always when he didn't take the time to consult with others. He had a sense of what was great but not of the beautiful. He had the most astonishing career of anyone in a thousand years. He committed three capital mistakes: Spain, Russia and the pope. Those were the reasons for his fall, which was no less extraordinary than his rise. Those three apart, he made few political mistakes, astonishingly few when you consider all the interests he had to deal with and the scope, importance and speed of events he was involved in. He was certainly a great man, an extraordinary man, almost as extraordinary for his talents as for his good fortune – in my view the most extraordinary man of our age and of many a century.

Even allowing for some embellishment by Holland, who actively opposed Napoleon's detention on St Helena on civil liberties grounds and whose equally aroused wife sent the prisoner the latest books to read to keep his spirits up, Talleyrand's tribute suggested his admiration had outlasted his hatred and scorn. If there wasn't a jot of sentiment to it, there was much plain awe. He kept to himself his personal part in ensuring Napoleon's end, showing no sign of remorse, yet no sign of satisfaction.

Some months previously, when news first arrived that Napoleon was ill, he'd observed, not unkindly: 'A cannonball four or five years ago would have brought a better end to this extraordinary life.' Now the most malicious dig he allowed himself was to express doubt on whether Napoleon had left any memoirs. Because he wrote so well himself, he'd always smiled at Napoleon's stiffness with the pen and his erratic spelling. He shook his head over prospects for the publication of imperial souvenirs. 'He wouldn't have been able to write them!' he told the countesses. 'He could have dictated something, but I doubt it.'

He was only half right in this. Napoleon did not produce his own memoirs, but he'd been dictating and reminiscing away for his life's worth on St Helena. Right to the end he blew hot and cold on Talleyrand, who hobbled no less relentlessly through his mind than he had during the harsh sled ride back from Moscow. To a ready scribe, his military aide, he called him a corrupt rogue with lips 'as tight as a cast-iron safe' – but only until dinnertime, after which he was 'an old gossip'. Napoleon was pretty sure that he had sold state papers to the English 'at a thousand francs a time'. 'I have never known anyone more deeply immoral,' the fallen emperor burbled. 'He lacks outstanding merit, and he hates work. But he has the gift of letting nothing show on his face, knowing when to say nothing – and staying awake until three in the morning, which allows him to keep his meetings secret. But of course, he comes from a great family. That makes up for everything. That gives the great nobility its advantage.'

It was odd that Napoleon with his efficient police spying apparatus never to his dying day suspected Talleyrand of spurring on Austria and Russia to defeat him, and of actively helping them do so over a period of at least five years. Had he stayed up past midnight himself, things might have gone better for him. The only treachery of which he accused Talleyrand was scheming to bring back the Bourbons to replace him. Moreover, as Napoleon avowed on St Helena, Talleyrand never double-crossed him quite as Fouché had: 'The Prince of Benevento had his master's confidence, Fouché never.' Only when it came to the two allied invasions did he point his finger at a handful of men he ranked responsible for his fall, starting with Talleyrand and a sensible pair of marshals who abandoned a hopeless fight. 'I pardon them,' he said in his last will and testament. 'May French posterity pardon them as I do.'

Also in his will, he at length accepted personal responsibility for the arrest and summary execution of the Duc d'Enghien, the ever-festering episode he'd long accused Talleyrand of inspiring. The deed was done, he said, to protect national security; he would do the same again if he had to. The gracious admission gave some satisfaction to the prince, though the stain he wore for involvement in the darkest affair of the Consulate never really went away, not in royalist eyes. Napoleon bequeathed a comfortable sum (most often 100,000 francs) to scores of Bonaparte family members, imperial dignitaries, generals and officials who served him well, ordering what remained of his fortune to be shared out among wounded French survivors of Waterloo. The handouts came from Napoleon's personal fund of six million francs still held in a Paris bank.

In view of the size of the fortune distributed, it was those who received nothing who took the eye. The prince of diplomats received not a sou and he wasn't surprised; he accepted that the emperor thought he'd received enough already. If there was one thing for which Talleyrand respected Napoleon, it was the wealth he'd heaped on him, or provided the key to, during his imperial service. Only years later, in his own will, did he fully air his gratitude:

> Forced by Bonaparte to choose between France and himself, I took the option prescribed by the most imperious of duties. But this I did in sorrow, only because it was no longer possible to treat his interests and those of my country alike, as I had in the past. I shall none the less remember to my last hour that he has been my benefactor, for the fortune I leave to my nephews comes to me largely from him. My nephews must not only never forget this, but they must teach it to their children and to their children's children, so that the memory endures in my family from generation to generation and that if ever a man by the name of Bonaparte finds himself in such a position as to need help or assistance, he may obtain from my immediate heirs or their descendants all manner of assistance it is in their power to give him. By this means more than any other will they show gratitude to me and honour my memory.

The biblical lilt suggested he was searching for atonement. Perhaps it was also meant to explain to certain people, such as the royal tax inspectors, where his riches came from. Beyond that it sounded sincerely grateful. It said something of Talleyrand, though, that his last word on

Napoleon concerned not their great policy clashes over war and peace, but money.

Another death in 1821, this one entirely unexpected, cut much closer to Talleyrand's heart. His 'angel', the Duchess of Kurland, just turned sixty, died at her castle in Bohemia on 20 August after a brief chest illness. He had been writing to her right up to her sudden death. His last letter sent in late July, when he had heard that she'd been unwell but was getting better, was a tender measure of his feelings for her: 'I have perhaps never felt so much how deeply I am attached to you. You are so good, you know so well how to care, how to give, that anyone who knows you can only adore you. Goodbye my good, sweet angel.'

The news of her death a fortnight or so later left him inconsolable. She was his second half, the beauteous half, the cherished recipient of his morning notes through thick and thin – through his worst trials with Napoleon, his most arduous diplomatic negotiations, his political ups and downs, his chest colds, his leg pains, his indiscretions, his confrontations with King Louis – and he held very little back from her. Only her daughter knew as much of his private thoughts. As he gazed now with Dorothy at a portrait he kept of the departed duchess, he was moved to tears, murmuring: 'I don't think there is a woman on earth more worthy of love.' In the days that followed he turned sadder still. He told Dorothy forlornly: 'I shall miss her until my dying day, which I now see approaching without pain.'

It was perhaps convenient, in these sorrowful circumstances, that Dorothy had just given birth to another of her offspring of mysterious paternity. This time the child, a girl christened Pauline, entered Valençay parish records as the daughter of Edmond, making her a legitimate Périgord. Again it was most unlikely that Edmond was the father: he and Dorothy didn't live together and were very soon to be legally separated. The prime candidate was a young marquis who sat in for Talleyrand in the Chamber of Peers and who spent hours on end talking with Dorothy in quiet corners.

The usual nonsensical story went the rounds that the father was Talleyrand himself, based on the close interest he showed in little Pauline from her infancy on. His tenderness wasn't hard to explain. She was half a Kurland girl! A little of his sadness over the duchess's death was lifted by her arrival. He called her 'my kitten' and from the start saw personally to her education, writing her nicely turned morning notes to widen her knowledge and give her a sense of history. He made sure that Dorothy, who wasn't the most fawning of mothers, kept his little favourite present all the time at Valençay and the Place de la Concorde residence.

For deaths were now fast accumulating around him, sending warnings of his own mortality. The indefatigable Mme de Staël, who seemed more than a match for any natural ailment, died not long before Napoleon; Choiseul, his lifelong friend from schooldays and a fellow diplomat of lesser renown, went with her; his young diarist friend Mme de Rémusat succumbed suddenly before 1821 was out, as did his saintly uncle, long promoted to Archbishop of Paris, who had eased his early, problematic way into the church, then manned his corner with the Bourbons. After that, the following spring, came the turn of Richelieu, the successor he so scorned, to whom Talleyrand accorded the economical epitaph: 'He was someone.' King Louis himself was in poor health and clearly hadn't long for this world. Why, Talleyrand was about to outlive even the stripling Tsar Alexander (the Russian autocrat died in the usual mysterious Russian manner four years after Napoleon).

It did not escape Talleyrand that he was older than most of those disappearing around him. His face was a baggy 'ruin', as a series of independent witnesses now concurred. A similar thought struck them: he looked like the devil! Beelzebub! The bad hoof, the smooth destruction of the features only confirmed it. It wasn't a blinding discovery. Napoleon, with a trace of awe, had always called him 'a devil of a man'. The Faubourg Saint Germain, with cruel respect, had long ago christened him the 'lame devil'. But these days the air of devilry seemed increasingly real, and it grew easier for his enemies to portray him as the artful, malevolent one with the forked tail. All the same, physically speaking, he was surviving better than most. Was it those chest-clearing morning snorts? The refusal to hurry? His sparing food habits? It was a fact that these days he never touched the copious fare he laid out for his constant flow of guests before the dinner hour struck. Whatever the trick, his survival talents as a statesman seemed to be widening to confront the advancing years themselves.

A sound constitution kept his appetite for power and influence alive right through the years of the Bourbon Restoration. If the truth of the matter was that he had been put out to grass, he took care to position himself in a fertile patch. He carried the Périgord burden: the conviction that as long as he lived, he was there to serve France. He had never been wrong yet.

In the venomous clash between hardline royalists and liberals that forever threatened King Louis' authority, he was bound to take the liberal side. Again and again, with leonine persistence, he came back to the issue of press censorship, a courageous stand in view of his Grand Chamberlain rank. Political ideas were bubbling anew after the intellectual blank of the Napoleonic era. The publishing trade, in books and newspapers, was straining at the leash. In this atmosphere it wasn't hard to see that continuing censorship would hurt the Bourbons more than it could help them. King Louis had to realise that; it was political folly not to. That the liberals, republicans and even nostalgic Bonapartists who defended the written word were also the monarchy's opponents was beside the point. For Talleyrand warned Louis: 'Without press freedom there is no representative government.'

This was the core of a memorable speech he made to the Chamber of Peers in July 1821 that swayed the censorship debate and made the political police a little less diligent in locking up people who wrote things that displeased the king's government. What sorrowed him, he observed in a sardonic opening line, was the 'complete futility' of the words he was about to pronounce. 'Freedom of the press is a necessity of the day. A government exposes itself when it obstinately rejects what the day proclaims is necessary.'

He also resolutely promoted in parliament his legitimacy principle, renewing his old efforts to force Louis to toe the line of constitutional monarchy. A good opportunity arose when King Ferdinand of Naples, purveyor to the Périgords of the Duke of Dino title, was squeezed by a local uprising into granting his people a constitution under which he grudgingly agreed to rule. This struck Talleyrand as setting an excellent example for Louis, who still insisted, for all his dabbling with democracy, that he ruled by the grace of God, not that of the people. The mystery of majesty wasn't mysterious at all, Talleyrand told the house of lords. It wasn't the will or the caprice of a king that was sacred. What was sacred was the law of the nation deposited with the sovereign. Through this charge the sovereign was indeed sacred – but the majesty of royalty was no more than the reflection of the majesty of the law. It was an argument with small appeal for royalist 'ultras'. To them, even to saddle a king with a constitution amounted to regicide.

Talleyrand was back at the ramparts when Louis and his government opted to go to war in 1823. It was hard to believe that France, still oppressed by war weariness, was already returning to it. Harder still to believe she was fighting in Spain, where Napoleon's empire came adrift. The purpose was to reverse a revolution against Ferdinand VII, Talleyrand's erstwhile long-staying guest at Valençay. Restoring the Spanish Bourbons to their throne seemed a bounden duty to Louis and his royalist supporters. What was more, since legitimate monarchs didn't like seeing their kind toppled, this was a French war-making enterprise that for once had the approval of Napoleon's victors – excepting England, which was wary of Ferdinand's blank disregard for constitutional rule.

The prospect of military adventure alarmed Talleyrand. Here they went again! As with press censorship, he became the strongest voice of opposition in parliament to war in Spain. In the salons, he argued:

> We shall have to fight insurrection, which is the worst kind of war. I predicted so before, when I tried to stop Napoleon meddling in Spain's affairs. Napoleon did not listen. In the hornet's nest he entered he ingloriously wore out his army. This was the beginning of his fall. Well now! We insist on going into Spain. History will repeat itself.

In the house of lords, he lamented: 'Sated with military glory, our country flatters herself that under her king's governance she can repair, at her peaceful leisure, all that we have suffered from war over thirty years.'

Reaction to his campaign was mixed. It was good to hear sensible Frenchmen calling him 'the tutor of the Restoration', or, more gratifying still, 'the prophet of Valençay'. Louis, on the other hand, was sorely tempted to send him into disgrace once more. 'Are you perhaps thinking of going back to the country?' the king inquired purposefully of his Grand Chamberlain. But Talleyrand enjoyed the prickly prophet role and the time he spent in Paris, which required him to keep on speaking terms with the court. He replied, 'No, Sire. Unless Your Majesty is thinking of Fontainebleau, in which case I should have the honour of accompanying him to discharge my duties there.' Rural Fontainebleau and its royal chateau were not a day's carriage ride from the capital.

Contrary to Talleyrand's predictions, Louis' war in Spain went off without major mishap. The Spanish populace responded more kindly to the white lily emblem of the French Bourbons than they had to Napoleon's eagles, in large part because Louis' commanders, imitating Wellington, paid Spanish peasants for what their forces took. At relatively little cost, France restored Ferdinand to his throne.

Still, Talleyrand could plausibly argue that each of the causes for which he campaigned during the Restoration was for King Louis' own good. At the same time, though, they had the effect of drawing him closer to an enigmatic royal figure who was born to differ with Louis and aspire to his place. This was the Duc d'Orléans, the head of France's secondary royal line and a man who so favoured constitutional monarchy that he was ready, in his quiet way, to fight for it. Despite his royal blood, Louis-Philippe d'Orléans had revolutionary form: his late father, Philippe Egalité, so named for his progressive views, had incurred the lasting wrath of émigrés during the Revolution for supporting the execution of Louis XVI. The son, by now a reserved man in his mid-fifties, remained the target of their mistrust – and he proceeded to earn it with his open sympathy for a model of monarchy from which King Louis shrank.

It was clear, though, that with the Duc d'Orléans radical politics had its limits: ordinary people scarcely knew him, nor he them. His constituency was the wealthy bourgeoisie, the business class, and he wasn't about to let it down. The Orléans family seat was the Palais Royal next to the Louvre, a stone's throw from Talleyrand's Place de la Concorde residence, and, as King Louis' reign stumbled, Talleyrand's brand new carriage, a glossy vehicle embossed with lions' heads, was seen drawn up there with increasing frequency. The Palais Royal seemed a risky destination for Louis' Grand Chamberlain, but he could tell which way things were moving and Louis-Philippe was preparing to make himself available.

The king died on 16 September 1824 with Talleyrand holding unhappy court at his bedside. Louis, fat and breathless, had been failing for months before succumbing to rampant gangrene. It was the Grand Chamberlain's duty to attend to his last sigh. This Talleyrand did ungrudgingly, the more so because the dying Louis had made him a most generous deathbed gesture, absolving him of blame in the killing of his royal kinsman the Duc d'Enghien. Twenty years after the event, the Enghien affair still refused to go away. It was an ugly wound on France which the ultras wouldn't allow to heal. Despite Napoleon's last testament, Talleyrand again found himself under heavy fire as Louis faded. It was perhaps the sharpest criticism he had yet faced over Enghien; one of Napoleon's former top generals was now directing the fire straight at him. Louis intervened to halt the clamour, ordering publication of his clement view on Talleyrand: 'His Majesty wishes the past to remain forgotten, excepting only for services rendered to France and to his person. The high rank you retain at court, Prince, is proof positive that the accusations which wound and afflict you have made no impression on His Majesty.'

After that, Talleyrand felt chained to the king's bedside. But it was an unpleasant wait. The odour of gangrene choked the death watch. Dorothy grew alarmed at the effect on Talleyrand, now seventy. What he told her of the experience she recorded in her diary: 'Continuous presence in the dying man's chamber, almost no rest, no sleep, and then the most lugubrious and frankly the most disgusting duties to fulfil for someone of the age and infirmity of M. de Talleyrand – this is more than enough to make me fear for his health.' The Grand Chamberlain survived it well enough. At Louis' burial at Saint Denis, he propped himself at the catafalque, holding the white emblem of the Bourbons as though he were one of the family.

The time wasn't yet ripe to push Louis-Philippe forward. King Louis' brother, the Comte d'Artois, was next in legitimate line to the throne and

Talleyrand, founder member of the legitimacy club, was in no position to argue with his ascent, though he was convinced it would end badly. Legitimacy was a wonderful principle to uphold when it was going to succeed, less so when doomed to fail. Artois came to the throne as Charles X, a king with if anything less sense of the political landscape than either of the brothers who preceded him. He had more charm than they, but none of their patience. Under King Charles, the ultras were back in charge, intent on restoring French glory and grandeur.

With only ten years separating his reign from the end of Napoleon's, it was risky for Charles to hold territorial ambitions, but impatience got the better of him. What drove him was a desire to undo as far as possible the recent treaties with the allies that kept France in check. He aimed to regain France's 'natural frontiers', dreamed of retrieving the lands on the left bank of the Rhine and taking Belgium back into the French realm.

Years before, Talleyrand might have agreed with much of this. But not now. Now it struck him as a rash, vainglorious challenge to Napoleon's victors that endangered peace. Furthermore, it took Charles' eye off worse problems at home where his desire to please the ultras and thoroughly disown the Revolution raised the hackles of the bourgeoisie and the populace alike.

Charles' five-year reign was a quick march to further revolution. It offered precious little joy to Talleyrand, though he retained his rank of Grand Chamberlain. Charles never thought of taking the exquisite title away from him. It seemed tattooed on his grand, baggy face. His renown was intact. Renown had its price though. Grand Bourbon ceremonies at the royal basilica of Saint Denis followed one on the other, requiring his attendance. Talleyrand was attired in his formal best on 20 January 1827 for yet another commemoration of the death of Louis XVI at the guillotine. As usual a large crowd gathered outside in drizzling winter weather to watch the high and the mighty come and go. After the mass, he limped from the basilica behind the royals and was looking around for his carriage when he felt a powerful blow to the side of the head which sank him to his knees on the dank cobbles. Grounded in his silken finery, he felt further vigorous blows crushing into his body, like the kicks of a horse. It all happened so fast that Talleyrand, stunned, winded, had no idea why he found himself lying there. Close onlookers thought he was assassinated. Guards tussled with an attacker who had broken blindside through their ranks to throw himself at his prey. As other guards rushed to help him, Talleyrand was able to make out a well-built young man in a high state of nerves shouting to the police, 'I had to give Prince Talleyrand a hiding. He has hurt me and my family.'

Back on his eternally unsure feet, Talleyrand discovered that no bones appeared to be broken. He was driven home, put to bed by doctors and given a soothing rubdown with unguents for his bruises. For a seventy-three-year-old he came through the assault almost unscathed.

His assailant, he learned, was Comte Marie-Armand de Maubreuil whose name he indeed recognised. The agitated Maubreuil swore that Talleyrand had commissioned him years earlier to assassinate Napoleon, then dropped him when the supposed plan somehow went awry. Maubreuil, a Breton aristocrat once cashiered from the Grand Army for going off the rails, had been voicing such charges since 1815. Now he claimed he had given Talleyrand 'a slap' at Saint Denis. He admitted that in his fury he had also kicked him, but his sole purpose was to deliver a slap to teach the prince a lesson and humiliate him. This was testimony that aggrieved Talleyrand, not only because he dismissed Maubreuil's charge as ludicrous. He did not want it thought he had been slapped. A slap was an insult, better resolved, even in this changing age, by duelling pistols than through a police tribunal. An outright physical assault was one thing; it was the sort of risk all public figures faced. But a Périgord did not receive a slap! King Charles had to be aware of this, and he made sure he was.

When Charles sent him a concerned message inquiring of his health and promising that Maubreuil would be punished, Talleyrand replied tartly from his bed, 'Sire, it was a punch.' And to the countesses who flocked to view his bandages he declared with some pride, 'He felled me like an ox.' To avert pernicious salon debate over what distinguished a slap from a punch and head off publicity for his assailant's strange charges, he asked the public prosecutor to drop the matter. It wasn't quite dropped – Maubreuil went to prison for a year or so and received a fine – but Talleyrand's reputation, like his bruised hide, emerged more or less intact.

The fall of the Bourbons by now seemed so preordained and inevitable to Talleyrand that he was able to watch it play itself out without alarm. When in Paris, he regularly sat at the whist table with King Charles, a card lover like himself, and it was all he could do to hold back from asking him outright why he filled his government with the most unpopular men in France, men whose sole merit he saw as blind obedience to the obstinate fellow sitting beside him. That didn't mean he had any clear idea of what would follow the Bourbons, despite the discreet coaching he was offering Louis-Philippe. From Valençay, he wrote to a politician friend in Paris: 'We are moving towards an unknown world without a compass or a pilot. Only one thing is certain: it will all finish with a shipwreck. England's revolution went on for half a century. Ours is nearing only its fortieth year and I can't for the life of me see its end. I doubt even whether the current generation sees it. We are entering new hazards.' He was fond of shipwreck metaphors. It was the pilot in him.

He was increasingly worried as the year 1829 drew to a close that his eyes might let him down at the very moment a pilot was needed. Well before Maubreuil set about him, his eyes had been bothering him. Now they were badly swollen and running. The ailment half-blinded him and at times made it impossible even to read. It pained him in head and spirit, though he tried to make light of it. To the same politician friend he'd advised of the imminent shipwreck, he wrote: 'I haven't written for a long time because I have a big bulge in the eyes. I haven't been able to read or write. I daresay it's not the worst moment for an eye infection, however, since it seems to me there isn't much to read . . . There is nothing being published that would hasten me back to Paris.'

Dorothy was deeply concerned. She wasn't long back from one of her protracted absences – this time in the Pyrenees, a quiet spot to round out another of her nine-month ailments. She had left little Pauline at Valençay with her doting great-uncle and a governess. The absence left her more than usually anxious about Talleyrand's wellbeing. She couldn't bear the idea of the old lion being removed from the hunt by failing sight. To show that her interest in his career was as alive as ever, she encouraged him to make sure there *were* interesting things being published. With the brilliant Thiers, who had an evident crush on her and was now a glowing name in opposition politics, she induced the sore-eyed prince to put his weight behind a new newspaper, *Le National*, a moderate sheet that took issue with the regime rather than yelled for its fall. Between them, assisted by two or three liberal wordsmiths, they created *Le National* at an attractive country chateau near Tours, not far from Valençay, which Dorothy had recently purchased so as to have her own property in France. Talleyrand confined his support to financial backing and advice. He was, after all, the Grand Chamberlain. Gradually his eyes improved as the new paper attracted a large and excited readership in Paris. Without crying it from the rooftops, Thiers was all for bringing Louis-Philippe to the throne. Readers appreciated the ferret-like editor: he was as adept with the memorable phrase as Talleyrand himself. The paper was an irritation to the king's government. But who was going to ban a newspaper backed by the champion of press freedom?

In July 1830 the ship of state finally ran aground. A workers' revolt in Paris against the Bourbon regime tottered into full-scale revolution, energised by a series of suicidal decrees signed by King Charles on 25 July. He suspended the limited press freedom he'd granted earlier, dissolved a newly elected parliament containing rather too much liberal bias and again fiddled with the electoral law to restrict the vote to the wealthy. Public anger boiled over in working-class Paris and its suburbs, with republicans and Bonapartists to the fore. Soldiers and rioters exchanged ceaseless gunfire around the Bastille. Barricades draped in the red, white and blue of 1789 went up on the boulevards. The king hadn't seen it coming. Having announced his decrees, he went hunting.

By chance Talleyrand returned to Paris from the country on the eve of Charles' ultimate imprudence. As the din of revolution approached the Place de la Concorde, his immediate thoughts were for practical matters of survival. After clearing his Bourse holdings he had Courtiade remove the gilt *HOTEL TALLEYRAND* plaque from above his main entrance. How could he be sure the revolutionaries would know which side the doomed king's Grand Chamberlain was on?

Now he was ready.

TWENTY-ONE

Last Performance

At the age of seventy-six, Talleyrand hobbled once more to the front of the world stage. He did so with a venerable reticence that scarcely hid his satisfaction. Fifteen years had passed since Napoleon's ultimate fall and here was the conqueror's old antagonist returning to power – flabbier, shoulders hunched, his mask more inscrutable than ever, but once more ready to put the world aright.

The revolution that upended France in the last days of July 1830 placed Louis-Philippe d'Orléans on the throne in place of Charles X, who abdicated and fled to England. In the nature of such transitions, it was far from smooth. Nor did it meet the aims of the new breed of revolutionaries. In Talleyrand's case, lending support to a takeover by a branch line of royalty meant bending his precious legitimacy principles. Fortunately he was able to find dual grounds for doing so. 'It is not I who have abandoned the king, it is the king who has abandoned us,' he declared, passing judgement on Charles' flight from the Tuileries Palace to the royal hunting castle at Rambouillet, thence to the Channel coast and England. A second consideration, perhaps stronger, was common sense: when circumstances demanded it, only fools refused to change their minds. The principle of legitimacy he'd advanced to lodge the Bourbons firmly on their throne at the Congress of Vienna had succeeded in trumping allied ambitions to dismember France. But now things were different. He told the harem: 'Today, sacrificing legitimacy can save and even strengthen the liberal monarchy.' Here in fact was a perfect chance to trim the monarchy to the constitutional size he wanted.

All the same, even after Charles fled, the Duc d'Orléans realised he had no constitutional right to replace him. Charles had complicated matters, in a last spurt of hubris, by naming his grandson as his successor. But a vacuum existed and Louis-Philippe gingerly filled it. His 'July Monarchy' headed off anarchy and further experimentation with a republican regime which many revolutionaries favoured. It was lucky for Louis-Philippe that the bloodlust of 1789 was largely absent in July 1830. In the end the habit he had of walking in Paris with a common man's umbrella was perhaps his best claim to the revolutionaries' sympathies, thence to the throne.

Once Talleyrand had got his principles in order, he pushed Louis-Philippe to act. As the claimant scratched his head at his private residence in the pleasant suburb of Neuilly, out of hearing of the gunfire in the streets of the capital, Talleyrand sent a message from the Place de la Concorde urging him to come into Paris immediately and put himself at the head of the insurrection. With the Bourbons gone for good – not, Talleyrand insisted, due to any subversive action of his – it was vital to forestall political bedlam. He recalled: 'All I could see was another republic and its dire consequences – anarchy, more revolutionary war and more of the misfortunes that France laid aside with such pain in 1815.'

For the Duc d'Orléans to take personal charge of the revolt on the streets wasn't possible, but he did hasten to his family seat at the Palais Royal at daybreak on 31 July to receive a deputation from parliament, and when the deputies offered him the vacated throne he did say he would give it urgent thought. He looked to Talleyrand before he leapt. The single hour he gave himself to consider his situation was time enough to send a messenger to the prince just down the road at the Place de la Concorde and ask for his final assessment of events. 'Accept!' said Talleyrand without a second's hesitation. Whereupon Louis-Philippe ventured to the Paris City Hall, climbed to the balcony and waved the revolutionary tricolour at insurgents massed below, an act sufficient in the heat of the moment to melt rebel hearts.

It was not a scene for the likes of Talleyrand to take part in. The news of it alarmed Europe. The allies who had defeated Napoleon at phenomenal cost could hardly be expected to embrace further revolution in France. Louis-Philippe was being hailed 'King of the Barricades' – with glee by the populace, with anguish by others at home and abroad. The label worn by the new king was in truth well wide of the mark, but no less disturbing to foreign powers for that. Even his formal title bothered foreign courts. To distinguish himself from Charles, who, like all French monarchs before him, was King of France by divine right, the Due d'Orléans was enthroned 'King of the French', by the grace of the street. The semantic distinction was supposed to lend him a popular, democratic touch, but it did him little good with foreign powers for which 'King of the French' was an awkward reminder of the expansive title Napoleon had carried – Emperor of the French.

In the days after the first heat of this new revolution died down, Talleyrand conferred at length with Louis-Philippe on the dark impression it left abroad. Would the other great powers be tempted to descend once more on France to resolve things to their liking? In the capitals of Europe there was grave talk of impending war. The more incensed revolutionaries, the Jacobin fire-eaters and their like, were singing of liberating peoples and restoring the foreign conquests of 1789.

It was up to the 'King of the Barricades' to make the leading foreign powers at least accept the fact of the revolution that brought him to the throne, and also to make sure they weren't about to intervene. In this, England had the whip hand. Talleyrand convinced the new king that England was the pivot for French world policy. By her liberal institutions and her own bygone experience of revolution she would naturally be least ill disposed towards the new regime in France, and might be talked into sympathising. An old flame leapt to life in Talleyrand: 'The desire to establish at last that alliance of France and England that I have always considered to be the firmest guarantee of the happiness of the two nations and of peace in the world'. Of course, he told the king, it would take someone of great experience, someone well known in Europe, to carry it off.

Louis-Philippe took him at his word. Instead of asking him to take over the foreign ministry, which he'd intended, he asked him to become ambassador to London. The London post, they concurred, was far more important at this extremely delicate juncture than the rest of French diplomacy combined. Anyone could be foreign minister! If things didn't work out with England, there would be no French policy worth its name to tend to.

Talleyrand hedged a little, protested that he was too old, too tired. It wasn't difficult, though, for the king to talk him into taking the post for which he'd written such exclusive candidacy requirements. Moreover, he would continue to receive his Grand Chamberlain stipend without even pretending to fulfil the outdated function. Perhaps Talleyrand would have preferred to resume his old trust as foreign minister; it would have saved his eyes and his tortured limbs. But the selection process had moved on. He rationalised his mission to London in time-honoured Talleyrand style: 'I was decided, in this circumstance as in others in my life, by the sense of duty and the thought of serving my country.' To his old friend the Duke of Wellington, currently England's prime minister, he fired off an intimate exhortation: 'We two shall maintain peace against the anarchists of France and troublemakers abroad.'

The return to England, with Dorothy present as his muse and deputy in all things, cloaked Talleyrand in power. It was no longer power of a conventional kind. It was the power of history. He *was* history. Not merely decades of it, but centuries. That was how this powdered relic of the *ancien régime*, weatherer of so many storms, the civilised world's avenger in the age of mighty Napoleon, appeared to the curious English. How convenient it was that Wellington was in charge, who knew about these things. The Tory prime minister had the cannons boom into an orange sky from Dover Castle as Talleyrand landed there at twilight on 24 September 1830. It was a salute to history. And how different it all was from the bleak day thirty-six years before when William Pitt, Wellington's distant predecessor, expelled him from the same shore for reasons that only his unshakeable admiration for England ever allowed him to digest. There were large obstacles ahead, but now he felt full of hope. Great responsibility was a wonderful tonic.

A serious new threat to harmonious relations with England arose, however, at the very time Talleyrand disembarked at Dover. Its name was Belgium. Dating from Napoleon's first victorious battles, that flat green land to the French north had become part of France herself. Then, at Lord Castlereagh's insistence in Vienna, it was merged with the kingdom of Holland. The English calculated that the union of the Low Countries would keep the port of Antwerp well and truly out of French hands, thus perpetuating its long-established role as England's trading gateway to the Continent. Now, in the late summer of 1830, the Belgians had revolted and were fighting for independence from Holland. In English eyes there was an evil fit in prospect here – a coalescence between what the Belgians were fighting for and what the revolutionary camp in Paris was seeking. It was a sure bet that once Belgium wrenched itself free of Dutch rule the French would want to have their old province back.

For all his high hopes, Talleyrand was in a squeeze. His difficulty was in having to reassure Wellington and his government that their fears were groundless while at the same time staunching French desires to recover Belgium. It was eerie how little Belgium tossed Talleyrand's grand career around and how it habitually ruptured the harmonious teamwork he sought between France and England. Belgium was the touchstone for cross-Channel friction. Revolutionary France's war with England broke out in 1792 over Belgium, specifically over Antwerp; hostilities came to an end close to a quarter of a century later in that same country, at Waterloo; and now it was Belgium that threatened to spoil things again. Anxious courts in Russia, Austria and Prussia awaited England's lead on how to handle the July Monarchy. Europe's peace depended on conciliation between France and Britain – in sum, on Talleyrand.

Londoners lined the streets to take a look at the famous statesman and his alluring companion in her Parisian robes. They applauded as his carriage went by when he presented his credentials to the king, the newly crowned William IV. They clapped in the streets again when he rolled up with Dorothy to attend grand state functions. From the crowds Dorothy heard cries of friendship for France, of admiration for her elegance and even 'Long live Talleyrand', which pleased him no end. He appeared to all the world to be the leader of France. Not everyone loved him – there was constant carping in the House of Commons over what some saw as government kowtowing to a legendary foreign rogue – but everyone seemed fascinated. The caustic London press christened him 'Old Talley', which he took to be a little distrustful, yes, but somehow amicable in its familiarity.

He wasn't all affection for Londoners either. Struck by the growth of the capital's population, he wrote home to Louis-Philippe's sister, Adelaïde d'Orléans, a private and uniquely useful channel of communication he was fostering with the king: 'Today London has 150,000 souls – if you can call souls the egotists who inhabit it. To my great astonishment, however, I have found a rather nice sun shining.' The familiar banter with the king's strong-minded sister was merely an additional mark of his standing.

Old Talley set out his sumptuous diplomatic stall at his embassy in Westminster, faithful to the dinner-table diplomacy that brought the powerful running into his embrace. The expense, Dorothy complained, was ruinous; providing decent food and wine for the upper-class multitude was so much more expensive in London than in Paris. In fact, she found everything three times more expensive in London, except for items made of cotton. She appealed through Adelaïde d'Orléans, who had more influence on her brother than his ministers did, for better financial support from Paris. Since people in London were indeed inclined to see Talleyrand as France's surrogate leader, as the man with his country's destiny in his hands, he had to play the part in leaderly spirit. And that is what he did.

From the start he plotted his course on his own or directly with Louis-Philippe, bypassing a spluttering foreign minister who took office in Paris, the Comte Louis-Mathieu Molé. Bitterly though Molé complained about Talleyrand making his own policy and keeping him in the dark, he was destined to remain there. A fortnight after Talleyrand's arrival in London, by which time he'd held numerous private talks with Wellington and other ministers, poor Molé, an otherwise sanguine soul, was unable to contain his irritation. The one note he'd received from Talleyrand hadn't even mentioned the Belgian crisis. He wrote to him: 'You will assuredly under-stand, my prince, my need to ask you for a quite different form of corre-spondence. Thus far, yours leaves me ignorant of the London government's dispositions.'

Talleyrand thought Molé had no business trying to meddle in his nego-tiations. He knew precisely what France's best interest was, and it was to be served by methods loftier than the pettifogging diplomatic channels Molé was insisting on. It was to be settled by great men of vision. By men with the power to decide things. His foreword to Wellington and leaders of the other European powers he was about to confront in negotiations reflected the cosy manner in which he aimed to conduct them: 'I am just a man of some experience come to sit with old friends to talk of general affairs.' No wonder Molé nettled him. In a superior huff he wrote back calling the minister's chastisement 'neither friendly nor ministerial':

If my manner of carrying out affairs is out of fashion, it is simpler to tell me so clearly. Let us, then, be open with each other. We shall do well only if we treat affairs with an ease born of confidence. You will find that I tell everything except what I find to be of no importance. That is how I worked with the Emperor and even with Louis XVIII. I realise that today's France no longer abides by this old tradition, that our country is in what they call flux, but for myself, here on the soil of old Europe, I believe it is necessary to let time take its course, and that to hurry things is so alien to English custom that it can only detract from the sort of weight we must give all our proposals.

Molé was soon obliged to give up. Treated by his chief ambassador as a lightweight, he was put aside in favour of an obscure army general. But Talleyrand then ran into further interference from a more difficult quarter – from Charles de Flahaut, his illegitimate son. Flahaut, now a richly decorated soldier-diplomat of forty-five, arrived in London for what Talleyrand perceived to be 'rather complicated' motives. He was pleased to see his son; he always was. He'd kept in touch with him from childhood, promoting his career with true paternal interest. In this case, though, Charles appeared to be an emissary for a faction within Louis-Philippe's government which proposed doing things with Belgium that Talleyrand found unacceptable.

The proposal Charles carried was to split the little country four ways, the largest part going to France, a slab to Holland to compensate for loss of the whole, another slab to Prussia so as to keep Berlin smiling – and the city and port of Antwerp to England. It dawned on Talleyrand that Charles was chosen to convince him of the merits of this scheme because, apart from being his son, he too knew certain English government grandees and hoped to be appointed ambassador in London once his father stepped down.

The prince was surprised and a little irritated by his son's pretension. He told him the plan was senseless, dangerous and contrary to French interests. There was only one solution to the Belgian question and that was the one on which he was close to obtaining English agreement: an independent and neutral kingdom of Belgium. France merely courted war in dreaming of taking back Belgium, or any part of it. Besides, much as he admired

England and sought the closest relations with her, France had expended centuries of blood and grief to remove the English from their territorial possessions on the Continent and he wasn't going to negotiate their repossession of Antwerp or anywhere else. 'I would rather cut off my fist than sign a deed that brought the English back,' he told his son with a final dismissive flourish.

Nonetheless, he sent Charles back to Paris with a long, reasoned letter for his sponsors explaining why France had to concentrate not on ogling Belgium but on building unshakeable relations with England. It all came down to civilisation. To protecting civilisation. France had to join with countries where civilisation was most advanced. 'This naturally means regarding England as the one to build our closest relations with. Let me point out that England is the sole power with which we share essential principles . . . the one power which, like us, frankly wants peace. Other powers abide by some sort of divine right; France and England alone no longer do so.' Others, he said, upheld their monarchies' divine right by the cannon; France and England upheld their principles through popular opinion.

In view of England's enduring fondness for the cannon and the sheer novelty of anything approaching popular democracy in France under the July Monarchy, Talleyrand's lecture sounded frankly idealistic. But such warm notions nonetheless appealed to the English, at least to the liberal fraternity. The solution he proposed for Belgium prevailed; it stood on his principle of non-intervention. The English came round to the view that their design for a greater Netherlands under the Dutch crown was unworkable. And a change of policy became a little easier still when Wellington's Tory government fell in the last days of 1830. Not that Old Talley's friend had been blocking a settlement. It was just that he was succeeded as prime minister by the Whig leader, Earl Grey, whom the prince also knew, having tasted his excellent blend of tea with him on several occasions during his exile in London long before. Grey's Whigs were more relaxed than the Tories over events in the Low Countries.

The Netherlands crisis rumbled on with occasional flare-ups despite the settlement. The Dutch couldn't quite reconcile themselves to relinquishing Belgium, and many of the French, republicans as well as royalists, never stopped dreaming of retrieving their former province to the north. As long as the settlement held, Talleyrand's stock was high in London. In the press, which otherwise blew hot and cold about him, he was portrayed with the world at his feet. 'He is the perfection of an aristocrat,' observed the visiting French writer Prosper Mérimée, a guest at one of his frequent embassy banquets. 'The English, who have great pretensions as to elegance and style, simply aren't up to him.' Mérimée observed that the most distinguished of English peers acted servile in his presence.

It surely wasn't the old prince's look that most impressed them, though this too may not have displeased the English taste for the eccentric. To Mérimée's eye he was now a 'big package of flannel enveloped in a blue habit topped by a death's head encased in parchment'. What better impressed was his manner and his wit; on politics, literature and cuisine no guest could match him. To confirm his standing with English gentlemen about town he frequented their London clubs, making the Travellers on Pall Mall his preferred late evening haunt. The Travellers Club modified its stairs to ease his tortuous passage to its whist tables where he played with passion and few words. In the absence of talkative ladies a London club was no substitute for a Paris salon, but he liked the Travellers setup nonetheless, in particular the furniture. 'A good armchair is a very good thing,' he wrote home to the harem. 'The English do everything better than we do.'

Dorothy made her own contribution to the style of the Talleyrand embassy, and not only through her talents as a society hostess. Stories of her stream of young lovers much impressed London ladies while testing their prudery. Talleyrand's otherwise reliable stand-in and chief secretary at the embassy, Adolphe de Bacourt, was her latest amour. Lady Grey, the prime minister's wife, defended her, not unbitchily, from the worst gossips, noting that she liked her a lot and that she was always of good humour and pleasing company. 'Since she never says anything that upsets me, why should I worry about lovers they say she has? I'm not proud of being different from her. I have been lucky, that's all.' Talk about Dorothy amused Talleyrand. With her as his adoring minder and political deputy, he possessed a love without being caught up in its emotional trials, which anyway had never much snared him and which snared him still less as he approached eighty.

Since the Belgian question cussedly refused to go away, he was kept on his painful toes through a second year in London. The iron strut that helped him walk more or less straight cut remorselessly into his calf, and he was under fire not only from French compatriots who imagined he'd robbed them of Belgium, but from English members of parliament who thought he had cast a spell on Wellington and Grey so as to deceive them. At the London end recriminations came to a head on 29 September 1831, when argument raged in the House of Lords over Talleyrand and his role. The most painful side of the debate for the prince was that the brother of his old partner Castlereagh, the Marquis of Londonderry, led the assault. The bristling conservative claimed Talleyrand had made England give way all along the line. Who could trust him? A man who had served four regimes! (Londonderry did not count well.) 'I do not think it would be possible to find anywhere in the world another character such as that of the wily individual who represents France here. It is sickening to see how our ministers pay eager court to such a man.'

This was good xenophobic stuff largely born of old hatred for Napoleon and no doubt for France in general, and it brought Wellington to his feet, despite the fact that Londonderry was a member of his Tory party. Wellington was no less aroused than Talleyrand's aggressor. White of face, the soldier said the prince had served his country with guile and steadfastness, always behaving with honour and uprightness towards others. 'In all conscience I declare to you that no man, public or private, has ever been depicted in falser colours.' Lord Holland, who had shared the news of Napoleon's death with Talleyrand in Paris, also leapt to his assistance, dismissing Londonderry's attack as shameful slander. Talleyrand was touched when he read reports of the scene. Wellington's support was particularly precious. His fragile eyes misting, he said: 'I am especially grateful to the duke. He is the only statesman in the world who has ever spoken well of me.'

Old Talley indeed had a prodigious gift for making others speak ill of him. But any maudlin thoughts he had on this matter in no way undermined the worth he believed he brought to serving France to her best advantage. This was evident from a heart-to-heart encounter he had at this very time with a second literary visitor to his embassy, the Romantic poet Alphonse de Lamartine. While Lamartine mixed verse with politics (he was destined to become a government minister), it was perhaps his familiarity with the heart and with tears that caused Talleyrand to look into himself and shrug off the devil's mantle in which so many people liked to cloak him. His judgement on himself was frank, but also positive. 'I open my name to all interpretations, all the outrages of the crowd,' he told the poet:

> They think I am immoral and Machiavellian, yet I am simply impassive and disdainful. I have never given perverse advice to a government or a prince, but I do not go down with them. After shipwrecks, you need pilots to rescue the shipwrecked. I stay calm and get them to port somewhere. No matter which port, as long as it offers shelter.

With age, the pilot metaphor clearly appealed to him more and more. Still, even the admiring Lamartine wondered how this rescuer of rudderless mankind was able to deal with the charges of corruption, of crimes even, that were so often thrown at him. How could he claim to be an honest man? Unruffled, Talleyrand replied:

> For statesmen there are many ways of being honest. Mine is not yours, I see, but one day you will hold me in greater esteem than you now think. My so-called crimes are fools' fantasies. Does an able man ever need crime? Crime is the resort of imbeciles in politics. Like the turning tide, it comes back on itself and drowns. I have had my weaknesses. Some call them vices. But crimes? Please!

To be sure, men such as he were a cut above crime. Nor did he need encouragement from Lamartine to applaud himself on his accomplishments while in England, though he did so leanly, content to say: 'I have done a little good. It is my best work.'

The same understated pride glowed through his report to the wrinkled harem in Paris on the Low Countries agreement he at length obtained for Louis-Philippe. 'It is the first treaty the king has made and it is useful to France, whose frontier is covered, and to Belgium, which it makes independent.' How succinct! How grand! Through that one line shone all his diplomat's talent for reducing the most complex questions to their essence. Louis-Philippe and his sister Adelaïde, with whom Talleyrand kept up the bantering correspondence he trusted she found flirtatious, were delighted with him. The bourgeois king called his accomplishment a great service to France; he had succeeded in reconciling London and the rest of the European capitals with his violently born July Monarchy.

That 'little good' he claimed to have done was one of his choicer understatements. From the time of his London embassy, France and England were never again to make war on each other. This was extraordinary. Scarcely credible. Through future decades, future centuries, Europe's oldest and most unforgiving rivals contrived through thick and thin to keep on the same side when the cannons roared. The mere prospect of this was something Talleyrand prized most when looking back on his life: 'From the beginning to the end of my career my dearest wish was an intimate alliance between France and England, convinced as I am that the peace of the world, the strengthening of liberal ideas and the advance of civilisation rests on this base.'

It was a most judicious moment to be fulfilling his dearest wish. Before he died a young woman little older than Pauline inherited England's throne at the outset of the longest reign in English history, and England, under Queen Victoria, was never more powerful and prosperous, nor more secure as an ally than a foe. The mistrust voiced by the Marquis of Londonderry never quite left English hearts, which prevented the two countries from co-founding an authentic European union when the time came for it and nothing short of unity in Europe would do. But the enduring peace that Talleyrand helped put in place between them, together with his eccentric belief that Europe's best interests were also France's best interests, were a sound enough base for European integration.

All of these were principles he developed from experience. Coping with Napoleon had shown him the madness of the opposite course. On European union he had a paternity claim.

As Talleyrand's dearest wish began to look attainable, near exhaustion, alas, cramped his style. His head and chest lost the fight with London weather. The Low Countries saga got him down. 'I am so fed up with the word Belgium,' he wrote to a countess friend, 'that I shall forbid three generations of Talleyrands ever to pronounce it.'

All-round fatigue induced him to take extended home leave through the summer and autumn of 1832, spent mostly resting up at Valençay and taking the sulphurous waters at Bourbon l'Archambault. By his side were Dorothy and young Pauline, whose education he lovingly attended to and whose pious nature so touched him that he wondered where it came from.

'I need to think of my legs, my eyes and take a look at my affairs,' he announced in advance of his home leave to the surviving dames of the Paris harem. He hardly bothered to reflect on a curious feeler from his old associate Charles de Rémusat, ever the chamberlain, on his readiness to head a new government Louis-Philippe was forming. Dorothy, who knew how tired he was, answered the discreet inquiry for him. 'M. de Talleyrand is much too determined not to be part of any government to be harried on this point.' In any case it was perhaps more a courtesy than a genuine proposition on the king's part. As far as Talleyrand pondered it at all, he brushed it off with scorn: 'They must think I'm very silly if they believe I want to take on the premiership. I have no desire to bring that carnival to the Rue Saint Florentin.' No, his rest programme for Valençay and the spa was well laid out: 'Early to bed, eat the strict minimum and avoid having to say anything remotely important.'

The regime worked up to a point, though he was besieged all along by Paris newspaper insults suggesting that the famous rest-cure patient had sold out his country from beginning to end – and that Belgium was the last straw. Nonetheless by mid-October he'd recovered his strength, was sleeping better and was able to return to his responsibilities in London where Louis-Philippe insisted he stay to maintain France's glossier standing in Europe.

He wanted to retire. He ached to retire. But he couldn't bring himself to do so. His Périgord blood and a turbulent series of rebounds in the Low Countries saga kept him going for another year before he again returned to France on leave in September 1833, this time thinking it would be permanent. Again it was not to be. By the New Year of 1834 he was back at his post in London, propelled there, he noted with greybeard pride, by Louis-Philippe's conviction that he was indispensable. He advised his embassy stand-in, Dorothy's latest favourite: 'I am returning to England for a few months. People seem readier than I am to believe that I am of some use.'

In February he turned eighty and felt it. His gait had an increasingly perilous wobble that threatened to ground him with each step. All the same he had a last diplomatic trick up his sleeve, one which the London government helped him play. The English planned to sign a friendship pact with Spain and Portugal to shield the Iberian peninsula from unwanted interference by other European powers. Talleyrand saw in this cosy triangular scheme a chance to complete a formal alliance with England. What he did was to square off the pact by bringing France in as co-signatory, which achieved his purpose. War with England was proscribed forever more, on paper at least. The Quadruple Alliance signed in London on 22 April 1834 was Talleyrand's last diplomatic act.

It was Dorothy who eased him over his reluctance to retire. She recognised his physical decline better than most. As she often did when she had something important to tell him, she wrote him a plainly worded note saying that he risked compromising his reputation and his career by staying on any longer. She reminded him he had only agreed to come to London to save his country as it shook from the tremors of revolution. For a man of his age, out of power for fifteen years, to have thrown himself into this undertaking was a mark of his boldness. 'You have accomplished it. Let that be enough! When you have made history, as you have, there should be no thinking of a future other than the one that history has prepared for you. Declare yourself old! Then people won't find you are growing old. Tell the world, nobly and simply, the hour has struck.'

Talleyrand wanted no more pushing to call it a day. By the end of August 1834 he was back in France for good.

He believed his four years in London had put him right back on the top rung of statecraft. All the same in his official letter of resignation to Louis-Philippe, a chatty, laconic note typical of Talleyrand, he ribbed the king for keeping him at it too long: 'The king too often forgets my great age in the bountiful indulgence he has shown me. He forgets that an octogenarian is not entitled to make mistakes, for what makes the mistakes of old age so sad is that they are irreparable.'

*　　*　　*

341

Retirement was better spent at Valençay than in Paris, and not only for the repose offered by the most serene countryside in all France. Abroad, the world honoured the prince of statesmen and lamented his departure; Wellington and Metternich led the chorus of praise, and even the testy Tsar Alexander's successor, Tsar Nicholas, joined in. At home, though, the political roisterers of Paris were less than unanimous in their respect. Their continuing abuse was hard to stomach. It seemed that those who hated him for keeping French hands off Belgium aimed to make sure the king would never again recall him to high office, which would have been all right by him had it not been for the gratuitous ferocity of the attacks.

The insults came at times from the unlikeliest quarters. The novelist George Sand, a Valençay neighbour of his with a rising literary reputation in Paris, celebrated a visit to his magnificent estate by publishing a vicious personal attack in a Paris periodical. She depicted him as a satyr, a reptile, a monster, 'a man born for great vices and petty actions'. She ended the article addressing him directly: 'And you, you savage, gorged old vulture, you will die a slow bitter death in your nest!' This wasn't very nice even by the harsh standards of grudge-slinging to which he was currently subjected. He was deeply shocked. Neither he nor Dorothy cared to respond, but their visitor's strange outburst helped lodge an unappealing portrait of Talleyrand in public opinion.

What could he do about it? The condition of France to which he returned was no help. The July Monarchy remained a contentious and tumultuous enterprise, and he had borne its banner before the world. Attempts to assassinate Louis-Philippe followed one on the other; governments came and went as the king's liberal instincts veered off course towards the inflexible. His odd reign liberalised inside out the charter by which the Bourbons ruled, but all it produced was an illusion of democracy that was probably as much the fault of the torn nation as his. There came a fleeting moment of satisfaction for Talleyrand when his protégé Adolphe Thiers, the forceful liberal whose career he and Dorothy had helped launch, became head of government in early 1836. But Thiers opted out within months and was replaced by none other than the aggrieved Molé, who was still smarting over the Talleyrand performance that cut short his first outing in government.

The truth was that Talleyrand was doomed to fight a losing battle for popularity and national honour in his time. It was now twenty-one years since Napoleon's ultimate fall at Waterloo and well over a decade since his death, but the conqueror was still astride his charger in the nation's heart. The slower France was to reassert her customary power and glory under the inept Bourbons and the struggling Louis-Philippe, the faster Napoleon's ghost rode. There came a hectic vision of this during 1836 when Napoleon's nephew, the otherwise obscure Louis-Napoleon Bonaparte, attempted a putsch against the July Monarchy; it failed but it was the sign of things to come. Popular nostalgia for Napoleon's legend, plus his nephew's astute promotion of it, would put Louis-Napoleon at the head of a second French Republic before the century was half out, then make him Emperor of France, albeit a less adventurous one than his uncle.

The peace Talleyrand fought for and achieved was one thing: it saved France and it saved Europe – for a good long time at least – from her murderous old self. In that, Talleyrand was the unshakeable patriot he never doubted he was – Périgord blood permitted nothing less. National esteem was another matter. It was the conqueror he brought down, not he, who won a lasting place in French hearts. Glory, even vainglory, was always a more exciting gift than the peace and quiet of the civilised life which Talleyrand aimed to bring Europe.

Years earlier, when he was first in disgrace with Napoleon, he had fallen into discussion with an inquisitive young Prussian countess on how posterity would see him. As a fan of Napoleon, she was disinclined to flatter Talleyrand. She suggested therefore that future generations would see him as a figure who wanted the world to argue about him forever. 'Yes, that's it, that's exactly it!' he said. 'I want people to go on arguing for centuries over what I have been, what I have thought, what I have wanted.'

He never claimed they would love him.

EPILOGUE

Talleyrand died at his Paris residence on the Place de la Concorde on 17 May 1838, his crippled frame worn out. He was eighty-four. The death was problematic, as it had to be. It required a negotiation. To the Catholic God, he was a sinner. A stupendous sinner. There wasn't much he hadn't done to offend the Almighty: a bishop defrocked, sacrilegiously wed, nationaliser of Church property, breaker of Church allegiance to Rome, and right-hand man of an emperor who humiliated and incarcerated the pope.

Against that charge sheet, he could say little more than that he was forced into the Church against his will and that he was a dissenting bystander in the miserable treatment of the pope, which he regarded as a cardinal error by Napoleon, as mad as his march on Moscow and his war in Spain. This was meagre ammunition for the defence, but Dorothy and the adolescent Pauline, who was increasingly more pious than the rest of the Kurland women, pressed him to seek heavenly grace. Talleyrand was ready to believe he wanted it – the mysteries of the Catholic faith had never lost their attraction for him – but he wasn't prepared to grovel for it. To do so would be a gift to his enemies, and it wasn't the time to invite their sarcasm and ridicule; deathbed conversions were the stuff of boulevard theatre farce. He could hear them saying he'd never stopped changing sides to his last gasp. They wouldn't understand. Through the ages a proper Périgord exit had demanded God's grace. He had the right, though, to bargain with God for his soul.

Sweet-natured Pauline he couldn't disappoint. His great-niece, already seventeen, was pleading with him to take her confessor as his. Even as he felt death's hand, while she was away taking the air on the Normandy coast, he kept up his flow of charming instructional notes to his young favourite, including the poignant:

When you are back in Paris, I shall take you to see the King of Siam's elephant. He exercises with such grace. Being huge doesn't stop him

345

being extremely agile. You know how, when you are pleased with an actor, you call him back after the play to applaud him. Well, here they call the elephant back after each performance and he comes to the front of the stage where he curls and uncurls his trunk to thank everyone. I am sure he will amuse you. Goodbye, dear child, I love you tenderly.

Did Talleyrand glimpse himself in the performance? It sounded like it. He too was a mammoth of sorts – and a lifelong performer.

Such were the qualities he displayed in his ultimate negotiation with God, conducted through an understanding Paris seminary head named Father Dupanloup whom Pauline and Dorothy managed to press upon him. Talleyrand approved of Dupanloup, who was in close contact with the papal nuncio, but he wasn't going to let him decide things. But for his defrocking and release from holy orders, he outranked him in the Church by several shades of red. Indeed Dupanloup, intimidated, recognised this from their first encounter in Talleyrand's salon at the Rue Saint Florentin, recalling: 'I doubt whether kings can be more kings in their palaces than Talleyrand was in his salon.'

The prospective bargain had two parts, one a retraction by Talleyrand of his sins against the Church, the second a letter to the pope requesting forgiveness. The devil was in the extent to which Talleyrand retracted.

All through April draft versions meandered back and forth between the dying prince and God's side, ending up unsigned in the lap of the defrocked bishop, who disputed words and corrected corrections with the obsessive care he'd lavished on his most painstaking international treaties, refusing as ever to hurry. The Vatican gave its final clearance weeks before Talleyrand agreed to stop reworking the texts in early May. Even then he refused to sign. When surgeons gouged a tumour from his lower back and his condition looked critical, he still wouldn't sign. He had Dorothy read the repentance papers out loud to him over and over so that he was sure he had the right nuances all through. In a final tweak, the immortal diplomat in him insisted on backdating the finished documents to the day two months earlier in March when he'd given a well-acclaimed discourse on statesmanship to the Institute, his last speech. That way, he said, no one could say he had 'reverted to childhood' in repenting.

Repentance in its final shape looked like a diplomatic victory for the prince, a half-victory at worst. It placed guilt for his churchly transgressions on the 1789 Revolution which, he maintained, carried all before it and still influenced things fifty years on. He allowed: 'At my great age and after long experience I have come to blame the excesses of the century that reared me, and to condemn outright the grave mistakes which over these long years have assailed [the Church] and in which I have had the misfortune to participate.' Never once, he said, had he stopped considering himself to be a son of the Church: 'I once more deplore those acts in my life which have aggrieved it.' In the letter to the pope, he expressed unbroken personal loyalty to the head of the Catholic Church but couldn't resist falling back on the reason why he hadn't appeared to live up to it: 'The respect I owe to those who bore me cannot prevent me from saying that my entire youth was directed towards a profession I was not made for.'

At last he appeared satisfied with the negotiation. So why wouldn't he sign? His will was settled: Dorothy was trustee of all his wealth, property and personal papers, which she was to dispose of among the Talleyrand-Périgord clan according to his written instructions; the descendants would have quite enough to help out any luckless Bonapartes who came knocking. What kept Dorothy and Pauline fretting was the danger, the horror as they saw it, of his dying without putting his name to the bargain with Dupanloup. Louis-Philippe and Mme Adelaïde broke with court protocol to attend him on his deathbed for a royal farewell; princes, ambassadors, statesmen, old friends and the odd surviving member of the harem stopped by for a last word. Even Molé, the prime minister, putting aside personal grievance, stood watch at his bedside next to the trembling Dupanloup.

It was the most public of deaths. But still Talleyrand refused to go public with his repentance. The shifting spectators wedged in the doorway between his bedroom and salon could only wonder what was going on behind those half-closed eyes. He was unlikely to be afraid. He had never shown fear. The whisper in the Faubourg Saint Honoré was rather that he knew the reaction his repentance would provoke and he was cutting things fine to foreshorten the scandal. More likely he just wasn't sure of his action, and never would be. Périgord pride prevailed to his last gasp. On 16 May, an overcast day, he told Pauline, as she began her daily ritual of imploring him to sign, that he would do so at dawn the next day, between 5 and 6 a.m.

On the stroke of five on 17 May he was awake. Dupanloup stepped forward with the papers. A forbidding flicker in Talleyrand's eye stopped him short. As six struck, Dorothy asked him if he wanted her to read him the texts one more time. He nodded, 'Yes, read it.' As she finished, she handed him pen and ink and he raised his hand slowly, not a tremor crossing his blank face, to inscribe on both documents the signature he reserved for state treaties: Charles-Maurice, Prince Talleyrand.

A few hours later he was dead.

* * *

They talked of his life. They talked of his pact with God. And they talked of the Devil, as many were inclined to do when they talked of Talleyrand. No sooner had he gone than the grizzled Pozzo di Borgo, the envoy of the Russian tsars, observed with a respectful smile: 'Now he is in hell, and I am sure the Devil is telling him, "Old Friend, you exceeded my instructions".'

In place of a formal bibliography I have endeavoured to cite in the notes that follow all the books and documents I have read or referred to in writing this life of Talleyrand. Those not mentioned in the notes are listed at the end.

Prologue: Paris 1809 (pages 1–10)

Page 7 *I came to meet him . . .* : The two books I chanced upon in Berlin are *Talleyrand, le Sphinx Incompris* by Jean Orieux (Flammarion, Paris, 1970) and *Talleyrand aux Etats-Unis* by Michel Poniatowski (Perrin, Paris, 1976). Orieux is the biographer most familiar to French history lovers; his is a colourful, unbiased treatment, the most readable there is. Poniatowski, a descendant of Polish royalty who played a Talleyrandesque role as leading minister to President Valéry Giscard d'Estaing in the 1970s, is of near equal historical interest for his original look at the newborn United States and Talleyrand's efforts to find a place in it.

      The most scholarly and exhaustive studies of Talleyrand's life, to both of which I also owe grateful acknowledgements, are *Talleyrand* by Georges Lacour-Gayet (four volumes; Payot, Paris, 1928) and *Talleyrand, le Prince Immobile* by Emmanuel Waresquiel (Fayard, Paris, 2003).

Page 8 *And what a flow of personal letters . . .* : A good many found their way into print towards the end of the nineteenth century as *Correspondance Diplomatique de Talleyrand* or *Lettres Inédites de Talleyrand*, addressed to the likes of Napoleon, French government ministers, diplomatic cronies, the Duchess of Kurland (his ultimate favourite, to whom he wrote daily – or twice daily – once he fell for her) and Louis XVIII. What exists can be seen in the Bibliothèque Nationale de France (BNF).

Page 8 *'No, no, no, that isn't . . .'* : The lesson on how to drink cognac is widely retold, including *Humeurs et Humour de M de Talleyrand* by

Gérard Sellier (Paris, 1992) – essentially a compilation of Talleyrand anecdotes.

Page 10 *Finally, money . . .* : The French government statistics agency, Insee, values the purchasing power of the franc in 1901 at 3.4 euros (2006). Since the franc held remarkably stable right through the nineteenth century there is some sense in applying a like rate for Napoleonic times.

Chapter 1: Born to Count (pages 11–19)

Page 13 *He did not remember seeing his parents . . .* : This and most other details of Talleyrand's life from early childhood to adolescence (including the patently false story of the origin of his deformity) are provided by his memoirs, *Mémoires de Talleyrand* (vol. 1, 1754–1807; vol. 2, 1807–15). There have been several editions of his memoirs since they first appeared in the second half of the nineteenth century. The one I have used for reference is edited by Paul-Louis and Jean-Paul Couchoud (Plon, Paris, 1957). Their work is particularly rich in annotations, commentaries, details on peripheral personalities cited by Talleyrand – and most of all in the provision of texts of his abundant correspondence, private and official. A corroborative account of the youth and early manhood is contained in *Talleyrand et l'Ancienne France* by Michel Poniatowski (Perrin, Paris, 1988).

Page 18 *This was 1769, the year Napoleon was born . . .* : Books on Napoleon by the world's historians may well outnumber the fighting men in his armies. More often than not I have referred to a crisp biography in French by Jean Tulard (Fayard, Paris, 1987) and one in English by Vincent Cronin (Collins, London, 1971).

Chapter 2: In the Black (pages 20–38)

Page 21 *There was also the girl . . .* : Talleyrand, *Mémoires*, vol. 1, p. 22. For Talleyrand's relations with women, see (among others): *Les Femmes de Talleyrand* by Baron Valentin de Vars (Kolb, Paris, 1891), and *Les Belles Amies de Talleyrand* by Jacques Dyssord (Nouvelles Editions Latines, 2001). Such books promote the womaniser reputation his enemies like to pin on him; they invariably get him wrong.

Page 26 *The salons where Talleyrand enjoyed his evenings . . .* : For descriptions of the prevailing salon society see *Les Salons Littéraires* by Roger Picard (Paris, 1942), and *Ces Bonnes Femmes du 18ème Siècle* by Serge Grand (Paris, 1985).

Page 29 *'I didn't say, "ah, ah" . . .'*: Talleyrand, *Mémoires*, vol. 1, p. 40.

Page 29 *They were one thing that irritated him . . .* : Talleyrand, *Mémoires*, vol. 1, p. 33.

Page 35 '*Suaviter in modo . . .*': Gouverneur Morris, Talleyrand's rival for the affections of Mme de Flahaut, is a sharp, if subjective observer of his quarry in candid souvenirs of his Paris stay, *Diary of the French Revolution*, edited by Beatrix Cary Davenport (1939). In this entry, dated 17 October 1789, Morris also writes that Mme de Flahaut eyes Talleyrand 'with a look very close to scorn' as regards his ability to satisfy her physical needs.

Chapter 3: A Good Revolution (pages 39–57)

Page 41 '*They were almost all lawyers . . .*': Talleyrand, *Mémoires*, vol. 1, p. 148.

Page 42 *At this decisive moment . . .*: See Jules Michelet, *Histoire de la Révolution Française* (re-issued by Laffont, Paris, 1979), vol. 1, p. 129. Michelet's history, first published in 1847, is the classic work on the period, a romantic masterpiece in two volumes.

Page 43 '*Please accept the truth, the revolution . . . is indispensable . . .*': Talleyrand, *Mémoires* (appended documents), vol. 1, p. 172. His support for the Revolution is expressed in a letter to the Comtesse de Brionne, a salon hostess and diarist.

Page 44 '*Now that all the efforts of wit . . .*': from Henry Bulwer-Lytton, *Essay on Talleyrand* (London, 1868), Preface. Until Duff Cooper produced his biography more than half a century later, Bulwer-Lytton's lengthy Victorian portrait was the most perceptive study of Talleyrand in English.

Page 44 *allowing his pectoral cross to retreat . . .*: Anecdote from Orieux, *Talleyrand*, p. 150.

Page 45 *That bothersome American . . .*: Gouverneur Morris, *Diary and Letters* (Library of Congress, New York, 1988), entry for 28 October 1789.

Page 48 *He had in fact saved the clergy . . .*: From Talleyrand's letter to Mme de Brionne (see above).

Page 51 *the personification of the liberal-minded . . .*: Bulwer-Lytton, Preface.

Page 54 '*Ah, it's you. I beg you, don't make me laugh' . . .*: Orieux, p. 174, citing the Marquis de La Fayette, *Correspondance* (BNF).

Page 54 *It was his lucky day . . .*: Orieux, p. 176. The original source for Talleyrand's 14 July antics is his longstanding friend and accomplice, the Comte de Vitrolles (*Mémoires*, BNF). Vitrolles, a Provençal nobleman with a talent for intrigue, will do him many important services over the years, in particular when it comes to hastening Napoleon's fall.

Chapter 4: Saved by a Passport (pages 58–73)

Page 59 *'I wanted to get away for a while . . .'*: Talleyrand, *Mémoires*, vol. 1, p. 191.

Page 60 *'It is precisely because it is so extraordinary . . .'*: Valdec de Lessart's note appears in *Talleyrand, Correspondance Diplomatique, Mission à Londres, 1792* (Pallain, Paris). Later this same year, as the Terror gets under way, de Lessart is forced to resign as foreign minister and is soon executed in prison.

Page 62 *His fallback was to listen . . .*: Orieux, p. 189.

Page 64 *He protected his rear . . .*: The judiciously argued document in question appears in the Talleyrand archives, French Foreign Ministry.

Page 65 *'I came upon the bishop Talleyrand . . .'*: Waresquiel, p. 164, citing Bertrand Barère, *Mémoires* (BNF). Barère is to become a prominent member of the Committee of Public Safety that unleashed the Terror.

Page 67 *'We have at last learned' . . .*: This Talleyrand proposal is addressed to the provisional government led by Danton, who has supplied his life-saving passport (French Foreign Ministry Archives; *Angleterre* Section).

Page 70 *For him, the Revolution had become a total calamity . . .*: Talleyrand, *Mémoires*, vol. 1, p. 195.

Chapter 5: America (pages 74–88)

Page 75 *In the Cornish inn . . .*: The curious encounter with Benedict Arnold is retold in full by Talleyrand himself: Talleyrand, *Mémoires*, vol. 1, p. 223.

Page 77 *Philadelphia, an industrious river port of shipwrights . . .*: For the look of Philadelphia, the yellow fever outbreak, etc, see *John Adams* by David McCullough (Simon and Schuster, New York, 2001), p. 78 onwards. Of the US founding fathers, Adams, Thomas Jefferson (both of whom became president) and Benjamin Franklin all completed notable diplomatic stints in pre-1789 France.

Page 77 *Morris warned the president . . .*: Gouverneur Morris, *Diary*, entry for 4 February 1792.

Page 78 *Land speculation, already an American standby . . .*: For full accounts of Talleyrand's trials as land speculator see *Talleyrand aux Etats-Unis* by Poniatowski, and also, in English, *Talleyrand in America as Financial Promoter 1794/96*, translated and edited by Hans Huth and Wilma Pugh (Library of Congress, Washington DC), consisting of his long, reflective reports on the early US property market, his descriptions of barely charted territory and his views on American economic prospects.

Page 78 *The country was a vast virgin forest . . .* : McCullough, p. 396; also Talleyrand, *Mémoires*, vol. 1, pp. 225–6.

Page 79 *'Luxury had come too soon . . .'*: Talleyrand, *Mémoires*, vol. 1, p. 228.

Page 79 *Each time he inhaled . . .* : Poniatowski, p. 212, drawing on the reminiscences of Talleyrand's bookshop-owner friend, Moreau de Saint-Méry, *Voyage aux Etats-Unis* (BNF).

Page 80 *'Come, come, great tidings from France . . .'*: The episode is recorded by the Comtesse Henriette-Lucy de la Tour du Pin, *Journal d'une Femme de Cinquante Ans*; see Poniatowski, pp. 165–7. Talleyrand hears the news in the company of the young countess, a free-thinking fellow exile of highest pedigree whom by happy chance he has just come across chopping meat in a forest clearing near Albany, where, with her husband Frédéric, she has temporarily chosen the life of a backwoods pioneer. Years later Comte Frédéric will serve as a chief aide to Talleyrand at the Congress of Vienna.

Page 80 *They smelled bad . . .* : See Talleyrand's report to Holland Land Co., reproduced by Poniatowski, p. 177.

Page 82 *He put a proposition to Hamilton . . .* : Talleyrand, *Mémoires*, vol. 1, p. 232. Discussions between Talleyrand and Hamilton centred on early, dreamy ideas for economic globalisation.

Page 83 *His compensation for boredom . . .* : For Talleyrand's liaison with the Caribbean negress, see Poniatowski, pp. 201–4, quoting Moreau, *Voyage aux Etats-Unis*. In his own memoirs Talleyrand ignores the episode entirely. Moreau takes great pleasure in comparing 'voluptuous' negresses with 'most beautiful white teeth' – the sort then congregating in Philadelphia – with colonial American women 'who lose their shape, their teeth and their hair' by the time they reach the age of forty.

Page 84 *it was a country where honest people could prosper . . .* : Talleyrand letter to the Comtesse Caroline de Genlis, a Paris salon priestess who is in exile in Copenhagen: Talleyrand, *Mémoires*, appended notes, vol. 1, p. 247. Mme de Genlis' own memoirs (BNF) are a chatty, perceptive walk through the turbulent age.

Page 84 *His intuition and acute sense . . .* : Alexander Baring's double-edged letter home regarding Talleyrand: Waresquiel, p. 185.

Page 86 *He saw the Directory as weak, 'perhaps ridiculous' . . .* : See private Talleyrand letter to Lord Lansdowne, 16 November 1795 (Lansdowne Correspondence, British Library).

Page 88 *the returning exile toured the commercial banks . . .* : Talleyrand, *Mémoires*, vol. 1, p. 253. That the remains of his Hamburg deposits are, as he puts it, 'extremely meagre', is confirmed by the story of how he loses his precious banknotes, which he no doubt enjoys telling at the time but which in fact only becomes Talleyrand lore years later after he relates it to participants at the Congress of Vienna.

Page 88 *Talleyrand obtained a nicely engraved passport . . .*: Waresquiel, p. 201.

Chapter 6: Encounter with a Warrior (pages 89–104)

Page 89 *On the stroke of the hour . . .*: Talleyrand's first meeting with Napoleon – like their pernicious merry-go-round of a relationship that ensues over the next eighteen years – is dissected by Emile Dard in his scholarly *Napoléon et Talleyrand* (Plon, Paris, 1935), pp. 14–19. I owe grateful acknowledgements to Dard, who examines this first meeting with the astute caution: 'It is unwise for two people to love each other before they know each other.'

Page 89 *'At first sight I found his countenance . . .'*: Talleyrand *Mémoires*, vol. 1, pp. 264–5, wherein he also gleefully records Napoleon's upstart claim that he, like Talleyrand, has an uncle in the Church.

Page 92 *'My dear child, that's all I have, twenty-five gold pieces . . .'*: Orieux, p. 257.

Page 93 *Talleyrand arrived at Barras' residence . . .* : Talleyrand, *Mémoires*, vol. 1, pp. 256–8.

Page 95 *'You are very curious!'*: The dialogue with the coachbuilder is a classic morsel of Talleyrandia, first retold in print, I believe, by Charles-Maxime de Villemarest, author of *Monsieur de Talleyrand* (Roret, Paris, 1834). Villemarest is a prolific wordsmith attached to Talleyrand as a diplomatic aide during his time as foreign minister.

Pages 98–100 *Pinckney was deeply shocked . . .* : For the notorious XYZ Affair (from the American viewpoint), see *Official Correspondence* between the Pinckney mission and US President John Adams (in both British Library and Library of Congress).

Page 100 *the social round was run by bourgeois women . . .* : Orieux, p. 322, citing the eagle-eyed Comtesse Adèle de Boigne, *Mémoires* (BNF). Mme de Boigne progresses with a true diarist's discipline from Bourbon court gossip to social commentator on the Directory and Napoleonic era, making herself a prime source for the social life of the times. It is she who analyses Talleyrand's attraction to Catherine Grand as a *coup de foudre*.

Page 103 *'She continually wounded Talleyrand . . .'*: Mme de Rémusat, *Mémoires 1802–1808* (BNF), p. 322. Claire de Rémusat, another busy diarist who becomes a confidante of Talleyrand, is the wife of the Comte Auguste de Rémusat, an administrator who becomes First Chamberlain to Napoleon as emperor. Although she is in the Bonaparte inner circle, she will share Talleyrand's eventual horror for the emperor.

Chapter 7: Minister of Civilisation (pages 105–19)

Page 106 *'At this moment a new enemy . . .'*: Talleyrand's speech introducing General Bonaparte and letting fly at England is published in the semi-official gazette, *Moniteur Universel*, 10 December 1797.

Page 109 *'Not Peru'*: Talleyrand, *Mémoires*, vol. 1, p. 265.

Page 110 *Talleyrand's tolerance of the Directory . . .*: Talleyrand, *Mémoires*, vol. 1, p. 299. The task he sets himself of 'bringing France back into European society' is a leitmotiv of the memoirs.

Page 111 *'Here, open my desk over there . . . you'll find 100,000 francs . . .'*: Orieux, p. 346. Orieux pins this episode on Talleyrand, *Mémoires*, though it does not appear in the Couchod version I have used as a reference.

Page 111 *'Better put off to tomorrow . . .'*: The advice, as well as a rundown on Talleyrand's office routine and his writing style, is found among *Lettres Inédites de Talleyrand* by Pierre Bertrand (Perrin, Paris, 1889).

Page 112 *He ranged over the world scene . . .*: The typically opinionated summary of geo-politics he composes for the Directors – including the tilt at America's 'fake neutrality' and the venomous blast at England – comes in a note contained in *Talleyrand sous le Directoire, Correspondance Diplomatique* (Pallain, Paris, 1891).

Page 113 *The news from Egypt . . .*: See Louis de Bourrienne, *Bonaparte Intime* (Edition Choisie, Paris), pp. 84–6. If Aboukir at once strikes Talleyrand in Paris as a disastrous turning point, similarly dire calculations very soon also occur to Napoleon in the desert, according to Bourrienne, who long serves as Napoleon's private secretary; they have been at military cadet school together. Keeping so close to Napoleon is bad for Bourrienne's nerves; he will die in a madhouse in Normandy. The twelve-volume memoirs he produces in 1829 (from which *Bonaparte Intime* is taken) are something of a shambles but are of interest for his recollections of his private discussions with Napoleon.

Page 116 *'I attest that any system intended to bring liberty by open force . . .'*: from a letter of 2 July 1799 (French Foreign Ministry Archives) addressed by *Citizen Talleyrand* to *Citizen Lacuée*, a member of the Council of Five Hundred. Napoleon wasn't listening. Nor, a while later, were Messrs George W. Bush and Tony Blair.

Page 117 *At 1 p.m. they heard a squad of cavalry . . .*: Talleyrand, *Mémoires*, vol. 1, pp. 301–2.

Page 118 *his resignation went so smoothly . . .*: Waresquiel, p. 263, citing the supposed target of the sweetener, Paul Barras, who charges in his *Mémoires* (BNF) that Talleyrand keeps the money for himself. It is also Barras who notes that Talleyrand, in an untypical piece of theatre, arrives to seek his resignation with two pistols bulging from his pockets.

Chapter 8: Napoleon Breaks His Leash (pages 120–36)

Page 120 *'Citizen Consul, you have entrusted me . . .'*: Bourrienne, p. 163. Talleyrand's manner of accepting the foreign ministry post and his proposal to relegate Napoleon's fellow consuls is similarly recorded by Baron Claude-François de Méneval, *Mémoires* (BNF). Méneval doubles with Bourrienne as a private secretary to Napoleon; he is usually at the warrior's side in meetings, and is a credible source.

Page 121 *'Talleyrand isn't wrong . . . he has got inside me . . .'*: Bourrienne, p. 164.

Page 125 *'he is launched on a course that can have no end . . .'*: Dard, p. 67. The conversation in which Talleyrand first begins to talk of Napoleon heading for a fall takes place with the prominent banker G.-J. Ouvrard, who covers his bets: he will lend Talleyrand a hand in suing for peace with England even while bankrolling Napoleon's Grand Army.

Page 126 *he sought to redeem himself in American opinion . . .* : See Talleyrand note to Napoleon, 7 February 1800 (French Foreign Ministry Archives, US Section). George Washington dies on 14 December 1799. The Washington statue that now adorns Paris will be erected more than a century after Talleyrand first proposes it.

Page 127 *The furniture was removed . . .* : Talleyrand, *Mémoires*, vol. 1, p. 307. The Austrian negotiator whom Talleyrand accompanies to the heavily stage-managed meeting with Napoleon is Ludwig von Cobenzl, an old schoolfriend of Talleyrand from Harcourt; Coblenzl will soon rise to Austrian foreign minister before Metternich takes enduring charge of Habsburg affairs.

Page 128 *'Now, I am going to give you great pleasure . . .'*: Orieux, p. 371.

Page 129 *Now his first diplomatic task, as he saw it . . .* : Mme de Rémusat, *Mémoires*, p. 226. She records the great efforts Talleyrand puts into preventing Napoleon from letting his quick temper shape policy. He tells her: 'In the post I occupy it is above all with Bonaparte that I negotiate.'

Page 133 *(A little girl, Charlotte . . .)*: Charlotte, adopted as Elisa-Alix-Sara de Talleyrand, is born in London in 1799, officially of parents unknown. Catherine's nebulously documented story makes Charlotte the illegitimate child of a well-born French woman in London who seeks a distinguished family to take charge of her. The only credible conclusion is that the unwed mother is in fact Catherine herself. As for Talleyrand, who makes no bones about having fathered Charles de Flahaut, he never remotely hints at having sired Charlotte and there is not a shred of evidence that he did so. All the same, he grows fond of her once she arrives with Catherine in his household, recounting: 'I tell her things she doesn't know and she tells me things I have forgotten, which I like.' He sees to her education, takes her with him on trips to the provinces and maintains her through womanhood, eventually marrying her off to a junior Périgord relative.

A more famous offspring attributed by wagging tongues to Talleyrand is the painter Eugène Delacroix (born 1798). This too is fable. Talleyrand habitually remains close to his kin, yet the sole verifiable link he has with the artist is an eventual admiration for his canvases. Tittle-tattle over the paternity derives from the fact that Talleyrand replaced the painter's father Charles Delacroix as foreign minister in 1797; it made salacious salon talk to suggest he also replaced Delacroix senior in Mme Delacroix's bed.

Page 134 *The faithful Courtiade, who never had a bad word . . .* : Orieux, p. 409. Courtiade's grouse that his master lets the side down in marrying Catherine Grand after all the fine women he has known is most likely hearsay, though it no doubt reflects the long-serving valet's true feelings.

Chapter 9: England's Baggage (pages 137–54)

Page 137 *'So you want war!'*: Orieux, p. 390. Accounts of Napoleon's rant at Lord Whitworth derive from a scene graphically depicted by Jacques de Norvins, *Histoire de Napoléon* (Paris, 1868).

Page 137 *'There are very few political transactions that don't benefit . . .'*: Letter from Talleyrand, *Correspondance Officielle* (Pallain, Paris).

Page 139 *Louisiana was the courtly name . . .* : The Louisiana Purchase is sparsely documented by Talleyrand's contemporaries on the French side (Méneval, *Mémoires*, takes a brief look). It is generously covered by US historians: *Purchase of Louisiana* by Daniel Goodloe (Southern History Association, 1900); *So Vast So Beautiful a Land* by Marshall Sprague (Boston, 1974); etc.

Page 142 *A contemporary police estimate . . .* : Waresquiel, p. 317. The prime source for such estimates is Etienne de Pasquier (*Mémoires*, BNF), an able soldier whom Napoleon appoints as police prefect for Paris. Pasquier keeps close tabs on Talleyrand as regards *douceurs* – details of which he dutifully communicates to Napoleon.

Page 145 *His whist partners were mystified . . .* : Orieux, p. 422.

Page 146 *'You have the right of self-defence . . .'*: This private letter to

Napoleon, dated 8 March 1804 – a week prior to the abduction of the Duke of Enghien – only comes to light some twenty years later, raising the possibility that Talleyrand's detractors have fabricated it in order to put blood on his hands. However, Méneval knows of it at the time, and indeed cites it, so it may be taken to be authentic.

Page 147 *the title of emperor pleased him less* . . . : For the tussle between Talleyrand and Napoleon over the most appropriate royal title, see Mme de Rémusat, *Mémoires*, p. 359.

Page 150 *He favoured velvet* . . . : Orieux, p. 425. The fortuitous resurrection of the Lyons silk industry is the most positive result of Napoleon's quest for impressive imperial apparel.

Page 152 *Talleyrand was alarmed* . . . : Talleyrand, *Mémoires*, vol. 1, p. 357.

Chapter 10: Austerlitz – and Trafalgar (pages 155–70)

Page 155 *Napoleon collapsed to the floor* . . . : The emperor's sudden collapse is retold in their memoirs both by Talleyrand (vol. 1, p. 359) and Mme de Rémusat (p. 61). Does Talleyrand obey the plea to keep it quiet? Probably not. But Mme de Rémusat will certainly have learned of it in any event from her husband Auguste, who, as first chamberlain, is the one other person present with Talleyrand to witness the emperor's fit. Rémusat may view his part in the drama as useful professional experience; he will soon be appointed Superintendent of Imperial Theatres.

Page 156 *He took Carême into his employ* . . . : The extreme care Talleyrand took to present a fine table is examined in *Talleyrand à Table* by François Bonneau (Paris, 1988). Talleyrand serves 'French style', which is to make an ostentatious display on the dining table of a vast array of soups, hors d'oeuvres, meats and fish all at once for guests to feast their eyes, then make their selection, whereupon they signal to their accompanying valets to serve them. Because food served French-style grows cold rather quickly and loses its succulence, 'Russian style' service is gradually replacing it at this time. 'Russian style' is basically the method used in restaurants today – less of a feast for the eyes but helpful in keeping food warm.

Page 158 *'You are the king of conversation . . .'*: Lacour-Gayet, p. 456.

Page 159 *This was his big diplomatic throw* . . . : For the entire peace plan, formulated as a letter to Napoleon, dated Strasbourg, 17 October 1805, see *Lettres Inédites de Talleyrand à Napoléon* by Pierre Bertrand, (Perrin Paris, 1889): pp. 156–65.

Page 164 *The Slovak boatmen* . . . : Talleyrand, *Mémoires* (appended correspondence), vol. 1, p. 392.

Page 165 *the government in Vienna released from state funds . . .*: Dard, p. 119.

Page 166 '*From the campaign of 1805 . . .*': Dard, p. 117 and pp. 155–61. Dard's search through Austrian foreign ministry archives shows that Metternich displays his talent for character-reading and for going straight to the heart of matters from the very outset of his long reign as statesman.

Page 166 '*You made me a treaty at Pressburg that displeases . . .*': Talleyrand, *Mémoires*, vol. 1, p. 364. Talleyrand is able to swallow the criticism because Napoleon follows it up almost at once by giving him the title Prince of Benevento.

Page 167 '*friendship with Mme Talleyrand was a calamity . . .*': Orieux, p. 444, citing the Duchesse Laure d'Abrantès. Mme d'Abrantès, whom it seems Catherine pestered, is another of the stinging social diarists whose souvenirs enjoyed much salon success in her time. She is the wife of one of Napoleon's most famous generals, Andoche Junot – ennobled as Duc d'Abrantès for his feats in Portugal – who at length puts an end to chronic money miseries by defenestrating himself.

Page 168 *Thus his balance sheet . . .*: Talleyrand's chart enumerating the transfer of souls in German lands is among territorial juggling curios found in *Lettres Inédites de Talleyrand à Napoléon* by Bertrand.

Page 169 *For his part, Talleyrand whispered in the ear . . .*: Dard, p. 140, quoting General A.-J. Savary, *Mémoires du Duc de Rovigo* (BNF), who succeeds Fouché as Napoleon's police minister and knows just what Talleyrand is telling foreign ambassadors.

Chapter 11: The Quartermaster's Two-step (pages 171–82)

Page 171 '*I shall send you a portfolio . . .*': Waresquiel, p. 360. From Napoleon's side, this marks the most vindictive moment thus far in his relations with Talleyrand.

Page 172 '*I swore inwardly . . .*': Talleyrand, *Mémoires*, vol. 1, p. 367. The decision to resign isn't quite the inward secret he calls it, nor is it sudden. Dard (p. 137) shows that even a stand-in Habsburg envoy in Paris is aware of it four months earlier. Writing in July 1806, the envoy says: 'He ardently desires to retire from a post which can no longer tempt his ambitions and whose burden weighs him down.'

Page 174 '*The door at last opened on an old gentleman . . .*': The less than flattering picture of Talleyrand at fifty-two is given by the Weimar envoy Friedrich von Müller, *Erinnerungen aus Kriegeszeiten 1809–1813* (extract reproduced in Talleyrand, *Mémoires*, vol. 1, p. 397). Müller, it must be said, is smarting at the time over a rebuke by Talleyrand, who was unhappy with the Duke of Weimar's support for Prussia at Jena.

Page 177 *the emperor was 'unamusable'* . . . : Mme de Rémusat, p. 342.

Page 177 *'Talleyrand procured her for me . . .'*: Dard, p. 146. The ungallant remark (*'Talleyrand me l'a procurée, elle ne s'est pas défendue'*) is recorded in the papers of Baron Gaspar Gourgaud, an imperial courtier who remained faithful to Napoleon after his fall.

Page 178 *'You are one of the first interests . . .'*: Talleyrand, *Mémoires* (appended letters), vol. 1, p. 400. Talleyrand's fatherly note to his natural son Charles, with its expressions of love, is one of many letters kept by Charles which found their way into storage in the home of Talleyrand's English friend, Lord Lansdowne, at Bowood, thence to the British Library, London. The note is accompanied by a droll description by Charles of his schooldays in England.

Page 181 *Franz's special envoy . . .* : The Austrian statesman sent to Talleyrand's side in Warsaw, Baron Alexander Vincent, is a discreet diplomat he knows from Paris (Dard, p. 148). His reports on Talleyrand's plan of action in the event of Napoleon's death – like his portrayal of Talleyrand as an enemy of Napoleon – are contained in Austrian foreign ministry archives. In his dealings with the Austrians, Talleyrand more usually operates through a trusty intermediary, Emeric von Dalberg, a German-born aristocrat conversant with all the courts of continental Europe.

Chapter 12: Disgrace (pages 183–96)

Page 183 *'I did not wish to be Europe's executioner . . .'*: Orieux, p. 468. This stark reason for resignation is attributed to Talleyrand by the historian–critic Saint-Beuve, who may have invented it; he was three years old when Talleyrand is supposed to have said it.

Page 183 *'During all the years I was responsible . . .'*: Talleyrand, *Mémoires*, vol. 1, pp. 373–4. His own brief account of his resignation is revealing for being among the most heartfelt passages in the memoirs.

Page 184 *'Things went well for me . . .'*: Napoleon's lament over Talleyrand's resignation is expressed in 1812 to his equerry Armand de Caulaincourt (*Mémoires du Général Caulaincourt*; reissue, Plon, Paris 1933; p. 257) following the Grand Army's retreat from Moscow. They are returning to Paris incognito in a hired farm sled, as Napoleon thinks back on what has gone wrong.

Page 184 *Perniciously, Metternich reported home . . .* : Dard, p. 160.

Page 189 *They were bored in his presence . . .* : Mme de Rémusat, p. 331.

She hears of Napoleon's pained outburst straight from Talleyrand, who still enjoys counselling the emperor on life's pleasures.

Page 193 *Be there by Monday night . . .* : Talleyrand, *Mémoires* (appended documents), vol. 2, p. 78. All Talleyrand himself says in his memoirs of the demeaning imperial order is: 'The emperor, hoping to make people believe that I approved his [Spanish] schemes, picked precisely on Valençay as a prison for Ferdinand VII.'

Page 194 *a library routine he fondly kept to . . .* : Talleyrand's library habits are recorded by the Duchesse de Coigny, *Mémoires* (Paris, 1817), p. 192. Like others in the tribe of blueblood women diarists of her day, Aimée de Coigny is a liberal-minded socialite who knows Talleyrand well.

Page 196 *Emperor – What do you mean by that?. . .* : Talleyrand, *Mémoires*, vol. 2, p. 66. Given the effrontery of Talleyrand's tone in this exchange – calling the emperor a cheat to his face – it is more than likely to have been inserted there later, or at least sharpened up, by Adolphe de Bacourt, his long-time secretary and executor of his memoirs. Bacourt no doubt ascribes more of his own insights to his master's pen elsewhere in Talleyrand's memoirs.

Chapter 13: Tea with the Tsar (pages 197–209)

Page 200 *'Sire, what is your purpose here?' . . .* : Dard, p. 207, citing Metternich's memoirs (of their eight volumes, vols 3 and 4 relate to Talleyrand). Metternich is not in fact present in this instance to hear Talleyrand's extraordinarily candid outburst, but gets it verbatim from Baron Vincent, his Habsburg predecessor as ambassador in Paris, who has been sent to Erfurt by Emperor Franz to keep his ears open.

Page 201 *'at Erfurt, I saved Europe . . .'*: The heavy pat on the back Talleyrand gives himself after Erfurt is recorded by Vitrolles, *Mémoires* (BNF), p. 445.

Page 204 *'I trust, Sir, you will be happy in the marriage . . .'*: See *La Duchesse de Dino* by Micheline Dupuy (Perrin, Paris, 2002), pp. 115–17. The Dino title is Talleyrand's. Dorothy takes it, years after her marriage to Edmond, when Talleyrand transfers it to his nephew.

Page 205 *He made her the target of intimate little 'morning notes' . . .* : A raft of billets-doux addressed by Talleyrand to Duchess Dorothea are contained in *Correspondance avec la Duchesse de Courlande* (Kolb, Paris, 1891).

Page 208 *In his coded messages, Metternich . . .* : Dard, p. 222. Metternich's switch to identifying Talleyrand as X is discovered by Dard in Austrian foreign ministry archives.

Page 209 *The mishap ensured* . . . : Dard, pp. 220–1. The interception of the joint Talleyrand-Fouché letter to Murat seems especially fortuitous, given Fouché's practical familiarity with police mail-spying methods.

Chapter 14: A Stockingful of Mistrust (pages 210–29)

Page 210 *Talleyrand waited patiently* . . . : In the scene at the Tuileries, the accusations and menaces Napoleon hurls at an unflinching Talleyrand are related verbatim by Pasquier (*Mémoires*, p. 358) and confirmed in the memoirs of Adolphe Thiers, then a budding Talleyrand political protégé, who recounts what Cambacérès is able to recall for him. Talleyrand himself is characteristically short on such detail in his own memoirs, referring to the event as merely one of the 'violent scenes' the emperor made in public (*Mémoires*, vol. 2, p. 146).

Page 210 *his habit when upset was to kick* . . . : Bourrienne, p. 218.

Page 213 *'Sire, I have obeyed Your Majesty's orders . . .'*: Lacour-Gayet, vol. 4, pp. 104–5.

Page 214 *'I shall do him no harm . . .'*: Orieux, p. 518. This crowning example of Napoleon's intrinsic clemency towards Talleyrand is relayed both by the emperor's step-daughter Hortense (*Mémoires de la Reine Hortense*, BNF) and by Comte Pierre-Louis Roederer, a writer-politician whom Napoleon confides in and who contrives, over twenty years, to serve almost as many regimes as Talleyrand.

Page 215 *'a few hundred thousand francs, say . . .'*: Dard, p. 227. Metternich's subtle, not to say slippery, efforts to settle on a suitable payoff for Talleyrand are documented in Austrian state archives. In this particular report, dated 31 January 1809, Metternich's encryption efforts make his message so hard to decipher that the Vienna foreign office asks him to resend it.

Page 217 *'Sire, Your Majesty has been gone . . .'*: Talleyrand's grovelling note, almost the reverse of his true thinking, is among *Lettres Inédites de Talleyrand à Napoléon 1800–1809* by P. Bertrand.

Page 223 *Sham governed the meeting* . . . : Talleyrand, *Mémoires*, vol. 2, pp. 148–50. The scene at Napoleon's marriage council is described in writing by several members of the high imperial entourage present, and Talleyrand perhaps overstates his own part a little.

Page 223 *. . . he sent to Vienna the army marshal . . .* : The Grand Army commander sent to take the hand of Marie Louise and bring her back to Paris is Louis Berthier, raised to Prince of Wagram following his illustrious role in the defeat of Austria there. (Five years later Berthier kills himself by jumping from a window after Napoleon, by then fallen, escapes from exile on the island of Elba and returns briefly to rule France.)

Page 223 *Amid gasps and sobs* . . . : Dard, p. 290. Some disgusted Habsburg aristocrats booked tickets to America to avoid the ignominy of seeing Napoleon marry into their royal family – or threatened to.

Page 226 *Sire, Your Majesty has shown an interest* . . . : Talleyrand's astonishing begging letter to Tsar Alexander, reproduced here virtually in full from Russian state archives, will remain a secret to all except its recipient and his courtiers until the tsarist press publishes it in 1897. Talleyrand's 'burn this' instruction therefore goes unheeded, though the tsarist court is gracious enough not to use it to compromise him during his lifetime.

Chapter 15: 1812 (pages 230–41)

Page 231 *'the emperor is mad, completely mad* . . .*'*: Tulard, p. 387. Marshal Marmont was in fact circulating this view in the salons a year or so before Napoleon's assault on Russia, covering his rear by attributing it to the defence ministry. As subsequent justification for his forecast that Napoleon will end up sending France 'flying arse over head', Marmont gets himself defeated by Wellington in a decisive battle in Spain, then, in 1814, surrenders Paris to the allies in Napoleon's face.

Page 235 *'the beginning of the end'*: Waresquiel, p. 420. Talleyrand's damning verdict prior to the Grand Army's march on Moscow is recorded by his niece-companion, Dorothy, in souvenirs published after Talleyrand's death in 1838. His longstanding diplomatic accomplice, Dalberg, is more explicit: 'Napoleon is a corpse. But he doesn't stink yet.'

Page 235 *She stirred hidden feelings* . . . : Waresquiel, p. 421. Talleyrand's passion for the Duchess of Kurland is described by an English observer, Lady Yarmouth, who notes, bitchily, in view of the fact that the duchess is now around fifty years old: 'Mr Talleyrand is tumbled in a very violent love with the duchess. Nothing seems to captivate him so much as old age.'

Page 236 *'Good God!* . . . *Bonaparte must be finished* . . .*'*: Orieux, p. 552. The future Louis XVIII's ironic greeting for Talleyrand's communication is recorded by Villemarest (*Mémoires*).

Page 237 *'What made him so impressive* . . .*'*: Dard, p. 289. Dorothy's focus on Talleyrand's taste for danger comes from her belatedly published souvenirs.

Page 238 *'The man has nothing more to do* . . .*'*: Mme de Coigny, *Mémoires*, pp. 210–11, quoting Talleyrand.

Page 240 *It was the worst military disaster . . .*: Tulard, p. 394. As regards numbers of Grand Army survivors, the authoritative Tulard counts only 18,000 men re-crossing the Niemen out of 380,000 soldiers who reached Moscow – a force previously reduced by 200,000 through death, disease and desertion in the early stages of the campaign.

Page 240 *The carriage was getting nowhere . . .*: The story of Napoleon's flight across central Europe in a farm sled and his harping on Talleyrand's role in his misfortunes is told by Caulaincourt in his *Mémoires* in the section entitled 'En Traineau avec l'Empereur'.

Chapter 16: A Conqueror's Fall (pages 242–61)

Page 243 *'Dishonour myself? Never! . . .'*: Tulard, p. 397. Napoleon's posture is recorded by Metternich, *Memoirs*. As a practitioner of the diplomatic art in the capital that will pioneer psycho-analysis, Metternich might have written a case sheet on Napoleon after this outburst.

Page 244 *Italy too dropped away . . .*: The story of Murat – an innkeeper's son who rises under Napoleon to Grand Army marshal then King of Naples – is that he bargained with Austria, half successfully at first, to help him bring the entire Italian peninsula under his control. The fact that his wife Caroline, Napoleon's sister, has been Metternich's mistress certainly offers him some leverage in this quest. Murat's initiatives typify the self-seeking attitude of members of the Bonaparte clan enthroned around Europe. After helping to drive Napoleon's forces out §of Italy, Murat disobliges his newfound Austrian allies by promoting Italian independence. A Habsburg firing squad ends his exploits for good in 1815.

Page 244 *'It is not without bitter pain . . .'*: Talleyrand, *Mémoires*, vol. 2, p. 267.

Page 245 *let down by all the ingrates . . .*: Dard, p. 314. It was no secret that Napoleon's marshals were sick of foreign wars. 'I see you no longer want to make war,' Caulaincourt in his *Mémoires* quotes the emperor as telling a gathering of his commanders during the 1813 truce. He accuses them of preferring to hunt or enjoy the good life in Paris.

Page 245 *'Oh, please! Let me be . . .'*: Orieux, p. 555. The woman who runs into Talleyrand and hears him speak so cuttingly of Napoleon is the Comtesse de La Tour du Pin (*Journal d'une Femme de Cinquante Ans*) – the same unconventional blueblood he once joyfully chanced upon during his exile in America (see notes to Chapter 5).

Page 245 *'You have made a mistake. You must say so . . .'*: Mme de Rémusat, vol. 2, p. 107.

Page 248 *French youths . . . were pulling their teeth . . .*: Tulard, pp. 413–14.

Page 248 *'Once invaded, France had so much piled against her . . .'*: Talleyrand, *Mémoires*, vol. 2, p. 268. The passage offers Talleyrand's most penetrating view of Napoleon's foibles.

Page 250 *he devised a coded message system . . .* : Mme de Coigny, *Mémoires*, pp. 239–42. It must be said that, even in code, Talleyrand is never quite as open with Caulaincourt as the emperor's aide appears to be with him.

Page 251 *Above all, there could be no smell . . .* : Talleyrand, *Mémoires*, vol. 2, pp. 306–11. Talleyrand's careful elucidation of his legitimacy principle has a key place in his memoirs and is held by some constitutional experts to be a classic definition of a complex issue.

Chapter 17: 'One More Frenchman' (pages 262–73)

Page 262 *The emissary's instructions were to bag them . . .* : Dard, pp. 355–6.

Page 263 *'Give him a response!'*: Talleyrand, *Mémoires*, vol. 2, pp. 319–21. Talleyrand's after-the-fact invention of the Comte d'Artois' homecoming speech is also nicely recounted in the souvenirs of the aide he gets to write it, Comte Jacques-Claude Beugnot (*Mémoires*, BNF), who becomes navy minister for his pains. The line 'Nothing has changed – except that there is one more Frenchman' will win the Bourbons more popular credit than any they subsequently utter from the throne.

Page 264 *they had . . . shared a mistress . . .* : The woman whose favours Louis XVIII, then France's dauphin, and Talleyrand, then a bishop, supposedly shared in the late 1780s was Comtesse Anne de Balbi, a witty lady-in-waiting at the Bourbon court and a high-stakes whist player who remained a friend of Talleyrand to the end.

Page 268 *Exhausted of men, finances and resources . . .* : Talleyrand, *Mémoires*, vol. 2, p. 325. No critic of Napoleon has ever delivered a harsher indictment of the emperor's legacy.

Chapter 18: The Congress of Vienna (pages 274–92)

Page 274 *Talleyrand got to Vienna . . .* : For the organisation and outcome of the Congress of Vienna, its issues, its colour, its participants – and for an examination of balance-of-power politics in general – the most illuminating work in English is Harold Nicolson's *The Congress of Vienna* (Constable & Co, London, 1946).

Page 274 *Talleyrand always moved in style . . .* : Isabey, the painter he takes with him to Vienna, having won fame as Napoleon's court portraitist, is otherwise out of a job; the pianist Sigismund Neukomm is a former pupil of Haydn.

Page 275 *'Allies? Against whom? . . .'*: Talleyrand, *Mémoires*, vol. 2, p. 396.

The harangue that changes the course of the congress is recorded in a letter to Louis XVIII (French Foreign Ministry Archives) and confirmed in official notes of the meeting taken by Friedrich von Gentz, Austria's secretary general of the congress.

Page 276 *A certain amount of cavilling* . . . : Nicolson, p. 147. The blabbermouth Spanish plenipotentiary who bores everyone to tears and thus effectively removes Spain from the decision-making process is Don Pedro Labrador, whom Wellington, an acquaintance from the Peninsular Wars, describes as 'The worst head I have ever met.'

Page 281 *'Vienna! My whole destiny* . . .': Dupuy, *La Duchesse de Dino*, p. 176.

Page 281 *Napoleon* . . . *struggled to adapt* . . . : For a graphic rundown on Napoleon's changing mood in exile on Elba, see Vincent Cronin, *Napoleon*, pp. 374–88.

Page 286 *'Alexander pipes down* . . .': Orieux, p. 613. The Talleyrand admirer who observes the tsar and the two kaisers seemingly struck dumb in his presence is France's Prince de Ligne, a genial old aristocrat on his last legs in Vienna, where he proceeds to die.

Page 290 *'Talleyrand is still the man who best knows* . . .': Dard, pp. 368–9. Napoleon attempts to send three emissaries to contact Talleyrand in Vienna, one of whom is his soldiering son Charles de Flahaut, who is halted at Frankfurt and fails to reach the Austrian capital. Of the two who get through, one sees Talleyrand, to no avail. As to the proposed bribe to Metternich, it is doubtful whether either emissary finds it possible to offer it.

Page 292 *he feared the king's faint-hearted run* . . . : Talleyrand, *Mémoires*, vol. 2, pp. 457–8. With scarcely veiled disdain, he scolds Louis on the manner of his flight and his return in a series of letters contained in *Correspondance Inédite de Talleyrand et du roi Louis XVIII*, edited by Pallain (Plon, Paris, 1881).

Chapter 19: Waterloo (pages 292–307)

Page 293 *'I am no longer a conqueror* . . .': Tulard, p. 430, citing Benjamin Constant, *Mémoires sur les Cent Jours* (BNF). Why the liberal Constant elects to bond with Napoleon during the Hundred Days, having loathed him until then, is a mystery he fails to illuminate in his memoirs.

Page 294 *'All the nations of Europe together form* . . .': Note from a collection of Talleyrand writings in Poniatowski family archives. The Poniatowski collection, into which many Talleyrand papers eventually found their way, have been mined by Michel Poniatowski to write four works that accompany Talleyrand through different phases of his life. Like other Talleyrand private jottings on Europe, the note in question points to him as a spiritual father of the European Union – a role that will be awarded him by an actual father, France's Maurice Schumann (*Talleyrand: Prophet of the Entente Cordiale*, Zaharoff Lecture, Oxford, 1976).

Page 297 *'Monsieur will forgive me . . .'*: Talleyrand, *Mémoires* (appended documents), vol. 2, p. 489.

Page 298 *'vice leaning on the arm of crime'*: Orieux, pp. 634–6, citing Chateaubriand, *Mémoires d'Outre-Tombe* (BNF). Chateaubriand's line on Talleyrand and Fouché appearing arm in arm before the king has become a classic epigram in French school history courses. The author seems to have made his disdain a little too apparent at the time, for he fails thereafter to land the grand embassy he seeks. Talleyrand prevails on the king to offer him Stockholm.

Page 300 *The prime minister's public ablutions . . .*: Orieux, pp. 641–3. The toiletry routine is observed in detail by both the Comte de Rémusat and Comte Louis-Mathieu Molé, a politician and regular visitor to Talleyrand's house at this time who notes (Comte Molé, *Mémoires*, BNF) the general unease at the sight of the 'claw'. Molé reveals that Talleyrand's elaborate precautions against falling out of bed derive from 'a morbid childhood fear' of doing so. (Molé will later become foreign minister and have a rancorous falling-out with Talleyrand, who looks down on him.)

Page 304 *'Such a wonderful country!'*: Talleyrand's oblique language in dismissing Fouché is reported by Vitrolles, *Mémoires*, pp. 197–200.

Page 305 *His choice was a twittish nobleman . . .*: Dard, p. 371. The story of how the Marquis de Montchenu was selected for St Helena comes very much second-hand, but sounds like Talleyrand.

Page 307 *'We leave without a single compliment . . .'*: Talleyrand, letter dated 25 September 1815, from *Correspondance avec la Duchesse de Courlande* (Kolb, Paris, 1891). A large selection of his 'morning notes' appears in this collection, the prime source not only for his relationship with Duchess Dorothea but also for his cryptic view of general events.

Chapter 20: National Grouch (pages 308–29)

Page 310 *he resembled an 'old rat' . . .*: Waresquiel, p. 533. The cruel observer is the visiting son of the US ambassador.

Page 310 *A beguiled Austrian statesman . . .*: Dupuy, p. 215. The suitor who finds Dorothy 'depraved' is Friedrich von Gentz, secretary general of the Vienna congress, who writes of her: 'As remarkable for the subtlety of her intellect as for the depravity of her heart, this woman both intrigued and amused me.'

Page 310 *Clam's child was not the last . . .*: Waresquiel, pp. 537–8, who lists the likely identities of those in Dorothy's illegitimate troupe. Apart from the two sons she first bears Edmond, the only subsequent child recognised as a Périgord is Pauline, born 29 December 1820, whom Talleyrand adores.

Page 312 *'a courage full of sang-froid . . .'*: Dard, p. 289. In her reminiscences, *Chronique de la Duchesse de Dino* (BNF), Dorothy is adamant in singling out what she regards as Talleyrand's most priceless asset – his courage.

Page 314 *So began one of Talleyrand's shabbier enterprises . . .*: Dard, pp. 372–84. Scores of Napoleon's original letters to Talleyrand in fact got left behind in Vienna when Metternich returned the bulk of them to Talleyrand; the rest either ended up in various collections of Talleyrand papers or were taken by his long-serving secretary, Gabriel Perrey, then sold over the years in dribs and drabs to private collectors.

Page 317 *But a shocking event . . .*: The Duc de Berry's killer, a saddler named Louis Louvel, had obtained a job in the royal stables; he had an obsessive down on the Bourbons, blaming them for the occupation of France by foreign troops. He stabs the duke to death as he leaves the Opera. Royal authorities seek to uncover a conspiracy but are obliged to conclude that Louvel acted alone.

Page 318 *'His genius was inconceivable . . .'*: Dard, pp. 388–9. Talleyrand's off-the-cuff tribute to Napoleon appears in Lord Holland's memoirs, *Diplomatic Souvenirs* (British Library).

Page 320 *'May French posterity pardon them . . .'*: In his will (article 6), Napoleon blames four men for having ensured that allied armies defeated him at a time when he felt he wasn't yet finished: besides Talleyrand, they are Grand Army marshals Marmont and Augereau and, for less evident reasons, the Marquis de La Fayette, the French star of America's War of Independence who was then shifting his sympathies back towards the Bourbon crown.

Page 321 *'I don't think there is a woman . . .'*: Orieux, p. 686, citing Dorothy's *Chronique de la Duchesse de Dino.*

Page 324 *'We shall have to fight insurrection . . .'*: Waresquiel, pp. 551–3.

Chapter 21: Last Performance (pages 330–43)

Page 331 *'All I could see was another republic . . .'*: Talleyrand, *Mémoires*, Supplement, p. 3. Talleyrand first completes his memoirs – most often presented in two volumes – in 1816 at Valençay, signing off as one who had performed in 'the great theatre of the world in one of the most extraordinary ages in all history'. This is a year after Louis XVIII has regained the throne a second time. In 1830–2 he pens brief supplementary memoirs (BNF) which contain the above pronouncement and others that follow. He has two reasons for adding to his memoirs: first, to defend himself in detail against the recurring 'hideous libel' that he is to blame for the execution of the Duc d'Enghien; second, to trace his diplomatic exploits during the July Monarchy.

Page 333 *They clapped in the streets . . .* : Talleyrand, *Mémoires*, Supplement, p. 6.

Page 336 *Grey's Whigs were more relaxed . . .* : Long before becoming Prime Minister, Grey, who liked his tea dark and was known for it, had served a stint as foreign secretary prior to Castlereagh. The latter committed suicide in 1822, seven years after the Congress of Vienna. Unpopularity at home turned him gloomy.

Page 337 *Talleyrand's otherwise reliable stand-in . . .* : The winsome Adolphe de Bacourt is to gain a lasting place in the lives of both Dorothy and the prince; on Talleyrand's death, he is delegated to classify his private and public papers – under the watchful eye of Dorothy, the executor of Talleyrand's will.

Page 337 *'I have been lucky, that's all . . .'*: Lady Grey's fork-tongued tribute to Dorothy is quoted by Orieux, p. 745.

Page 338 *'They think I am immoral . . .'*: Orieux, pp. 758–9, quoting the poet-politician Lamartine. Talleyrand's thoughts on morality, honesty, crime and not going down with sinking ships are recorded first hand by Lamartine in his *Entretiens Familiers de Littérature* (BNF).

Page 339 *It was a most judicious moment . . .* : Queen Victoria comes to Britain's throne at the age of eighteen in 1837 when Talleyrand has under a year to live. She is one year older than Pauline.

Page 341 *It was Dorothy who eased him . . .* : Dupuy, p. 289. Dorothy herself has mixed feelings about leaving England, partly because it means a break with her embassy amour, Bacourt. 'Goodbye England, but not to the memory of four beautiful years here,' she writes on the departing Channel ferry.

Page 343 *Popular nostalgia for Napoleon's legend . . .* : Louis-Napoleon, son of Napoleon's brother Louis, hoists himself to the head of the Second Republic that brings King Louis-Philippe's reign to an abrupt halt in 1848. Four years later he has himself named emperor as Napoleon III (the fictional title of Napoleon II having been settled on Napoleon's deceased son by the Empress Marie Louise).

Louis-Napoleon was a curious blood link between the Talleyrand and Bonaparte clans: his mother Queen Hortense, the Empress Josephine's daughter and wife to Louis Bonaparte, bore another son, illegitimate, by Charles de Flahaut, Talleyrand's illegitimate son. This child, Talleyrand's natural grandson, was therefore Emperor Napoleon III's half-brother and became a prominent businessman-statesman in the Second Empire as the Duc de Morny (1811–65). His playboy style somewhat diminished his political weight, but he remained an enduring influence on the emperor.

Epilogue (pages 345–8)

Page 348 *'Now he is in hell . . .'*: Orieux, p. 817, quoting Pozzo di Borgo's memoirs.

Among other works I have consulted but have not cited in the foregoing notes are, in chronological order of publication: Damas Hinard, *Napoléon, Ses Opinions et Jugements* (Paris, 1838); Georges Paleologue, *Le Diplomate Romantique* (Paris, 1926); Bernard de Lacombe, *La Vie Privée de Talleyrand* (Plon, Paris, 1933); André Castelot, *Talleyrand: ou le cynisme* (Perrin, Paris, 1980); and François Furet, *La France Revolutionnaire* (Hachette, Paris, 1988; English translation, Blackwell, 1992).